The Liberal Democrats

The Liberal Democrats

Edited by

D. N. MacIver

PRENTICE HALL
HARVESTER WHEATSHEAF

LONDON   NEW YORK   TORONTO   SYDNEY   TOKYO   SINGAPORE
MADRID   MEXICO CITY   MUNICH

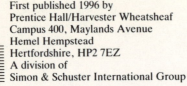

First published 1996 by
Prentice Hall/Harvester Wheatsheaf
Campus 400, Maylands Avenue
Hemel Hempstead
Hertfordshire, HP2 7EZ
A division of
Simon & Schuster International Group

Printed and bound in Great Britain by
T J Press (Padstow) Ltd

Library of Congress Cataloging-in-Publication Data

Available from the publisher

British Library Cataloguing in Publication Data

A catalogue record for this book is available from
the British Library

ISBN 0–13–227802–2

1   2   3   4   5   00   99   98   97   96

This book is dedicated to the memory of

my father

Contents

vii

Tables and Figures

Tables

Figures

The Contributors

Lynn Bennie is a lecturer in politics at the University of Aberdeen and is co-author of a number of articles on party membership, including the Liberal Democrats.

Duncan Brack is a research officer at the Royal Institute of International Affairs, Chatham House and formerly director of policy at Liberal Democrat headquarters.

John Curtice is senior lecturer in politics at the University of Strathclyde and is co-author of *How Britain Votes, Understanding Political Change* and *Labour's Last Chance*.

Stephen Ingle is professor of politics at Stirling University and is author of several articles on politics and literature and political parties and of *British Political Parties*.

Tudor Jones is a lecturer in politics at Coventry University and author of a forthcoming book on British social democracy.

Don MacIver is a lecturer in politics at Staffordshire University and author of a number of papers on political parties and nationalism and editor of a forthcoming book on *The Politics of Multinational States*.

Vincent McKee is sometime lecturer in politics, formerly a Liberal Democrat parliamentary candidate and author of a number of articles on factionalism in political parties.

Colin Rallings and **Michael Thrasher** are at the University of Plymouth and are directors of the Local Government Elections Unit. They have written extensively on elections.

Wolfgang Rüdig is a lecturer in politics at University of Strathclyde and has written several articles on political parties and the Green Movement.

Michael Steed was formerly lecturer in politics at Manchester University and is now honorary lecturer at the University of Kent. He has written extensively on parties and elections. He was president of the Liberal Party, 1977–78.

John Stevenson is at Worcester College, Oxford, and author of *Third Party Politics*, a history of the Liberal party, the Alliance and the Liberal Democrats since 1945.

Michael Temple is a lecturer in politics at Staffordshire University and has written a number of articles on local government politics, hung councils and coalitions.

Preface

The Liberal Democrats are the newest of the major political parties in Britain, but they have not yet been treated to a comprehensive study. This book is an attempt to fill that gap. When I proposed the idea I was delighted to have it accepted by Harvester Wheatsheaf. No doubt it will be well supported, although a little delayed, by their decision to commission parallel volumes on the other two major parties.

The book is an assessment of the Liberal Democrats by a group of professional political scientists. It has not been written from any particular point of view or a shared political outlook. It consists of a number of separate contributions which are intended to make a coherent study and contributors were given guidelines to facilitate this purpose. They have worked diligently to produce what was asked of them and they have each presented their own analysis and conclusions. The credit for any merits the work may have thus belongs to them, although responsibility for any shortcomings in the coherence and completeness of the work as a whole remain with myself.

The completion of this work has involved the cooperation and support of many to whom I am considerably indebted. I must first gratefully acknowledge the help of Graham Elson and staff at Liberal Democrat headquarters who gave me access to recent files and some confidential material and granted permission to use the party logo on the cover. I am grateful to the contributors for carrying out the tasks I asked them to undertake and especially those who completed their contributions on time. I have to thank Hannon Rose for his kind interest and encouragement and for his helpful comments on the introduction. I also wish to thank colleagues at Staffordshire University for reading parts of the manuscript and particularly David Morrice, David Dunn and Michael Brereton for their comments. Duncan Brack, John Curtice, Vincent McKee and Michael Temple also commented on some of the chapters. Others helped in other ways. particularly Jean Edwards who typed some of the manuscript. I have a particular debt to Geof Bridgewood of the Design and Print Unit at Staffordshire University for his indispensable advice and assistance in preparing camera ready copy. Finally, I have to thank Clare Grist and the staff at Harvester Wheatsheaf for their thoroughness, patience and support during the preparation of the book.

D N MacIver
December, 1995

Introduction

The Liberal Democrats in British politics

During the last quarter of the twentieth century there have been substantial changes in the structure of party politics in Britain. During the 1940s, 50s and 60s a pattern was established in which British elections were dominated by two major parties, the Conservative Party and the Labour Party, and characterised by a high degree of class-based voting. In the 1970s a change began to appear in this pattern. Class partisanship seemed to weaken and the major party share of the vote decreased, never to return to its pre-1970 level. These changes were emphasised by the regional polarisation of party support in England, the rise of political nationalism, particularly in Scotland, and the growth of support for third parties, first the Liberals and then the Liberal Democrats.[1]

From this process of change the Liberal Democrats emerged as a result of the union of the historic Liberal Party and the more recently formed Social Democratic Party (SDP). The Social and Liberal Democrats, as the party was first called, were formed in 1988 and adopted the short title of Liberal Democrats in 1990. The early years of the new party were marred by schismatic bickering and recrimination caused mainly by the refusal of the Owenite minority to accept the decision of the SDP to proceed with the merger.[2] Consequently the boost expected from the merger was lost and the new party made little headway in its first two years, coming well behind the Greens in the European elections of 1989. These difficulties were overcome, however, and, under the 'fresh and energetic'[3] leadership of Paddy Ashdown, the Liberal Democrats advanced through a series of local and by-election successes to emerge as an effective electoral challenge to the major parties. It is not yet clear how the Liberal Democrats will develop or what impact they will eventually make on the party system, but they claim to offer a distinctive political programme which has already attracted considerable public interest.

The Liberal Democrats first came into the public eye at the Eastbourne by-election in 1990[4] and have rarely been out of it since. A well-directed public relations effort, reinforced by electoral success and an increasing influence in local government, have ensured them continuous media attention. In a situation of considerable uncertainty

1

about the likely development of the party system, the performance of the Liberal Democrats raises a number of questions, not least about their own prospects. One recurrent question is whether they should be regarded simply as another third party or whether their success heralds a new pattern of politics. In either case it is important to examine the development of the Liberal Democrats and assess their significance in contemporary British politics. That is the purpose of this book.

The book begins with an account of the development of Liberal and third party politics since 1945 which culminated in the formation of the Liberal Democrats. It then addresses three sets of questions concerning the new party. First, it discusses the political heritage of the party, its traditions and political philosophy and considers whether it has been able to develop these into a coherent set of ideas and policies with the substance, cogency and electoral appeal to make an impact on contemporary politics. The book then looks inside the party at the organisation, members and groups that make it up and considers how far the party has succeeded in overcoming its early divisions. It also assesses how well the organisation serves the membership and the objectives of the party. A survey of members and a study of the plurality of groups in the party reveal some interesting and possibly unexpected features of the Liberal Democrats today. Finally, the book examines the competitiveness and behaviour of the Liberal Democrats in the arena of party competition. A discussion of the origins and evolution of their unique political strategy is complemented by an examination of their electoral support and their performance at elections. The Liberal Democrats' only experience of power is in local authorities, frequently in hung councils, and a review of this experience provides the most comprehensive analysis currently available of the practice of the Liberal Democrats in government.

The remainder of this introductory chapter develops these themes, previews the findings of the contributors and raises some of the issues facing the Liberal Democrats as the newest of the major parties in contemporary British politics.

Political roots of the Liberal Democrats

From the early twentieth century until the First World War Liberal ideas and the Liberal Party dominated British politics. The Liberal Party, however, emerged from the war bitterly divided by personal and policy issues, its finances severely depleted and its organisation, both nationally and locally, in decay.[5] Damaged in both their internal cohesion and external support by the experience of the war and the policy and personality conflicts it created in their party, the Liberals found not only that their appeal was diminished but also that various parts of their agenda were being adopted and their traditional ground colonised by the Conservatives and Labour. The Conservatives were presenting themselves as the party of the middle class, sound finance and the business interest, while Labour was pitching for the working-class vote and making a strong showing on social and international issues. This was complicated by the increased importance of class politics in the post-war years, which Liberals and Liberalism generally failed to address effectively. After the major challenges of the pre-war and wartime years, Liberalism seemed overwhelmed by the new challenges of collectivism, class politics and the rising popular expectations which led to the preoccupation with economic growth as a policy priority. It was not that Liberals or Liberalism had been unaware of these challenges or had sought to avoid them. Indeed, it may be argued that before the war the Liberal Party, despite the middle-class character of its local organisation, had demonstrated that it could also contest and hold working-class seats. Moreover, the evolution of social Liberalism in the late nineteenth century enabled Liberals to produce a coherent and potent response to the challenge of collectivism by mobilising the resources of the state to empower individuals and communities to find their own solutions to collective problems. However, this approach had always divided the party between classical (or economic) and social Liberals and, in the strained conditions of the 1920s, activists and supporters from both these sections of the party began to break away, some motivated by ideological and others by class issues.

The Liberal Party declined steeply during the inter-war years, entering the First World War as the party of government and emerging from the Second World War with only 12 parliamentary seats.[6] The heaviest losses occurred in the 1920s, with party organisation in decay after the war,[7] and there were only 59 Liberal MPs by the end of the decade. Liberals were again divided in the 1930s on issues of monetary policy, social security and free trade, divisions which were further complicated by personality conflicts and links with other parties. The experience of the National government and the Ottawa agreements split them into the Samuelite traditional radical free trade Liberal Party and the Simonite protectionist Liberal National Party, allied to the Conservatives, with Lloyd George leading a little group of his own. Thus Liberals in the inter-war years were faced not only by problems of unity, organisation and resources, but also by a problem of identity. It was not until the late 1950s and 1960s that a new generation, determined to restore the Liberal Party, refashioned Liberal ideas and traditions to produce a new Liberal identity based on a commitment to constitutional reform, regional devolution, European integration, industrial democracy, investment, environmentalism and education.[8]

While the progress of the Liberal Democrats thus represents a considerable growth and consolidation of third party support in Britain, it is also the culmination of a significant Liberal resurgence. In the 1951 general election the Liberal Party polled 2.5 per cent of the vote and barely more than a handful of seats in the House of Commons.[9] This was the very nadir of the long and painful decline of a great and historic party and the consequence of the collapse of activity, organisation and finance, especially at local level, with the result that the party could contest only one in five seats in 1951. After that a major effort was made to rebuild the party and restore the organisation. Some have argued that the turning point came at the Inverness by-election in 1954, when the Liberal candidate polled 36 per cent of the vote but did not win the seat.[10] Others have looked to the Torrington by-election in 1958, when the Liberals did win the seat, although they were unable to hold it at the subsequent general election.[11] It is not absolutely clear, however, that either of these events could be presented as the start of a recovery. The Inverness by-election possibly marked the end of the party's decline but there were several years before there was substantial evidence of a recovery. Such evidence came in the early 1960s when the revival of Liberal fortunes was borne out by strong opinion poll ratings, significant gains in local government elections and the landmark by-election victory at Orpington. This performance was sustained over the following decade and in the general election of February 1974 the party was within decimal points of 20 per cent of the vote. Since then the Liberal Party, either alone or in alliance with the SDP or in the phoenix form of the Liberal Democrats, has been a significant factor in British politics.

This revival of fortune was attributed to many causes from protest voting by disillusioned major party supporters to a modest realignment in some sectors of the electorate. However, it was also due to the renewed vitality of the Liberal Party and persistent efforts of successive Liberal leaders, from Jo Grimond onwards, who were determined to restore Liberalism as a major force in British politics. What Grimond sought was an electoral realignment which would enable the Liberals to win over a substantial section of Labour support. His view was based on the assumption that Liberal support had leaked to other parties, especially Labour, and could be won back.[12] One consequence of operationalising this approach was David Steel's caution about accepting Labour dissidents into the Liberal Party and encouraging instead the formation of the SDP in the hope of splitting the Labour Party and initiating a realignment of the left in British politics. This approach led directly to the formation of the Liberal/SDP Alliance and eventually to the amalgamation of the two parties in the Social and Liberal Democrats.[13]

The Liberal Party and realignment

The Liberal Party had long sought the kind of restructuring or realignment of politics which the Alliance seemed to make possible. For Liberals, however, realignment always meant more than simply winning over support from the Labour Party. Most Liberals did not place themselves on the left–right spectrum which embraced the Conservative and Labour Parties. Liberals regarded both these parties as centralising, statist and potentially authoritarian and unsympathetic, if not actually opposed to the radical, individualist and community values of the Liberal Party. Moreover, they saw the left–right spectrum itself as presenting a narrow and dogmatic, if not essentially misleading view of the substance of politics. Realignment, therefore, meant a realignment of ideas and values as well as a realignment of political support.

This image which the Liberals had of themselves was never accepted or projected by the media. They were usually presented as a 'centre' party, but the Liberal Party was never a centre party in conventional ideological terms and rarely a centre party on particular issues. The centre label was simply a convenient device by which apologists for the major parties and some political commentators accounted for the Liberals in their own scheme of politics. Some Liberals, however, who thought of their party as a moderate force, especially on economic and social policy, may have been prepared to accept a description of themselves as centrist. This tendency was reinforced by the alliance and subsequent merger with the SDP, which did see itself as a centre party. The Alliance tended to emphasise the common ground between the parties, mainly economic and social issues, on which the Liberal Party was generally on the centre-left. Moreover, many Liberals accepted the merger because they believed it gave them an opportunity to attract a new body of support.

Liberals had always been ambitious for their party beyond its resources and, while it remained a minor party, it always tried to make an impact on politics. In this it was only partly successful. The party never built the strength and concentrations of support that would have given it effective representation in parliament and never achieved the pivotal influence that some Continental third parties achieved and which Liberals so envied in the German Free Democrats. There have been three general reasons for this lack of success. First, the Liberals found themselves marginalised in a predominantly class-based structure of partisanship and by an electoral system which seriously disadvantaged minor parties. Although since the late 1950s the Liberals have consistently polled a considerably higher share of the votes than the German Free Democrats, they have never gained a fraction of the latter's parliamentary representation. As a minor party they could make little impact on the parliamentary process and were then further marginalised or ignored by a political press that tends to be Westminster-centred and obsessed by the government/opposition spectacular. Secondly, the task which the party set for itself of recovering from near oblivion in the early 1950s to challenge a well-entrenched two party system could only be achieved in decades, if at all. Thirdly, the Liberals did not always present a clear and consistent message and frequently failed to coordinate effectively, with the result that their efforts sometimes made little impact.

It would be mistaken, however, to conclude that the Liberals failed completely. In four distinct ways the Liberal Party has made a significant contribution to British politics in the second half of the twentieth century. First, the party's consistent advocacy of constitutional and political reform has had far-reaching effects on the British political agenda and is now widely accepted. Secondly, it has developed a new style and approach to politics rooted in its commitment to participation, decentralisation and community politics which have fundamentally altered the style and discourse of political campaigning in Britain and are now increasingly emulated by other parties. Thirdly, it has often been a policy innovator, pioneering and developing new policies well ahead of the other parties. Finally, by keeping its conception of politics alive and constructing an effective organisation, it was in a position to provide the basis for a new alternative party when the need and the opportunity arose.

The British Liberal Party was unique amongst Liberal and centre-left parties in the western world, and particularly in Europe, for several reasons: its deep historical roots and long traditions; its loyalty to a clear and consistent set of values, albeit a set of values whose interpretation and application were frequently contested even within its own house; its early anticipation of social democracy and its development of social democratic values within a Liberal framework; its ability to gain support from the British electorate and thus survive as a significant, if marginal, political force; and its success in developing the common ground with the SDP and thus restoring the unity and coherence of the centre-left in British politics.

The SDP and the Alliance

The SDP was formed after a split which resulted from a shift in the balance of power in the Labour Party. The Labour Party was an uneasy coalition of three elements; first was the liberal social democratic 'right wing', regarded by many in the party as rather highminded and elitist; secondly, the democratic socialist 'left wing', ranging from radical methodists to soft Marxists; and finally, the 'labourists' claiming to represent the interests of the trade unions and the working class. Between the mid-1930s and the mid-1960s the social democrats had a dominant position in the party through their alliance with the trade unions. In the late 1960s and 1970s there was a shift of ideological alignment within both the party and the unions which challenged the predominance of the right and gave the left an opportunity to exercise more influence. Moreover, the left wing leadership which emerged in the 1970s and early 1980s was more tough-minded than its predecessors and more determined to assert its claims. The focus of their challenge was the ideological orientation of the party and the selection and political accountability of the leadership and MPs.

Things came to a head over a cluster of constitutional reforms proposed by the left in 1980–81. After a special conference on the constitution in January 1981, which many of the social democrats saw as a defeat, a number of them detached themselves from the party and established the Council of Social Democracy, soon to become the Social Democratic Party. The leading members of the group, the Gang of Four (Roy Jenkins, David Owen, William Rodgers and Shirley Williams), justified their position and presented their political credo in the Limehouse Declaration, published on 25 January 1981. They proclaimed themselves in favour of proportional representation, regional government, a market economy and community politics. These ideas, of course, were congenial to the Liberal Party which was already gaining from the electoral effects of the divisions in the Labour Party and was hoping to benefit further.

Many of the SDP MPs were in close touch with the Liberals even before their defection, but most, of whom David Owen was the most single-minded, were more concerned to build their own party than to ponder their relations with the Liberals. Liberals on the whole were less than welcoming to the new group, but the Liberal leader, David Steel, had been involved with the Social Democrats, especially Jenkins and his supporters, from the beginning and was determined to create an alliance between them and his party, which he thought would provide the necessary boost to propel the Liberals into major party status. The two parties published a joint prospectus on policy on 16 June and a formal Alliance was endorsed by both in September. Their opinion poll ratings quickly accelerated and they were soon enjoying significant local and by-election victories with the help of the highly professional Liberal by-election machine. For a few months between early in the summer of 1981 and the spring of 1982 the prospects for the Liberal/SDP Alliance seemed to be bright. The two parties in the Alliance attracted more support than they did separately. The parties did offer each other significant advantages. Through the Liberals the SDP gained access to a national organisation, a growing activist network with extensive local experience and a campaigning machine with a strong track record, especially at parliamentary by-elections. For the Liberals the advantage of the SDP was the novelty and apparent freshness of its appeal, the political experience of its leaders and the professional approach of its central organisation. Moreover, the Liberals hoped that the SDP could give them access to a section of the vote that had been denied to them since the 1930s.

The alliance with the SDP, therefore, was possibly the greatest opportunity the Liberals ever had of making the electoral breakthrough they had so long sought, but it was for the most part an opportunity lost. Many Liberals were doubtful about the SDP, which they regarded as a Westminster creation over-promoted by the media. However, they generally responded to David Steel's enthusiasm and leadership and during these years the party probably functioned more effectively as a national forcethan ever before. The frictions which developed between the two parties, personalised around Steel and Owen, were due mostly to a split within the SDP on the appropriate posture to be adopted towards the Liberals. Owen and Jenkins had each conceived the formation of the SDP independently, but differently, and had divergent visions of its development which they both regarded as legitimate. Owen and his supporters simply despised the Liberals and refused to take them seriously. Like Jenkins, however, most of the SDP considered effective cooperation with the Liberals as an essential condition of success. Moreover, Owen frequently made policy pronouncements on his own on such matters as defence and nuclear power, the future of the Alliance and the possibility of coalition with the Conservatives, which brought him into direct confrontation with Steel during the 1987 election campaign. These differences were never resolved and were probably not even properly addressed, which led to confusion within the SDP, between the SDP and the Liberals and amongst potential voters with disastrous consequences for both the Alliance and the SDP itself.

The SDP was different in many ways from the existing parties including the Liberals. It was conceived not only as a new party but also as a modern party which would bring modern ideas and methods to the rather stuffy world of party politics. Its founders believed that a party that was going to change the face of British politics should look the part. Thus it was intended that the SDP should be democratically based, independently financed and professionally organised. An elaborate effort was made to create a democratic constitution which provided amply for membership participation but reserved the preponderant power to the national leadership. The constitution provided a decision-making system based on one member one vote and a postal ballot. The organisation was based on multiconstituency area parties (although it was also possible to organise single constituency local parties), a relatively powerless regional tier and a national conference with consultative rather than decision-making powers. The most significant arena of debate was the Council of Social Democracy and decision-making power was concentrated in the National Committee, dominated by the Gang of Four, and particularly the Policy Sub-Committee, chaired by the leader. In reality, therefore, the SDP was an elitist, centralised and patrician party in which the strategic and the more important tactical decisions were usually taken at the centre. Both party members and MPs were considerably more deferential to the leadership than their Liberal counterparts. Some elements of the SDP constitution were transferred to the Liberal Democrats, however, giving the new party an organisational and managerial strength which the Liberal Party never really had.

Formation of the Liberal Democrats

The Liberal Democrats might have emerged some years earlier had it not been for the difficulties that beset the Alliance in the mid-1980s. The two Alliance partners differed in their constitutions and organisations and this was reflected in some significant respects in their underlying principles and working practices. The Liberal Party had a devolved and participative structure in which the local associations had considerable autonomy and the annual delegate assembly controlled policy, although the leader had extensive discretion and freedom of action. The SDP, on the other hand, was a more centralised party: the local and area organisations were more dominated by the centre and, although the membership had some countervailing power through conference, the leadership generally had a monopoly of initiative and decision.

There were also differences in the political ethos and self-images of the two parties. The SDP regarded itself as a centre party, occupying the middle ground between Conservatives and Labour, upholding the essence of the post-war consensus and thus, according to its enemies, proposing 'a better yesterday'. On the other hand, the Liberals, whom the press had cast as a protest party, were used to seeing themselves as an innovative and progressive party, offering a radical, non-socialist alternative to the major parties. The differences between the Liberals and the SDP, however, were probably less in practice than either the press or the representatives of the two parties sometimes appeared to believe. Policy differences were most evident on defence and environment issues, but there was a broad similarity of views on Europe, the mixed economy, the welfare state and education, while the SDP readily embraced the long-established Liberal programme on electoral and constitutional reform.

Few of the differences between the parties were fundamental but they were undoubtedly complicated by the personality clashes and other conflicts between the two leaders. It is possible that the problems of the Alliance would have been reconciled by clear, purposeful and sensitive leadership but this, unfortunately, was lacking. There was possibly some virtue in the dual leadership while the two leaders were in sympathy and agreement, but dual leadership only compounded the problems when they were not.[15] Steel and Jenkins subscribed to much the same liberal creed and a very similar prognosis of British politics. These similarities may have led them to a number of shared policy positions and common purposes, in particular that the Alliance was intended to pave the way to a fusion of the two parties. There was no such meeting of minds between Steel and Owen. Unlike Steel, Owen never saw the Alliance as a stepping stone to the creation of a new party and insisted on his own distinctive position, sometimes at the expense of Alliance unity. The consequent friction in the leadership exasperated many Social Democrats, alienated rank-and-file Liberals and possibly undermined the effectiveness of the Alliance. These problems were never overcome within the Alliance and were only resolved when Steel pressed the issue of merger and Owen excluded himself from the new party.

The political developments which led to the formation of the Liberal Democrats are outlined by John Stevenson. As the post-war period began, the Liberals were in the last stages of a long decline which reached its nadir in 1951. Once the Liberals overcame the threat of extinction, their fortunes began to recover later in the decade when they began to perform effectively in by-elections, culminating in the celebrated victory at Orpington in 1962. From then the Liberal revival was fully under way, encouraged by Jo Grimond who became leader in 1956. The Liberals continued to make gains through the 1960s and came near to a breakthrough in 1974 when they polled nearly 20 per cent in the February general election. In the two steps forward, one step back character of the Liberal advance, however, they fell back again in 1979 but came close to another breakthrough in 1983 by which time they had formed the Alliance with the Social Democrats. The Alliance did not live up to the expectations of its supporters and it was dissolved in a merger of the parties in 1987–88. The Alliance failed to break the mould of British politics but it was not entirely without success. Whether Liberals alone would have achieved what the Alliance did is debatable but the short-term effects of the SDP and the Alliance on the Labour Party may have contributed to realignment. Stevenson concludes that the Liberal Democrats occupy a position stronger than that of the Liberals in the post-war period and that this growth has been self-generating and independent.

The heritage and philosophy of the Liberal Democrats

The Liberal Democrats claim to incorporate two political traditions which, having been organisationally separated and in some ways opposed for several decades, were now brought together in a framework which could nourish the growth of their shared values.[14] The first of these was the rich and varied Liberal tradition which had well-established roots in all sectors of British life and society. Liberals traced their ideological origins through Edwardian radicalism back to John Stuart Mill and the nineteenth-century liberals and before that to the Whigs. Some even believed themselves the heirs to an unbroken tradition reaching back to Locke, Milton and the seventeenth-century radicals. Liberalism in this tradition was an individualist and reforming creed, which prized freedom as its fundamental value and was deeply suspicious of any institutionalised power, especially that of the state. Liberalism was all about freedom, free enterprise, free markets, free trade and personal freedom. Freedom was understood as the empowerment of individuals and informed a complex range of human, interpersonal, community and civic values which were expressed in the Liberal policy priorities of equality of opportunity, diffusion of power, extension of democracy, participation and pluralism. The tradition was, of course, contested and, throughout the history of the Liberal Party, there were frequent and prolonged arguments about the implications of these ideas and how they should be applied. The most significant of these was between classical and social Liberals over the idea of positive freedom, ie.the idea that collective action could empower individuals and remove obstacles to the full realisation of their potential.

The other tradition to be incorporated in the new party was the social democratic tradition, which had many affinities with social Liberalism, although these were often understated because of their long political separation. British social democracy, like most British political traditions, was largely home-grown and owed much to the Liberal tradition, including some of its intellectual roots and basic ideas. In the 1920s many Liberals of a social democratic inclination, including some leading individuals and several MPs, left the Liberal Party for Labour, believing it to offer better political prospects at that time. Thus Liberal social democracy found a home, though not always a welcome, in the Labour Party. There were, of course, other sources of British social democracy, in particular the tradition exemplified by the Fabians which was less individualist and community-oriented and more state oriented and more influenced by Continental revisionist ideas. There was also a significant input from the democratic socialist strand stemming from the Independent Labour Party (ILP), although its adherents had more in common with the radical tradition and were to some extent influenced by Marxism.

Both the political style and the policy agenda of any political party are likely to be heavily influenced by its traditions and political heritage. In the first chapter of this book Michael Steed evaluates the significance of Liberal tradition and its influence on the style and philosophy of the Liberal Democrats. He shows that this tradition had very deep roots in British politics and traces its origins back to the seventeenth century. He demonstrates how the tradition has been passed from generation to generation and from one institutional form of liberalism to another, 'from Whig to Liberal, and Liberal to Liberal Democrat, to form a continuous institutional tradition'. He asserts the importance of the Liberal tradition in keeping the party alive: its survival in adversity is 'a tribute to its own faith that what it stood for was important, distinctive and attractive'. For the bearers of the tradition it meant a commitment to certain political values and principles, particularly the idea of freedom. The distinctive features of Liberalism were its concern for constitutional and political reform, social justice and peace as great objectives of policy. The development of new Liberalism revitalised the Liberal tradition and enabled it to adapt to meet the political demands of industrialised mass society. Always the watchword was freedom and its development in Liberal thought and philosophy which was reflected in 'a deep belief that political structures matter more than economic ones'. This meant that Liberalism was more in tune with the 1960s' demand for participation and in 1969 it became the first party to install a one member one vote system into its constitution.

A party with the long history and pluralistic origins of the Liberal Democrats is likely to draw on a rich store of political ideas. This is examined by Tudor Jones, who finds that Liberal Democrat thought is rooted in the two parallel and related traditions of social liberalism and social democracy, which the party has sought to reunite and synthesise. The origins of both these traditions lay in the late nineteenth-century evolution of the idea of positive freedom and the enabling state. Jones shows how social liberalism, which grew out of the ideas of Green, Hobhouse and Hobson were developed by Keynes, Beveridge and others within the inter-war Liberal Party and made a significant contribution to the political philosophy of British social policy after the Second World War. He then discusses the emergence of British social democracy from 'an ideological synthesis of Edwardian New Liberalism, Fabian Socialism and Keynsian economics' to form a non-Marxist reformist socialism. These ideas were revitalised and restated 'as a body of theory and a set of policies' by Crosland and his colleagues within the Labour Party in the 1950s. It was this approach which the Social Democrats brought with them from the Labour Party including particular commitments to the mixed economy, constitutional reform and the decentralisation of power which enabled them to cement the Alliance with the Liberals. Jones explores the common ground between social liberalism and social democracy and outlines the body of ideas which clearly distinguished the Alliance from the doctrinaire libertarianism of the right and the fundamentalist socialism of the left. Finally Jones assesses the contemporary concerns of this renewed tradition of thought and their articulation in the philosophy and ideology of the Liberal Democrats today.

These concerns are the subject and the substance of Liberal Democrat policy, which is discussed by Duncan Brack, who explains that it was systematically derived from the party's core values of liberty, equality and community. Liberal Democrat policy has tended, therefore, to emphasise greater dispersal of power, redistribution of wealth and increased participation. Policies are important to a political party because they represent its promise to the electorate, they are an expression of its ideology and values and they are the outward mark of its distinctiveness. They are part of the kaleidoscope of impressions that together form the overall image of the party in the mind of the electorate. Having first resolved the political differences outstanding from the Alliance, the Liberal Democrats made painstaking and assiduous efforts to develop their own policies and establish their distinctive political image. Three areas of economic policy, environment and education were given special attention and their review of these areas marked a return to Liberal ideas and priorities as compared with the Alliance. These three areas, together with electoral reform and Europe made up the five 'E's of the Liberal Democrat manifesto, which was generally well received by the press although the *Financial Times* found it incoherent. One of the recurrent and more galling frustrations experienced by the Liberal Party was that although it had a host of distinctive policies, these were rarely discussed by other parties or the media who then claimed that it was not clear what the Liberals stood for.

Inside the party

If it is assumed that party ideology will have a profound effect upon party organisation, the Liberal Democrats are no exception, having enmeshed their philosophy of participation within the formal organisation of the party. The most noteworthy features of the Liberal Democrat organisation, according to Stephen Ingle, are its federal structure and its absolute commitment to participative politics, empowering the membership more than any other party. Ingle outlines the structure of party organisation, giving particular attention to the local parties, the conference, the executive and the leader and describes the key processes of policy-making and candidate selection. He then discusses two separate but closely associated parts of the organisation. First he assesses the organisation and management of the parliamentary party and examines the Liberal Democrat claim to be a principal opposition. Secondly, he considers the organisational support for community politics which he finds to be flawed in some cases (in particular in the Tower Hamlets case) but recognises the party's efforts to deal with this. Ingle concludes that the party organisation is generally in good shape and has given effective support to the party's objectives and campaigns.

This seems to be confirmed by the reactions of party members, who seem relatively satisfied with the service they get from the party organisation. According to Bennie, Curtice and Rüdig's survey, it also appears that the party has a reasonably stable and active membership base. The social profile of Liberal Democrat members shows that they are predominantly middle aged and middle class and almost half are women. Former Liberals outnumber former Social Democrats by four to one, but about half the membership did not belong to either of the predecessor parties and these new members are more like Liberals than Social Democrats. Liberal Democrats have the most highly educated membership of all the parties and there is also a significant religious influence with the proportion expressing a strong religious commitment being twice that of the electorate at large. Since the Liberal Democrats depend heavily on membership for both campaigning and financial support, it is fortunate that just over half the membership is classed as active, rather more than other major parties. The burden of activism, however, is borne disproportionately by a relatively small number of members, of whom 6 per cent regularly spend 20 hours per month on party work. This uneven level of commitment is echoed in the uneven commitment of members to the policies of the party. While 80 per cent support a Bill of Rights and 93 per cent support proportional representation, almost one-third are opposed to devolution and about half are opposed to the party's official position on European union. On the other hand, there is strong support for the party's economic and social policies on which 'the political attitudes of Liberal Democrats are well within the traditions of social liberalism' and 'are more likely to have something in common with Labour than with the Conservatives'.

Political parties are not monoliths and the Liberal Democrats have a pluralistic culture which enables a diversity of groups and political activities to flourish within their constitution. This is the conclusion of Vincent McKee, who discusses factions and groups within the Liberal Democrats. He finds that the party constitution provides well for a wide diversity of activity and argues that this is 'an effective check on central regulation' which 'strengthens accountability of the Liberal Democrat leadership'. In these respects one of the most powerful organisations is the Association of Liberal Democrat Councillors (ALDC) which has a nigh autonomous role in the management of local government campaigning and political support. The party recognises a considerable number of organisations which represent particular interests within the party including students and trade unionists, Greens and Christians, candidates and agents. Not all organisations are equal and while some enjoy the patronage of the party hierarchy, others are refused recognition. In addition to the official and unofficial special organisations, McKee identifies two others which he describes as ideological tendencies like LINk and Chard, and elite fellowships such as the Gladstone Club and A1 which is inherited from the Alliance. Generally the Liberal Democrats are comfortable with diversity and pluralism of both ideas and interests in such a way that sectionalism is not a serious issue and the unity of the party is not threatened.

Party competition

While the Liberal Democrats believe that they are the guardians and advocates of a renewed liberal and social democratic tradition, which provides the framework of their ideology and the basis of their public policy, they are also eager to gain power, but it is not clear how they can do so with only a score of seats in the House of Commons. Although they have an increasingly strong base in local government, they have not made a significant impact at general elections. They have considerably less than a quarter of the popular vote and lack the concentrations of support and the electoral strongholds which the other parties can rely upon to provide a base of 'safe' seats in Parliament. They have sought, therefore, to devise a strategy which will increase their parliamentary strength and enhance their chances of entering government. The basis of Liberal Democrat strategy is Ashdown's endorsement of Grimond's declared objective of political realignment. In the chapter on strategy, MacIver discusses the origins of this idea and its development in the Liberal Party. He then examines the effectiveness of the community politics and political cooperation strategies which were intended to accomplish it and the efforts to combine and develop these strategies into a new, integrated campaign strategy in the 1990s. During and after the 1992 election it was clear that the issues and choices facing party strategists were complex and full of uncertainty and risk. How can the party increase its share of the vote? How can it increase its share of parliamentary seats to reflect the share of the vote it has already? Should it seek to negotiate a share of power within the existing system while advocating proportional representation or simply press on in the hope of eventually storming its way to a share of power sometime in the future? A cursory review of these options highlights the paradox in the overall situation of the Liberal Democrats and reveals the frustration of a third party operating in an electoral system which appears to diminish the party's performance and marginalise its significance.

The social profile of the Liberal Democrats' electorate is in many respects similar to that of their membership. The electoral support for the Liberal Party was notoriously volatile, mainly middle class and evenly spread both territorially and socially. That this was a source of weakness for the party was frequently demonstrated, especially in the Liberal surge of 1974. This picture was modified only marginally by the Alliance. Contrary to some expectations, the SDP failed to attract more working-class support; indeed the Liberals attracted more working-class votes than the SDP in 1983. The Liberal Democrats wished to build a more stable and more reliable base of support than either of their predecessor parties. What has become clear, however, is that the Liberals, the Alliance and the Liberal Democrats occupy a distinctive and coherent ideological position which can be described as centre on economic and social issues (the familiar left– right) and liberal on liberal–authoritarian issues like welfare spending, law and order and civil liberties. This pattern, first identified in 1983, 'also appears to have been present in 1992', when despite the narrowing of the ideological distance between Labour and Conservative, the Liberal Democrats seem to have made significant inroads into Labour's traditional ideological support. Liberal Democrats have also built a more solid territorial base with a significant bridgehead of support in the south west and west of England and growing potential elsewhere. Despite this social, regional and ideological consolidation, there are still a number of weaknesses in the Liberal Democrat vote, notably volatility, instability and lack of commitment and social reinforcement compared with the Labour and Conservative Parties. Curtice concludes, however, that Labour and the Conservatives may not be capable of inflicting as much long-term damage on the Liberal Democrats as some commentators have suggested.

The Liberal Democrats have been as eager for electoral success as their predecessors and have experienced much the same disappointments when opportunities and expectations have been unfulfilled. The consequence of electoral failure is that their principal project of establishing themselves as a major party will also fail. It is fitting, therefore, that they should be judged on their electoral performance. This is the view of Colin Rallings and Michael Thrasher who find that the 'Liberal Democrats meet with different levels of electoral success in different electoral contexts'. Their greatest success has been in achieving a better conversion rate of votes to seats than the Alliance and in overcoming, to some extent at least, the difficulties of the electoral system which tends to work against third parties. With the Labour revival, however, the days of plenty enjoyed by the Alliance are over and the new party has to find a way of making more gains on a smaller share of the vote. In this they have had some success in both parliamentary and local government elections and Rallings and Thrasher believe they should be particularly satisfied with their performance at the local level. In both parliamentary and local by-elections they have also achieved considerable success, although in their more recent outings they have been pressed very hard by Labour. Even in European elections, where in the past they have had little to show for their efforts, they have made some gains but they still underperformed. At the 1993 European elections their share of the vote fell by 10 per cent compared with their share at the local government elections a month earlier, whereas, if it had remained the same, they might have gained considerably more than the two seats they actually won. Thus it is clear that, despite their campaigning successes, the Liberal Democrats have an uphill struggle to win a solid base of support that can be relied upon in all electoral contexts.

Electoral success may be an elusive and fickle friend to the Liberal Democrats, but it is only a means to gain power or a share of power, which was mostly denied to the Liberal Party and the Alliance. For the Liberal Democrats, however, opportunities 'to demonstrate their competence in government proliferate'. Their success in local elections has enabled them to take control of local authorities and even more extensively to share power in hung councils. Thus they have been able to demonstrate their 'very real commitment' to more democratic local government through their practice of participation, local devolution and community councils. In his study of the Liberal Democrats in hung councils, Michael Temple finds that the success of the party at the local level is indisputable and it is involved in more administrations than any other group. They are 'generally the most successful of the three major parties in hung councils' and 'are far more likely to achieve their budgetary aims'. They do sometimes overestimate their bargaining position, however, and underestimate the annoyance which their success induces in other parties, who tend to accuse them of irresponsibility and opportunism. On the other hand, their more open approach to inter-party cooperation gives them an advantage in partnership negotiations in which they are usually closer to Labour than to the Conservatives, although their supposed preference for arrangements with Labour is exaggerated.

Prospects of the Liberal Democrats

New parties in British politics are unusual, and successful new parties are rare. The relative success of the Liberal Democrats may be accounted for in terms of a number of specific conditions. First, although the Liberal Democrats may be a new party, they have an old and well-established pedigree based on their political and organisational continuity with the Liberal Party. The persistence and revival of the Liberal Party in the post-war period ensured that the Liberal alternative never wholly disappeared from the awareness of the electorate.[16] The Liberal Democrats are thus the heirs to a great political tradition that is well recognised by the British public, though possibly not as well understood. Secondly, the decline in support for the major parties since the mid-1970s and the increased volatility of the British electorate have created conditions more favourable to political change than in previous decades.[17] In addition, the intensity and vehemence of the constitutional and policy disputes in the Labour Party in the 1980s weakened the solidarity of that party, alienated many voters and created an enhanced opportunity for an alternative left-of-centre party. Thirdly, the launch of the SDP in 1981 and the formation of the Alliance with the Liberal Party created a new and highly visible political force which was clearly attractive to voters. Thus the Alliance may have boosted the cause of third party politics and created a new interest in the possibility of political realignment.[18]

The much sought realignment has not been accomplished by the Liberal Democrats, at least not in the form envisaged by its progenitors. On the other hand, while there has not been a structural realignment of British politics, there has been a realignment of ideas which was, to some extent at least, influenced by the Alliance and the Liberal Democrats. The call for a dialogue and a coalition of ideas canvassed by Ashdown in 1992 has been taken up by Tony Blair and some elements in the Labour Party. This has clear dangers for the Liberal Democrats of being outflanked or even overwhelmed by the larger party, but they are conscious of these dangers and have tried to deal with them and have so far fared reasonably well in competition with Labour. However, while the two parties have demonstrated the possibilities of working together on the Scottish Convention and some other occasions, they remain independent and fiercely competitive.

The next general election will be crucial to the Liberal Democrats' future, and their prospects are uncertain. The Boundary Commission's recommendations may bring them some advantages and one informed observer forecast that they could win about 35 seats.

The party's own forecasts are, unsurprisingly, more optimistic, claiming it could win up to 50 seats even on a national poll rating of only 15 per cent. As always for third parties, the truth is that the outcome for the Liberal Democrats depends to a large extent on the performance of the other two parties. In this respect the Liberal Democrats may not be any better placed than the Liberals or the Alliance were and may have to face many of the same problems and frustrations as they did. Thus only time and events can confirm John Stevenson's assessment that the Liberal Democrats have a stronger and more secure place in British politics than any of their predecessors.

Whatever the outcome of the next general election, it is very likely, even certain, that the Liberal Democrats will remain a significant third force in British politics, offering a distinctive alternative to the major parties, with the resources and capabilities to maintain a formidable record of success at by-elections, a substantial share of power in local government and sufficient presence in Parliament to retain the respect and support of voters, command the attention of the media and exercise some influence on the course of public affairs. Whether the party can go beyond this and break through to the 'big time' depends, like its election prospects, partly on the fortunes of the other parties and the opportunities thus created, but even more, perhaps, on the effectiveness of its own performance. In this respect a great deal depends on the extent to which the party has clarified and resolved the issues which have been identified and discussed in this book. From this viewpoint, there are three general sets of issues to be considered, relating first, to ideas, secondly to organisation and thirdly to strategy.

First, can the party bear out the views of Michael Steed, Tudor Jones and Duncan Brack that it has a consolidated political tradition and coherent philosophy that can support a unified ideology and policy programme? Can it confidently say that it has a distinctive image with electoral appeal and that voters have a clear perception of its political identity and what it stands for?

There does appear to be some evidence to support the Liberal Democrats' claim that they have developed a coherent ideological position, rooted in the philosophical foundations of the progressive radical tradition of British politics. Its particular synthesis of social liberalism and social democracy gives this ideology a depth, strength and coherence which is, if not unique, at least unusual in contemporary political parties. This is due in large measure to the efforts to capitalise on the party's heritage and tradition which provide a rich store of principle, ideas, rhetoric and example which has been applied to the development of policy. The party has made a conscious effort to develop a clearly visible image which distinguishes it from both the Conservatives and Labour. While the Liberal Democrats have been diligent and thoughtful in both the development and presentation of their message, however, it is not yet clear that they have overcome the communication gap that has handicapped them in national politics in the past. It may be, therefore, that there is still some work to be done in this corner of the vineyard.

In some respects, however, the problems of the Liberal Democrats could be viewed as the problems of success. With the Conservative Party now claiming, at least officially, to be a party of the centre right and the Labour Party declaring itself to be a party of the left and centre and occupying much of the Liberal Democrats' policy space, the centre ground has become heavily contested. Although the agenda of the 'radical centre' has been shaped by the Liberal Democrats and their predecessors possibly more than any other group, this does not mean that they will reap the political rewards. There is another perhaps less obvious danger for the Liberal Democrats as a party of the centre-left. As Labour moves more to the right, it may leave the Liberal Democrats, not as less powerful competitors in the centre of national politics, but exposed on the left and appearing too radical to appeal to their potential electorate.

The second issue facing the party is whether it has resolved the differences inherited from its predecessors, the Liberals and the Social Democrats, about political priorities and party management? Can it uphold the contention of Ingle, Bennie *et al.* and McKee that it has a democratic and effective organisation, with a strong pluralistic culture and a clear sense of purpose, serving a satisfied membership and committed to a participative and campaigning style of politics?

The evidence presented here is that the party is united and comfortable with a lively, diverse and pluralistic membership in which factionalism and internal divisions are not a problem. It has built an effective organisation with a participative and democratic ethos which appears to give satisfaction to the members. There are no grounds for complacency, however, and there are a number of issues which probably should be kept under review. The current imbalance of the federal structure might be examined with a view to operationalising it fully by further empowering the English regions, a crucial question for a party committed to a federal form of regional government, especially with the prospect of an autonomous Scotland seeming ever closer. The extent to which the party organisation itself has cultivated a centralised, elitist and top-down decision-making and management style in some respects remote from the membership cannot be entirely welcome in a party dedicated to participative democracy.

Similarly, the uneven burden of party work placed on a relatively small activist base and the limited rank-and-file participation in policy debate, must be a cause for concern in a party with a large policy repertoire and a commitment to a policy-oriented, campaigning style of politics. Finally, although they have been relatively successful in membership recruitment, the Liberal Democrats cannot afford to relax their customary zeal about membership, which is the main resource of the party and provides its lifeblood in both finance and active personnel. In this respect the party faces possibly severe competition on the one hand from a resurgent Labour Party, eager to expand in all directions by any means, and on the other from a mobilised Green Party with potential but hitherto untapped support in the British electorate. The Liberal Democrats may be able to rely on considerable reserves of active commitment from the membership, but there are grounds for some concern. The membership survey revealed significant dissonances between the views of the members and official policy on a number of important issues. On the other hand, while the members appear to favour a closer working relationship with Labour, it is not clear that the voters will do the same. The evidence from the past, such as it is, would suggest that they may not.

The third issue facing the party is its approach to party competition. Has it determined whether it is a radical or a centre party and accordingly, has it worked out a coherent and realistic strategy for expanding its vote, winning elections and gaining power? Can it sustain the analysis and conclusions of MacIver, Curtice and Rallings and Thrasher that it has developed a single-minded and coherent strategy, a clear and self-consciously distinctive electoral base and that it is capable of continuing to win parliamentary seats even if its share of the vote does not increase?

The Liberal Democrats do seem to have acquired and developed a social base of support that is more coherent and probably more reliable than any that the Liberals ever had. They have consolidated one or two regional bridgeheads that may provide them with the concentrations of electoral support that were always denied to their predecessors. They have greatly extended their influence in local government and, if the expectations of the community politics strategy are borne out, they may be able to convert this into a stronger position in national politics. They have consciously evolved and refined a strategy designed to maximise the advantages to be gained from these circumstances. These developments do not in themselves ensure that the Liberal Democrats can avoid being characterised as simply another third party, but they do enhance their capability and effectiveness in the arena of party competition. Their strategy relies on the conversion of their strong local government base into majorities at parliamentary elections, the effective exploitation of regional concentrations of support, the targeting of winnable seats and the wider application of the campaigning style and the techniques of community politics. This strategy may cease to be a singular advantage if it is countered or even copied by other parties increasingly aware of its effectiveness or if the Liberal Democrats themselves experience even a marginal loss of electoral support.

All these observations, like all observations in politics must be provisional and speculative, but they do constitiute a relatively optimistic prospect for the Liberal Democrats. While the party can take encouragement from its performance to date, there remain problems and dangers facing it, many of which are actually beyond its control. On the other hand, how it responds to these problems and how it deals with matters that are within its control could have a very important bearing on its future and determine its ability to take advantage of whatever opportunities the fortunes of politics make available to it.

Notes

1 For a concise and comprehensive discussion of these developments, see Ian Budge *et al.*, *The Changing British Political System*, Longman, 1988.

2 S.J. Ingle, "SLD and SDP: End of a Chapter or End of the Book?', in *Talking Politics*, Vol. 1, No. 2, 1988–89; R. Liddle, 'Democracy – David Owen Style', *New Statesman*, 21 August 1987.

3 David Steel, *Against Goliath*, Pan Books, 1991, p.365.

4 *Guardian*, 20 October 1990; *New Statesman*, 26 October, 1990.

5 A very readable, though not entirely dispassionate account of this episode is provided in Trevor Wilson, *The Downfall of the Liberal Party 1914–1935*, Collins, 1966.

in Trevor Wilson, *The Downfall of the Liberal Party 1914–1935,* Collins, 1966.

6 For a recent discussion, see Paul Adelman, 'The Decline of the Liberal Party 1910–1931', in *Modern History Review*, Vol. 1, No. 2, 1989

7 Local Liberal Party organisations were closed during the First World War and never wholly recovered, while Conservative and Labour organisations remained active and built up their resources during the war.

8 Jo Grimond, *The Liberal Future*, Faber and Faber, 1959, G. Watson (ed.), *The Unservile State,* Allen and Unwin, 1957.

9 D.E. Butler, *The British General election of 1951*, Macmillan, 1952.

10 Michael Steed, 'TheElectoral Strategy of the Liberal Party', in Vernon Bogdanor *Liberal Party Politics*, Clarendon, 1983, pp. 77–78.

11 John Stevenson, *Third Party Politics since 1945,* Blackwell, 1993.

12 Jo Grimond, *The Liberal Challenge*, Hollis & Carter, 1963, p.309. A more complete account is provided in Ian Bradley, *The Strange Rebirth of Liberal Britain*, Chatto & Windus,1985.

13 Jeremy Josephs, *Inside the Alliance*, John Martin Publishing, 1983, p.1–38. Cf David Steel, *Against Goliath*, Pan Books, 1991, pp.261–300.; Hugh Stephenson, *Claret and Chips: the Rise of the SDP*, Michael Joseph, 1982, p.29.

14 Roy Jenkins, *A Life at the Centre*, Macmillan, 1992; David Owen, *Time to Declare*, Penguin, 1992; and David Steel, *Against Goliath*, Pan Books, 1991.

15 See Peter Clarke, 'Liberals and Social Democrats in Historical Perspective', in Vernon Bogdanor (ed.), *Liberal Party Politics,* Clarendon Press 1983; Peter Clarke, *Liberals and Social Democrats*, Cambridge University Press, 1978; Robert Behrens, 'Social Democracy and Liberalism', in L. Tivey and A. Wright, *Party Ideology in Britain*, Routledge, 1989; Michael Meadowcroft and David Marquand, *Liberalism and Social Democracy*, Liberal Publications, 1981.

16 William Wallace, *op. cit.*; Michael Steed, 'The Liberal Party', in H.M. Drucker, *Multi-party Britain*, Macmillan, 1979; A. Cyr, *Liberal Party Politics in Britain*, John Calder, 1977. Cf. D. Butler and D. Stokes, *Political Change in Britain*, Penguin, 1969, Ch. 11; this passage is still of interest although it has been heavily criticised for its methodology and the reliability of its evidence.

17 A. Heath *et al*, *Understanding Political Change*, Pergamon, 1991, pp.10–31.

18 Ian Bradley, *Breaking the Mould,* Martin Robertson, 1981, pp.90–91; A. Heath, *et al.*, *How Britain Votes*, Pergamon, 1985, p.3 and pp.170–175.

Part One

The Development of
the Party

CHAPTER 1

Liberals to Liberal Democrats

John Stevenson

The outcome of the 1992 election confirmed the Liberal Democrats as an effective third party in British politics, but denied them the opportunity to participate in power through a 'hung' parliament, the role they had sought for a generation of third party politics.[1] In hindsight, however, taking the history of the Liberal Party since 1945, this may have been disappointing but not entirely unsatisfactory. In the years immediately after the Second World War the Liberal Party as a force in British politics seemed doomed to extinction.

Probably the most useful way of examining the history of third party politics since 1945 is to consider it in four phases: the period up to 1958 when the decline of the Liberal Party apparently continued the trends of the inter-war years; the period from 1958 to 1981 when the Liberal Party revived; the period from 1981 to 1988 when the formation of the SDP and its alliance with the Liberals brought the highest level of third party support for decades; and the period since 1988 when a new, merged party, the Liberal Democrats, was formed.

The threat of extinction

By the Second World War the writing seemed to be on the wall for the Liberal Party. Beneath the sorry tale of decline at parliamentary level lay the decay of grass-roots organisation. While the Conservative Party under Baldwin and Chamberlain consolidated its position as the party of the shires and the urban middle class and Labour reinforced its hold on the industrial heartlands, from the 1920s, the Liberals were quite literally being squeezed out and their support increasingly reduced to the Celtic fringe and a few independent bastions in England. The Second World War did little to interrupt that decline. The thousands of young men and women who voted for the first time in 1945, the children of the Depression, looked to the Labour Party to build the 'New Jerusalem'.

23

The 1945 election result was a disaster. Only 12 Liberal MPs were returned in 1945, and of the 475 Liberal candidates 319 – two-thirds – lost their deposits. The total Liberal share of the vote was just 9 per cent.[2]

During the early 1950s the Liberals were further reduced: to nine seats in 1950 and to six in 1951. When Churchill in 1951 offered the Liberal leader Clement Davies a place in his government and the offer was refused, it looked like a brave gesture from a dying man. At the 1955 election the party, fielding 110 candidates with 60 lost deposits, remained at six MPs and accounted for less than 3 per cent of votes cast. Labour and Conservatives between them now accounted for over 96 per cent of the vote. In the era of two-party dominance the Liberals appeared irrelevant, a 'party living on its traditions with virtually no organization whatsoever'.[3] In local government they were equally weak. Only 2.2 per cent of councillors elected in 1950 were Liberal; by 1955 it was down to 1.5 per cent.[4] Moreover, the party was adrift on policy. Its progressive clothes had been stolen by Labour in the post-war years, and those who rejected socialism found an attractive option in a Tory party influenced by Liberal ideas and led by moderates like Eden and Macmillan.

This nadir in Liberal fortunes preceded the first hints of a turn-around. In 1956 Clement Davies was succeeded by Jo Grimond, who quickly proved himself an attractive and vigorous leader. Aged only 43 in 1956, his seat in Orkney and Shetland gave him a secure basis from which to revitalise the party. Grimond gradually fashioned the Liberal Party as a party of the radical non-socialist centre-left, the position it has persistently claimed for itself ever since. Grimond was fortunate in coming to the leadership at a time when disenchantment with the Conservative government created opportunities for the Liberals. Even before Grimond came to the leadership the Liberals had scored some impressive results in parliamentary by-elections. Then, early in 1958, Ludovic Kennedy achieved second place at Rochdale with 35 per cent of the poll and two weeks later Mark Bonham-Carter achieved a breakthrough when he won Torrington from the Tories.

Liberal revival

The Torrington by-election marks the beginning of the second phase of Liberal politics after the Second World War. Between 1929 and 1958 the Liberal Party did not win a single by-election. After 1958 it was to receive much-needed publicity and welcome boosts to its confidence through its ability to overturn large majorities at by-elections. In 1962 the party achieved another spectacular success when Eric Lubbock won Orpington – the first Liberal breakthrough in the Conservative suburbs and a source of considerable optimism. The Liberals were beginning to act as a vehicle for anti-government protest. There was a more substantial basis to the Liberal revival, however, as shown in a doubling of the party's share of the vote in the 1959 general election.

The history of the party in the 1960s was a mixture of continued by-election successes, as in 1965 when David Steel won Roxburgh, Selkirk and Peebles, and a gradual increase in its share of the vote at general elections and the number of MPs returned: nine MPs in 1964, rising to twelve in 1966. The decade ended with a setback, however, when the Liberal vote fell in 1970 and the party was reduced to only six seats, demonstrating the switchback character of the Liberal revival. Although David Steel subsequently described the result as a disaster,[5] the Liberals, with over two million votes, were clearly recovering from the collapse of the 1950s.

One problem for the Liberals in late 1960s and 1970s was that they were challenged in the Celtic fringe by the Welsh and Scottish Nationalist Parties who threatened them in areas where they had been able to maintain an electoral base.[6] A second problem was that the Liberal party still lacked a clear identity for many voters; its capacity to act as a vehicle for protest was not yet matched by its ability to project a distinctive positive image. The paradox was that, while the Liberals seemed best able to capture new votes in middle-class, suburban, Tory seats, it had made little progress in its assault on Labour areas. Thus, when Jo Grimond resigned as leader in 1967, many commentators argued that his dream of a radical alternative to Labour had failed to materialise. The new leader in 1967 was Jeremy Thorpe. Once again the party had chosen a young leader, only 38 years old when chosen. Educated, like Grimond, at Oxford, he was a trained lawyer and a presentable television and media performer.

The late 1960s and 1970s brought a younger generation of Liberals to the fore, one by-product of student activism. The Young Liberals began a pronounced leftwards trend which caused considerable discomfort for the older generation. However, there were some lasting results. The Young Liberals placed increasing emphasis on what was known as 'community politics', direct action campaigns on local issues, sometimes dubbed 'pothole and pavement' politics by its enemies. It brought the Liberals into the forefront of grass-roots politics involving organisations such as tenants' groups, community associations and conservation lobbies. At the local level, Liberals were also able to take advantage of the decay and complacency of the major parties, particularly in urban areas. The *Focus* leaflet, a community newsletter, became the hallmark of local Liberal campaigning. Decayed and moribund local Labour parties, as in Liverpool, soon found themselves facing a powerful Liberal challenge. An important result of this was that the Liberals began to build a strong base of local councillors in places like Liverpool, Leeds and Birmingham.

A series of by-election victories in 1972–73 was followed by the Liberals winning fourteen seats in the 1974 election, obtaining over six million votes, one-fifth of all votes cast. The defeated prime minister, Edward Heath, opened talks about a coalition with the Liberals in order to preserve his government in power, but these broke down with Heath's refusal to promise electoral reform. The Liberals seemed on the verge of breakthrough to a share of power. Then, in 1976, there was another setback as the party was rocked by the personal scandal surrounding its leader Jeremy Thorpe, forcing his resignation and casting the Liberal brief once again into the doldrums.

Following an interregnum David Steel was elected leader through the operation of a newly devised electoral college. He was the first leader of a British political party in the twentieth century to be elected by a democratic procedure. Steel's election as a fresh, young leader with impeccable credentials as a 'son of the manse' finally buried the Thorpe affair. Behind Steel's clean-cut image, however, was the skilled politician who was determined to exploit the weakness of the Labour government to give the Liberal Party some share of power and the discipline of responsibility. In 1977 he was given a chance when prime minister James Callaghan sought a pact with the Liberals. The so-called 'Lib/Lab' pact gave the Liberals a consultative role, but no seats in Cabinet or a promise of proportional representation. Many Liberals believed a better deal could have been struck and there was much criticism of the pact at grass-roots level. The Liberals withdrew from the pact in 1978, but at the 1979 election they found their image smeared by their association with Labour. As their share of the vote fell by two million to 14 per cent to return only eleven MPs, another bid for decisive influence appeared to have failed.[7]

The SDP and the Alliance

The defeat of the Labour Party in 1979 brought to a head the strains and bitter conflicts between left and right within the party. Two effects of this contributed to the formation of the Social Democratic Party (SDP). First, Roy Jenkins, former deputy leader of the Labour Party, in his Dimbleby Memorial Lecture of 22 November 1979, after discussing the matter with David Steel, argued the need for a new centre party with a programme of radical, social and constitutional reform. The new party would seek to attract support from left and right and those who had hitherto played little part in politics. Jenkins' vision had roots in Dick Taverne's breakaway Democratic Labour, victor in the 1973 Lincoln by-election and ultimately in the broadly based Gaitskellite social democratic tradition which many felt was stifled by the Labour Party's close identification and constitutional entanglement with the trade union movement.

The other factor was the increased leftwards drift of the Labour Party and the formation in 1977 of a centre-right pressure group, Campaign for a Labour Victory, founded by Ian Wrigglesworth, John Cartwright, William Rodgers and Alec McGiven,[8] which became a vehicle for facilitating a breakaway from the Labour Party. The election of Michael Foot as leader on 10 November 1980, seen as a shift to the left, was followed by an acrimonious dispute over the procedure for choosing the leader in future. The alternative of one member one vote, as opposed to a system which gave a weighting to the trade unions, became the issue on which some MPs decided whether or not to stay in the Labour Party.

A week after the electoral college decision, the' Gang of Four', Roy Jenkins, David Owen, William Rodgers and Shirley Williams, issued the Limehouse Declaration on 25 January 1981 setting up an interim body called the Council for Social Democracy, which attracted the support of nine Labour MPs. The Liberals under Steel supported the creation of a non-socialist alternative to Thatcherism. An opinion poll in the *Sun* gave a putative Liberal–Social Democratic arrangement 51 per cent of popular support. One hundred prominent people gave their backing to the Council for Social Democracy in an advertisement in the *Guardian*, calling for funds and members. Shirley Williams resigned from Labour's National Executive and, on 2 March, twelve Labour MPs resigned the party whip. On 26 March the new Social Democratic Party was formally established, headed by a group of talented figures with Cabinet experience and consisting initially of fourteen MPs, one Conservative and thirteen Labour, the largest defection of MPs from the Labour Party since 1931.[9]

Almost immediately the question of an alliance with the Liberals arose. The Liberals were already the beneficiaries of Labour's disarray and the growing unpopularity of the Conservatives, and in the May 1981 local elections they recorded a net gain of 250 seats. Discussions between the Liberals and the SDP proceeded informally. A fortuitous opportunity came for Steel to consult with Shirley Williams and Bill Rodgers at the annual Anglo-German conference at Koenigswinter. The ground rules for the Alliance were laid, including arrangements to conduct alternate by-elections as they arose, an agreement on a share-out of constituencies in the event of a general election, and the decision to issue a joint statement of principles which was published as *A Fresh Start for Britain* on 16 June.

On 16 July 1981 the SDP had its first opportunity to test electoral support. In the safe Labour seat of Warrington where Liberals had hitherto obtained only a small vote, Roy Jenkins came within 1,700 of winning and rightly claimed a moral victory. This encouraging result helped to create a euphoric optimism for the prospects of 'breaking the mould' of British politics. At the Llandudno Liberal conference in September, the unratified alliance with the SDP received overwhelming support, culminating in David Steel's words, 'Go back to your constituencies and prepare for government'. The Alliance was then endorsed at the first SDP conference, a three-part event held in Perth, Bradford and London. Further defections from Labour brought the total of SDP MPs to 21. On 22 October Bill Pitt, a local Liberal, secured the first by-election victory for the Alliance in Croydon North-west.

Alliance support surged to an unprecedented level for a third party. In February 1981, just before the SDP was formed, the Liberals stood at 20 per cent in the opinion polls, against 36 for the Conservatives and 35 per cent for Labour. By October, Gallup was polling 40 per cent for the Alliance, reaching an astonishing 50 per cent in December.[10] In the 214 local government by-election contests between July and December 1981, Alliance candidates won almost half the seats.[11] Several opinion polls in the autumn and early winter of 1981 forecast a sweeping Alliance victory at a forthcoming general election. In a headline-grabbing by-election, Shirley Williams at Crosby in November 1981 converted a Conservative majority of over eighteen thousand into one of more than five thousand for the SDP. Jenkins' victory at Hillhead was narrower, but it confirmed the ability of the SDP to create the same 'bandwagon' effect as the Liberals.

The mould unbroken?

During the winter of 1981–82, when it seemed that the Alliance could sweep all before it, problems emerged. The agreement concluded between the Liberals and the SDP to contest half of the parliamentary seats at the forthcoming election with the arrangements to be worked out at a regional level brought some tensions to the surface. Many Liberals who assumed that the SDP as a new party would contest a selection of seats, perhaps up to a hundred in the first instance, were quickly disabused. The compromise of a 50/50 share-out created problems at local level for the Liberals, some of whom would have to accept giving up seats where they had worked for years. On the other hand, SDP newcomers to politics were less than ready to yield primacy to Liberal candidates and constituency organisations which claimed established tenure with little electoral success to show for it.

These frictions meant that negotiations over seat allocation proved long and time-consuming, exacerbated by differences in the organisation of the parties at local level. For a party like the Liberals, heavily dependent on relatively small numbers of activists, most of whom knew each other, there were real difficulties in relating to a party which was organised locally on the basis of area committees, sometimes responsible for several constituencies, which paid more attention to instructions from headquarters than had ever been the case amongst the Liberals. There were also complaints from Liberals that some of the local SDP were, in fact, their old enemies from local Labour politics in new guise, including Labour MPs and councillors who joined the SDP because they were threatened with deselection. These were minor irritants, greatly outweighed by the infusion of new supporters and activists,[12] but they had some effect on the support enjoyed by the Alliance in the opinion polls which, by early 1982, had been trimmed back to more like parity with the other parties, settling eventually at about half its peak level. Some attributed this change of fortune to the 'Falklands factor', but, in fact, the decline in Alliance support had already begun in early 1982, before the Falklands factor began to intervene (Table 1.1).

Table 1.1 Voting intentions according to Gallup, March 1981–July 1982

		Conservative%	Labour%	Alliance%
1981	March	30	34	32
	April	30	34	32
	May	32	35	29
	June	29	37	30
	July	30	40	26
	August	28	38	32
	September	32	36	29
	October	29	28	40
	November	26	29	42
	December	23	23	50
1982	January	27	29	39
	February	27	34	36
	March	31	33	33
	April	31	29	37
	May	41	28	29
	June	45	25	28
	July	46	27	24

Source: D. Butler and G. Butler, *British Political Facts, 1900–1994*, Macmillan, 1995,

In line with the polls, Alliance support fell to 28 per cent in the May 1982 local elections – the first national test of Alliance support. However, the two halves of the Alliance polled differently. More SDP seats were lost than gained as defecting Labour councillors were defeated, and the Liberals gained nearly five times as many seats as the SDP. The Alliance seemed set for a hard slog rather than a meteoric rise to power as it had promised a few months earlier. The Alliance also trailed in by-elections at Mitcham and Morden on 3 June, lost its deposit at Coatbridge and failed with the veteran Dick Taverne at Peckham. It had to wait for its next success until February 1983, when Simon Hughes secured Bermondsey with 58 per cent of the vote.

In the 1983 general election the Alliance mounted the most successful third party campaign in British post-war history but was still unable to 'break the mould' of British politics. The result was a triumph for the Conservatives, giving them a majority of 140 seats, on the basis of a simple plurality of 42 per cent of the vote. Labour plummeted to 28 per cent, its worst figure since 1918, while the Alliance with a strong surge in the last few days of the campaign ended at just over 25 per cent. This was the best third party showing since the 1920s, but it produced a meagre return of 23 seats. Labour with only just over 2 per cent more of the vote had 209.[13] The even spread of Alliance support meant that the 7.75 million votes cast for the Alliance were not translated into a proportionate share of seats, although they retained some of their by-election gains. The Alliance made further gains in Wales, the West Country and the Scottish borders, where the Liberal vote was most concentrated. The SDP, considered as a separate force, fared less well. Only five of their sitting MPs were returned and two of the Gang of Four, Shirley Williams and William Rodgers, lost their seats.

The Alliance manifesto *Working Together for Britain* included some points from the earlier joint statement *A Fresh Start for Britain*, such as proportional representation, devolution, freedom of information, industrial partnership and commitment to the EC, all of which had been Liberal policies for decades. It was well received and contained a number of policies which firmed up previous Liberal positions on economic expansion, incomes policy and trade union reform. In the midst of record unemployment the Alliance promised a programme of economic expansion to create a million jobs over two years.

The Alliance divided

The Alliance remained in a frustrating position between 1983 and 1987. While it consolidated its position in local government and scored occasional by-election successes, its credibility as an alternative governing party remained in doubt. Moreover, David Owen's assumption of the leadership of the SDP in place of Roy Jenkins in 1983 created difficulties. Steel had close relations with Roy Jenkins, but less so with the other members of the Gang of Four, especially David Owen. Jenkins and Steel saw the SDP playing an interim role in the realignment of British politics, bringing in defectors from the Labour Party and hitherto uncommitted voters and potential activists leading eventually to a merger with the Liberals. Owen, on the other hand, a dominant and ambitious personality, well connected in the media, with strong views on issues such as defence and economic policy, was a strong advocate of the SDP's claim to a permanent distinct identity and opposed to a merger with the Liberals. This difference in approach and emphasis was to bedevil relationships between Owenites and Jenkinsites over the next few years.

During the summer and autumn of 1986 disagreements over defence policy threatened a major rift in the Alliance. The strong unilateralist and pacifist elements in the Liberal Party were increasingly roused by what they saw as David Owen's pre-emption of nuclear policy and David Steel's apparent compliance on a Euro-bomb. The resulting revolt of the Liberal assembly at Eastbourne in September 1986, passing a non-nuclear amendment on defence policy in defiance of the party leadership, brought this rift into the open. Its immediate effects on the opinion polls demonstrated the vulnerability of Alliance support to disunity within its ranks. Although a compromise defence policy was patched up by the beginnng of 1987, in time for a relaunch rally, there remained an underlying concern that tensions over defence and the dual leadership would impair the performance of the Alliance.

There were optimistic signs, however. The build-up of support at local level continued. In 1987 the Alliance gained 400 council seats and more councils passed either into Alliance control or, more often, into no overall control. By-elections were also encouraging, particularly from the summer of 1986. On a swing of almost 20 per cent, the Alliance secured a major success at Ryedale in May, collapsing the Conservatives and squeezing Labour with a near miss, within one hundred votes, at West Derbyshire on the same day on a swing of 12 per cent. In a more difficult contest there was another good showing at Newcastle-under-Lyme in July on a swing of 17 per cent. An SDP gain at Greenwich in late February 1987 was followed in March by the successful Liberal defence of Truro (Table 1.2).

The overall electoral position, however, was not especially favourable. The best by-election successes were against the Conservatives, but, with the economy moving ahead and privatisation and council house sales popular with the electorate, the Conservative lead in the polls seemed secure.Although the new Labour leader, Neil Kinnock,was try-

Table 1.2 Alliance by-election performance, July 1985–March 1987

Date	Constituency	% change in Lib/SDP vote
4.7.85	Brecon and Radnor	+ 11.4
6.12.85	Tyne Bridge	+ 11.4
10.4.86	Fulham	+ 0.6
8.5.86	Ryedale	+ 19.8
8.5.86	Derbyshire West	+ 12.3
17.7.86	Newcastle-under-Lyme	+ 17.7
13.11.86	Knowsley North	+ 19.8
26.2.87	Greenwich	+ 27.8
12.3.87	Truro	+ 3.1

ing to modernise his party, he was still burdened by the unpopular policies which had dragged Labour to defeat in 1983. The May 1987 municipal elections were encouraging for the Conservatives, giving them sufficient confidence to call a general election in June 1987.

The Alliance campaigned on a manifesto *Britain United: The Time Has Come*. The Alliance sought, if it held the balance of power, to curb the excesses of both main parties and to initiate its Great Reform Charter, proposing electoral reform, repeal of the Official Secrets Act, a Freedom of Information Act, regional government and fixed-term parliaments. The arrangement agreed at the outset of the 1983 campaign, when Jenkins had been designated 'Prime Minister in waiting', was replaced by a joint leadership of the campaign by David Owen and David Steel. The offer to work with other parties attracted inevitable media attention, but it was not clear that the Alliance leaders had an agreed strategy for its implementation. While David Steel remained judiciously uncommitted, apart from ruling out support for certain Conservative policies, David Owen seemed to indicate that he regarded the Conservatives as preferred partners because of his own views on nuclear weapons and his distrust of Labour on that issue. Many regarded this as a dangerous breach in the carefully contrived Alliance position, which made it difficult for Alliance candidates to capitalise as effectively as they might have done on the anti-Conservative vote and probably damaged the prospects for an advance on the 1983 result. Another factor was the presidential nature of the election campaign. The Conservative campaign was built around Thatcher as one of the most determined of Britain's post-war leaders. Labour responded by presenting Neil Kinnock in similarly presidential terms with slick party political broadcasts and well-managed rallies. In contrast, the Alliance's joint leadership failed to make a distinctive impact.

With 22.7 per cent of the vote the Alliance obtained only 22 seats. The Conservatives, staying ahead in the polls almost throughout the campaign, scored another smashing victory by almost one hundred seats. Labour, though fighting what many saw as an excellent campaign, secured just over 30 per cent of the vote, not sufficient to trouble the Conservatives, but enough to win 229 seats.[14] After a second general election, it was evident that the Alliance had failed to break the mould of British politics. To many it seemed a good moment for taking stock and rethinking the Alliance's position.

Making a new party

The opportunity to rethink came more quickly than almost anyone expected. The weekend following the general election, David Steel called for a 'democratic fusion' of the two wings of the Alliance and appealed directly to SDP members for their support. David Owen immediately declared against a merger and called for a ballot of SDP members. At a special conference in January 1988 the Liberals, with a small dissenting minority, formally agreed to a merger with the SDP to form a new political party. Local parties were already coming together and, despite resistance from Owen and others, the SDP membership approved a full merger in a ballot declared on 2 March, thus overcoming the final obstacle to the launch of the Social and Liberal Democrats (SLD) on 3 March.

The SDP ballot, while showing a comfortable majority (65.3 per cent) for merger, also revealed a substantial minority for continuing the SDP as a distinct party. On 8 March this took effect when Owen relaunched the SDP with himself as leader and John Cartwright as president.

The merger issue brought the tensions between Steel and Owen to a head but left a legacy of wrangling, bitterness and disillusionment. Thus the launch of the Social and Liberal Democrats was not propitious. During the first year there was a collapse of support in opinion polls and a steady loss of members and activists. The SLD and the SDP seemed intent not only on splitting the former Alliance vote but also on reducing their combined support and actually on destroying each other.

Under the temporary joint leadership of David Steel and Robert Maclennan the new party faced two tests. The first was the local elections of May 1988, in which, as anticipated, the new SLD lost ground, with a net loss of over sixty council seats, but taken over the broad spectrum of seats being defended, the losses were fairly marginal. More encouraging was that the party secured a vote considerably better than its opinion poll ratings, while the weakness of the 'continuing' SDP, which lost heavily, was ruthlessly exposed.

The second test was the question of leadership, held in abeyance until after the local elections had been fought. As widely anticipated, David Steel declared that he would not be a candidate for the leadership. By the opening of the eight-week election campaign in June 1988, the two candidates were Paddy Ashdown and Alan Beith. In a series of 'hustings meetings' up and down the country, it soon became apparent that there were few differences of principle between the candidates: more ones of personality and strategy. Ashdown's insistence that the SLD must replace the Labour Party was met by Beith's argument that such a strategy was unrealistic. The outcome, however, was a decisive victory for Ashdown by six votes to one.

Ashdown had an unusual background to succeed the past leaders of the Liberal Party and the Alliance. A former marine commando and executive, he was seen as an attractive, fresh personality who had come from third place to a winning position in his own constituency of Yeovil by classic community campaigning. As an MP of only five years' standing and a largely unknown quantity to the electorate he was bound to face difficulties in establishing his credibility as the effective leader of a new third force.

The first conferences since the break-up of the Alliance were eagerly awaited to see how the ex-partners would fare. The SDP's conference at Torquay in September 1988 was notable for David Owen's clear declaration that his party would continue. The SLD conference at Blackpool in the same month debated the short name by which the party would be known and, by a clear majority accepted the short title of The Democrats. With by-elections and European Parliament elections pending, however, the future of the old Alliance partners still appeared to hang in the balance. The new SLD and the continuing SDP faced each other in their first by-election at Kensington and neither emerged creditably. The SLD was unable to repeat the bandwagon effect of earlier by-elections, its only crumb of comfort being that the SDP candidate obtained fewer votes and almost lost his deposit. The Richmond and Epping Forest by-elections seemed to show that the existence of two parties claiming to stand as an alternative to Labour and the Conservatives was likely to damage both. A good second place at Epping by the SLD might have been a victory in other circumstances. At Richmond, the SDP was able to take second place over the SLD, exposing how effectively their intervention could spoil any advance by the Democrats.

The Social and Liberal Democrats, however, were stronger than their poll ratings and parliamentary by-election results showed. In the 1988 local elections the SLD put forward over 1,700 candidates, the SDP only 280. The SLD had 303 elected, the SDP only 4. In local by-elections from March 1988 to March 1989, the SLD elected 87 councillors against the SDP's single success. The SLD share of the vote was also much higher than its poll ratings suggested, at an average of 30.8 per cent in seats contested over the twelve months to March 1989. It was the local strength of the SLD, resting on the earlier successes of the Liberals which gave it some resilience during its most difficult period. The 1989 May local elections saw this disparity between the former Alliance partners confirmed. The SLD defended 619 seats compared with the SDP's 31. In the previous twelve months the SLD contested 307 of 394 by-elections, while the SDP could manage only 47. By April 1989, the SLD fielded 2,254 candidates in the 3,565 by-elections contested. The May local elections saw the SLD lose more than a hundred seats, considerably less than the 200 losses Ashdown had predicted as late as January. While the opinion polls showed support in single figures, the average share of the poll in the May elections was 20 per cent.[15]

The next test of strength came a month later in the European Parliament elections of June 1989. The initial background to the elections seemed promising. The Owenite SDP decided to withdraw as a national force following its evident inability to contest anything like a full slate of local council seats. However, the SLD was faced with serious financial problems and organisational fatigue. It was decided not to put much central effort into the elections, leaving it to local parties to find the substantial deposits required for European parliamentary constituencies and meet the cost of the campaigns themselves. At a critical juncture in the life of the new party this was an understandable decision. Unfortunately it occurred just at the point when a new force was appearing on the scene. The sudden revival of environmental concern in 1988–89 brought about by new evidence of global warming and damage to the ozone layer gave an enormous boost to the Green Party. From a minor force as fringe candidates in local elections, their support mushroomed to fill the vacuum left by the disarray in the old Alliance partners. In the European Parliament elections it was the Greens who were to demonstrate just how much damage the disputes over the merger had done to the Social and Liberal Democrats, beating them into fourth place. The SLD received only 6 per cent of votes cast while the Greens scored almost 15 per cent.[16]

Suddenly, all the media attention previously concentrated on the Alliance switched to this new phenomenon. The Green Party attracted a flood of new members, some of them ex-Liberals disillusioned by the more professional ethos which Ashdown was attempting to instil into his struggling party. The national opinion polls showed the Greens ahead of the SLD, now well down in single figures. As well as losing support, the SLD's financial difficulties were so serious that many of the headquarters staff had to be sacked and the network of regional agents disbanded. Membership fell to about seventy-five thousand, some five thousand fewer than voted in the leadership contest in 1988.

The local election results proved a more reliable guide than the European Parliament elections to the fate of the SLD as the major third party. The SDP was now clearly in decline and it had in effect quit the scene as a national force as its poll ratings fell and it failed to secure any by-election successes. The Social and Liberal Democrats moved swiftly to prove their 'green' credentials. They were in a particularly strong position to do so, being able to demonstrate that they had taken up environmental issues before anyone else and had put green policies into practice in local government. By the September 1990 conference, the SLD was hanging onto its modest share of the poll ratings. These ratings were now barely in double figures but they were clear of the Greens and 'others' by a few percentage points.[17] What was more serious was the still widespread confusion about the identity of the party, a confusion compounded by the change in its name. The short title of Democrats had been agreed without enthusiasm by the majority, primarily as a gesture to the sensitivities of former SDP members, concerned about a 'takeover' by the Liberals. The gesture was a failure, however, and instead of becoming an icon of recognition, the new name became a liability. It created dissatisfaction and embarrassment amongst party members and sheer bewilderment amongst the electorate. Gallup revealed the depths of the credibility gap facing the party when it found that nearly three-quarters of its respondents in September 1990 either did not know the new party's name or got it wrong.

Fashioning the Liberal Democrats

It was clear to both the leadership and the membership that the party must establish its identity and project a new image. The first step was to adopt a name and title with which the membership would be comfortable. Thus the party agreed on Liberal Democrats, a name which found favour with members from both sides of the former Alliance. After much discussion and redrafting, the party then published the document *Our Different Vision*, an attempt to state the party's distinct philosophy and political position. Although these developments occurred when the Labour Party was recovering and making some gains, the Liberal Democrats were also able to benefit from the growing unpopularity of the Conservative government. The poll tax was the crucial issue, its unpopularity surpassing the government's worst fears, while its identification with Mrs Thatcher seriously damaged her own popularity as well as that of the government. Her speech at the Conservative Party conference in October 1990, likening the Liberal Democrats to the 'dead parrot' of the Monty Python sketch, unintentionally highlighted this. The parrot returned to haunt her, a week later, when the Liberal Democrats scored a major by-election victory at Eastbourne, overturning a Conservative majority of 17,000 in a seat in which the Liberal Democrats had a sustained record in local government and their candidate, David Bellotti, was well known as a county councillor. Suddenly, from a point where they had been written off as serious contenders, the Liberal Democrats were back in the headlines.

Eastbourne helped to convince a sizeable proportion of Conservatives that Mrs Thatcher's style of leadership and the poll tax were likely to deny them victory at the next election. The resignation of Geoffrey Howe on 1 November and his sensational Commons attack on Mrs Thatcher plunged the Conservative Party into a leadership contest from which John Major emerged as the new leader.[18] The first by-election of his premiership in Ribble Valley in rural north Lancashire in March became a virtual referendum on the poll tax. Ribble Valley was the thirteenth safest Conservative seat in the country with a majority of almost twenty thousand, but it became the second great victory of the Liberal Democrats in their new image. Two days after the result, the end of the poll tax was announced by the Environment Secretary, Michael Heseltine, and in the subsequent budget the Chancellor put an additional 2.5 per cent on VAT to fund an immediate poll tax reduction of £140. Apart from the Orpington by-election which heralded Macmillan's unprecedented Cabinet reshuffle, probably no sequence of by-elections had more direct impact on the course of politics than Eastbourne and Ribble Valley. Eastbourne probably put Thatcher's continued premiership in question, while Ribble Valley certainly destroyed the poll tax.

The Liberal Democrats now began to benefit from the afterglow of by-election success. They entered the local council elections in May 1991 anticipating a modest loss of seats. Because of the operation of the local government electoral cycle, the Liberal Democrats were defending seats won when the Alliance was in full swing four years earlier. The widespread gains surpassed all expectations and the surge of support continued into the 1991 autumn conference season, at the start of which the Gallup rating was 17.1 per cent, whereas a year earlier it scarcely reached double figures.[19] Although the party's overall poll ratings slipped back from the conference-time high-points, they still averaged 14 to 15 per cent at the beginning of 1992.[20] Poll evidence also suggested that increasing numbers of the electorate were now able to distinguish the party and had some idea of its policies. Moreover, Paddy Ashdown registered a high level of personal support as leader of the Liberal Democrats, with 58.6 per cent of respondents in the December 1991 Gallup poll thinking he was giving the party good leadership, a higher rating than either of the other party leaders.

The improvement in the position of the Liberal Democrats was matched by the demise or decline of competing parties. The SDP gave up the fight after the summer of 1990, while the surge of support for the Greens dissipated. The Liberal Democrats were now the only effective third party competing for votes throughout mainland Britain and, in the run-up to the 1992 election, they were in reasonably good spirit. The sequence of by-election successes which had marked their revival was confirmed by another success at Kincardine and Deeside in November 1991, turning a Conservative majority of two thousand into a Liberal democrat majority of nearly eight thousand. This result enabled the Liberal Democrats to strengthen their position in Scotland, first by forcing the Scottish

Nationalists into third place and secondly, overtaking the Conservatives as the second largest party in Scotland.

Facing the electoral challenge

The picture presented by many commentators in the pre-election period was that, coming from the brink of oblivion in 1988–89, the Liberal Democrats were a force to be reckoned with, though probably less formidable than the Alliance. Hence the ITN *Guide to the 1992 Election* predicted that the Liberal Democrats were unlikely to win the 23 per cent of the vote gained by the Alliance in 1987, because much of that support came from disaffected Labour voters who had returned to Kinnock's 'new model' Labour Party. The potential limitations on the Liberal Democrat revival could be seen in the pattern of by-election successes. In the 1987–92 Parliament, Liberal Democrat gains were at the expense of the Conservatives and they also made some inroads into the Labour vote, especially at Liverpool Walton in April 1991 (although they were unable to prevent Labour retaining that seat), holding Hemsworth in November or making gains at Monmouth in June and Langbaugh in November. What was not yet clear, therefore, was whether, faced with a revived Labour Party, the Liberal Democrats could recapture the appeal of the Alliance and compete effectively for the anti-Conservative vote. On the evidence of opinion polls and by-election results, Labour and the Liberal Democrats appeared to be rivals competing for the anti-government vote.

On the other hand, experience suggested that pre-election polls tended to underestimate the Liberal Democrat vote. While some commentators felt that breaking the 20 per cent barrier was unlikely, such predictions had frequently been confounded by the result. Moreover, it was recognised that the Liberal Democrats could increase the number of their seats, even on a reduced share of the vote, by concentrating on specific targets. A 5 per cent decline in share of the vote in the 1991 council elections brought the Liberal Democrats over five hundred gains through effective targeting. The Liberal Democrats' position as the main challenger, in a swathe of some twenty seats where a swing of only 4 per cent would net them the victory, offered the alluring prospect of an increase in the number of seats even on a lower share of the vote.

In private briefings as late as January 1992, Ashdown was ready to play down expectations of the forthcoming election. His message was that the next election but one was the real prospect for his party, as a result of either a hung Parliament or a further Labour defeat which would bring them to accept electoral reform. With all the opinion polls making a hung Parliament or a very small Conservative majority the most likely outcome of the election, these were not unrealistic projections. Thus when the election was eventually called for 9 April, the Liberal Democrats already felt on an upward swing.

The Liberal Democrats' manifesto contained few surprises, but the main feature was their pledge to place one penny on the standard rate of income tax to fund increased spending on education and training. Ashdown's energetic campaigning, firm and credible commitments on policy, and the offer to participate in any coalition which would create a stable platform for economic recovery and electoral reform seemed to present a coherent message. The electorate appeared to respond and three out of the four polls taken in the final week of the campaign showed Liberal Democrat support at 20 per cent. Most remarkable of all, the last weekend of the campaign was dominated by the constitutional issue in an atmosphere in which every poll pointed to an indecisive outcome. Kinnock was forced to edge nearer the Liberal Democrats, offering them a place on the Labour Party's Plant Commission on electoral reform in what were widely regarded as the first moves in post-election manoeuvring between Labour and the Liberal Democrats. For their part, the Conservatives were forced into ever more vehement defence of the constitutional status quo, launching an attack on proportional representation as likely to produce unstable governments. For the first time ever, electoral reform was actually an issue in a general election.

The results were disappointing, giving the Conservatives an overall majority of 21 seats, while the Liberal Democrats secured just 20 seats on the basis of 18.3 per cent of the vote, more than one million down on 1987. The by-election gains of 1990–91 at Eastbourne, Ribble Valley and Kincardine and Deeside were lost as well as three gains made in 1987. While the Liberal Democrats did well in the south west, winning back Devon North and Cornwall North, they lost Southport and two seats in Wales. They took only two of their target seats, Cheltenham and Bath, but missed four others by less than a thousand votes, two of which, Portsmouth South and Stockton South required swings of less than 1 per cent. Other three-way marginals, including Edinburgh West, Colne Valley and two of the Plymouth divisions were equally disappointing.

The overall tally of lost seats and missed opportunities was more discouraging because the Labour Party's advance enabled them to gain second place in another 75 seats, putting them second in 186 constituencies as compared with 145 for the Liberal Democrats. The reality was that Labour had made significant gains overall and now occupied a more challenging position than previously in southern England. Most disheartening of all, the prospect of a hung parliament predicted in the exit polls vanished like a mirage as the results came in, depriving the Liberal Democrats of any role to play in the next government.

Ashdown struck a bullish note in his immediate post-election pronouncement. The result, he argued, confirmed that Labour could not win power on its own. Even with a recession and the legacy of the poll tax, Labour had been able to obtain only 35 per cent of all votes cast. Labour's attempt to prove itself a viable alternative government in its own right looked shattered. Secondly, Ashdown reinforced the traditional message about the unfairness of the electoral system, which had 'cheated' the Liberal Democrats out of most of the one hundred seats they would have gained under a proportional representation system.

The most important feature of the 1992 election result for the Liberal Democrats was the re-establishment of the party as a viable third force after the traumas of the merger. Subsequently, by continued by-election gains such as Newbury and Christchurch, by winning their first European Parliament seats in 1994 and by returning a record number of councillors in the May 1995 local elections, the Liberal Democrats established themselves as permanent and significant actors on the political scene. Compared with the low-point of its fortunes in 1988, twenty MPs, over one hundred thousand members, and the possible consideration of proportional representation by one of the other parties seemed a satisfactory outcome. Even in 1995, however, after fifty years of third party politics, the realisation of the larger hopes of Grimond, the Alliance leaders and Ashdown himself for a realignment of the left still seemed a long way off.

Conclusion

The Liberal Democrats in the mid-1990s occupy a position which is far stronger than that of the Liberals in the post-war period. By any objective standard, whether share of the vote, number of MPs, number of local councillors, by-election successes or party membership, there were substantial gains. However, the pattern of that advance was uneven and spasmodic, characterised by by-election victories and surges of support, followed by disappointing general election results. Thus the Liberal, Alliance and Liberal Democrat revivals have appeared to proceed at two steps forward and one step back, cumulatively impressive though experiencing short-term reverses.

What is also clear, however, is the dependence of the Liberal Democrats, as of the Alliance and Liberal Party before them, upon the fortunes of other parties. Revivals have usually occurred in the context of mid-term disillusion with Conservative governments. The decline of the Labour Party in the 1980s offered the prospect of winning support from disillusioned Labour voters. These prospects dimmed as Labour survived the defection of the Gang of Four and, under a succession of new leaders, refashioned itself into a party of the centre-left, increasingly like the Liberal Democrats.

The growth of third party support, however, has not simply been a reflection of the popularity of other parties but has been to a large extent self-generating and independent. The weakness of third party support in the post-war period reflected the inherent weakness of Liberal Party organisation and activity as well as the strength of Labour and the Conservatives. Arguably, the incremental rise of third party support since the 1960s has been due to the increasing ability and growing success of the Liberals, the Alliance, and Liberal Democrats in turning their potential support to account and retaining a significant portion of it through each revival and subsequent reverse.

Notes

1 For election results, see D. Butler and G. Butler (eds), *British Political Facts, 1900–1994*, Macmillan, 1995, p.219.

2 For the party's history up to the 1945 election, see J. Stevenson, *Third Party Politics since 1945: Liberals, Alliance and Liberal Democrats*, Blackwell, 1993, pp. 14–23.

3 R.S. Milne and H.C. Mackenzie, *Marginal Seat: A Study of Voting Behaviour in the Constituency of Bristol North-East at the General Election of 1955*, The Howard Society, 1958.

4 This compared with pre-war figures in 1935 and 1938 of 10 per cent and 7 per cent respectively.

5 D. Steel, *Against Goliath: David Steel's Story*, Pan Books, 1989, p. 66.

6 The SNP, for example, raised its candidature from five in 1959 to twenty in 1966.

7 For Liberal performance in 1979, see J. Rasmussen, 'David Steel's Liberals: Too Old to Cry, Too Hurt to Laugh', in H.R. Penniman (ed.), *Britain at the Polls, 1979: A Study of the General Election*, American Enterprise Institute, 1981, pp. 170–1.

8 For this link see G. Daly, 'The Campaign for Labour Victory and the Origins of the SDP', *Contemporary Record*, Vol. 7, No. 2, 1993, pp. 282–305.

9 See Witness Seminar, 'The Launch of the SDP, 1979–81', *Contemporary Record*, Vol. 7, No. 2, 1993, pp. 417–39.

10 Butler and Butler, *op. cit.*, p. 256.

11 Stevenson, *op. cit.*, p. 78.

12 See Witness Seminar, *op. cit.*, pp. 449–59, for discussion of the seat allocation issue.

13 Butler and Butler, *op. cit.*, p.219.

14 *Ibid.*, p.219.

15. *Ibid.*, p.258.

16 *Ibid.*, p.221.

17. *Ibid.*, p.258.

18 Conservative support rose ten points in Gallup, October 1990 to February 1991, *ibid.*, p. 258.

19 *Ibid.*

20 *Ibid.*

CHAPTER 2

The Liberal tradition

Michael Steed

The Liberal Democrats, though constituted only in 1988, are heirs to one of Britain's oldest parties. The Liberal Party was not just long-lasting for a political party, it had to survive most of this century out of office. After 1922, it only shared peacetime office briefly in 1931–32 and limited access to power during the Lib–Lab pact of 1977–78. What kept the party going?

Political parties change continuously, not only when a name is altered or a new constitution is adopted. A party must adapt as the political context or voters' demands change, while new leaders often seek to freshen up its image. At the same time, any lasting organisation develops a collective, if also selective, memory of its experiences and achievements. Such a memory can play a powerful role in maintaining the commitment that holds a party together, especially in adversity. A political party must motivate members who give their time, and often cash, for no material reward or career prospects. Motivation is made easier by building on a tradition, emphasising historical and ideological continuity which leaders and members share. This chapter explores how the Liberal tradition contributed to sustaining the party for so long while on the margins of British politics.

The 1936 Liberal convention

On 18 June 1936, there was a by-election in Lewes, Sussex, where the 1992 general election Liberal Democrat vote was to be 34.5 per cent and the Labour vote just 9.5 per cent. At the 1936 by-election no Liberal candidate stood, and the Labour vote was 34 per cent in a straight fight with a Conservative. Indeed, of the ten by-elections held in 1936, a Liberal candidate stood in only one, polling 4 per cent in Ross & Cromarty. As an electoral force, Liberalism seemed utterly exhausted. In the previous decade many erstwhile Liberals had duly decided they could better pursue their political beliefs and

41

prospects by joining the Labour Party or by working, within the Liberal National group, in close consort with the Conservatives.

On the day that Lewes voted, a two-day Liberal convention opened at the Kingsway Hall, London, with the ostensible purpose of bringing under a single umbrella the various bodies which then made up the Liberal Party. Strictly speaking, it founded the Liberal Party as an organisation, giving it for the first time an overall constitution, with a preamble setting out its aims and objects in a sort of mission statement. More importantly, it was a defiant decision by those Liberals present to maintain a separate party in existence. It was nearly twenty years before there was any real response from the electorate, in the form of a run of good by-election results in the winter of 1955–56, since when the party has slowly re-established itself, particularly in local government. Since that turning point, people sympathetic to its outlook or its policies have had reason to support it and to seek political careers through it.

However, it is less obvious why anyone should have thought such a career choice worthwhile during the wilderness years. A study of the British party system published in 1953 commented: 'one of the saddest aspects of the decline of the Liberal party is that so many brilliant men now in the prime of life are condemned to political futility because they belong to a party that has no hope of office'.[1] Yet not only did such leading figures persist in their commitment, but the party was remarkably successful in attracting fresh young blood. At the 1950 election, when it attempted a comeback, 42 per cent of its candidates were under the age of 40 and 13 per cent under 30.[2] Unlike many organisations in decline, the Liberal Party was never a dwindling band of ageing supporters. By the 1960s, its vigorous youth movement was one of the party's most notable features.

This is one reason that we should not neglect the party's continuity. Each generation of leading Liberals had attached themselves to the cause two or three decades earlier. On the whole, those who led the party, nationally or locally, into the alliance with the SDP joined it well before 1974, when its score of the six million votes encouraged academics and journalists to speculate that the Labour/Conservative two-party system was under threat. The leading figures in the party which they joined chose to be Liberals during the party's leanest times, yet also when they were able to meet legendary Liberal intellectuals and men who had served in Liberal governments. Occasional recruits were welcomed from other parties, but between the adhesion of the Peelites and the launch of the SDP, the Liberal Party was not influenced significantly by members from a different political tradition. Successive cohorts of leading Liberals who, by their example and their words, helped to attract and mould the attitudes of successive waves of new recruits represent a continuous as well as a distinct tradition.

A small political party with bleak electoral prospects, which is neither a one-issue party nor one based on a particular section of society (most small parties in western democracies are in effect one of these) has an acute problem. The Liberal Party's survival in adversity is a tribute to its own belief that what it stood for was important, distinctive and attractive. The Liberal tradition had to be strong, and deeply held, otherwise the party would not have been around when circumstances began to favour its revival, and Britain's third party today would not have had a Liberal title. Thus the determination of the Liberals of 1936 to preserve their party helps to explain why the Liberal Democrats exist today.

As part of the run-up to the 1936 convention, *The Liberal Magazine* invited ten leading Liberal intellectuals and parliamentarians to state why they were Liberals.[3] Three themes stand out among the responses: an emphasis on freedom or individualism, the claim to be the heirs of great philosophers (most commonly Locke and John Stuart Mill), and references to historic achievements or roots. Ernest Barker, Professor of Political Science at Cambridge University, took these back furthest: 'I found that the Liberal Party went back to the Green Ribbon Club of 1675 [and] had been a continuous force in English history, acting for causes I believed to be good – free churches, free parliaments, free trade and the freedom of labour'. Another, Francis Hirst (editor of *The Economist* from 1907 to 1916), put the sense of inherited tradition more personally: ' I was brought up in a Liberal atmosphere. Cobden, Bright and Gladstone were our household gods'. Liberal heroes were important to the making of tradition. John Morley, Gladstone's biographer, saw biography as a way of creating heroes; he duly became 'custodian of the Gladstonian legacy'.[4] Hirst had, as a young graduate, helped Morley with research on Gladstone, and regarded himself as Morley's disciple 'as he was a disciple of Cobden and J.S. Mill and as they were disciples of Adam Smith and Jeremy Bentham'.[5]

An earlier link was attached to the office of Liberal Party president, created in 1936. Isaac Foot, founder of the Cromwell Association in 1936, and the president of the Liberal Party in 1947–48, presented an early copy of the *Areopagitica*, Milton's eloquent defence of the principle of freedom of speech, to his successor as a symbol of the office. This was publicly signed by each president on taking office until 1987,[6] thus itself creating a tradition.

Affirming that freedom was the core of Liberalism defied the conventional view that politics was a polarised choice between left and right, the extremes of which were communism and fascism. Liberals simply did not accept the analysis which located them in the middle of that spectrum and preferred a political landscape in which totalitarianism, whether right or left, was the opposite extreme to their own ideal society. Somewhere between Liberalism and dictatorship, therefore, they saw the Labour and Conservative Parties lying together. At the founding congress of the Liberal International in Oxford in 1947, Gilbert Murray opened his inaugural address with the words, 'The great division in Europe is not socialist against capitalist ... The real division in Europe is the conflict between freedom and tyranny'.[7] Many Liberal speeches have been made in similar tones, often attaching high significance to the word association of 'liberty' and 'libera'.[8]

The preamble to the 1936 constitution began with the declaration of the party's devotion to freedom:

> The Liberal Party exists to build a Liberal Commonwealth, in which every citizen shall possess liberty, property and security, and none shall be enslaved by poverty, ignorance or unemployment. Its chief care is for the rights and opportunities of the individual, and in all spheres it sets freedom first.[9]

The preamble was amended and expanded in later years, especially when the party comprehensively revised its constitution in 1969 (see page 57). Echoes of it can still be found in the preamble to the Liberal Democrat constitution of 1987 (see page 245). However, the 1936/69 preamble, which followed the inspired and lucid prose of its drafter, Ramsay Muir, was more incisive and succinct. Only two substantial changes were made to Muir's draft by the 1936 convention.[10] One, adding a statement of Social Liberalism, is discussed later (see page 54). The other, encapsulating the nearest to a single-issue identity which the Liberal Party has ever had, added specific commitments to free trade. The reverence for free trade is unsurprising. Conflict over free trade underlay the realignment of parties in the 1840s out of which the Liberal Party emerged. Threats to free trade provided the Liberal Party with its biggest electoral triumph in 1906, helped it to reunite in 1923 and led to the departure of the Liberal ministers from the National Government in 1932. Yet, by the 1950s there was widespread agreement in Britain that worldwide free trade was a desirable objective and few still saw free trade as the essential distinguishing mark of the Liberal Party.

Free trade is symbolic of a bigger problem about Liberal identity. Once freedom became a consensual value in western democracies, the Liberal emphasis on it did not distinguish the party clearly enough to outsiders. Rather, it fed the argument that as much of what the Liberal Party had pioneered became widely accepted, the party ceased to have a function. It also failed to do justice to the richness and complexity of the Liberal tradition. In the survey of the party's history that follows, we therefore emphasise four elements in the record of the party's aspiration and achievement that most explain its distinctiveness and its place in Britain's three party system. These are its pursuit of constitutional reform, its commitment to social justice, its view of the character of Britain and its concern for peace.

The roots of Liberalism

Early expressions of Liberal ideas can be traced further back even than the Green Ribbon Club or the Cromwellian period. We could start with the Lollards, whose locally based preachers opposed war, condemned ecclesiastical wealth and power and emphasised everyone's right of access to the scriptures, thus beginning a tradition of British dissent, out of which Liberalism grew.

Eccleshall's collection of extracts from Liberal thinkers commences with the Civil War period, adding to the *Areopagitica* a quotation from the Levellers.[11] Another collection agrees that 'English Liberalism was born out of the 17th-century struggle for freedom of conscience and the resistance of Parliament to the arbitrary authority of the King', but its extracts only commence with Charles James Fox's speeches during the French Revolution.[12] Fox indeed came to be seen as an inspiration by Liberals, but it is strange that such a collection ignores the influence of Locke. Russell, on the other hand, who is both an historian of that period and a leading Liberal Democrat parliamentarian, does emphasise Locke, not just as a political philosopher but as an organiser of the early Whigs. Russell insists that the Whigs are the start of 'a continuous institutional tradition'. The Liberal Democrats, he claims, 'inherited the machinery, the membership and the goodwill of the Liberal Party as clearly as the Liberal Party inherited the membership, the machinery and the goodwill of the Whigs'.[13]

Historians of the nineteenth century dispute that the changeover from Whig to Liberal was so simple and there are important discontinuities between Whig and Liberal. There was far more continuity of ethos in the transition from Tory to Conservative; the Conservatives remained the party of squires and county, as the Tories had been before them. The Whigs' aristocratic style of politics, however, had little in common with the party of self-made middle-class leaders and democratic spirit which succeeded them. The foreign and economic policies of eighteenth-century Whig governments in no way anticipated those of nineteenth-century Liberal ones: there was a revolution in thinking between mercantilism and free trade. As the Liberal Party formed between 1857 and 1868 it brought together several distinct strands, only one of which was Whig.[14]

In due course the Whig strand distanced itself from the new party. This was already evident at the first Gladstonian victory in 1868, when the party lost ground in some counties where its support was over-dependent on Whig magnates. During Gladstone's first two governments it became increasingly clear that the majority of Whig/Liberal peers were attached more by historic sentiment than agreement with government policy. With Gladstone's conversion to Irish Home Rule most of these peers became Liberal Unionists, and in due course part of the huge Conservative majority in the House of Lords.[15] As a group the Whigs disappeared. In general political discourse the word 'Whig' became obsolete, while among Liberals it came to be used dismissively for party colleagues considered out of touch or out of date. In contrast, 'Tory' has continued to be used as a substitute for Conservative.

Although the Whig contribution to the Liberal Party was limited, significant differences between Whig and Tory three centuries ago were carried into the nineteenth-century dichotomy between Liberal and Conservative. They became an essential part of the Liberal tradition, a Whig heritage that can still be traced in the Liberal Democrats, and a fascinating example of how enduring political divisions and alliances can be.

The key political difference was over the constitution. Tories defended a traditionally royalist or monarchist view while Whigs championed parliamentary supremacy and the rule of law. In time this Whig view became the orthodoxy defended by Tories, and Whigs moved to more advanced views. Some Whigs, notably Fox, were involved in the brief outburst of agitation for reform in 1780. By 1830 the cry for reform had become the Whig cause and brought the Whigs back to power after a generation in opposition. The 1832 Reform Act maintained the Whig tradition of cautious movement from inherited, outdated institutions towards ones which were more rational and more democratic. That tradition moved fully into the Liberal Party, through which the pressure for the next two Reform Acts was expressed. A Liberal belief in constitutional reform and a constant search for more effective democratic institutions, in contrast to a Conservative faith in tradition and distrust of constitutional change, have lasted until today.

Conflicts of ideas in the late seventeenth century were as much over religion as politics. Both Whigs and Tories were parties of the Anglican establishment, but with significant differences of emphasis. The term Whig derived from a derisory Gaelic word for a Scottish presbyterian rebel; the Whigs took a more temporal view of the relationship between religion and the state which accepted the expediency of a church establishment which could be Calvinist in one part of Britain and episcopal in the rest. They were also the defenders of the 1689 Toleration Act which gave protection to dissenters. Conversely, the Tories reflected a more fervent and doctrinal Anglicanism. This Whig alliance with Scotland's character and English non-conformism, greatly strengthened in the early nineteenth century, was to make a profound mark on British Liberalism.

The difference between Whig and Tory over religion was also an incipient debate on the nature of Britishness. Jews had been allowed back in England by Cromwell, and French persecution of Protestants was bringing Huguenot refugees. The argument over naturalisation in the 1690s prefigures precisely the 'Tebbit test' of the 1990s. Those who welcomed the cultural and economic enrichment of British society were pitched against those who feared it. One contemporary description of the party system pinpointed 'a material difference between the Tories and the Whigs' as the Whigs 'being civil and friendly to Foreigners, whom they love, cherish and esteem' whereas the Tories 'are their declar'd enemies, treating all nations (unless you except the French Papists) with the utmost inhumanity, scurrility, and contempt'.[16] These profound dissonances between Whig and Tory over the religious and cultural character of Britishness are reflected in differences between Liberal and Conservative today in outlook and policy.

A century later, in the 1790s, reactions to the French Revolution opened up further differences between Whig and Tory. The Whigs split in 1794, with the Foxite Whigs the 'party of peace and civil and religious liberty', although Derry argues that Fox was guided by expediency rather than principle. However quintessentially Whiggish this was, Fox's stance came to be seen by Victorian Liberals as part of their heritage; his opposition to the Tory government's suppression of freedom of speech 'provided...a memorable historical mythology ... and became an integral part of essential whiggery'.[17] His criticism of the war with revolutionary France also established the patriotic legitimacy of opposition to a government's policy of war.

Formation of the Liberal Party

As the turmoil of the French revolutionary period was settling down, the word 'Liberal' entered the political vocabulary. It was first used in French and Spanish around 1810 to describe the reformers who championed ideas of popular sovereignty, individual freedom and constitutional rule enshrined in the 1812 Spanish Constitution. The first recorded use in British political debate was in 1816 when the poet Robert Southey referred scornfully in the *Quarterly Review* to 'the British Liberales'.[18] It was not until the 1830s that the anglicised form was commonly used.

Curiously, the word 'Radical' moved in the opposite direction. The English political term had been in use for half a century before it appeared pejoratively in French political dialogue around 1820 and was then adopted by the reforming forces themselves in the 1830s.[19] This terminological exchange reflects the fluidity of political labels at this period, and more significantly how, in contrast to its earlier specifically British roots, by this stage there was a pan-European inspiration of what came to be called Liberalism in

English but might have become here, as in French, Radicalism. Some five generations later the accidental way in which such labelling differences arose and then became loaded with significance was to cause confusion and difficulty as the Liberal, Radical and similar parties within Europe sought to form a common organisation.[20]

Within British domestic political discourse, the word 'radical' continued to be used inside the Liberal Party. Joseph Chamberlain's Radical Programmers of the 1880s resemble the Radical Bulletin Group within the Liberal Party of the 1970s in having a standpoint critical of the leadership and a feeling that the party's home was on the left. However, there is no continuity of organisation or thought and the repeated use of the label does not mean there is a coherent radical tradition within the party. Yet it was the early nineteenth-century Radical contribution which gave the Liberal Party much of its character. From the Radicals came an analysis which emphasised freedom as the engine of progress as well as a moral principle. The Radicals also bequeathed a popular campaigning style of democratic politics, the cutting edge of Victorian Liberal economic and financial policy and the distinctive thrust of its foreign policy.

There was never a Radical Party in the modern sense. Individual MPs and writers worked together as Radicals over issues such as penal reform and widening the franchise for several decades. In the 1840s the leading parliamentary and popular campaigners, Bright and Cobden, took their inspiration from the philosophic or Benthamite Radicals. They saw themselves as a 'school', of which they were 'chief professors' and did not 'purpose to make a trade of politics'.[21] They were sometimes known as the Radical Party, and also as the Manchester School or Party. From the Benthamite Radicals came also the most notable Liberal philosopher, John Stuart Mill. Mill's all too brief service as Liberal MP for Westminster (1865–68) emphasised his unsuitability for the rough and tumble of electoral politics, but his works *On Liberty* (1859) and *Considerations on Representative Government* (1861), published at the point when the Liberal Party was coming to recognise itself as such, became foundation texts of British Liberalism. It was Mill, a Radical, who gave clear meaning to the central Liberal concern for freedom.

Meanwhile the governments formed by Grey, Melbourne and Russell between 1830 and 1852 were Whig in personnel and style, though sometimes described as Liberal.[22] The Aberdeen government of 1852–55 was a coalition of Whigs and Peelites, with leading Radicals opposing it, especially over the Crimean War. Its successor, under Lord Palmerston, initially had the same political basis but was almost immediately transformed into a Whig administration by the withdrawal of the Peelites.

The Peelites, amongst whom Gladstone was by now the most prominent, did not contribute large numbers to the formation of the Liberal Party. Nevertheless, what they stood for should not be underestimated for its part in Liberalism's success in dominating British politics for many decades. Sir Robert Peel's conversion to the repeal of the Corn Laws in 1846 was, because he split the Tory Party, possibly a mistake for a party leader. For Peelites, however, it was an act of statesmanship, a demonstration that there were issues and interests which mattered more than party or political careers. Although the Peelites became by definition free traders, their route to that conclusion had been very different from that of the Radicals. They represented pragmatic reaction rather than philosophical reasoning; the wise instincts of a governing class rather than the populism of agitators. Gladstone himself was a deeply conservative man who saw the need for dramatic changes; he conveyed boldness and trust in a remarkable combination. In due course he came to define Liberalism in moral language and to embody distinctive Liberal ideas and principles, but there is a sense in which he remained at heart a Peelite.

Outside Parliament the forces that were to sustain Gladstonian Liberalism were active. The Quaker-led Peace Society campaigned for peace as an objective of foreign policy from 1816. From 1838 Cobden's Anti-Corn Law League and from 1853 the non-conformist Liberation Society developed popular agitation as a political method, with the focus on swaying votes at elections and the passage of reforms in Parliament. The growth of the press, especially in the large new industrial cities, was also crucial. After the repeal of stamp and paper duties (the 'tax on knowledge') in 1855, many local Liberal newspapers were founded and expanded rapidly. Campaigning editors remained a significant influence within Liberalism during the next century. These developments laid the foundations for the type of democratic politics, mobilising popular support through campaigning and education about issues, that not only formed the character of the Liberal Party, but also assured the transition from aristocracy to mass democracy in Britain without a revolution. An alternative path, represented by the Chartists of the 1840s with their challenge to Parliament, petered out and contributed little to the Liberal tradition.

In Parliament, a key date is 6 June 1859. Following the inconclusive outcome of the April 1859 election, a combination of Radicals and Peelites agreed to vote with the Whigs to bring down the minority Conservative government. Gladstone was not party to this agreement, but by joining Palmerston's goverment based on this combination, he signified his adhesion to the Liberal cause. In some respects, especially Palmerston's foreign policy, this was the last Whig government. In others, especially the combination of Whigs, Radicals and Peelites, it was the first Liberal government.

In 1860 the Liberal Registration Association (later the Liberal Central Association) was formed and Liberalism acquired a national organisational identity, and a party headquarters. But this was a whip-run, top-down body. Local party members only became involved in a national body when their representatives, working from bottom-up, formed the National Liberal Federation in 1877. This is as good a date as any to identify as the point when the Liberal Party became a fully fledged modern political party.

Thus the Liberal Party came together. It bore the hallmarks of the diverse forces, attitudes and types of political activity which had contributed to its formation. Its deep and bitter divisions after 1916 are regarded by some historians as contributing to its downfall. So too are the profound philosophical differences over the meaning and direction of Liberalism which occurred during the two decades which preceded that split. In truth, however, the Liberal Party was never united in the way that is said to be required for parties to merit success today. Yet there was a Liberal prime minister in a Liberal-dominated parliament for twenty-seven of the fifty years between 1868 and 1918. For half a century, the formula of vigorous internal debate within a broad unity of thought and purpose worked well enough.

Gladstonian Liberalism

The unity of purpose owed much to Gladstone's towering leadership. It is well summed up in his classic slogan: Peace, Retrenchment and Reform. The crusade for free trade explained the power of the association between the first two of these objectives. The argument advanced ceaselessly by Cobden and his disciples was that removing barriers and increasing trade would bring not only prosperity but peace.

On the whole since the Great War, and certainly since Hiroshima, peace has been a universally shared objective in British politics, albeit one fraught with difficulty of achievement. In Cobden's time it was very different. In a country which had been fighting wars of imperial expansion for centuries and where the hero's funeral accorded to the Duke of Wellington in 1852 had reawakened the national memory of almost a thousand years of war with France, to make peace the object of policy challenged the established order of politics much as *The Origin of Species* challenged established theology. The argument for peace, although supported by pacifists on moral grounds, was argued principally from rational and economic premises. Britain's best interests would be secured by expanding trade peacefully, not by expanding the area ruled by the British flag. Cobden also appealed to Whig tradition, exploring the parallel between Fox's opposition to the war with France and his own criticism of the Crimean War, concluding that, 'the annals of Parliament do not record a nobler struggle in a nobler cause'.[23]

Gladstonian Liberal governments were not pacifist. Arms were used to defend British interests, though more as a last resort than with Whig or Conservative governments. Liberals refused to glorify Empire, enabling Disraeli to make imperialism an emotive difference between the parties. Instead Gladstone's role in bringing an end to the dispute with the US government over the *Alabama* by accepting a costly international arbitration settlement was lauded by his biographer: 'the result did something to impair the popularity of Mr Gladstone's government, but his association with this high act of public policy is one of the things that give its brightest lustre to his fame'.[24] For possibly the first time, but certainly not the last, the difference between Liberal and Tory was defined as whether it was in the true national interest to secure peace through support for international order or to insist on the rights of sovereignty.

Retrenchment included fighting the demands on the public purse by the military and saw financial savings in the pursuit of peace. Gladstone's final resignation in 1894 followed his failure to carry his colleagues in opposing an increase in the naval estimates. He agonised: 'My name stands in Europe as a symbol of the policy of peace, moderation and non-aggression. What would be said of my active participation in a policy that will be taken as plunging England into the whirlpool of militarism?'[25]

Retrenchment also built on Gladstone's record in pursuing the greatest possible economy in public expenditure, allowing repeal of many taxes on consumption and reductions in income tax which climaxed in his 1874 election pledge to abolish income tax. However, he did not repeat the pledge and by 1894 the Liberal chancellor and later party leader, Sir William Harcourt, moved sharply towards more progressive taxation in his 'Death Duties Budget'.[26] The earlier Liberal principle of minimising government expenditure went with a desire to avoid government involvement in private economic activity. This did not necessarily mean lack of concern with social problems; rather it meant a strong belief that such problems were best tackled by voluntarism. Even at this period though, only a few Liberals took the extreme position of pure *laissez-faire*; those that did criticised such Gladstonian legislation as the Employers Liability Act 1880 or the Irish Land Act 1881, both of which interfered with private contracts.

Reform continued to be a foremost objective. It moved from making the House of Commons and local government more representative to wider constitutional questions. By the time the Second Reform Bill was under debate, advanced Liberals were advocating women's suffrage[27] and proportional representation.[28] Devolution followed suit as Gladstone called for 'arrangements under which Ireland, Scotland, Wales, portions of England, [could] deal with questions of local and special interest'[29] even before his conversion to Irish Home Rule. With the Liberal Unionist secession in 1886, the Gladstonian party became strongly identified with this cause; its 1892 election victory provided a Commons majority for Irish Home Rule, but this was vetoed by the House of Lords. The restless 85-year-old Gladstone wanted a dissolution on the issue of curbing the Lords power, anticipating the battle of 1909–11, and used his final address to the Commons for a vigorous assault on the peers.

It may be that if Gladstone had succeeded in implementing Home Rule, Ireland would have developed peacefully with a devolved parliament within the United Kingdom. It may be that by the 1890s both Irish Nationalist and Ulster Unionist passions were too strong for this solution to have worked. However, as bloodshed and bitterness have dogged British–Irish relations from 1916 to the present unresolved conflict in Northern Ireland, Liberals have recalled Gladstone's search for a constitutional solution to the Irish problem with justifiable pride and contrasted it with the inflexible Conservative defence of the Union. When devolution within Great Britain came back on the political agenda in the 1970s, Liberals with a sense of history often pointed to the lessons from Ireland. Certainly, of all issues which are still current in British politics, the contrasting Whig/Liberal and Tory/Unionist attitudes towards devolution provide the most striking continuity over centuries.

For campaigning Gladstonian Liberals, reform was bound up with the identification of privilege as the enemy. Bright's oratory was particularly notable for pitching Liberal demands against privilege. The language used was not that of egalitarianism: wide differences of wealth were seen as inevitable, but they had to be justified on a rational basis and to contribute to the general good. It was no defence to point to hallowed tradition or to quote the *laissez-faire* principle. If inequalities resulted from inherited status, nepotism, limitations on political rights or restrictive laws which carried no general benefit to society, they were vigorously denounced. Privilege was proclaimed a prime obstacle to progress: once privilege was abolished, men would be fully free and enabled to better their lot in life.

This approach enabled the Liberal Party to unite the demands of the new manufacturing and growing professional classes with those of the peripheral parts of Britain and the non-conformists who still encountered discrimination, and to combine them to popular feelings of resentment against the better-off. That resentment might have been mobilised on a class basis and from the 1870s there were socialists active on the political fringe seeking to do so. However, Liberal language eschewed class politics, identifying concentrations of land-ownership, the wealth and legal position of the established Churches in England and Wales and the way that political institutions and antiquated laws worked to the benefit of the few, particularly the aristocracy, as the equivalent of what others would call the class enemy. The 1867 Reform Act gave the Liberal Party a more working-class electoral base and threw it into a natural alliance with the emerging trade union movement; electorally it was strongest in big cities and industrial regions. However, the party always saw itself as acting in the interests of society as a whole, and like society, was essentially middle class in its leadership.

A stronger pattern, despite the party's nationwide appeal, picked up the Whig alliance with Scotland and dissent. Late nineteenth-century Liberal electoral strongholds were in Wales (which had gone solidly non-conformist), in much of Scotland, of the north of England and in Cornwall. Conversely, the party was weak in most of the south east and, among the big cities, Birmingham (after 1886) and Liverpool.[30] There is some socio-economic explanation for this geography, but it reflects more strongly the cultural differences over Church and State, the Empire and Ireland, that lay at the heart of the Liberal/Tory dichotomy.

New Liberalism

By the time Gladstone retired, the party was in the throes of a vigorous debate over its purpose. The context was changing: the increasing flexing of trade union muscles; the growing awareness that social problems were not easing with greater prosperity; the shift from economics to sociology as the source of theories of how progress was to be achieved. Among Liberal intellectuals a new school was growing. This school, New or Social Liberalism, whose leading proponents were T.H. Green, L.T. Hobhouse and J.A. Hobson, was to have as profound an impact on the character of twentieth-century British Liberalism as the Manchester School had on Gladstonian Liberalism.

In 1902, in his book *Liberalism*, a young philosopher/politician in the party set out how he thought Liberalism should be developing.[31] Herbert Samuel was of the generation who had been directly inspired by Gladstone's final years, but looked forward to careers in a post-Gladstonian party. He was to become party leader in 1931, and was still a guiding spirit as politics moved into the television age; in 1951 he presented, for his party, the first ever television election broadcast. As much as anyone, Samuel symbolised the generation who sacrificed career to keep the party alive in the 1930s.

Samuel demonstrated that social reform had been steadily moving up the Liberal agenda, citing numerous measures of the 1892–95 government in his book. He met head-on what he saw as the traditional Liberal distrust of the state, arguing that, having replaced an aristocratic and corrupt regime with a democratic parliament and competent administration, Liberals should now use the machinery they had reformed. Samuel's book's structure emphasises the shift: after a short introductory section, a set of chapters headed 'state action' takes up half the book; classic Liberal concerns of the constitution and imperial and foreign policy are relegated, and retrenchment does not even figure in the index.

Yet the platform on which the Liberal Party won its greatest election victory did not reflect this enthusiasm for expanding the role of the state to tackle social ills. As Russell's analysis of candidates' election addresses shows,[32] the classic Liberal causes still dominated the way the party presented itself. Free trade (mentioned by 98 per cent) was the rallying cry, followed by four issues mentioned by over three-quarters, two reflecting non-conformist priorities (amending the pro-Anglican Balfour Education Act and Licensing Reform) and two classically Gladstonian in moral tone: Ireland and Chinese labour in South Africa. The issues that Russell groups as 'Poor Law reform and pensions' came sixth, appearing in 69 per cent of manifestos, but unemployment legislation (41 per cent) and workers' compensation (22 per cent) were well down, outnumbered by candidates who thought it worth reiterating support for retrenchment (54 per cent). What triumphed in 1906 was not Social Liberalism.

The 1906–14 Liberal government achieved little progress on the issues dear to Liberal hearts – education, temperance, Ireland or constitutional and electoral reform. Its major achievements were the social reform priorities of the New Liberals. By introducing old-age pensions and a national insurance scheme against unemployment, sickness and industrial injuries and by establishing a nationwide network of labour exchanges it laid the foundations of the welfare state. To finance this, taxation was sharply increased and made more progressive by being concentrated on land, inheritance and higher incomes. This government, along with Gladstone's and the 1945 Labour government, is rightly regarded as one of Britain's major reforming governments.

Subsequently Liberals have taken great pride in this achievement, yet it nearly never happened. After two years in office, facing the Unionist blocking strength in the Lords, the government had failed to deliver to its own supporters and was losing ground badly in by-elections. Then the new Chancellor of the Exchequer, David Lloyd George, introduced his People's Budget, galvanising his party, reviving its populist campaigning style and producing an electoral turn-round in by-elections. Fighting on this Social Liberal platform linked to an old battle against the power of the peers, the Liberal Party went on to win two more elections. Three victories in a row is not common in British democratic politics: the Conservative Party has managed it twice, and Labour never. Perhaps more significantly, to judge from by-elections in the 1911–14 period, the shift in Liberalism's appeal stemmed the growth of the Labour Party.

The somewhat accidental and electorally opportunistic manner of this reversal of the principle of retrenchment should be matched by a more sympathetic interpretation. Liberalism had wrongly been written off after Gladstone's final retirement, when the party had appeared to be profoundly divided. Its capacity to regather, redefine itself and recover so fully was not chance. It followed rather from the flexibility, breadth and strength of its appeal, which were derived from the way the party was formed. It was in the process of absorbing and expressing the reasonable demands of the working class in a more effective way than the latter's ultimate choice was to do. The Labour Party, by replacing Liberalism's pluralism with a stifling and centralising collectivism, divided the left and so handed power to the Conservative Party for most of the twentieth century.

As one historian concludes: 'only the greatest catastrophe in modern European history could arrest the Liberal Party's gradual digestion of the last in the long line of sympathetic but fractious groupings on its left – the British labour movement ... the schism which resulted was to inflict a lasting impoverishment on the British left'.[33]

Whether the Great War, and its consequences, eclipsed the Liberal Party or whether the rise of a distinct Labour Party was inevitable, is debatable. For the Liberal Party, the fact that it had gone so far down the Social Liberal road by 1914 became an important part of its own tradition. Liberals did not see themselves as socialist, firmly rejecting state or collective ownership of the means of production, distribution and exchange (the defining phrase widely used in political debate for twenty-five years before it was put into the Labour Party constitution in 1918). Nevertheless, they knew they had pioneered the welfare state and believed that Liberalism had in effect embraced the better part of what was later called social democracy. The sense that Labour's insistence on creating a rival party had betrayed the true interests of the progressive wing of British politics lingered long. Following the May 1955 election, the 84-year-old Samuel rightly concluded that Labour's defeat marked the start of a period of decline and concluded 'they pushed their way in. Now it is our duty to push our way back.'[34]

Labour's rise ensured that the distinctive Liberal agenda of constitutional reform was pushed out of mainstream political debate. The 1906–14 Liberal government achieved only one major reform: establishing the supremacy of the elected chamber over the unelected. However, Liberal MPs kept up pressure for more. By 1914, Irish Home Rule, with a limited Ulster opt-out, had been passed over the Lords veto and was only suspended for the duration of the war. Bills to establish a Scottish Parliament and to abolish plural voting were passed by the Commons but failed to pass the Lords. A Royal Commission on Electoral Systems, set up in 1909, reported in favour of a limited reform, the alternative vote; in 1917 a Speaker's Conference recommended a comprehensive set of electoral reforms, including votes for women; most were implemented but not the proposed element of proportional representation. Another Speaker's Conference, in 1920, put forward rather unworkable proposals for legislative devolution to England, Scotland and Wales, but the Labour Party, initially favourable to Liberal ideas on devolution and electoral reform, lost interest in the 1920s. The Liberal Party did not: for some fifty years, up to 1974, the most consistently distinctive feature of its general election manifestos was the regular call for Scottish and Welsh devolution and for proportional representation through the single transferable vote. For those who believed in constitutional reform, especially these priorities, the Liberal Party remained the party to join.

The Liberal commitment to peace was, in some part, taken up by Labour. It had been put under severe strain during the South African war of 1898–1902. The Liberal Imperialists (who included Gladstone's successor, Rosebery, and Asquith) were convinced that the party could not regain power without embracing some of the imperial outlook about which Cobden and Gladstone had been so sceptical. Others, including Lloyd George, felt obliged to oppose both a war of conquest of the Boer Republics and the British army concentration camps. Up to 1914 the Liberal government wrestled with the growing tension in Europe as it sought in vain to avoid the whirlpool of militarism. In a re-run of the issue which brought Gladstone's final resignation, the cabinet divided in

1909 over the Sea Lords' demand for increased naval expenditure, with Britain's two future war leaders, Lloyd George and Churchill, leading the opposition.[35]

When war broke out, the bulk of the Liberal Party rallied to the defence of Belgium against German aggression, but the custodian of the Gladstonian legacy, Viscount Morley, resigned in protest. Some of the pacifist protest in due course moved into the Labour Party.[36] But the party's mainstream supported vigorous prosecution of the war whilst trying to withstand the militarisation of life that followed; Liberal MPs were deeply divided over the introduction of conscription. In essence, the Great War was a repudiation of some of the deepest values of the Liberal Party and engendered an atmosphere of patriotic fervour in which its rivals prospered.[37]

Survival in third place

Despite successive electoral defeats, after 1918 Liberalism displayed energy and conviction in developing its programme. The Liberal Summer School Movement provided an intellectual focus,[38] firmly rooted in the Social Liberal approach. Its committee initiated the Liberal Industrial Enquiry of 1928, often known as the *Yellow Book*,[39] summarised in a famous pamphlet by Lloyd George for the 1929 election *We Can Conquer Unemployment*. In 1934, the party produced a comprehensive survey of policy, *The Liberal Way*, which anticipated much of the 1945 Labour government's achievements in planning and welfare legislation, but not in nationalisation; it even included firm support for 'a minimum wage ... enforceable at law'.[40] This is unsurprising since the two figures most prominently involved in engineering the consensus on which the Attlee government built were also Liberals. J. M. Keynes had played a central role in the Liberal Summer School Movement, while Sir William Beveridge was elected a Liberal MP in October 1944.

Thus Social Liberalism became central to the party's identity. At the 1936 Liberal convention the following words were added to the draft preamble to make this clear:

> a country in which the powers of the State will be steadily used to establish social justice, to wage war against poverty, to ensure that the country's resources are wisely developed for the benefit of the whole community, and to create the positive conditions which will make a full and free life possible for all citizens ...

Yet the fact that this section was not in the original draft and had therefore to be moved as an amendment, albeit from the platform, is indicative of some hesitation. While the majority of Liberals were confident in seeing a positive role for the state in pursuit of social justice, there remained a minority who distrusted it.[41]

The Liberal Party reinforced its proprietorial attitude to the welfare state with Beveridge's prominent role in its 1945 election campaign; but the public knew the post-1945 welfare state was set up by another party. Liberal support for a Keynesian economic programme made the party's stance in 1929 highly distinctive; but by 1945 this, too, was part of the post-war consensus. For a new recruit to the party from the 1940s onwards, the Social Liberal record might be a source of historic pride but it did differentiate the party. It was accordingly neglected in the outside view of the party, and many long-standing members of the Labour Party were to be surprised when, in 1981, through the SDP, they started mixing with Liberals as allies and discovered the strength of the Social Liberal tradition.

In one respect, however, the party maintained a highly distinctive Social Liberal approach. The *Yellow Book* and *The Liberal Way* had advocated worker participation in industry as the alternative to socialism and capitalism. The party put forward various proposals, from statutory works councils and worker-directors to wider share-ownership and profit sharing. The former reflected traditional Liberal ideas of citizenship and democracy, the latter a distributive emphasis on spreading ownership of property. Such policies became a central feature of Liberal manifestos in the 1950s, and gave Liberals confidence that they had a better way than what they saw as the sterile argument over nationalisation on which the other two parties concentrated.[42]

Between the wars, a similar consensus around collective security and support for the League of Nations seemed to smother the distinctiveness of the Liberal concern for peace. Yet the party itself continued to insist that its outlook was different: *The Liberal Way* asserted in 1934 that 'the main line of division in politics in all countries will in future be that between those who cling to the out-of-date and ruinous conception of a narrow and selfish nationalism, and those who accept and welcome the growing interdependence of the world and make it the basis of their policy. Liberalism stands unwaveringly for the international view'.[43]

After 1945, two successive leaders, Clement Davies and Jo Grimond, often repeated this claim. The party's internationalism certainly made its stance on a number of issues highly distinctive. Thus it opposed the independent British nuclear deterrent, arguing that collective security through NATO under the protection of the US nuclear umbrella was sufficient. In the run-up to the 1967 devaluation, it questioned the established, consensual view that defending a fixed rate for sterling was a British interest. It opposed the 1964 Labour government's initial commitment to British bases in the Indian Ocean and its support for the US war in Vietnam, sharing these positions with the Labour left, though not necessarily from the same analysis. Its Cobdenite and Gladstonian heritage meant that it understood much more readily than the two larger parties how Britain needed to adjust to post-imperial reality.

From this stance, the Liberal Party derived its most distinctive policy of the second half of the twentieth century. It was always the most sympathetic of British parties towards European integration. It may seem strange that the party historically so identified with free trade should have become such a strong and consistent supporter of a European Customs Union. Indeed, some die-hard supporters of free trade within the party fought hard in the 1950s for a purist opposition to the Common Market.

We can trace how the mainstream Liberal tradition moved through Philip Kerr, Marquis of Lothian, who had been Lloyd George's private secretary and was one of the Liberal ministers who resigned in 1932 over free trade. At that stage the Liberal commitment to peace through free trade had become a faith in the League of Nations. However, as Lothian argued by 1935 'the fatal fact of national sovereignty' was destroying the League and leading to another war; 'the only final remedy for war is a federation of nations'.[44]

The logic of *The Liberal Way*'s internationalism was that the party would embrace federalism, as several Liberals did when the Federalist Movement in Britain suddenly burst into activity in 1938–41. After the war the party became committed as, from 1948 onwards, the Federalist Movement concentrated on European integration. Hence, Davies enthusiastically supported British membership of the supranational European Coal and Steel Community in 1950, later hailing it as 'the finest step towards peace in the world which has ever been made'.[45] There is a clear line of descent from the Anti-Corn Law League and the Peace Society to modern Liberalism's wholehearted commitment to the European Union.

Another line of descent leads from the original Whig/Tory dichotomy over Britishness. A century ago Liberals and Unionists were divided in their response to the wave of East European Jewish refugees arriving in Britain, while in 1892 the Liberal voters of Finsbury Central elected an Indian to sit in the Commons and advocate independence. By the late 1950s Liberals were rewarded with special strength in Jewish areas such as Finchley, while in 1968 they were the only party to fight for the rights of British passport-holders of Asian descent.[46] For many Liberals at this period opposition to racist policies in Southern Africa or on immigration became a litmus test of their detestation of Conservatism, and of the contempt for the Wilson government they shared with many on the Labour left.[47] There is a clear continuity with the Gladstonian conscience about subject peoples and with the 1906 campaign on Chinese labour in South Africa. However, the link is also with the Liberal sense of the place of Scotland, Wales and the English regions in Britain, and with internationalism. From the original 1690s' Whig view of foreigners onwards, the Liberal tradition has echoed the internally varied character of Britain and the inclusiveness of Britishness. As such questions of identity are among the most profound of political issues, the Liberal Party attracted those with a similar outlook, and repelled those who wanted Britain to be exclusive and homogeneous.

Conclusion: the imprint of history

Such lines of descent explain what so many observers have found puzzling about the position of the Liberal Party in the party system. The Liberal Party is often seen simply as a centre party, but on the issues which mattered to it, it could be found at either end of the spectrum. On Europe it only found itself part of a centre consensus when, by the time of the 1975 referendum, both other parties had moved towards it. At the 1959 election it was pitched against them when it led a solitary campaign for British entry to the Common Market. At other stages, Liberal MPs provided a Conservative government with the critical votes for European Community legislation, against bitter criticism from the Labour Party, as at the second reading vote in February 1972, and again on the paving motion on the Maastricht Bill in December 1992. Yet on most end-of-empire issues it found itself closest to the Labour left. Its Social Liberal track record placed it in the centre on many domestic issues; but its internationalism placed it where it could be closest to, or furthest from, the Labour left. It had contributed massively to establishment thinking, yet continued to challenge it.

Its deep belief in constitutional reform also pitched it against the conventional wisdom that British political institutions were functioning well. In the 1960s, it embraced English regionalism and begun to advocate an entrenched charter of human rights. At its Edinburgh assembly in 1968 it brought these reforms together with its long-standing commitments into the framework of a proposed federal structure for the government of the United Kingdom and thereon advocated a comprehensive package of constitutional reform, much of which was to be adopted by the non-party pressure group Charter 88 twenty years later.

This action reflected a deep belief that political structures matter more than economic ones, in contrast to Labour's radicalism over economic structures and its conservatism over political ones. It meant the Liberal Party found itself naturally more in tune with 1960s' demands for participation, a demand articulated strongly by Grimond.[48] The young recruits that this attracted in the 1960s developed the party's decentralist and participatory thinking into the community politics strategy adopted in 1970. They also argued vigorously for reform within the party, making it the first to put a one member one vote system of selecting parliamentary candidates into its constitution in 1969 and to involve party members in the election of its leader from 1976. Only later did the SDP and the Labour Party flatter by imitation.

The rapid and rejuvenating growth in party membership during the Grimond era changed a small party kept going by the strength of non-conformist and Scottish presbyterian commitment, but these had moulded an ethos which included a deep respect for individual opinion and for decision by open democratic debate as well as belief in personal accountability for one's own actions. So a 1960s' recruit attracted by the party's European, anti-racist or participatory outlook but also advocating sexual freedom and chafing at Britain's restrictive licensing laws could feel at home in the party that once embodied Victorian respectability and campaigned strongly against alcohol. This was symbolised by a one-word change in the preamble in 1969. 'Unemployment' remained in the trilogy of enslavement identified in 1936 but by then was not a problem. So it was replaced by 'conformity'. The Liberal Democrat preamble still pinpoints the evils of 'poverty, ignorance and conformity', as if recalling a piece of timeless Gladstonian rhetoric.

The 1936 emphasis on 'setting freedom first' made the Liberal Party a natural home for new or uncomfortable ideas. Consequently, the party became the first to adopt a gay rights policy in 1975 and the Liberal Democrats the first to debate decriminalisation of drugs in 1994. In addition, the party's reputation as a party of principle in a party system dominated by producer parties and divided by class made it the natural home for 1960s' post-materialist values. So the party of the mid-Victorian manufacturing classes became the greenest of Britain's main parties by the mid-1970s.

Such recruits maintained its middle-class character, and gave it a special attraction to the growing professional middle classes. Previous research identified the middle-class nonconformist vote as the most distinctively Liberal segment.[49] These, however interesting, are details. The party's major characteristic in an otherwise class-divided electorate was always its ability to appeal equally to all social groups. In this, its Social Liberal heritage shows strongly; it always proclaimed a socially-inclusive agenda at elections. Its reward was continued nationwide support across all social categories. This was a weakness as well as a strength. Under the British electoral system, evenly spread support can be grotesquely under-represented, as the party was cruelly reminded especially in 1964, 1974 and 1983. On the other hand, there were periodic hints of its capacity. However, of the first four by-election gains of the revival, two (Orpington, 1962 and Birmingham Ladywood, 1969) were in areas with no Liberal tradition: the first, one of the most staunchly Conservative suburbs, the other archetypically inner-city Labour. A party that could win both these seats could win almost anywhere; ludicrously small respresentation in the Commons deterred potential recruits less when a party could demonstrate such potential.

The other two, however, in pockets of strong Liberal tradition in the Celtic fringe (Torrington, 1958 and Roxburgh, 1965), reminded the party of what saved its representation at Westminster after 1945. From then to 1992 there have been 157 occasions on which a Liberal or a Liberal Democrat MP has been elected at a general election; of these more than two-thirds have been in rural parts of the Celtic fringe while only eight, or just 5 per cent, have been in the Midlands or south east. Conversely, almost half the House of Commons sits for constituencies in the Midlands or south east, and only 7 per cent of it for the rural Celtic fringe.

The imprint on the party's leadership was strong. Of the eleven leaders who followed Gladstone, one was a Scottish peer, five were Scotsmen representing Scottish constituencies, two similarly Welsh and one was Jewish (the only practising Jew ever to lead a British political party). Of the three more conventionally English leaders, two were Yorkshiremen by birth and all sat for Celtic fringe constituencies. After Gladstone left Greenwich in 1880, the Liberal Party never had as leader an MP for a seat in the four-fifths of England which lies south of Lancashire and east of Devon.

Thus the Liberal tradition left a party with broad, mass support but dependent, because of the voting system, on a geographical fringe and on cultural minorities for its presence at the centre. However, it also left a party which had a strong, distinctive appeal on important issues neglected by the larger parties, but one whose contribution on the socio-economic issues which were then central to election campaigns was drowned in the prevailing consensus. Though caricatured as a party of fringe issues and protest, it always insisted on presenting its Social Liberal policies as if it were about to form a government, and never lost the memory of having come into being as a party exercising power. Having inherited this will to win, the party always sought a route back to power and so embraced an alliance with the Social Democratic Party in 1981.

The logic of an effective alliance led to merger and in January 1988 the Liberal Party agreed to dissolve its identity into a new party, the Social and Liberal Democrats or SLD. The SLD adopted the short title of the Democrats in September 1988 and then changed in October 1989 to the present Liberal Democrats. The confusion of names reflected a confusion of identity and purpose. Did the party really see itself as something quite new (Democrats), as heir to two distinct and relevant traditions (SLD) or did it want to emphasise its Liberal inheritance? The result of the postal ballot amongst the party's membership which resolved the issue (70.7 per cent Liberal Democrats; 29.3 per cent Democrats) indicated that the new party's core faithful were still attached to the Liberal label and the tradition it bears.

Notes

1   Ivor Bulmer-Thomas, *The Party System in Great Britain*, Phoenix House, 1953, pp.284–5.
2   H.G. Nicholas, *The British General Election of 1950*, Macmillan, 1951, p.44. Only 22 per cent of Labour candidates were under 40, and 5 per cent under 30; of Conservatives, 31 per cent and 6 per cent respectively.
3   *The Liberal Magazine*, Vol. XLIV, April 1936, pp.89–95; May 1936, pp.132–4.
4   D.A. Hamer, *John Morley: Liberal Intellectual in Politics*, Clarendon Press, 1968, p.288.
5   Francis Hirst, *Richard Cobden and John Morley*, Cobden Club, 1941, p.11.
6   On behalf of the former presidents, the final president of the Liberal Party, Adrian Slade, gave the *Areopagitica* to the National Liberal Club, where it is displayed.
7   Quoted in the account of the founding of Liberal International by its first secretary-general: John H. MacCallum Scott, *Experiment in Internationalism*, Allen & Unwin, 1967, pp.51–2.
8   This is, for instance, the starting point of the opening chapter of George Watson (ed.), *The Unservile State: Essays in Liberty and Welfare*, Allen & Unwin, 1957, p.13.
9   The text of the Liberal Party constitution adopted in 1936 is catalogued as P12787 in the Gladstone Library, originally formed by the National Liberal Club and now held by the University of Bristol.
10 For the text of the draft preamble and of all amendments proposed to it, see P8630 in the Gladstone Library.
11 Robert Eccleshall (ed.), *British Liberalism: Liberal Thought from the 1640s to 1980s*, Longman, 1986.
12 Alan Bullock and Maurice Shock (eds), *The Liberal Tradition from Fox to Keynes*, Clarendon Press, 1956, p.xx.
13 Conrad Russell, *The Liberal Cause: The Three Century-long Tradition of Liberal Democrats*, Unservile State Papers, No. 35, Hebden Royd, 1990, p.3.
14 The period identified by the seminal study: John Vincent, *The Formation of the Liberal Party 1857–1868*, (2nd edn), Harvester, 1976.
15 The slow expiry of the Whig Party is best covered in Donald Southgate, *The Passing of the Whigs 1832–1886*, Macmillan, 1962.
16 Patricola, *The State-Anatomy of Great Britain, containing a particular account of its several interests and parties*, printed for John Philips, London, 1716/17, p.15. Patricola was the *nom de plume* of John Toland, a free-thinking disciple of Locke.
17 John Derry, *Charles James Fox*, Batsford, 1972, p.332, p.381 and p.334 respectively.
18 George Watson (ed.), *op. cit.*, p.13.

19   Jean-Thomas Nordmann, *Histoire des Radicaux 1820–1973*, La Table Ronde, 1974, pp.22–34.

20   Michael Steed, 'The Liberal Parties in Italy, France, Germany and the UK', in Roger Morgan and Stephano Silvestri, *Moderates and Conservatives in Western Europe*, Heinemann, 1982, pp.163–4 and 178–9.

21   From Bright's letter to Cobden (April 1857) in John Morley, *Life of Richard Cobden*, Chapman & Hall, 1881, Vol. II, p.194.

22   Thus *Whitaker's Almanac* had, for decades until it expunged such historical lists in its 1995 edition, recorded Lord John Russell's 1846–52 government as the last Whig one and Lord Palmerston's of 1855 as the first Liberal one, but assisted the reader with the accompanying explanation that 'In 1828 the old party of the Whigs became known as Liberals'. Several other standard reference sources are similarly confused.

23   From Cobden's pamphlet '1792 and 1853, in Three Letters', quoted in Morley (1881) *op. cit.*, Vol. II, pp.133–6.

24   John Morley, *Life of Gladstone*, Lloyd's Popular Edition, 1908, Vol. II, p.16.

25   Quoted in Morley (1908) *op. cit.*, Vol. II, p.560.

26   The significance of this budget has been overshadowed by the 1909 People's Budget; it was described by his biographer as 'the zenith of his career'. A.G. Gardiner, *The Life of William Harcourt*, Constable, 1923, p.280.

27   J.S. Mill in particular advocated women's suffrage (see his trenchant essay 'The Subjection of Women', published in 1869) and from this period most Liberal electoral reformers such as Thomas Hare also advocated votes for women. However, the Liberal Party never made this majority view the party's policy.

28   Mill and other reformers secured early experiments in more proportional systems such as the limited vote in some parliamentary elections in 1867 and the cumulative vote in school board elections in 1870, but such reformers did not agree on one system and proportional representation, whilst favoured by the majority of Liberal MPs in free votes, did not become party policy until 1922.

29   W.E. Gladstone, *Midlothian Speeches 1879*, Leicester University Press, 1971, p.87.

30   The local tradition of long-standing Conservative strength in Liverpool is ascribed by H.J. Hanham (*Elections and Party Management*, Harvester, 1978, p.285) to the 'ineradicable association' of Liberalism with the anti-slavery movement, later reinforced by its sympathy for the Catholic Irish cause. The consequent Conservative predominance lasted until 1964; only after that did Liverpool, the city in which mid-nineteenth century Liberalism was weakest, acquire its modern Liberal support.

31   Herbert Samuel, *Liberalism*, Grant Richards, 1902. Samuel's revealing subtitle was 'An attempt to state the principles and proposals of contemporary Liberalism in England'; the introduction was by Asquith.

32   A. K. Russell, *Liberal Landslide: The General Election of 1906*, David & Charles, 1973, p.65.

33   Brian Harrison, 'A Genealogy of Reform in Modern Britain', in Christine Bolt and Seymour Drescher (eds), *Anti-slavery, Religion, and Reform*, Dawson/Archon, 1980, p.145.

34   Quoted in John Bowle, *Viscount Samuel*, Gollancz, 1957, p.354.

35   George L Bernstein, *Liberalism and Liberal Politics in Edwardian England*, Allen

& Unwin, 1986, p.176.

36   Roy Jenkins, writing as a young Labour intellectual, lamented that anti-militarism was 'emotionally much the strongest strand' in Labour's traditional thinking on foreign policy, blaming this not on socialism but on the Liberal inheritance in his then party (*Pursuit of Progress*, Heinemann, 1953, pp.1–2).

37   The thesis that the Liberal Party was destroyed by the Great War is expounded in Trevor Wilson, *The Downfall of the Liberal Party 1914–1935*, Collins, 1966.

38   The lectures delivered at the first Liberal Summer School held at Oxford in 1922 were published as *Essays in Liberalism*, Collins, 1922.

39   The *Yellow Book* was reprinted with a foreword by David Steel to mark the centenary of the founding of the National Liberal Federation: *Britain's Industrial Future, being the Report of the Liberal Industrial Inquiry of 1928*, Ernest Benn, 1976.

40   *The Liberal Way* (foreword by Ramsay Muir), Allen & Unwin, 1934, p.172.

41   For a view which emphasises divisions within Social Liberalism see Michael Freeden, *Liberalism Divided: A Study in British Political Thought 1914–1939*, Clarendon Press, 1986.

42   For a good exposition of this Liberal emphasis on co-ownership see Elliott Dodds, *Let's Try Liberalism*, Simpkin Marshall, 1944.

43   *Op. cit.*, pp.62–3.

44   Marquis of Lothian, *Pacifism is Not Enough Nor Patriotism Either*, Clarendon Press, 1935, pp.40–1.

45   Quoted in Alan Butt Philip, 'The Liberals and Europe', in Vernon Bogdanor (ed.), *Liberal Party Politics*, Clarendon Press, 1983, p.220.

46   One of the issues on which future the Liberal leader cut his teeth: see David Steel, *No Entry*, Hurst, 1969.

47   For two Liberal leaders taking a stand of principle against racialist policies in Southern Africa was arguably their finest hour: for Davies his solitary consistent opposition to the British government's acceptance of the Apartheid regime's veto on the paramount chief of Bechuanaland having a white wife, and for Jeremy Thorpe his advocacy of force in 1965 to avert the Rhodesian settler seizure of independence.

48   See especially Jo Grimond, *The Liberal Challenge*, Hollis & Carter, 1963, which is given the alternative title on the dust jacket of 'Democracy through Participation'.

49   David Butler and Donald Stokes, *Political Change in Britain*, Macmillan, 1969, pp. 126–7.

CHAPTER 3

Liberal Democrat thought

Tudor Jones

In their philosophical stance, the Liberal Democrats have aspired to create a fusion of two interrelated ideological traditions in British politics – social liberalism and social democracy. This chapter examines the historical and intellectual development of those traditions within the Liberal Party and the Social Democratic Party and traces the roots of Liberal Democrat political thought to that dual inheritance and demonstrates how values and principles drawn from it have shaped the aims, character and broad policy approach of the new party.

Social Liberalism

The origins of the social liberal tradition in Britain can be traced to the fragmentation of British liberal ideology that occurred in the 1880s. Much scholarly debate has focused on this question.[1] Until the 1970s, historians of political thought stressed the transition from the old, individualist classical liberalism to the new, collectivist social liberalism. However, more recent accounts have pointed to the lack of a clear distinction between the two stages or schools of liberalism.[2] Indeed, Eccleshall maintains that the polar concepts most commonly used in exploring that distinction, namely, individualism and collectivism, and negative and positive liberty, tend to conceal the continuities between the old and new liberalism.[3]

This chapter follows Vincent in maintaining that the distinction between classical and social liberalism is valid but 'should not be taken as hard and fast'.[4] It also seeks to illustrate Clarke's observation that the new or social liberalism 'represented a discovery of the old liberal values in a collectivist context'.[5]

The social factors that shaped the emergence of social liberalism in Britain in the late nineteenth century included the growing awareness of poverty and unemployment as acute social problems within industrial cities; the downturn in economic growth as the

63

result of the Great Depression; and the rise of an increasingly organised and partly enfranchised working class.

All these forces gave rise to tensions between the new liberalism, formulated between 1880 and 1914 by political thinkers such as T.H. Green, D.G. Ritchie, L.T. Hobhouse and J.A. Hobson, and the old classical liberalism. Classical liberal positions, notably support for an unregulated market economy, a negative conception of liberty as the absence of constraints on the individual, and a commitment to a limited state, were all severely challenged by the problems generated by industrialisation and urbanisation.

In response to these ideological tensions there was a growing trend in British liberal thought after 1880 towards an emphasis on greater state responsibility for working and living conditions. To some extent that approach was itself a development of liberal arguments for increased state intervention, evident in the practice of the Gladstone administration of 1868–74, that had been strengthened and legitimised by the extension of representative democracy.

After 1880, however, the movement towards a new, more collectivist form of liberalism gradually gathered pace, at both policy-making and theoretical levels. In policy terms, for instance, its ideas were embodied in Joseph Chamberlain's Unauthorized Programme of 1885 and in the Newcastle Programme adopted by the National Liberal Federation in 1891. The increasing state intervention advocated by liberals during this period assumed two main forms: first, state responsibility for the regulation of industrial conditions, and secondly, state involvement in the provision of health, education and welfare services.

Among the earliest theoretical justifications for this growth in state activity, and hence for the renunciation of the extreme individualism of some nineteenth-century liberals, was that provided by the Oxford philosopher T.H. Green, who argued for a positive, although limited, role for the state. In certain situations, Green maintained, the state was required to free its citizens from social obstacles that prevented them from making the best of their lives. Public health and education services, for example, should thus be available to all unless supplied by voluntary action. Furthermore, Green developed an idealist notion of the state, assigning to it a positive, ethical role in society as the embodiment of its members' wills and aspirations. The state was therefore envisaged by Green not just as the remover of restrictive barriers in the path of its citizens but also as 'an instrument of the common good', concerned with realising certain common purposes in society.

Moreover, for Green, individual freedom and the common good were indissolubly linked. As members of a community, with clear duties towards it, individuals acquired true freedom – that is, their capacity for moral, intellectual and cultural self-development – in their pursuit of the common good. Green's ultimate political ideal was therefore 'freedom in its positive sense: the liberation of the powers of all men equally for contributions to the common good'.[6]

The practical implication of this positive conception of freedom was that from the 1880s Green and other liberals were turning more and more to consider the social and economic constraints on the individual's opportunities which had arisen from industrialisation. In, for instance, his highly influential lecture on *Liberal Legislation and Freedom of Contract* (1881), Green advanced the case for government action, on grounds of extending positive liberty, with regard to protection for landed tenants in Ireland, the provision of compulsory education, regulation of public health, and control of conditions and hours of work in factories.

Green's concept of positive liberty – the individual's opportunity for self-development – was to be the key concept of the new or social liberalism from 1880 to 1914. It pervaded the thinking of later political philosophers such as Hobhouse and Hobson as well as that of practising politicians such as Samuel, Haldane, Asquith, Churchill and Lloyd George. It provided, too, the main ideological justification for the ambitious programme of social and industrial legislation enacted by the Liberal governments from 1906 to 1914.

Leonard Hobhouse, philosopher, journalist and sociologist, under the influence of Green's version of philosophical idealism, made more explicit his mentor's break with classical liberal assumptions. In his classic work *Liberalism* (1911) and other writings, he firmly placed the concept of liberty in a social context. Freedom, Hobhouse stressed, amounted to the individual's ability to develop his or her individuality or potentiality, which in turn depended upon social and economic circumstances. He thus reformulated liberalism by extending its central concept of liberty to embrace not just civil and political freedoms but also liberation from social and economic impediments.

Hobhouse travelled further down the collectivist road than Green. He believed in the evolution of society from one based on competitive individualism towards a more advanced stage of development resting on altruism and mutual responsibility. Advocating greater state intervention in promotion of an extensive programme of social reform, he developed Green's positive conception of liberty to accord with his own theory of progressive social evolution.[7] He distanced himself further, too, from Green's influence by underlining the imperfections of a free market economy. The role of government, Hobhouse maintained, involved devising remedies for those defects – not just through the Liberal government's measures but also through additional radical social and fiscal reforms such as a comprehensive welfare system and redistributive taxation to achieve it.

Hobhouse's case for a more interventionist state promoting positive liberty was reinforced by Hobson, another major Edwardian liberal theorist. An influential economist as well as political thinker, Hobson argued in *The Crisis of Liberalism* (1909) that the New Liberalism involved 'a fuller appreciation and realisation of individual liberty contained in the provision of equal opportunities for self-development'.[8] In order to promote such opportunities there was a need for a greater measure of selective state intervention. However, 'Liberals must ever insist,' he stressed, 'that each enlargement of the authority and functions of the State must justify itself as an enlargement of personal liberty, interfering with individuals only in order to set free new and larger opportunities.'[9] Underlying this view of the relation between state intervention and individual freedom was his conviction that the emphasis in liberal thought should be shifted away from 'the aspect of liberty which consists in absence of restraint' to its other aspect 'which consists in presence of opportunity'.[10]

Sharing Hobhouse's belief that liberals should turn away from any residual commitment to the *laissez-faire* doctrine, Hobson, too, exposed the flaws of unregulated capitalism: its waste, instability and tendency towards unemployment. Believing that liberalism was now formally committed to 'a new conception of the State',[11] he not only defended recent Liberal social legislation but also proposed a radical programme of social and economic reform, including redistributive taxation, improved public education, public ownership of transport and public regulation of monopolies.

Both these prominent New Liberal thinkers were thus seeking to reinterpret British liberalism in order both to justify existing Liberal government practice and to promote liberal collectivist policies designed to foster equal opportunities for positive liberty. The 'new conception of the State' which they both favoured was in essence that of an enabling state, an idea that stretched back in British liberal thought not just to Green but also to the later writings of John Stuart Mill.[12] For the state's widening range of social and economic responsibilities – centred particularly on the provision of public services and on some political control of the economy – was defended by the New Liberals on the grounds of the enlargement of individual freedom.

Hobhouse and Hobson were therefore revisionist liberals in the sense that they were seeking to adapt liberal ideas and values to meet the radically changed circumstances of a democratic and collectivist age. They shared the nineteenth-century classical liberal commitment to personal liberty. They were revising, however, the classical liberal interpretation of liberty, viewing state activity as capable in some social and economic areas of enhancing, rather than undermining, individual freedom, which they reinterpreted positively as opportunity for self-development, rather than the mere absence of state coercion.

The new social liberalism expressed in the ideas and writings of Hobhouse and Hobson was manifested, too, at a legislative level in the achievements of the reforming Liberal governments of 1906 to 1914, notably, in their introduction of old age pensions in 1908 and national health and unemployment insurance in 1911, and in other collectivist innovations such as labour exchanges, wages boards and legal protection of unions' right to strike. There was in fact an interaction during this period between Liberal theory and practice.[13] The policies and legislation of Liberal governments, influenced by New Liberal ideas, invited both a reformulation of liberal theory and a theoretical justification for enacted and proposed reforms.

The broader ideological significance of Edwardian New Liberalism was that, by developing a radical, yet non-socialist, response to the social and economic problems of industrial capitalism, it had thereby provided the British Liberal Party, as Curtice has noted, with 'an intellectual tradition which has put it on the "social" or "left" end of the family of liberal parties and ... a philosophy which was close to that espoused by many social democrats in the emerging Labour Party'.[14]

Without exploring here the implications of the second part of that observation, the point can at least be made that the emergence of the New Liberalism created the theoretical basis for cooperation with reformist socialists within the Labour Party, who included Hobson's friend Ramsay MacDonald. For while the New Liberals recognised the merits of the market economy in furthering wealth-creation and therefore rejected the socialist principle and policy of widespread public ownership of the means of production, they shared the reformist socialists' desire to reduce social and economic inequalities and to promote social reform. In pursuit of those goals, however, the New Liberals were, as Clarke has observed, essentially 'moral reformists' who believed that social ills could be remedied through the free will and participation of active citizens, whereas Fabian socialists were 'mechanical reformists' who maintained that social reforms could best be achieved through manipulation and regulation from above by specialists and experts.[15]

By the 1920s, however, with the Liberal Party in sharp electoral decline, any prospects of a progressive, cross-party alliance in British politics receded. Instead, there was a subsequent drift of social liberals – including Hobson, Haldane and Trevelyan – into the Labour Party. Nevertheless, British Liberalism continued to display its intellectual vitality during the 1920s, particularly through the Liberal Summer Schools, regularly attended by, among others, John Maynard Keynes.

By the end of the decade Keynes had emerged as the major intellectual influence on British Liberalism. He contributed to *Britain's Industrial Future* (1928), the so-called Liberal *Yellow Book,* based on the party's Industrial Inquiry initiated by Lloyd George. This amounted to a comprehensive programme for managing British capitalism without recourse to the orthodox socialist remedies of large-scale public ownership or central economic planning. The programme's key policy proposal – for a Board of National Investment – anticipated Keynes's own argument, deployed in his seminal work *The General Theory of Employment, Interest and Money* (1936), for public investment as a means of reducing unemployment.

In ideological terms, Keynes saw the central task of social liberalism in the 1930s as one of controlling and reforming a market economy which had produced instability and high levels of unemployment throughout the industrialised world. The theoretical basis for such an ambitious project had already been laid in his essay, *The End of Laissez-faire* (1926), which provided both an incisive critique of unregulated capitalism and an attempt to set out, in Bentham's phrase, 'the Agenda of the State' which ought, Keynes argued, to relate 'to those functions which fall outside the sphere of the individual, to those decisions which are made by no one if the State does not make them'.[16]

In his major treatise, *The General Theory*, Keynes proceeded to specify the economic 'agenda of the state', which he considered appropriate for the times. Developing new methods and ideas for effecting the transition from 'the economic anarchy' of the prevailing system of 'individualistic capitalism', he rejected the traditional socialist policy instruments of public ownership and central state planning on the grounds that they would prove bureaucratic, inefficient and authoritarian.[17] In their place he advocated more indirect yet more effective methods of controlling the market economy. These would involve the use of fiscal and monetary policy, including, in particular, government management of demand – and hence, of investment and consumption – to levels at which full employment could be attained.

Keynes's theoretical work thus provided a movement away from classical liberal economic thinking with its belief in an unregulated market economy. He offered in its place a new theory of state intervention as the means of achieving a more humane and efficient form of managed capitalism. In this respect his ideas can be regarded as extending the social liberalism of the Edwardian period into the field of economic policy.

For in the manner of Hobhouse and Hobson, he sought to conserve the benefits of the market economy – its capacity for promoting productive efficiency, innovation and personal choice – while correcting its social and economic deficiencies.

The practical effect of Keynesian economics was its profound influence on the management of western economics from 1945 until the mid-1970s. Its intellectual impact was felt not only within the theoretical writings and policy proposals of British Liberalism: it also shaped the thinking, after 1950, of revisionist social democrats such as Anthony Crosland in the British Labour Party.

During the 1940s William Beveridge fostered the spirit of Keynes's social liberalism in the field of social policy. In his two major reports *Social Insurance and Allied Services* (1942) and *Full Employment in a Free Society* (1944), he recommended a comprehensive system of social welfare and endorsed Keynes's central economic ideas. In a collection of articles and speeches entitled *Why I am a Liberal* (1945), he gave ideological shape to his own policy proposals, depicting them as cornerstones of a radical, interventionist programme that would aim to liberate Britain from 'the giant social evils of Want, Disease, Ignorance, Squalor and Idleness'.[18]

Like Keynes, Beveridge presented his version of social liberalism – which he referred to as 'Liberal radicalism' – as an enlightened middle way between the extreme individualism of free-market Conservatives and the doctrinaire collectivism of state socialists 'who desire extension of state activity for its own sake'.[19] His approach would certainly involve an extension of the responsibilities and functions of the state into both economic and social policy areas. But that state activity would be justified not for its own sake but rather by the enhancement of personal liberty and the promotion of social justice that it would make possible.

This liberal collectivism of Keynes and Beveridge was far-reaching in its influence since it provided the intellectual and policy foundations of the post-war collectivist consensus in British politics, built upon the threefold commitment to the managed, mixed economy, the welfare state, and full employment, and enduring until the 1970s.[20] Yet, ironically, as the post-war Liberal Party gradually revived in the late 1950s after its electoral nadir of 1951, it found itself searching for a distinctive political and ideological position within a consensus originally designed by its own social-liberal intellectuals.

Jo Grimond, whose leadership from 1956 helped to spark the party's electoral and intellectual revival, sought to imbue it with a clear identity and purpose in his various writings and speeches.[21] His efforts were reinforced in 1957 by the publication of *The Unservile State: Essays in Liberty and Welfare*, the first full-scale study of British Liberal attitudes and policies since the 1928 *Yellow Book*. What emerged from these writings was a clear shift to a more decentralist version of liberalism. While maintaining a commitment both to collective provision of welfare services and to some degree of public control of the economy, Liberal contributors to *The Unservile State* displayed a marked hostility to the bureaucracy and centralised power inherent in modern state collectivism. In their place they projected the vision of a decentralised, participatory society in which power and responsibility, ownership and wealth, were all widely dispersed.

The practical policy implications of this decentralist approach amounted to a range of proposals for the political and economic decentralisation of power, which included devolution of government from Westminster, a revival of local government and industrial co-partnership.

Under Grimond's leadership this vision of a decentralised society and state helped to provide British Liberalism with its own ideological and policy space on a political landscape still dominated by the two major parties. That modest but significant achievement became linked after 1959 to a clear strategic aim. For after the general election of that year Grimond hoped that a realignment of the left would take place, with the fundamentalist Labour left splitting off from the Labour Party, leaving 'a radical party on the left of centre of British politics but free of socialist dogma'.[22] The Liberals' role, in his view, would be to serve as a catalyst for bringing about that new progressive grouping, appearing, in his words, as 'a non-socialist radical alternative' to the Conservatives.

Hopes of that realignment of the centre-left faded after Labour's electoral successes in 1964 and 1966. However, as the Liberal Party enjoyed another revival in the early 1970s, its distinctive emphasis on decentralisation and participation was increasingly expressed in a new strategic context – that of community politics.

Endorsed at the 1970 party assembly, community politics emerged as a dual strategy, to be applied both inside and outside established political institutions. Its stated aim was to 'help organise people in communities to take and use power, to use our political skills to redress grievances, and to represent people at all levels of the political structure'.[23]

In practice, that meant building a more participatory society and democracy through local community structures, such as neighbourhood councils and various cooperative ventures, designed to give people in local communities a greater influence over decisions affecting their lives.

The social factors that had given an impetus to this approach included the growth of large-scale institutions and organisations in contemporary society; the individual's increasing powerlessness in the face of insensitive decision-making by those bodies; and the apparent indifference or passivity of the ruling political parties in British cities with regard to the views or needs of individual citizens.

In the face of these developments, community politics was conceived as no less than 'an attempt to regenerate democracy and recast democratic institutions so that power is driven downwards to the most basic level possible'.[24] As a strategy and political approach it was thus commended by Liberals as consistent both with the party's traditional commitment to decentralisation[25] and with its radical ideological heritage.[26]

This principled endorsement of community politics tended to obscure some of the difficulties engendered by the strategy: the differences of opinion, for instance, between Liberals who regarded it as a supplement to parliamentary activity and those in the party who promoted it as a radical alternative; as well as tensions between its localist approach and the national focus and synthesising responsibilities of the parliamentary party and leadership.

Nevertheless, the local campaigning style of community politics, based on its concern for wider participation, together with the broader Liberal emphasis on political decentralisation and reform, provided a distinctive flavour and idiom for British

Liberalism throughout the 1970s and 1980s. Those features were further enhanced during the period by a sustained commitment to the traditional Liberal principle of international cooperation, expressed, for instance, in an unequivocal support for British membership of the European Community, and by an increasingly firm attachment to the cause of environmental protection.

If, as Eccleshall has maintained, liberalism as a political ideology can be viewed as a succession of strategies both 'for expanding the freedoms to which individuals are considered to be equally entitled' and 'to encourage the spread of self-government throughout society',[27] then the Liberals' decentralist approach appears, in its aims and values, consistent with his characterisation. It takes its place, along with the commitments to positive liberty, the enabling state, a reformed, managed capitalism, and a welfare state or society, as a significant part of the ideological and strategic development of social liberalism in Britain since 1880.

Social democracy

THE SOCIAL DEMOCRATIC TRADITION IN BRITAIN

The term 'social democracy' is descriptively imprecise and its usage has varied according to historical circumstance. Before 1914, as an ideological position it usually denoted organised Marxism. After the 1917 Russian Revolution, however, it came to mean organised, non-Marxist reformist socialism.

Social democracy in this latter sense is, as Padgett and Paterson have observed, 'a hybrid political tradition [which] is inspired by socialist ideals but is heavily conditioned by its political environment, and it incorporates liberal values'.[28] The social democratic project may thus be defined as 'the attempt to reconcile socialism with liberal politics and capitalist society'.[29]

More specifically, after 1945 social democracy came to mean not just non-Marxist, reformist socialism but also, in Hamilton's definition, 'a non-transformative type of socialism or social reformism',[30] for its primary objective has been 'amelioration of injustice and the promotion of common welfare and a measure of equality rather than transformation of the economic and social structure'.[31] In practice, its non-transformative approach has entailed pursuing its reformist aims within the context of a mixed economy rather than upon the traditional socialist basis of the public ownership of the means of production.

In Britain, social democracy gradually emerged in this century as an ideological synthesis of Edwardian New Liberalism, Fabian collectivism and Keynesian economics.[32] The simultaneous development of early Fabianism and New Liberalism, albeit along different lines of approach, helped to give shape to a non-Marxist form of reformist socialism.[33] In the 1930s that position was strengthened by Keynes' economic theories formulated in his *General Theory of Employment, Interest and Money*. His arguments, deployed against both free-market Conservative and fundamentalist socialist views, were embraced by young Fabian intellectuals such as Hugh Gaitskell, Douglas Jay and Evan Durbin, who were eager to introduce into the Labour Party Keynesian ideas on macroeconomic intervention.

In the post-1945 period social democracy in Britain became synonymous with the revisionist tendency within the Labour Party during the 1950s and early 1960s. This constituted an attempt to reformulate democratic socialist principles and revise Labour policies through a new analysis of the changed economic and social conditions of postwar British society.

As it was developed throughout the 1950s, Labour revisionism steadily acquired its distinctiveness both as a body of theory and as a set of policies. Its central ideas and arguments were most thoroughly and coherently expressed in Anthony Crosland's major work *The Future of Socialism* (1956). The period from 1956 onwards, following Gaitskell's accession to the party leadership, witnessed its increasing prominence as a major ideological influence within the Labour Party. For during those years revisionist ideas – on public ownership, economic strategy and social policy – were developed and promoted by Gaitskell and his supporters, notably Crosland, Douglas Jay and Roy Jenkins, and incorporated into party policy statements.

Revisionism involved two major, highly controversial deviations from accepted Labour orthodoxies. First, it repudiated the traditional view that socialism could be adequately defined as, or at least identified with, the public ownership of the means of production. It thereby questioned the established Labour commitment to extensive public ownership as a precondition of achieving all major reformist objectives.

Secondly, revisionism diverged from orthodox Labour thinking by presenting a distinctive ethical reinterpretation of socialism in terms of values and ideals such as personal liberty, social welfare and, in particular, social equality. The traditional doctrine of public ownership – enshrined in clause four of the party constitution – was therefore viewed as one important means among several others for realising those socialist values and ideals.

The intellectual foundation of the first part of the revisionist project – its repudiation of the orthodox identification of socialism with public ownership – was provided by Crosland in *The Future of Socialism*. In an analysis of changes within post-war capitalism, Crosland argued that a transfer of economic power away from the pre-war capitalist class had occurred in three directions: towards the state, the trade unions and salaried managers within private industry.

As a result of this shift of power, the nature of capitalism, in Crosland's view, had been radically altered. In addition, he argued, Keynesian techniques of economic management had resolved many of the deep-seated tensions of capitalism, for full or near-full employment had been attained, and governments appeared to have the policy instruments for achieving sustained economic growth.

Central, therefore, to revisionist social democracy as formulated by Crosland was the belief that a democratic government had the ability to control, by Keynesian methods, private economic power and thereby pursue desirable social objectives within a mixed economy. Keynesianism thus provided the economic cornerstone of revisionist social democracy since it offered both the means by which governments would seek to achieve economic growth and full employment and the economic surplus, derived from rapid growth and hence buoyant tax revenues, which could be redirected into higher social expenditure.

The main features, then, of this social democratic model, which substantially influenced Labour thinking and policy from 1956 until the 1970s, were: a rejection of the traditional association of socialism with wholesale public ownership; an ethical reformulation of socialist aims; the acceptance of a state-regulated yet market-oriented mixed economy; a commitment to full employment and sustained economic growth as the central objectives of economic policy; and the promotion of the welfare state, financed by both economic growth and redistributive taxation, as the main instrument of social welfare.

Aside from the Labour Party's internal developments, Keynesian social democracy, as Marquand and others have termed it,[34] acquired, too, a broader ideological identity, for it could also, as Wright has observed, 'offer itself as the progressive, modernising wing of the post-war consensus, employing the techniques of economic management and social engineering to ensure that welfare capitalism delivered on its promises'.[35]

Developing this interpretation further, Marquand has even depicted Keynesian social democracy as the governing philosophy underlying that collectivist consensus. According to this view, the term provides 'shorthand for a set of commitments, assumptions and expectations, transcending party conflicts and shared by the great majority of the country's political and economic leaders, which provided the framework within which policy decisions were made'.[36]

On a deeper ideological level, that set of governing ideas and policy commitments comprised 'a philosophy of the middle way' since its various adherents were agreed in 'repudiating the dichotomies of market versus state; capital versus labour; private enterprise versus public ownership; personal freedom versus social justice'. Instead, they believed that elements of both capitalism and socialism could be combined 'in a synthesis more benign than either'.[37]

However, in the face of the harsh inflationary pressures of the 1970s which followed the oil price crisis of 1973, Keynesian social democracy, in both its broader and its more specific ideological forms, appeared to lose its political and intellectual coherence and appeal by the mid-1970s. For the apparent demise of Keynesianism seemed to discredit the Croslandite social democratic goal of promoting social welfare and a more equal distribution of wealth and resources through high social expenditure on the basis of economic growth.[38]

Moreover, the strains of office to which the Labour governments were subjected between 1974 and 1979, resulting from the economic stagnation, sterling crises and bitter industrial disputes of those years, further undermined the key underlying assumptions of revisionist social democracy, namely that rapid and sustained economic growth could be achieved; that governments had the capacity to achieve such growth; and that the egalitarian and welfarist objectives of social democracy could be fulfilled through the political and administrative machinery of the British state.

By the late 1970s some social democratic politicians, notably David Marquand, Evan Luard and John Mackintosh, recognising the significance of those developments, began to develop a critique of the centralist and corporatist tendencies of state socialism.[39] Furthermore, Marquand identified as one of the main causes of the decline of revisionist social democracy the dominant influence of the Fabian element in its inheritance, for while the decentralist New Liberal influence had been largely neglected, the pervasive Fabian impact on social democracy had in practice degenerated into a centralist, bureaucratic form of social engineering.[40]

The wider consequence of this perceived dissolution of revisionist social democracy by the end of the 1970s was the increasing ideological polarisation of British politics. Social democracy found itself under challenge on its left from a revived fundamentalist socialism which, with the aid of a quasi-Marxist analysis of monopoly capitalism, promoted an alternative economic strategy based on widespread public ownership and on greater public control of private industry. On its right flank, meanwhile, social democracy found itself under increasing pressure after 1975 from the revived free market doctrines of Thatcherite Conservatism.

Surrounded by these hostile forces, social democrats appeared by the late 1970s increasingly isolated within the Labour Party. This process had in fact begun in the early 1970s, following Labour's major split over entry into the European Community in October 1971. Social democrats found themselves identified almost exclusively with the European issue, with the substantial pro-EC minority within the Parliamentary Labour Party drawn mainly from their own ranks. Their influence was eroded, too, as the focus of power within the party shifted in the early 1970s away from the parliamentary party towards the left-leaning extra-parliamentary party conference and trade unions.

Social democratic decline within the party became even more apparent after Roy Jenkins' unsuccessful bid for the party leadership and subsequent departure for the EC Commission in 1976 and following the deaths of Crosland in 1977 and Mackintosh in 1978. The Labour left's major constitutional and policy victories in 1979–81 precluded any significant recovery of the social democratic position. Its declining intellectual influence, too, had already been symbolised by the demise in December 1978 of *Socialist Commentary*, once the leading revisionist journal.

Nevertheless, two leading social democrats made important contributions to the wider national debate, whilst pointing towards future political possibilities. In his 1979 Dimbleby Memorial Lecture *Home Thoughts from Abroad*, Roy Jenkins emphasised the deleterious effects of the polarisation of British politics and the rigidity of the adversarial two party system. To counteract those trends, Jenkins advocated the formation of a new party of what he called the radical centre, committed to a programme of social and constitutional reform and to a political approach in which state intervention and market forces complemented each other. With a more specific focus, David Marquand, in his 1979 essay in *Encounter*, tried to disentangle the causes of polarisation within the Labour Party. He underlined the defensive posture of social democrats within a party that had become increasingly left-wing in its composition, proletarian in its ethos and anti-intellectual in its instincts. He concluded gloomily that he did not believe 'that the job of revising welfare-state social democracy can be done within the formal framework of the Labour Party or that active Labour politicians can contribute much to it'.[41]

In the same essay Marquand stressed the need for working out the purposes of 'a new-model libertarian decentralist social democracy'.[42] Yet, in reality, little systematic attempt was made to revise Croslandite social democracy to meet the changed economic and political circumstances of the late 1970s. Future political developments, which both Jenkins and Marquand had anticipated, were to make that ideological task more urgent.

SOCIAL DEMOCRACY IN THE SDP

The foundation of the Social Democratic Party (SDP) in March 1981 was accompanied by several attempts to provide it with a clear political and ideological identity. The statement *Twelve Tasks for Social Democrats,* published to coincide with launch of the SDP, together with major works by three of its founder-leaders – David Owen, Bill Rodgers and Shirley Williams – sought to provide an ideological justification for the new party's stance in British politics.

In those works there appeared to be an initial tendency, as Behrens has noted, to invoke 'the authority of dead heroes' of democratic socialism.[43] Owen, for example, championed 'the radical democratic libertarian tradition of decentralised socialism',[44] which for him was epitomised by G.D.H. Cole's Guild Socialism. Williams quoted R.H. Tawney with approval, while Rodgers revealed that Durbin's *The Politics of Democratic Socialism* 'remains for me the plainest declaration of one large part of my faith and purpose'.[45]

Such genuflections served to fuel the suspicions of some Liberals that these leading Social Democrats might be seeking a new political vehicle for resurrecting Croslandite social democracy with its centralist and statist methods. Yet by the early 1980s it became clear that the SDP's most influential politicians and thinkers were engaged in developing a critique of the bureaucratic centralism and statism of established Labour policy.

This undertaking was underlined by their common emphasis on the principle of decentralisation, already affirmed by Marquand, Luard and Mackintosh in the late 1970s. Owen's celebration of the decentralist tradition was thus designed to revive 'the concept of fellowship and community within a participatory democratic society'.[46] In contrast to Fabian collectivism, the 'deeply centralist' dominant tradition of the Labour Party,[47] the decentralist philosophy which he commended to Social Democrats would require 'a detailed programme of legislative and administrative reforms to diffuse power in Britain'.[48] Williams, too, argued for a wider diffusion of power through the extension of industrial democracy and wider popular participation in public policy-making and on public bodies. For 'a successful democracy needs open discussion involving as many groups of concerned and interested people as possible'.[49]

The SDP's official statements of principle and policy echoed that concern. Part of the Limehouse Declaration thus affirmed the new party's support for 'the greatest practical degree of decentralisation of decision-making in industry and government', while *Twelve Tasks for Social Democrats* recommended that 'decisions should more often be made at local level, involving people affected by them'.

Some problematic issues were embedded in this decentralist approach: the possible tensions, for instance, between the decentralisation of public services and the social democratic commitment to equality of treatment and opportunity, tensions which might arise as a result of disparities in health-care provision between different localities or regions. Both Owen and Williams candidly stressed the need to face what Owen called 'the genuinely conflicting arguments and attitudes that are posed within the centralist/ decentralist dilemma'.[50]

Nevertheless, the emphasis on decentralisation had now been established as an essential element in early SDP thought. It was reinforced, as part of the social-democratic critique of an overcentralised and bureaucratic state, by a willingness to embrace a market-oriented mixed economy. For Marquand that, indeed, was one of the most distinctive and important principles of social democracy. In 1980 he had maintained that 'clause-four socialists and defenders of the mixed economy... are on different sides of the deepest gulf in present-day British politics', and that 'the most obvious distinguishing feature of social democracy is a positive commitment to the mixed economy'.[51] A year later, a few months after the new party's foundation, he was promoting the mixed economy as a source of both prosperity and personal freedom, something which should be regarded as 'neither a staging post on the road to full socialism nor a regrettable compromise between economic sin and economic virtue, but an entity in its own right, positively desirable in and for itself'.[52]

Another distinctive Social Democratic emphasis, again arising from the reaction against an overcentralised and ossified political system, was a commitment to constitutional and political reform and hence to a programme of measures that included electoral reform, devolution of government, a Bill of Rights to protect personal and civil liberties, freedom of information legislation, and parliamentary reform.

These three fundamental commitments – to the decentralisation of power, to a market-oriented mixed economy and to constitutional reform – were underpinned by an equal commitment to the related but distinct values of personal freedom and social justice. Taken together, this set of governing principles and beliefs served two important political purposes. First, it cemented the alliance with the Liberals in 1981 by making clear that a wide common ground of principle and policy was shared by the two parties. Second, by maintaining an unequivocally reformist or radical stance, based not just upon a commitment to constitutional and social reform, but also rooted in an underlying decentralist and libertarian approach and ethos, it clearly distinguished itself and the Alliance both from the revived fundamentalist socialism of the Bennite left and from the free-market Conservatism of the Thatcherite right.

In spite of internal strategic differences over whether the SDP should project itself as a centrist or a left-of-centre party, a distinctive ideological space seemed, therefore, to have been reserved for Social Democrats and Liberals to occupy comfortably during a period of sharp polarisation in British politics. From that vantage-point the Alliance could thus mount a concerted attack on a two party system which had broken down 'because it is rooted in outdated battles of class and ideology, and provides no outlet for the vast numbers of people who want individual freedom to go hand-in-hand with social justice, who want the state to back industry without trying to take it over, who want power to be given back to communities instead of concentrated in Whitehall'.[53]

Liberal Democrat values

After the acrimonious process of merger between Liberals and Social Democrats in 1988, the newly formed party, which adopted the short title of Liberal Democrats after a postal ballot in October 1989, found itself, like its predecessor parties, facing the problem of establishing a distinctive political and ideological identity. This task was made more pressing in view of the steady movement of the Labour Party after 1987 back into the middle ground of British politics and, so it increasingly seemed, into the mainstream of European social democracy.

In its search for a clear identity, Liberal Democrats sought to emphasise the values of community and citizenship, promoting them as alternatives to the tenets of both the free market and state collectivism. Allied to the inherited commitment to the principles of decentralisation and wider participation, that emphasis helped to distinguish the new party from the centralist and corporatist tendencies of Labourist socialism as well as from the economic individualism of Thatcherism.

In his influential book *The Unprincipled Society* (1988), David Marquand placed a central emphasis on the concept of community. 'How can a culture,' he asked, 'permeated by possessive individualism restore the bonds of community?'[54] The model of society favoured by free-market Conservatism, the dominant ideology of the 1980s, precluded any possibility that self-seeking, separate individuals could share any sense of common purpose. Such a model was unable, Marquand argued, to 'accommodate the notion that a political community is, among other things, a web of reciprocal duties and rights: that rights imply duties, and that the health of the community depends as much on its members' willingness to perform duties as on their ability to perform rights'.[55]

This stress on the importance of the value of community was echoed in the party's 1989 policy document *Our Different Vision*, which set out the Liberal Democrats' core themes and values. 'We stand,' it declared, 'for three basic values – liberty, equality and community.'[56] Those values, drawn from the party's 'overlapping traditions of social liberalism and social democracy',[57] were interrelated. For liberty, in both its positive and negative aspects, entailed equality of opportunity since 'if some have greater opportunities than others, then some are less free than others'.[58] Moreover, liberty and equality without community were 'hollow' since individuals were social creatures not isolated atoms, who could fulfil their potential 'only as members one of another'.[59] Individuality was indeed best expressed and fostered within communities, whether based around locality, workplace or mutual interests.

Such sentiments were endorsed in the preamble to the party's constitution which declared that:

> The Liberal Democrats exist to build and safeguard a fair, free and open society in which we seek to balance the fundamental values of liberty, equality and community.[60]

The importance of community, it was argued, needed to be re-emphasised in Liberal Democrat policy as 'the buffer between the individual and the state and the framework within which the individual will, in the main, exercise power and understand responsibilities'.[61]

One of the main implications of this emphasis was the promotion of the related idea of active citizenship. Liberal Democrats stood, the 1989 statement declared, 'for equal citizenship – the badge of belonging to a political community and the means through which political communities take shape'.[62] For community and citizenship were interdependent since political communities 'belong to citizens and are renewed by citizens', while citizenship was 'exercised in and through a community'.[63]

In his book *Citizens' Britain* (1989), party leader Paddy Ashdown developed the same theme. In the more democratic and participatory society which he wished to see emerge in Britain, he looked forward to a revival of a sense of 'the importance of an active life as members of a community and the value of shared resources'.[64] At the heart of such a society he envisaged the need for a new concept of citizenship which would imply 'a new settlement of the terms of the basic contract which defines the citizen's relationship with government and with each other'.[65]

For Ashdown, this new view of citizenship would embrace three elements: first, rights – of a civil, political and economic nature; secondly, entitlements, which 'give us the opportunities and resources we need to be valued and valuable members of society', and thirdly, responsibilities, complementing those rights and entitlements, and to be recognised at the level of the community.[66]

The most distinctive aspect of this conception of citizenship was Ashdown's notion of entitlements, which aimed to define the citizen's right of access to health, education and welfare. It was government's task to guarantee that right of access to such public services or goods, the 'basic "entry ticket" to society', as a later party document described it.[67]

What, in fact, would be the wider role of government in this 'citizens' Britain'? The days of the corporate state were over, Ashdown stressed, but it was 'not sufficient to define the role of government simply as an idle bystander, while the free market is allowed to run rampant, with the powerful winning and the weakest going to the wall'.[68] In line with his central emphasis on citizenship rights and entitlements, he argued that the chief function of government should instead be 'to enhance, enable and empower the individual'.[69]

In the social policy field this meant that government should define and establish its citizens' social entitlements without acting as a monopoly provider of services. In the field of economic policy, too, the primary task of government was 'not to be a participant but to be an enabler and, especially, to be the regulator which ensures that the working of markets is not only free but also fair, open and honest'.[70]

With regard to markets, their important benefits were recognised and emphasised not just by Ashdown but also in successive statements of party policy and principle. The competitive market economy was regarded as essential for generating prosperity and economic efficiency, for maximising choice, for stimulating innovation and for ensuring the decentralisation of economic power.[71]

At the same time, however, it was stressed that 'the market should be our servant not our master'.[72] The role of government was therefore viewed as crucial in 'making the market work properly'.[73] As the party constitution made clear, Liberal Democrats pursued their economic and industrial·aims 'within a competitive environment in which the state allows the market to operate freely but intervenes where necessary'.

Such intervention, the 'Agenda of the State', should take three main forms. First, government action was required, preferably of a regulatory kind, in cases of market failure or deficiency in order, for instance, to prevent monopoly and to promote competition and to ensure that externalities, particularly environmental costs and benefits, were incorporated into market decisions.[74] Secondly, government should supply public goods or services which the market by itself could not provide comprehensively or sufficiently, such as infrastructure, education and training, health-care and environmental protection.[75] Thirdly, and most broadly, it was the role of government to set a long-term framework of policy for sustainable economic development within which the market could operate.[76]

Moreover, in performing those various economic and social tasks, the enabling state was required to operate within a reformed constitutional framework, for since the party's foundation, Liberal Democrats have affirmed their commitment to two interrelated principles inherited from the Liberal Party and the SDP, namely political decentralisation and constitutional reform.

In ideological terms, the decentralisation of political power is viewed by Liberal Democrats as intimately connected with the promotion of the fundamental values of liberty and community underlying a pluralist democracy. By decentralising government, it is argued, the powers of individuals and communities can be increased and the spirit and development of community can be fostered. In order, too, to control the powers exercised by government, an historic liberal aim, those powers 'are best discharged as near as possible to the individuals and communities they most affect'.[77]

Such beliefs underpin the broader commitment to the principle of constitutional reform which since 1989 has been translated into proposals for radical political reform, for, indeed, a 'new political settlement'[78] that would be codified and guaranteed by a reformed and written constitution.[79]

The need for such a settlement has been made all the more pressing, in the Liberal Democrat view, in the light of political developments since 1979 which both undermined civil liberties and threatened the foundations of pluralist democracy. In the Thatcher era there had been not only an unprecedented degree of centralisation of power on Whitehall, but also a lengthy period of one-party rule resulting in untrammelled executive power, which had eroded the checks and balances implicit in a system of alternating party government.

The new constitutional settlement advocated by Liberal Democrats would aim, therefore, to make secure the vital principles of a pluralist liberal democracy by 'embracing clear and explicit protections of basic human rights; the greatest possible devolution of power from the central state to the localities, regions and nations of Britain'; and 'reform of Parliament to democratise the House of Lords and give the House of Commons effective powers to scrutinise and control the executive'.[80]

In practical policy terms that entailed proposals for a new voting system based on proportional representation; for the incorporation of the European Convention of Human Rights into UK law, with its eventual entrenchment as a UK Bill of Rights; for devolution of government through the creation of a Scottish Parliament and a Welsh Senedd; for the replacement of the House of Lords by an elected second chamber; and for the enactment of freedom of information legislation.

This far-reaching programme of political reform would seek to realise the Liberal Democrat vision of 'a modernised, rights-based and decentralised constitution' that would both redefine the relationship between the state and its citizens, safeguarding their rights and liberties, and shift power away from Westminster and Whitehall to 'the individual communities, regions and nations of the UK'.[81]

Conclusion

All of these distinctive ideas and emphases – community, active citizenship, an enabling state, a publicly regulated market economy, political decentralisation and constitutional reform – helped to make clear where the Liberal Democrats stood in a changing political landscape. On all these points of principle, too, they have remained true to their radical ideological heritage, to the intertwined traditions of social liberalism and social democracy.

What, however, appears less clear is how significantly such ideas have distinguished Liberal Democrats from a Labour Party which, since 1987, has assumed an increasingly social democratic image and character. The enabling state and a publicly regulated market economy, for example, were central themes in Labour's major policy review documents after 1987,[82] while the concepts of community and citizenship have permeated the speeches and writings of Tony Blair since 1992 and particularly since his election as party leader in 1994. The Liberal Democrats' programme of constitutional reform, too, with the exception of a firm commitment to proportional representation, has been gradually embraced by the Labour Party since the late 1980s.

Arguably, there has still been evident in Liberal Democratic thought a greater commitment to the decentralisation of power and to the rights and liberties of the individual, embodied, for instance, in the party's proposals for devolution of government and for a Bill of Rights, as well as a stronger emphasis on environmental concerns. Nevertheless, the degree of policy and even ideological convergence which has steadily emerged between the two parties raises the question of the extent to which the distinctiveness of the Liberal Democrats' position and purpose has been eroded by Labour's neo-revisionist social democracy under Kinnock, Smith and Blair.

If such a risk of an erosion of ideological identity does now present itself, then in a sense that constitutes a new expression of the recurrent problem that faced the Liberal Party in the past: that of having its political clothes stolen by other parties. For as Stevenson has noted, the old Liberal Party, possessing no copyright on political ideas, was in many ways 'more important as a source of ideas which have entered the mainstream of political debate than as a vehicle for carrying them out'.[83]

A more optimistic view, however, would interpret the increasing common ground between Liberal Democrats and Labour as the basis for a continuing dialogue of ideas which could even herald the rebirth of a centre-left, progressive alliance, tentatively promoted in the 1890s and 1900s but destroyed by the tactical pressures of party politics in the 1920s.

Assuming that the Liberal Democrats will none the less strive to maintain their political independence, it does at least seem likely that, like the Alliance before it, the new party may have succeeded in reuniting, within its own thinking and policy, two related ideological traditions – social liberalism and social democracy – which throughout most of this century have been forced to find separate partisan expression.

Notes

1 For an examination of contributions to the academic debate, see A. Vincent, 'The New Liberalism in Britain 1880–1914', *Australian Journal of Politics and History*, Vol. 36, No. 3, 1990.

2 See A.Vincent, *Modern Political Ideologies*, Blackwell, 1992, Chap. 2; G.L. Bernstein, *Liberalism and Liberal Politics in Edwardian England*, Allen & Unwin, 1986; R. Leach, *British Political Ideologies*, Philip Allan, 1991, Chap. 3; H.J. Schulz, *English Liberalism and the State: Individualism or Collectivism*, Heath, 1972.

3 See R. Eccleshall, *British Liberalism*, Longman, 1986, p.7.

4 A. Vincent, *Modern Political Ideologies*, p.31.

5 P. Clarke, 'Liberals and Social Democrats in Historical Perspective', in V. Bogdanor (ed.), *Liberal Party Politics*, Clarendon Press, 1983, pp.29–30.

6 T.H. Green, *The Works of Thomas Hill Green*, ed. R.L. Nettleship, Longmans, Green & Co., 1888, Vol. 3, p.372.

7 See, for example, H. Samuel, *Liberalism: An Attempt to Restate the Principles of Liberalism in England*, Grant Richards, 1902.

8 J.A. Hobson, *The Crisis of Liberalism*, 1909; edited and with introduction by P.F. Clarke, Harvester Press, 1974, p.xii.

9 *Ibid.*, p.94.

10 *Ibid.*, p.92.

11 *Ibid.*, p.xii.

12 See, for instance, the third and later editions of J.S. Mill's *Principles of Political Economy* and his posthumously published *Chapters on Socialism*.

13 See M. Bentley, *The Climax of Liberal Politics, 1868–1918: British Liberalism in Theory and Practice*, Edward Arnold, 1987.

14 J. Curtice, 'Great Britain: Social Liberalism Reborn?', in E.J. Kirchner (ed.), *Liberal Parties in Western Europe*, Cambridge University Press, 1988, p.95.

15 P. Clarke, *Liberals and Social Democrats*, Cambridge University Press, 1978, pp.5, 65.

16 J.M. Keynes, *The End of Laissez-Faire*, Hogarth Press, 1926, pp.46–9.

17 See J.M. Keynes, *The General Theory of Employment, Interest and Money*, Macmillan, 1936, pp.377–383.

18 W. Beveridge, *Why I am a Liberal*, Herbert Jenkins, 1945, p.33.

19 *Ibid.*

20 See D. Kavanagh and P. Morris, *Consensus Politics from Attlee to Major*, Blackwell, 1994.
21 See, for instance, J. Grimond, *The Liberal Future*, Faber & Faber, 1959; *The Liberal Challenge*, Hollis & Carter, 1963.
22 J. Grimond, *Memoirs*, Heinemann, 1979, p.216.
23 Community Politics Strategy Resolution, Liberal Party Assembly, 1970.
24 S. Mole, 'The Liberal Party and Community Politics', in V. Bogdanor (ed.), *op. cit.*, p.259.
25 *Ibid.*; A. Beith, *The Case for the Liberal Party and the Alliance*, Longman, 1983, p.104.
26 See, for example, B. Greaves and G. Lishman, *The Theory and Practice of Community Politics*, Hebden Royd, 1980; D. Thomson, *The Stocktroops of Pavement Politics*, Hebden Royd, 1985.
27 Eccleshall, *British Liberalism*, p.5; 'Liberalism' in Eccleshall *et al.*, *Political Ideologies*, Hutchinson, 1984, p.50.
28 S. Padgett and W. Paterson, *A History of Social Democracy in Postwar Europe*, Longman, 1991, p.1.
29 *Ibid.*
30 M.B. Hamilton, *Democratic Socialism in Britain and Sweden*, Macmillan, 1989, p.11.
31 *Ibid.*, p.12.
32 See D. Marquand, 'Inquest on a Movement', *Encounter*, July 1979, p.9.
33 See P. Clarke, *Liberals and Social Democrats*, Cambridge University Press, 1978, for an exploration of the common ground, and points of divergence, between social liberals and reformist socialists in Britain.
34 See D. Marquand, *The Unprincipled Society*, Jonathan Cape, 1988; S. Holland, *The Socialist Challenge*, Quartet Books, 1975.
35 A. Wright, 'Social Democracy and Democratic Socialism', in R. Eatwell and A. Wright (eds), *Contemporary Political Ideologies*, Pinter, 1993, p.91.
36 D. Marquand, *The Unprincipled Society*, p.18.
37 *Ibid.*, p.19.
38 *Ibid.*
39 See D. Marquand, 'Inquest on a Movement'; E. Luard, *Socialism without the State*, Macmillan, 1979; D. Marquand (ed.), *John P. Mackintosh on Parliament and Social Democracy*, Longman, 1982.
40 See D. Marquand, *The Progressive Dilemma*, Heinemann, 1991, p.212.
41 D. Marquand, 'Inquest on a Movement', *Encounter*, July 1979, p.18.
42 *Ibid.*
43 R. Behrens, 'The Centre: Social Democracy and Liberalism', in L. Tivey and A. Wright (eds), *Party Ideology in Britain*, Routledge, 1989, p.78.
44 D. Owen, *Face the Future*, abridged and revised edn., Oxford University Press, 1981, p.3.
45 W. Rodgers, *The Politics of Change*, Secker & Warburg, 1982, p.4.
47 *Ibid.*, pp.25, 31.

46 D. Owen, *op.cit.*, p.3.
48 *Ibid.*, pp.27.
49 S. Williams, *Politics is for People*, Penguin, 1981, p.187.
50 D. Owen, *op. cit.*, p.27; Williams, *op. cit.*, p.207.
51 D. Marquand, 'Taming Leviathan: Social Democracy and Decentralisation', unpublished lecture, 1980, pp.3–4.
52 D. Marquand, *Russet-coated Captains: The Challenge of Social Democracy*, SDP, 1981, p.12.
53 *Britain United: The Time Has Come*, SDP/Liberal Alliance Programme for Government, 1987.
54 D. Marquand, *The Unprincipled Society*, pp.223–4.
55 *Ibid.*, p.67.
56 *Our Different Vision: Values and Themes for Social and Liberal Democrats*, Hebden Royd Publications, 1989, p.1.
57 *Ibid.*, p.9.
58 *Ibid.*
59 *Ibid.*
60 Preamble to the Constitution of the Liberal Democrats: the Federal Party.
61 *Facing up to the Future: Enduring Values in a Changing World*, Liberal Democrat Publications, 1993, p.11.
62 *Our Different Vision*, p.10.
63 *Ibid.*
64 Paddy Ashdown, *Citizens' Britain*, Fourth Estate, 1989, p.22.
65 *Ibid.*, p.32.
66 *Ibid.*, p.36.
67 *Challenge, Opportunity and Responsibility*, Liberal Democrat Publications, 1992, p.11.
68 Paddy Ashdown, *op. cit.*, p.43.
69 *Ibid.*
70 *Ibid.*, p.42. On this point see also, *Our Different Vision*, p.17.
71 See *Challenge, Opportunity and Responsibility,* p.11; *Facing up to the Future*, p.13; *Changing Britain for Good*, Liberal Democrats' 1992 general election manifesto.
72 *Changing Britain for Good*, p.6.
73 *Ibid.*
74 See *Challenge, Opportunity and Responsibility*, p.11; *Facing up to the Future*, p.13.
75 *Ibid.*; *Changing Britain for Good*, pp.6–7.
76 *Challenge, Opportunity and Responsibility*, p.11.
77 *Ibid.*, p.21.
78 *Here We Stand: Proposals for Modernising Britain's Democracy*, Liberal Democrat Publications, 1993, p.3.
79 See *Here We Stand*; *We, The People – Towards a Written Constitution,* Hebden Royd, 1990.
80 *Our Different Vision*, p.11.
81 *Here We Stand*, p.3.

82 See, for instance, *Meet the Challenge, Make the Change*, Labour Party, 1989; and *Looking to the Future*, Labour Party, 1990.

83 J. Stevenson, *Third Party Politics since 1945*, Blackwell, 1993, p.135.

CHAPTER 4

Liberal Democrat policy

Duncan Brack

Policies are important to a political party for a number of reasons. Most obviously, a party's policy programme represents its promise to the electorate: the proposals it intends to implement when it achieves power. It is also an expression of the party's ideology, the policy stances it derives from its basic philosophical beliefs and values. Particular policies can be used as advertising messages, highlighting the party's 'unique selling points'. Policies can contribute to general debate, sometimes being adopted by other parties if they deem it politically or electorally wise.

In these different ways, policies form part of the kaleidoscope of impressions that together form the overall image of the party in the mind of the electorate; other components of the image include the record of the party in central and local government, the qualities and behaviour of the party's spokespersons and representatives at national and local levels (most importantly its leader), and the portrayal of the party in the media.

These are external uses of policy; but policies are also tools of communication *within* a party. They can be politically educational in either of two directions. The party's leaders can use policies to teach the membership the campaigning and policy messages of the day; and the membership can signal to the leadership what it thinks and believes, particularly in response to leadership initiatives. Policy as an expression of ideology is also important internally: it can act as a credo, a reaffirmation of belief, a morale-raising message that the activist is not alone.

The values that different parties give to these uses of policy vary, reflecting the different natures, beliefs and compositions of the parties. Compared to the Conservative and Labour Parties, the Liberal Democrats have been more attached to policy detail, more

The author wishes to express sincere thanks and appreciation to Paddy Ashdown MP, Sir William Goodhart, Sean O'Grady, Matthew Taylor MP and Patrick Wintour, who were interviewed in connection with this chapter and who subsequently provided advice in its drafting; and also to Michael Hart, Don MacIver, Ben Pimlott, Ben Rich, Neil Stockley and William Wallace who similarly offered invaluable advice and help. Responsibility for any errors of fact or interpretation remains with the author.

internally democratic in how policies are drawn up, and more ideological in their development – though not in their use in campaigning. In turn this is a reflection of the different philosophy, internal structure, social and geographical composition, and political circumstances and history of the party. All these factors join together to result in policies that are different in important ways from those of other British political parties. This chapter examines these policies, how they have been derived and used, why and how they are different and their contribution to recent British politics. First, we examine briefly how they have developed.

From Alliance to Liberal Democrats

The policy inheritance of the Liberal Democrats was not a happy one. The birth of the Social and Liberal Democrats was intended to be accompanied by a statement setting out the party's initial policy stance and general aims. This document, however, drawn up by the Liberal and SDP leaders David Steel and Robert Maclennan over the winter of 1987–88, almost brought disaster to the entire merger process. Entitled *Voices and Choices for All,* but universally referred to as the 'dead parrot' document,[1] its story has been told elsewhere.[2] Its proposals, amongst others, for the retention of Trident, taxation of child benefit and the extension of VAT, not to mention its vacuous sub-Thatcherite rhetoric, ensured its suppression by horrified Liberals and Social Democrats alike.

Its replacement, *A Democracy of Conscience,* was accordingly designed to be as anodyne as possible. Adopted along with the new party's constitution in the two parties' merger ballots, it described the familiar Liberal/SDP Alliance agenda. Constitutional reform (proportional representation, a Bill of Rights, freedom of information, decentralisation of power) took pride of place. Economic policy was based on investment in infrastructure, training and R&D, social policy on greater state investment and administrative reform (particularly of the tax and benefits system), environmental policy on recycling and renewable energy, and international policy on support for NATO and the European Community.

All of the policy differences between the Alliance partners were thus left unresolved. The philosophies and policies of the Liberal Party and the SDP, though alike, were in important respects not the same. Liberals had held to a firm belief in liberty throughout their years in the political wilderness, underpinning their central commitment to a redistribution of power within society in the interests of individuals and communities. A belief in individual rights rather than group interests, a decentralist and environmentalist economic policy, and an international policy based on supranational institutions and laws rather than the bargaining strengths of nation states, all followed. As the party of Keynes and Beveridge, however, in economic and social terms it was for most of the post-war period[3] a social liberal (rather than European-style classical liberal) party, advocating a fairly high degree of state intervention in the economy and state provision of social services.

The SDP, most of whose leaders shared a background in the Labour Party, identified itself strongly with the post-war Butskellite consensus formed around the mixed economy, the welfare state, state action to maintain full employment, and progressive redistribution of resources following from economic growth. After he replaced Roy Jenkins as leader, however, David Owen strove to differentiate his party more sharply from Labour. Economic policy accordingly veered to the right, adopting a more free market and less state interventionist approach, for which Owen used the slogan 'social market economy'.[4] The SDP was notably more managerialist and less decentralist than the Liberal Party and rather less internationalist, though it shared a commitment to the economic and political development of the European Community.

Policy disagreements derived largely from the different characters of the two parties' memberships.[5] The Liberals tended to be the party of the periphery, geographical, social and cultural, and gathered electoral support throughout the 1970s from uncommitted protest votes and single issue enthusiasts. By contrast, the SDP was the party of the meritocratic centre – the professional middle classes, alienated from the traditional left/right polarisation of politics – and accordingly much less ready than the Liberals to embrace the need for radical change, adopting an essentially technocratic reformist stance. Under the Alliance, however, electoral support started to cohere, becoming increasingly concentrated in the professional and public sector middle classes and in all classes the more highly educated: the upwardly mobile meritocrats.

The most high profile policy difference between the two Alliance partners lay in the area of defence, where the Liberals tended to be much more hostile towards nuclear weapons than was the SDP; this was a key factor in the Social Democrats' split from Labour. The fault line here, however, really lay within the Liberal Party, which in 1984 had reversed its previous opposition to the British independent deterrent but in 1986 voted against a joint Alliance commission proposal for European cooperation in nuclear forces.[6] The Social Democrats' insistence on the inclusion of support for NATO in the new party's constitution (from which it could only be removed by two successive conference votes, the second by a two-thirds majority) was based entirely on distrust of Liberal leanings on defence. A much clearer party-based difference lay in the issue of nuclear power, to which the environmentalist Liberals were almost wholly opposed, and to which the more pro-technology SDP was largely in favour. Other disagreements took place over economics, where the SDP added detail to sometimes rather vague Liberal policy but watered down support for industrial democracy; over health, where the SDP was more market-oriented (supporting an internal market in the NHS before the Conservatives), and over foreign policy, where the SDP dissented from Liberal ideas of a federal Europe.

It would be wrong, however, to overemphasise these differences, particularly in comparison with the arguments over party structure which nearly wrecked the merger process. In most policy areas, disagreements were trivial or non-existent, and the experience of working in alliance over six years itself brought the two parties closer together – for example on constitutional reform, which both came to accept as a crucial cornerstone of the policy programme. The structure of the Alliance itself magnified disagreements, as policy disputes which would have passed unnoticed within a single party assumed the proportions of a major split in the context of two. Indeed, one of the arguments used in favour of merger was that policy differences could henceforth be settled by debate and democratic vote rather than through haggling and horse trading between negotiating teams.

The first two years of the Liberal Democrats' existence did indeed see the resolution of the policy differences outstanding from Alliance days. Disagreements over defence and environmental policy were significantly dampened by the progress of events. The ending of the Cold War took almost all of the heat out of the defence dispute and allowed the party to be much more imaginative about the possibility of future disarmament negotiations, and bolder about defence cuts than would have been realistic even a few years before; this helped to reconcile pro-disarmament activists to the policy of retention of the Trident submarine force.[7] Similarly, the evidence of the huge costs of the nuclear industry which led the government to withdraw the nuclear power stations from electricity privatisation in 1989 reinforced Liberal concerns over pollution and civil liberties, and a commitment to phase out nuclear power accordingly passed with ease at the spring conference in 1990.[8] On health and European policy, the new party adopted essentially the former Liberal position, those Social Democrats who were most favourable to an internal market in the NHS and opposed to a federal Europe having largely followed David Owen into the political wilderness (and also because by this stage the internal market was Conservative policy).

In three areas, though, the Liberal Democrats diverged from the direction of previous Alliance policy-making. Alliance *economic policy* had followed an orthodox Keynesian demand management approach, relying on increased state spending (on infrastructure, training and R&D and regional development) to boost the economy and reduce unemployment, and an incomes policy to control inflation. Throughout 1990 and 1991, the new party's economic policy developed in a less interventionist, more free market, direction, largely at the instigation of party leader Paddy Ashdown. Competition policy – a tougher line on mergers, the breaking up of the privatised utilities – was emphasised. The possibility of private investment in public services, such as the franchising of particular rail routes, was floated. Encouragement was to be given to the decentralisation of pay bargaining. Control over interest rates was to be taken out of the hands of politicians through the grant of operational independence to the Bank of England with a mandate to maintain price stability.[9] This was coupled with a continued commitment to Europe through support for economic and monetary union, and an attempt to integrate environmental into economic policy through market-based mechanisms such as energy taxation. This stress on markets can be seen as a return to older Liberal themes, and indeed was more in tune with the economic policy of Continental European liberal parties such as the German Free Democrats. It is ironic that it was the merger with an explicitly social democratic party that enabled Liberal economic policy to move in this direction.[10] It was also, of course, more in tune with wider economic debate at the time, and helped to distinguish the Liberal Democrats from Labour. The policy was attacked by its opponents within the party as a move towards the Conservatives, but at the 1991 autumn conference, the new policy[11] was adopted overwhelmingly and most attempts to amend it voted down.

Environmental policy became a central theme of the Liberal Democrats. Here they built on Liberal roots[12] but developed proposals much further and in a manner informed by the new market-based approach to economic policy. Environmental taxation, grants and subsidies and systems of tradable emissions licences for industry were all examples. The party's energy paper of 1990 was the first of many to propose a shift in the burden of taxation from income and labour to pollution and resource depletion; subsequent papers proposed taxing energy and petrol.[13] Liberal Democrat local authorities exhibited a consistent record of environmental action, and the stance was reinforced by the hyperactive and popular environmental spokesman in the Commons, Simon Hughes. The environmentalist Jonathon Porritt complimented the party on its environmental policies at a rally at the spring 1991 conference, and former Friends of the Earth director David Gee gave the 1992 election manifesto 9 marks out of 12 in a specially constructed environmental checklist, compared with 11 for the Green Party, 3 for Labour and 1 for the Conservatives. Although these developments were undoubtedly given momentum by the Greens' trouncing of the party in the 1989 European elections, it seems likely that they would have occurred anyway, given the strong green lobby within the party.[14] As the Green Party went into rapid decline in the 1990s, several of its activists found a natural home in the Liberal Democrats.

Education was the third new Liberal Democrat area, not so much in the details of policy but in the pride of place it was accorded in spending commitments. This was exemplified by the striking proposal to raise income tax by one penny in the pound to pay for the extra investment needed. (The party was always careful to say 'if necessary', but this caveat was usually ignored and by the 1992 election it clearly was necessary.) First floated in Paddy Ashdown's speech to the party conference in autumn 1990, this was taken up and pushed heavily by the new education spokesman, Matthew Taylor. It fulfilled a number of desirable objectives. It enabled the party to 'capture' a policy area that, unlike environment and constitutional reform, proved salient to much of the electorate. It created an impression of commitment to the long-term good of the country. It helped to build an image of preparedness to take unpopular decisions and honesty in putting them to the electorate. Above all, it was completely distinctive, no other party promising to raise the basic rate of income tax, and easily memorable.

These three policy areas, together with the more traditional themes of electoral and constitutional reform and Europe, formed the five 'E's on which the Liberal Democrat manifesto for the 1992 election, *Changing Britain for Good,*[15] was built (see Appendix for summary). The manifesto contributed to the positive impact of the election campaign, which lifted the party from an opinion poll rating of about 15 per cent at the start of the campaign to a peak of 21–22 per cent before falling back to 17.8 per cent on polling day. The *Guardian* and the *Independent*, the two newspapers most sympathetic to the party, were generally supportive. 'The Liberal Democrat essay far out-distances its competitors with a fizz of ideas and an absence of fudge,' stated the *Guardian.*[16] 'Across a spectrum of issues,' commented the *Independent*, 'the Liberal Democrats are more in sympathy with the spirit of the times than either of the two big parties'.[17] The policy most highlighted for comment was the penny on income tax for education, seen initially as a risky move but recognised by the end of the campaign as highly popular. The proposals for public investment, environmental policy and constitutional reform were also identified as distinctive: 'Here, ranged at the radical end of the spectrum, are many of the answers beyond Labour's mumbles,' believed the *Guardian*.[18] 'This is a package which Labour might dearly have loved to introduce, but for its electoral impact'.[19] The *Financial Times*, however, was not so convinced. The Liberal Democrats were 'a fruitful source of ideas,' it observed. 'some of which are bright and some of which are incomprehensible'.[20] The FT's analysis found the manifesto intellectually inconsistent (though it noted the programme's appeal to many different audiences): 'It is not a cohesive ideology. Instead, bright wheezes have been costed and reworked to fit into a framework that has common strands but cannot be defined in conventional terms or in a single phrase.'[21]

From philosophy to policy

The *Financial Times* was probably right to believe that Liberal Democrat philosophy could not be defined easily in 'conventional terms', if by this it meant the orthodox left/ right political continuum. (Liberal Democrat activists would probably take this as a compliment.) This does not in itself, however, prove its incoherence.

The Liberal Democrats have made a systematic effort to derive their policy proposals consistently from a core philosophy. This exercise is in sharp contrast to the other main parties; unlike them, the Liberal Democrats have lacked the benefit of an instinctive understanding of 'what the party stands for' amongst the electorate, the media and even their own members and activists (particularly in the immediate post-merger period). Five party conferences since 1988 have seen debates around 'themes and values' documents,[22] and almost all of the party's policy papers contain a section relating the specific proposals to one of these papers or to the preamble to the party's constitution, which itself sets out a summary of the party's enduring beliefs: 'The Liberal Democrats exist to build and safeguard a fair, free and open society, in which we seek to balance the fundamental values of liberty, equality and community, and in which no-one shall be enslaved by poverty, ignorance or conformity. We champion the freedom, dignity and well-being of individuals and their rights to develop their talents to the full. We aim to disperse power, to foster diversity and to nurture creativity. We believe that the role of the state is to enable all citizens to contribute fully to their communities and to take part in the decisions which affect their lives.'[23] *Facing up to the Future,* the latest and most coherent of these 'philosophy' papers, highlights the enduring values of liberty, equality and community.

Liberty is the traditional Liberal creed of freedom from arbitrary interference from the state and from the majority: 'a society which gives individual men and women opportunities to pursue their aims, develop their talents and fulfil their potential'.[24] The key to the creation of this liberal society is the dispersal of power, and, above all, its use by individuals themselves. This is the core of the Liberal Democrat philosophy, setting it apart from both Conservative and Labour beliefs: political power is not to be wielded on behalf, or for the greater good, of the people but *by* the people themselves, who are the only true judges of their own best interests. This belief underpins the constitutional reform agenda of the party.[25] Structures of government are to be decentralised, to regional, local and neighbourhood levels, so that ordinary citizens can more easily influence them, and a political environment created in which citizens can exercise power themselves, through voluntary bodies, housing associations, user groups, employee participation and ownership, and mechanisms of 'direct democracy', such as referendums and US-style citizen's initiatives. Where power must be exercised through representative government, Liberal Democrats aim to make it more representative and accountable: through electoral reform (via the single transferable vote, which affords the greatest degree of choice to the voter), decentralisation, reform of the House of Lords, the democratisation or abolition of quangos, and freedom of information. In order that individuals may be secure within this free society, the potential for the abuse of power is to be countered through a Bill of Rights to protect individual liberties, comprehensive redress mechanisms and a reformed system of administrative law to regulate public agencies, together with a written constitution setting out a clear definition of the responsibilities and duties of different levels of government.

Equality, the second of the triad of core values, is derived from this commitment to liberty: individuals cannot attain true freedom if they are constrained by poverty, unemployment, sickness or ignorance. The state is therefore justified in taking action to ensure that every member of society enjoys 'access to the essential requirements for making choices in their lives: a basic income, good education, necessary social services and a chance to develop and use their talents for their own good and the good of society'.[26] This approach justifies a redistributive tax policy, a social security system which avoids dependency and promotes opportunity, employment-generating investment in infrastructure and reductions in labour taxes (paid for by energy taxation), investment in health and social services and in 'social infrastructure' such as child care, and an active urban and rural development policy targeting specific areas of deprivation and lack of opportunity. Above all else, it argues for investment in education and training, the key, as the party sees it, to individuals' future self-development and also to the country's economic success. However, this commitment to equality is not derived from a belief in social justice for its own sake; it is identifiably the New Liberal desire to set people free to develop and fulfil their own potential.[27] The Liberal Democrat belief in equality is clearly not in equality of *outcome,* which compromises the primary belief in liberty; it is in equality of *opportunity* – which is why education, which attacks inequality less directly than, say, tax and benefits policy, is accorded such a high priority.

The last of the three Liberal Democrat core values, community, is to provide the framework within which individuals exercise these freedoms and enjoy these opportunities. It relates most obviously to the liberty-derived desire to decentralise power to the local and neighbourhood level, and the development by the Liberal Party since the 1970s of the theory of 'community politics' and a belief in individual empowerment. Policy proposals therefore advocate not only the creation of political structures of power at the community level, but also the promotion of community structures themselves. This includes an emphasis on local economic development and investment in community facilities, a neighbourhood-based approach to tackling crime (through crime prevention schemes and community policing), a planning policy aimed at creating localities with a mixture of housing, jobs, services and facilities (which also has environmental benefits), and the promotion of workplace communities through employee participation in decision-making, share-ownership and profit-sharing.

The concept of community can also be expressed in its original, French revolutionary, sense of fraternity: human beings' duty to their fellows, the obverse of their entitlement to liberty. This has deep historical roots, originating in the Gladstonian and nonconformist belief in voluntarism and the moral duty of the better-off to assist those less fortunate than themselves. Translated into the late twentieth century, it is expressed as society's responsibility to ensure equality of opportunity for all its members; the Thatcherite view that there is no such thing as society is instinctively repugnant to Liberal Democrats. Similarly, the present generation has a duty to the future; hence the commitment to education, and hence also the strong environmental strand that has become one of the main distinguishing characteristics of the party's policy, a development reinforced by its localist, decentralist nature. Liberal Democrat environmental policy is based on the concept of sustainable development – 'development that meets the needs of the present without compromising the ability of future generations to meet their own needs'.[28] Policy is designed to reduce pollution and conserve non-renewable resources, and to promote a sense of individual and community responsibility for protecting the environment.

Liberal Democrat economic policy, at least since 1991, has adopted a preference for market mechanisms, relating this to the party's belief in liberty: 'the operation of competitive markets in the economy is essential to generate prosperity, to maximise choice, to decentralise economic power and to stimulate innovation and adaptability'.[29] State power is needed to ensure the market works properly, to remove distortions and correct market failures; the party favours an active fiscal policy, with higher levels of tax and public spending than either of its opponents. State power, however, is suspect and 'bureaucratic failure is just as frequent and can be just as damaging as market failure.'[30] It should operate, therefore, where feasible in a near-market or regulatory way (for example via the internalisation of uncosted externalities, such as energy taxation to correct for pollution, or through the regulation of natural monopolies) rather than through direct state intervention or ownership. It is also to be constrained: control over interest rates should be taken out of the hands of politicians, and economic policy should be guided by clear rules such as a long-term 'savings target' for private and public sectors as a whole.[31] This is the area, however, in which most conflict has occurred within the party, and where the policy gap between leadership and membership is probably widest. The 1992 conference took the unusual step of defeating a Policy Committee proposal, on limited rail privatisation,[32] and came within a handful of votes of referring back a consultation paper,[33] mainly on the basis of its excessively pro-market stand. In 1994 the conference voted against the wishes of the parliamentary party in favour of a regional minimum wage.

Internationalism was a consistent characteristic of both the Liberal Party and the SDP. The Liberals were the first British party to call for UK entry to the European Community, and Labour hostility to the EC was a major factor behind the SDP split. This position derives from a general commitment to peaceful coexistence and cooperation amongst nations and peoples, and to the rule of law, inherent in the belief in liberty and community. Liberal Democrat international policy therefore stresses the construction of effective international institutions, at European and global levels, to deal with international problems of environmental degradation, poverty, security and peacekeeping. At the same time, it is true to its decentralist and democratic beliefs in arguing for a federal European Union, where power is exercised at EU level only where necessary and where EU institutions are subject to strong European Parliament control. In effect the party wishes to see power shifted both upwards and downwards from the centralised British state. Defence policy concentrates on European cooperation and a desire to see more effective UN peacekeeping; areas of controversy centre as much around levels of defence spending and controls on the international arms trade as around nuclear weapons. Free trade, one of the historic rallying cries of the Liberal Party, is still held to in the sense of an open, rules-based and multilateral trading system, though with some modification in the pursuit of environmental sustainability.

Does this attempt to derive Liberal Democrat policy from core philosophy result in a coherent package of proposals? The answer is broadly yes, particularly in the areas of political and institutional reform, environmental policy and foreign policy. The attempt made in *Facing up to the Future* to relate the whole set of policy propositions to the three core beliefs of liberty, equality and community is not a complete success – stances such as internationalism and environmentalism cannot easily be derived directly from these – but this is just another way of saying that Liberal Democracy cannot be summed up in three words. The simultaneous commitments to decentralisation and to further European integration have been attacked by the party's political opponents, but are hardly a contradiction in the true meaning of the term 'federalism'. Coherence has been most questioned in the field of economic policy, where commentators – the *Financial Times* at the election, *The Economist* in early 1994[34] – have queried the combination of higher state spending and a preference for market mechanisms. In post-war British politics, this is not an orthodox combination, but increasing social spending and investment in infrastructure hardly constitutes a threat to the private sector in an economy with unemployed resources; indeed, this is a classical Keynesian stance. There seems no obvious reason why this should not sit comfortably with a disinclination to intervene at the micro level, a commitment to greater competition in the economy and an independently governed monetary policy. It does imply a growth in the public sector in relation to its current size (albeit a much more decentralised one) and can therefore be criticised by those who believe that liberty demands small government. This is not, however, an automatic equivalence, and the Liberal Democrats (and their predecessor parties for at least the past ninety years) have been quite explicit in their belief in activist government. Differences in the leadership's and membership's attitude to the value of market mechanisms, however, have not helped to clarify the party's stance. Other commentators have not shared these doubts. The *Independent* in 1992 believed that the Party was 'alone in understanding that the market can be a potent ally in serving social ends'[35] and Hugo Young congratulated it for putting forward a package which was 'more honest and coherent than other programmes'.[36]

The process of policy development has undoubtedly succeeded in resolving the policy conflicts between Liberals and Social Democrats which the new party inherited; although there is of course still disagreement over the future direction of policy, it is not conducted in this context. The policy platform is also distinctive. It is clearly different from that of the Conservative Party in almost all aspects. Despite Labour's recent policy changes, some of which have drawn on existing Liberal Democrat policy (see further below), important distinctions remain here also, both in policies (particularly in environmental, European and international policy and constitutional reform, and in taxation and expenditure) and in values. The distinction that Peter Clarke (following Hobhouse) makes between 'mechanical reformists' imposing reform from above and 'moral reformists' seeking reform through popular assent and participation[37] is a valid description of the contrast between Liberal Democrat and Labour attitudes to politics, and has been demonstrated on many occasions in local government. Although the two parties do currently share many policy positions, they are not in general derived from the same beliefs.

Communicating Liberal Democrat policies

As the third party in a system which in parliamentary terms is still essentially designed for two parties, and lacking a sympathetic media, the Liberal Democrats only rarely achieve much prominence for their policy proposals. Policy paper press launches usually pass largely unheeded by non-specialist journalists, except at election times, when the broadcast media is required to give greater parity of coverage. The success of the party in establishing the one penny on income tax for education proposal as an issue in the 1992 election was notable for its rarity. The Liberal Democrats have subsequently used the same proposal in local election campaigns and in single issue campaigns between elections. Environmental policy has also been employed in this way; these are, of course, the two out of the five 'E's which have most resonance amongst the electorate, particularly at local level.

'Policy', however, in the sense that it has been used so far, has not often featured very highly in Liberal Democrat local election and by-election campaigns. These tend to concentrate on local issues such as hospital closures or road developments, the local roots of the candidate, the hard work and commitment to the constituency of the candidate and the campaign team and the record of local Liberal Democrat councillors and councils. National issues do, of course, often impinge on parliamentary by-elections: the Ribble Valley campaign in February 1991 was heavily influenced by the approaching demise of the poll tax, Kincardine and Deeside in November 1991 focused on the government's NHS reforms, and Newbury and Christchurch in 1993 both saw VAT on domestic fuel and power used as a weapon against the Conservatives. These are all negative issues, where the party primarily campaigned in *opposition* to the government's proposals (though local income tax featured as the Liberal Democrat alternative to the poll tax in Ribble Valley), but since by-elections are increasingly used by the voters, and presented by the media, as opinion poll-type opportunities to cast a verdict on the government of the day, this is hardly surprising. It is true, however, that the party's *positive* appeal is largely presented in local terms.

This has led to the inevitable attacks from other parties that the Liberal Democrats 'mean all things to all men', advocating different policies in different parts of the country.

It would be remarkable, however, if local variation were *not* the case for an avowedly decentralist party. The national party exercises no control over manifestos for local government elections (though a national 'action plan' is produced) – since campaigns tend to focus so heavily on local issues, it would be wholly impracticable for it to do so, not to mention contrary to its principles – though provisions do exist for action where the fundamental values of the party are thought to be contravened.[38] (By-election campaigns, by contrast, are run by the national party.) As the third party in local government (second since May 1995), Liberal Democrat council groups have not unsurprisingly attacked whoever is in power in their area. Increasingly, they have found themselves holding the balance of power between Labour and Conservatives. The fact that they criticise or cooperate with them in different ways in different places is no more remarkable that the fact that in some places the other two parties cooperate to exclude the Liberal Democrats, or that Liberal Democrat administrations are attacked by both. The party's critics have not succeeded in showing that Liberal Democrat councils follow fundamentally opposed policies in different parts of the country. (Indeed, the Conservatives have attempted to argue in both directions, claiming that the Liberal Democrats are nothing more than Labour's junior partners.)

The party has more credibly been accused of opportunism in some of its campaigning. The attacks in the Newbury and Christchurch by-elections on the government's plans to impose VAT on domestic fuel and power appeared to contradict the party's position in favour of raising the price of energy for environmental reasons. Though the campaign's position was technically correct,[39] it gave the impression that the party had never contemplated higher energy prices, which was not true. Similarly, the 1994 European election campaign, which concentrated on domestic issues, tried to play down the Liberal Democrats' longstanding support for a federal Europe and promoted the idea of a referendum following the 1996 intergovernmental conference,[40] gave the impression of an attempt to cash in on the government's domestic problems while hiding its own (electorally unpopular) European enthusiasm. But while these strategies led to some unhappiness within the party, and may have caused some loss of green and Euro-enthusiast votes, they arguably also contributed to two by-election victories and the gain of the first ever Liberal Democrat European seats: in Paddy Ashdown's phrase, 'a price worth paying'.[41] In the final analysis, a political party exists to win elections, and all parties find it necessary to modify their positions in order to do so. Moreover, by-elections are particularly important to the Liberal Democrats, lacking consistent levels of media attention. There is no evidence that the party has compromised its fundamental beliefs in its campaigning, though in a party which gives policy and philosophy as high a priority as do the Liberal Democrats, this is always likely to prove a continuing internal tension. It also jars somewhat with the honest and forthright image the party has tried to develop in putting over its national policy programme.

The party's structure has exacerbated this tension, by creating something of a division between policy-makers, campaigners and communicators, and failing to implement management strategies to bring them together. The result is that the three groups have sometimes seemed to be working entirely in isolation of each other. 'It cultivates an atmosphere of mistrust between policy bods, campaigners and communicators,' believed

Ben Rich, the party's former deputy director of policy. 'Each assumes that the other knows nothing about their work and cannot appreciate their needs .... as a consequence our campaigning can often be characterised by our opponents as thin and opportunist, while policy statements lie untouched.'[42] The recent appointment of a director of strategy and planning may help to resolve these tensions, and general election campaigns always help to integrate the different elements. Still, Paddy Ashdown admits that this is an organisational and cultural problem which the party has not yet got quite right, though it is improving.[43]

Realising that a concentration on local issues in campaigns does little to build a national picture of the Liberal Democrat programme for government, the party's Campaigns and Communications Committee has made attempts to give a more coordinated direction to policy-making, campaigning and communicating. The 'core message' exercise of 1993–94 aimed to link different policies to a common, central purpose, creating a firm background image of the party that was comprehensible, consistent and distinct. Its conclusion is familiar from the examination of Liberal Democrat ideology above. 'Every single policy that the Liberal Democrats are committed to shares the same, simple objective: to liberate, to equip, to encourage and empower every single person in this country. For all to realise their own potential. For everybody to be a somebody. Add it all together and what will you find? A vast, irresistible national recovery.'[44] This message can be linked back to the party's values: liberty, liberating individuals' ability to exercise power on their own behalf; equality, affording every individual the opportunity to make the most of their skills and talents; and community, in the sense of investment in Britain's future prosperity. In turn, it was linked forward to policy proposals: most obviously, investment in education, but also in infrastructure and encouragement for individual enterprise (government creating the conditions for individuals to flourish); action on health and crime (to remove barriers of ill health and insecurity); a commitment to Europe (to widen individual opportunity); and to constitutional reform (to create a political system enabling individuals and communities to flourish). Many of the developments and elaborations of the Liberal Democrat philosophy were missing, the inevitable result of simplification and distillation, and as a result the exercise was not wholly successful in deriving justifications for the party's positions on environmental or foreign policy. Still, it was a reasonably consistent attempt to turn policy principles into campaigning and communicating tools.

As such, it was used fairly consistently from late 1993 onwards in TV broadcasts, campaigning materials produced by the Association of Liberal Democrat Councillors, and policy documents – notably the European election manifesto, where it largely determined the title *Unlocking Britain's Potential.* Other than this, however, it was not taken up widely. Paddy Ashdown felt that while the exercise was helpful internally in defining the party's central unifying theme, it failed to arrive at an external description or slogan which the public could readily understand and appreciate.[45] The parliamentary party proved unenthusiastic even about the concept of a single unifying message and failed to employ it: an indication of the problems of central coordination in a decentralist party. It hardly helped that the new Labour leader Tony Blair employed very similar language in his attempt to define New Labour. The party still faces a continuing problem in establishing an instinctive public understanding of 'what the Liberal Democrats stand for', and may perhaps never manage to do so (except in particular areas of local strength) until it takes or shares power at national level.

Party structure

The structure of the policy-making process of the Liberal Democrats is described in Chapter 5. In practice, it represents a balance of power between five elements: the party leader, the parliamentary party, the Federal Policy Committee (FPC) and its policy working groups, the Federal Conference Committee (FCC), and the Federal Conference. Of these, the FPC exerts the greatest influence, deciding what policy papers the conference will debate, the membership of the working groups which draft them and the final contents of the papers themselves, and of election manifestos. The parliamentary party is well represented on the FPC but has otherwise largely exercised a negative, blocking power, attempting to prevent the adoption of policies which it perceives as electorally harmful – with mixed effect. Owing to lack of time or of inclination, only a few MPs have played an active role in the party's policy-making process, though in practice they exercise a wide degree of discretion in interpreting and adapting (and often inventing) policy in their role as spokespersons. This has on occasion led to statements which conflict with party policy, a practice which the party is in effect powerless to prevent but which has as yet created no major problems.

The part played by the party leader has been quite different. In the early years of the Liberal Democrats, Paddy Ashdown had a crucial role to play in drawing together a coherent policy programme out of the wreckage of the Alliance. His views – expressed through a series of books,[46] and of booklets produced by his office, in his conference speeches, and as chair of the FPC – helped to determine the direction and main themes of the party in the run-up to and during the 1992 election. This was particularly true of economic policy, where he provided the main impetus for the market-oriented approach.[47] He first floated the ideas of higher income tax for education, road pricing, and the various uses of information technology. This influence continued after the election, when he chaired the working group responsible for drafting the 'philosophy' paper *Facing up to the Future*; he was also largely responsible for the policy proposals for referendums and for a limited element of tax hypothecation. Ashdown has been able to stamp his ideas so firmly on the party's policy programme largely because of the respect and admiration he has enjoyed amongst party members – 'ordinary Party members will take things from him for which they would have lynched David Owen', commented *The Economist* in 1991[48] – but also because of his position as chair of the FPC, and that body's key role in determining policy.

There are signs, however, that this position may have started to change. Ashdown has become more hostile to conference resolutions, most notably the September 1994 votes in favour of a Royal Commission to investigate decriminalisation of cannabis, and in favour of a regional minimum wage.[49] He has also increasingly disagreed with FCC decisions on the selection of motions for debate. This breakdown in sympathy between the leader and the conference may be due in part to increasing disaffection amongst those party members hostile to Ashdown's strategic edging of the party towards closer relations with Labour; partly it is also simple bad judgement[50] probably deriving from the gradual isolation from the party's grass-roots which is common to all political leaders; and partly it is perhaps an increasing impatience with the relatively slow internal process of policy-making and internal political education, as his own time as leader gradually runs out.

What these policy defeats do not signal, however, is the growth of an 'anti-Ashdown' tendency within the party. Conference did not vote, for example, against the minimum wage option favoured by Ashdown because they wished to record a vote of dissent with his leadership – they simply thought he was wrong, and had few inhibitions about saying so. In the final analysis, although the FPC exercises the major influence over Liberal Democrat policy through its control over the policy paper process, it is conference which provides the bedrock. No proposal becomes party policy unless it has been adopted by conference; and conference itself has the power to decide policy independently of the FPC,[51] through voting on policy resolutions put forward by constituency parties and other party organisations. The selection of the conference agenda rests with the FCC, a committee elected primarily by the conference itself, and one which has in practice proved willing to select motions for debate in the face of parliamentary party opposition.

The relative powers of the different elements involved in policy-making thus result in a party which is relatively internally democratic, particularly when compared with the Conservative and Labour Parties. In comparison with the pre-merger SDP, from which the policy-making structure was mainly adapted, power has shifted from the leader and the policy committee to the conference; in comparison with the Liberal Party, power has shifted from both the conference and the leader (who exercised a formal veto over manifesto contents) to the policy committee. Yet although the potential for conflict between the various elements clearly exists, the main characteristic of the Liberal Democrat policy-making process is how rarely it has emerged. In the seven-year history of the party, only one conference (Harrogate, September 1992) has seen any number of FPC proposals voted down,[52] and this probably owed more to post-election disappointment and a desire to flex muscles suppressed during the run-up to the election than to any systematic opposition to the leadership. This is reinforced by the absence of policy-oriented factions within the party; although there is disagreement on particular policy details, there is wide consensus on the overall direction, and no coherent and consistent critique of the policy programme. The policy-making structure itself, which incorporates most potential critics through the working group system, helps to maintain this state of affairs. Where there has been conflict, it has generally emerged between the parliamentary party and/or the leader and the conference. (Clashes between the MPs and the FPC have also taken place, but not in public.) After the leadership defeats of September 1994, some argued that the conference was returning to the bad old days of the Liberal assembly, supposedly dominated by anarchic community politicians openly contemptuous of their MPs. Always a caricature of Liberal conferences, there is little evidence that this is the direction in which Liberal Democrat conferences are developing. What is true, however, is that the conference possesses a degree of self-confidence that is difficult to deflect. Debates are generally serious, well-informed and relatively uninfluenced by pressure from above.[53] If the conference believes something is wrong, it will vote against it whatever the parliamentary party and the committees may say.

This self-confidence and relatively democratic internal structure also help to give the policy-making process a life and momentum of its own. Although the selection of topics for conference debate is certainly influenced by the party's campaigning and communicating priorities, it is not directed by them. Liberal Democrat conferences have regularly debated topics which have nothing to do with any wider communications strategy, and are often issues which the party leadership would rather not see discussed.[54] The conference, FPC and FCC all display an independence which the parliamentary leadership often finds irksome but in practice can do little to stop; and if the committees were to display a greater degree of subservience, conference would probably become more rebellious.

Despite this evidence of a relatively high degree of inner party democracy, the extent of policy debate within the party is limited. Although conference has the power to amend FPC policy papers, the detailed nature of their contents make it unlikely that a large proportion of conference representatives read and understand them thoroughly before the debate. Beyond the federal, state and regional party conferences, there is little evidence of wide policy debate within the party at large. Local parties are usually too small and too preoccupied with fundraising and local campaigning to spend much time debating national policy issues. The FPC is certainly aware of this problem, and has implemented various reforms to the process in an effort to widen debate and consultation within the party. Of course, the system has its advantages: in the absence of broad media coverage, policy papers have helped to convince interest groups and specialists of the seriousness of the party's policy commitments and have helped develop a degree of coherence amongst the party's spokespersons and candidates. Nevertheless, in pushing through particular policy proposals, most of the cards lie with the 'policy leadership', the FPC and its working groups plus those parliamentary spokespersons astute enough to know how to use the system. Thus in the Liberal Democrats, in sharp contrast to the Liberal Party under Thorpe and Steel, most of the radical ideas have emanated from the leadership, with the conference exercising a more conservative brake. Where the conference has been more radical than the 'establishment' would have liked, it is almost invariably the parliamentary party – the most conservative element in the system – that has felt itself to be the loser.

Party composition

The composition of the Liberal Democrats – membership – is important in affecting both the party's policies and the way those policies are developed and discussed. As shown in Chapter 6, the party's membership can be characterised as the educated, professional and public sector middle classes, and, as Chapter 9 demonstrates, Liberal Democrat electoral support is also drawn heavily from these groups. Using a social value analysis, party supporters can be identified mainly with the 'inner directed,' as opposed to the 'outer directed' and 'sustenance driven,' group, motivated by personal growth and self-expression, individual freedom and responsibility, and by people and change; they are much less concerned with consumption, status and security. In almost all its features, and particularly in its stress on education, environment, internationalism, local communities and constitutional reform – and perhaps most important, in its recognition of the *need for change* – the Liberal Democrat policy programme fits the concerns and interests of this group remarkably well. As the amorphous and protest-based electoral support enjoyed by the Liberal Party, and then the Alliance, has gradually solidified and concentrated in particular social groups, the Liberal Democrats have become a real reflection and advocate of their interests: not a class-based party in the sense of the Conservative or Labour Parties of the 1950s, but a modern group-based party nevertheless.

This is not a new phenomenon. The impetus for the social reformism of the New Liberals of the turn of the century came from the professional middle classes: journalists, writers and lecturers, lawyers and doctors with a social conscience. The Liberal Summer Schools and Lloyd George's 'coloured books' showed the intellectual strength of the Liberal Party of the 1920s despite its electoral decline. The post-war revival under Jo Grimond once again attracted the same elements into the Liberal Party, and in the 1980s, the membership of the new Social Democratic Party appeared, as Hugh Stephenson argued, 'to be the professional middle classes jumping at the chance to have their *interests* represented and protected in the political system by a party they have themselves created, thus ending their effective exclusion from existing party politics'.[55] The SDP proved a magnet for policy intellectuals who were likely to be alienated by the instinctual and dogmatic Thatcherite approach to politics and who created a structure of rigorous, technocratic and detailed policy-making which was largely inherited by the Liberal Democrats.

This, however, is not the whole story. The Liberal Democrats are the party not just of the intelligentsia but also of local government, the legacy of the community politics-oriented, decentralist Liberal Party of the 1970s and 1980s. The local government success of the Liberal Democrats has been such that about one in every twenty party members – and a much higher proportion of activists – is a councillor on a principal local authority.[56] This local council bias reinforces the party's already strong decentralist ethos, and the interest it shows in debating local authority policy areas of education, environment, housing and social services. In turn this concentration on primarily social issues leads to an awareness of the defects and drawbacks of a market-based economy and a belief in an activist social and economic policy. This helps explain both the caution displayed by much of the membership to the policy leadership's embrace of market economics and the combination of market mechanisms and active fiscal policy which forms Liberal Democrat economic policy. The presence at conference of large numbers of councillors used to running or influencing local authorities also helps to explain the lack of deference displayed towards the parliamentary leaders, many of whom wield less real power in political life.

In terms of electoral strategy, any concentration of support is of course welcome. In terms of British electoral geography, there are severe drawbacks to a voter base that is not *geographically* concentrated. Here the Liberal Democrats have also been successful, with electoral support increasingly concentrated in the South of England, and particularly in the south west and in rural areas. Of the party's twenty-three MPs, sixteen represent predominantly rural constituencies, and only three hold seats in the big cities. Here the party's policy programme is not a good match to the pattern of support, probably because its membership and activist base are not themselves particularly rural. Although agriculture has always been given a relatively high priority in policy-making, but the party's proposals for sweeping reforms of the Common Agricultural Policy are not necessarily the best way to attract rural support. Many of the issues over which conference and the FPC have clashed with the parliamentary party concern topics where urban and rural interests are believed to diverge: they include environmental taxation of transport fuel, hunting with hounds, and the transport of live animals.[57] This is a continuing tension within the party that cannot easily be resolved until the Liberal Democrats win enough urban seats for the rural predominance of parliamentary seats to end.

Conclusion: the uses of Liberal Democrat policy

The Liberal Democrats (and their predecessors) possess a continuing record of influencing general political debate in Britain. 'Possibly the Liberal Party cannot serve the state in any better way', said John Maynard Keynes in 1926, 'than by supplying Conservative Governments with Cabinets, and Labour Governments with ideas.'[58] Seventy years later, the Conservatives no longer attract Liberal Democrat defectors, but Labour still borrows the party's ideas. In its climb back from the electoral disaster of 1983, Labour's development of policy on Europe and on constitutional reform has without doubt been heavily influenced by Liberal Democrat policy proposals. Indeed, a *Guardian* editorial described the Labour conference of 1991 as a 'shameless political ram raid' on Liberal Democrat constitutional proposals.[59] Much to Liberal Democrat irritation, many political commentators write as though this is the party's *raison d'être*. 'To deserve to be taken seriously, Liberal Democrats must put forward radical ideas,' stated the *Financial Times* in 1994. 'That above all is their role.'[60]

The party's impact on the Conservatives has been much more limited. As noted above, the current Conservative ideology and policy programme are largely hostile to those of the Liberal Democrats. Such impact as there has been – on the replacement of the poll tax, on support for the Maastricht legislation, on the policy of a referendum on further European integration – have stemmed more from the government's political weakness at particular times than from any Conservative desire to appropriate Liberal Democrat policies.

In recent years, however, the Liberal Democrats have enjoyed another external forum in which to deploy their policy programme. As the second party of local government, the party now has the opportunity to put a section of its policy programme into practice. Although this development is still too recent for much detailed comparative work to have been carried out, Liberal Democrat authorities do appear to be implementing many of the party's local policy proposals, giving a higher priority than other parties to education, environmental policy, the decentralisation of service delivery and decision-making and to opening up the work of councils to public scrutiny and access.[61]

It is in the *internal* uses of policy, however, that the Liberal Democrats have been most distinctive. The development and debate of a relatively detailed policy programme plays a noticeably more important role within the Liberal Democrats than it does in the Labour or Conservative Parties. This was just as true for the party's predecessors, the Liberal and Social Democratic Parties, and stems from the same reasons. All these parties have been third parties: they did not, and could not realistically expect to, form the government of the country. The Liberal Democrats cannot promote their message or boost the morale of their own supporters in terms of their government record; they have to rely instead on developing, refining and publicising their policies. In the early days of the party, policy development was crucial in cementing the merger, and resolving the conflicts, between Liberals and Social Democrats. The control of local authorities which the party now exercises may in time come to change this emphasis on policy in the abstract, but this is too recent a development, and too limited in terms of policy areas, for it to have occurred to any significant extent as yet.

Policy is also important to the Liberal Democrats because the party is largely composed of people for whom policy debate matters. Partly this is due to their social and educational backgrounds, as has been seen above, and partly to the party's third party status. The pursuit of power and personal ambition, or the management of government, cannot be motivations for Liberal Democrats in the same way as they can be for Conservative and Labour politicians. Policy development and debate offer an alternative driving force. This is a self-reinforcing process: since policy is important to the party, the organisation is structured so that policy debate is encouraged; and because policy is seen to be important, policy intellectuals are more likely to be attracted to the Liberal Democrats than to either of the other two parties, both as members and voters.

This is not to argue that the Liberal Democrats is a party of policy enthusiasts pure and simple. It also possesses an effective campaigning ability that has delivered electoral success in local government and in an increasing regional concentration of support. In effect, the party displays a mixture of cultures, of policy puritanism plus campaigning ruthlessness: people for whom elections are to be won to put policies into practice, together with people for whom policies exist to help win elections. The policies that each group desires to develop are different, and are developed and promoted in different forums. Tensions between the two have occasionally surfaced, and seem likely to do so with ever-increasing frequency as the party becomes more successful in elections. The two cultures can coexist, however, because the Liberal Democrats do not exercise power at national level, and have done so widely at local level only recently. The constraints that accompany the realities of power have therefore not yet infected the policy process. When and if they do, one can expect much greater tension, and associated clashes, within the party structure.

Equally, it is this mixture of cultures that gives the Liberal Democrats their real political strength. Policy-making without campaigning would lead to a party that really was nothing more than a source of ideas for others. Campaigning without policy development would be mere local populism. If the party can succeed in integrating these different abilities, realising their strengths while avoiding their weaknesses, then Liberal Democrat policies may come to be treated as more than just hypothetical.

Appendix: Summary of 1992 election manifesto

CHANGING BRITAIN FOR GOOD

Economic policy

An emergency programme of capital investment, funded by reversing the government's pre-election tax cuts plus a small increase in borrowing. Increased spending on public transport, housing, hospitals and schools, and on energy efficiency and conservation, aiming to reduce unemployment by an estimated 600,000 over two years. More investment in research, innovation and design.

A more competitive economy: the break-up of the monopoly providers of services such as British Telecom and British Gas, a new Restrictive Practices Act and a merged Monopolies and Mergers Commission and Office of Fair Trading. Encouragement for decentralised wage bargaining.

The promotion of enterprise: encouraging small businesses and the self-employed, freezing business rates for a year, relieving administrative burdens, legislating to make interest payable on overdue debt and establishing new regional development and local enterprise agencies.

Policies for long-term economic stability, including an anti-inflation strategy resting on an operationally independent Bank of England and the entry of sterling into the narrow band of the exchange rate mechanism (ERM). Taxes and public spending to be set to reach a medium term savings target for the economy as a whole.

Encouragement for partnership in industry, promoting profit-related pay and share-ownership schemes and guaranteeing employee rights of participation in decision-making in their enterprises.

Environment

A new Department of Natural Resources with sole responsibility for environmental protection and an independent Environmental Protection Agency, the adoption of 'alternative indicators' (environmental quality, standards of life, etc.) to supplement GDP, and a reliance on market mechanisms (including energy taxation, and a system of tradable emission licences for industry) where feasible to control pollution.

An EU-wide energy/carbon tax to increase incentives for energy efficiency measures (the revenue to be used to compensate those on low incomes and to reduce VAT), investment in energy conservation and efficiency, greater spending on renewable sources of energy and the phasing out of nuclear power.

Investment in public transport, promising an additional £1.75 billion for railways and other environmentally friendly forms of transport over two years. A phased increase in petrol taxation (with compensation for those with no alternative to private cars), the graduation of car tax and vehicle excise duty according to fuel efficiency, and the introduction of road pricing to tackle congestion.

Reform of the Common Agricultural Policy, replacing price support with incentives for environmental and social objectives, encouragement for forestry and fishing, and improved countryside protection policies.

Education and training

Increased investment in education, with priority going to pre-school education (a guarantee of access to two years for every child), 16–19 year olds (the equivalent of at least two days a week education or training for all 16–19 year olds in work) and adult education (financial support for pat-time study). To be funded through raising income tax by one penny in the pound, with additional support available from the emergency capital investment programme for school and college buildings.

A training levy for firms equal to 2 per cent of payroll, minus approved expenditure on training.

Support for local management of schools, a more flexible national curriculum, the abolition of grant maintained schools and city technology colleges, the phasing out of the assisted place schemes, and a review of the charitable status of independent schools.

A single Department of Education and Training, a better resourced HM Inspectorate of Education and Training and a new General Teaching Council to improve professional qualifications and set standards for teacher training and retraining.

Social policy

Higher funding for the National Health Service, including an annual real increase to match the costs of new technology and the growing number of older people; increased emphasis on health promotion and patients' rights and choices; the abolition of most of the government's reforms, including the internal market, GP fundholding and NHS trusts.

Investment in a new partnership housing (public–private) sector and relaxed controls on capital receipts to boost house building and renovation. 'Housing cost relief' weighted towards those most in need and available to house buyers and renters, to replace mortgage interest tax relief. Action to combat homelessness, and higher energy standards for all housing.

A law and order policy concentrating on crime prevention, such as Neighbourhood Watch and Safer City programmes. A redeployment of police resources to increase police presence in local communities. A new Ministry for Justice and a post of Public Defender, responsible for investigating miscarriages of justice.

Reform of the social security system, with the long-term aim of a 'citizen's income', payable to all irrespective of sex or status. Increases in the basic state pension and an end to the contributory principle ('means testing'); higher child benefit; a new disability income scheme and a new carer's benefit. The reform of personal taxation through the integration of tax and national insurance, the removal of the ceiling on employee's national insurance contributions and a new higher rate tax band on earnings over £50,000 p.a.

An attack on discrimination through the incorporation of the European Convention on Human Rights into UK law and a new commission on human rights; a guarantee of equal pay for work of equal value and improved child care support; reform of immigration legislation to render it free from racial discrimination; and equal rights for gay men and lesbians.

European and foreign policy

Support for European integration and the development of a federal, decentralised EU: acceptance of the Maastricht timetable for economic and monetary union, renouncing the British opt-out; a common voting system (of proportional representation) and greater powers for the European Parliament; and active EU scientific, environmental, regional and social policies (with rejection of the Social Chapter opt-out).

A defence policy resting on common EU foreign and security policies, including cost-sharing arrangements. A UK defence policy review aiming if possible for spending reductions but considering the potential for increased UK contributions to UN peacekeeping. Maintenance of the Trident nuclear deterrent but with the total number of warheads limited to no more than the Polaris total, and proposals for new strategic weapons talks including all nuclear powers. Action to curb the arms trade, and support for a more effective UN.

Increases in the overseas aid budget to reach the UN target of 0.7 per cent of GNP over five years, with particular support for countries respecting democracy and human rights and aid projects promoting environmental sustainability and population control. Support for the GATT Uruguay Round and for a resolution of the international debt crisis.

Electoral and constitutional reform

The cornerstone of the entire manifesto: 'We recognise that Britain's success in the next century will depend not just on changing what we do, but in changing the way in which we do it.' A full programme of constitutional reform, including the following.

Proportional representation (preferably by the single transferable vote system) for all elections at local, national and European levels, fixed-term parliaments and replacement of the House of Lords by a democratic senate.

Home Rule for Scotland and Wales, with a Scottish Parliament and a Welsh Senedd, preparation for regional government in England, reformed and strengthened local government (a unitary system, together with local neighbourhood councils) and the replacement of the poll tax with local income tax.

A Freedom of Information Act, the evolution of the European Convention on Human Rights into a UK Bill of Rights, and a written constitution with a supreme court.

Manifesto costings

Following the precedent set by the Liberal/SDP Alliance in 1987, the manifesto was accompanied by a costings supplement setting out the proposed variations in spending, taxing and borrowing, from the government's five-year forward programme. The key points were as follows.

A programme of mainly capital investment to act as a Keynesian fiscal stimulus and covering education and NHS buildings, housing, training, energy conservation and public transport (mainly rail). This investment reached a peak of over £5 billion in year 2, falling rapidly thereafter. It was to be funded principally by a reversal of the pre-election income tax cuts, a relatively small increase in the PSBR (£2 billion in year 1, falling to a £2.25 billion reduction in year 5) and the revenue flowback deriving from the lower unemployment resulting from this expansionary package,

A significant increase in spending on education, rising to £3.75 billion by year 5. In year 1, this was to be funded entirely from the proceeds of a one penny increase in the basic rate of income tax; in later years, largely from revenue flowback and reversed tax cuts.

Substantial reforms to the personal taxation and social security systems, the increases in benefits being entirely paid for by the integration of tax and national insurance and the new higher rate band.

The phased introduction of an energy/carbon tax, road pricing, and cuts in nuclear research, paying for various environmental grants and subsidies, higher spending on renewable energy and urban public transport, compensatory measures and cuts in the standard rate of VAT (0.5 per cent in year 2, another 0.5 per cent in year 4). (Total environment-related spending also included elements of the fiscal stimulus package.)

Smaller spending increases in various business support schemes, the science budget, the NHS, police and crime prevention, arts and overseas aid, paid for primarily by large cuts in military R&D, revenue flowback and reversed tax cuts.

Notes

1 Thanks to Des Wilson, the chair of the group appointed by the Liberal and SDP Policy Committees to draw up its replacement. Referring to a Monty Python sketch in which John Cleese played a pet shop customer sold a dead parrot, Wilson declared that *Voices and Choices for All* was 'as dead as John Cleese's parrot'. The parrot was to feature once again in the history of the Liberal Democrats. In 1990, Mrs Thatcher informed the Conservative conference that the entire party was 'as dead as John Cleese's parrot' – a week before the Liberal Democrats won the Eastbourne by-election, taking the seat from the Conservatives; next day's *Evening Standard* carried the headline: 'The Parrot Twitched'.

2 In Rachael Pitchford and Tony Greaves, *Merger: The Inside Story,* Hebden Royd, 1989.

3   At least since the departure of the 'economic liberals' in the 1950s: see William
    Wallace, 'Survival and Revival', in Vernon Bogdanor (ed.), *Liberal Party Politics*,
    Clarendon Press, 1983.

4   What Owen actually meant by the 'social market' varied significantly depending
    on which political party he wished to use it to attack. For a full analysis, see Duncan
    Brack, *The Myth of the Social Market: A Critique of Owenite Economics*, LINk
    Publications, 1989.

5   See Duncan Brack, 'A Comparative Look at the SDP', *Radical Quarterly* special
    edition, *Where Next?*, 1987.

6   Widely but wrongly reported, both at the time and subsequently, as a vote in favour
    of unilateral nuclear disarmament. For a full account see Michael Meadowcroft,
    'Eastbourne Revisited', *Radical Quarterly* 5, Autumn 1987.

7   Firepower would be limited to that of the Polaris fleet it was replacing; Federal
    Green Paper 7, *After the Cold War*, 1989; Federal White Paper 3, *Reshaping Europe*,
    1990.

8   See Federal Green Paper 12, *Energy and the Living World*, 1990.

9   Incomes policies had already been explicitly dropped in the party's first economic
    policy paper, Federal Green Paper 10, *Britain's Industrial Future*, 1989, which
    otherwise was fairly standard Alliance material.

10 Paddy Ashdown believes that this was one of the main SDP contributions to the
    party (conversation, 4 April 1995).

11 Set out in Federal White Paper 4, *Economics for the Future*, 1991.

12 The Liberal Assembly in 1979 declared that economic growth as conventionally
    defined was neither indefinitely possible nor desirable.

13 See Federal Green Papers 12, *Energy and the Living World*, 1990, 19, *Vehicles for
    Change*, 1991, and 23, *Costing the Earth*, 1991.

14 The Green Liberal Democrats, the Party's internal environmental pressure group,
    was one of the largest and most active in the Party's early years.

15 *Changing Britain for Good*, Liberal Democrat Publications, 1992. The mnemonic
    five 'E's structure was largely developed by Lord Holme, the party's manifesto
    coordinator, and first trailed in the 'pre-manifesto' paper *Shaping Tomorrow, Starting
    Today*, Liberal Democrat Publications, 1991, debated at the Party's spring conference
    in 1991. The sixth chapter of the manifesto, 'Britain's people', was added to cover
    the remaining policy areas (mostly social policy), but emphasis was always placed
    on the first five.

16 Leader, *Guardian*, 19 March 1992.

17 'The case for the Lib Dems', leader, *Independent*, 8 April 1992.

18 'The time, and the price, of change', leader, *Guardian*, 8 April 1992.

19 'The Paddy package', leader, *Guardian*, 17 March 1992.

20 'Lib-Lab, or nothing at all', leader *Financial Times*, 17 March 1992.

21 Ralph Atkins, 'Ashdown's Mixture Lacks Cohesion', *Financial Times*, 17 March
    1992.

22 September 1988 (*Themes and Values* consultation paper); March 1989 (Federal Green
    Paper 7, *Our Different Vision*); September 1992 (*Challenge, Opportunity and*

Responsibility consultation paper); September 1993 (*Facing up to the Future*).

23   First paragraph, preamble to the federal party constitution, Liberal Democrat Publications, 1993.

24   *Facing up to the Future*, Liberal Democrat Publications, 1993, p.11.

25   See Federal White Paper 6, *Here We Stand*, Liberal Democrat Publications, 1993.

26   *Facing up to the Future*, p.11

27   'Liberals must ever insist', wrote J. A. Hobson, 'that each enlargement of the authority and functions of the State must justify itself as an enlargement of personal liberty, interfering with individuals only in order to set free new and larger opportunities.' (*The Crisis of Liberalism: New Issues of Democracy*, P.S. King & Son, 1909).

28   The definition of the Brundtland Report of 1987, quoted in Liberal Democrat Policy Paper 8, *Agenda for Sustainability*, Liberal Democrat Publications, 1994.

29   *Facing up to the Future*, p.13.

30   *Ibid.*, p.13.

31   See *Economics for the Future*.

32   Part of Federal Green Paper 26, *After Privatisation*, Liberal Democrat Publications, 1992.

33   The forerunner to *Facing up to the Future*, entitled *Challenge, Opportunity and Responsibility* but memorably referred to by one conference speaker as 'fudge, mudge and bollocks'.

34   'Paddy's Balancing Act', *The Economist,* 5 March 1994. Not a very impressive piece of analytical writing, it contained several inaccuracies and criticised as interventionist precisely the same economic policies the magazine had welcomed as 'rediscovered free-marketry' two and a half years earlier ('Paddy's People', *The Economist*, 14 September 1991).

35   'The case for the Lib Dems', *Independent,* 8 April 1992.

36   Hugo Young, 'From Ashdown to Ashes', *Guardian,* 18 March 1992.

37   Peter Clarke, *Liberals and Social Democrats,* Cambridge University Press, 1978, p.65.

38   These were exercised in 1993, when an enquiry into a by-election campaign in Tower Hamlets found that a number of local campaigners were guilty of 'pandering to racism' (*Political Speech and Race Relations in a Liberal Democracy: report of an inquiry into the conduct of the Tower Hamlets Liberal Democrats in publishing allegedly racist election literature between 1990 and 1993*, Liberal Democrats Tower Hamlets Inquiry, 1993).   Disciplinary action was pursued against the individuals involved, and the national party imposed an agent on the Tower Hamlets parties for the local election campaign the following year. The enquiry also triggered off an internal review of the party's approach to community politics.

39   Contrary to Conservative claims, the party had never supported the imposition of VAT on fuel; successive policy papers clearly made the case for an EU-wide energy/carbon tax, and the 1992 manifesto proposed to use part of the revenue to reduce the standards rate of VAT.

40   See the European election manifesto, *Unlocking Britain's Potential*, Liberal Democrat Publications, 1994.

41 Conversation with Paddy Ashdown, 4 April 1995.

42 Ben Rich, 'Why Alan Leaman Needs Three Shredded Wheat for Breakfast', *Liberator* No. 227, March 1995, p. 24.

43 Conversation with Paddy Ashdown, 4 April 1995.

44 Liberal Democrat party political broadcast 20 April 1994.

45 Conversation with Paddy Ashdown, 4 April 1995.

46 *Citizen's Britain: A Radical Agenda for the 1990s*, Fourth Estate, 1989; *Beyond Westminster: Finding Hope in Britain*, Simon & Schuster, 1994; *Making Change Our Ally*, Liberal Democrat Publications, 1994.

47 See Paddy Ashdown's speech to conference, September 1990.

48 'Paddy's People', *The Economist*, 14 September 1991.

49 See Policy Paper 9, *Working for Change*, 1994, para 8.1.5 option A.

50 For instance, the two 'leadership defeats' (on drugs and the minimum wage) at the September 1994 conference were not in the slightest bit surprising, making the leader's (and the parliamentary party's) reaction to them rather puzzling.

51 The provision contained in the party constitution adopted at merger which gave the FPC the power to remit to itself for further consideration any motion on the conference agenda aroused widespread hostility and was hardly ever used; it was abolished during the party's review of its constitution in 1993.

52 The FPC was instructed to produce two policy papers it did not want (on genetic engineering, and on prostitution – subsequently Federal Green Paper 29, *The Challenge of Genetic Engineering*, 1993 and Policy Paper 3, *Confronting Prostitution*, 1994); the section of the policy paper on utilities (Federal Green Paper 26, *After Privatisation*) dealing with railways was defeated and the section on coal barely survived; and the consultation paper *Challenge, Opportunity and Responsibility* narrowly escaped a reference back. This hardly represented a major disaster, and the other three papers presented by the FPC were adopted by their customary overwhelming margins. The defeat of the rail section of *After Privatisation*, however, is notable for being the only occasion (to date) on which any significant element of a policy paper has been rejected by conference.

53 Although this was less true in the party's early days and partly depends on the stage of the electoral cycle; both FCC and conference representatives generally try to avoid negative publicity in the run-up to a general election.

54 Prostitution in September 1992 and March 1994, drug abuse and the monarchy in September 1994, are all examples.

55 Hugh Stephenson, *Claret and Chips: The Rise of the SDP*, Michael Joseph, 1982, p.173.

56 County, district, London borough or unitary authority, i.e. not including parish, town or community councillors.

57 The recent formation of the Liberal Democrat Forum for the Countryside, with financial backing from the countryside lobby, is likely to intensify the internal debate; the all-party Political Animal Lobby already part-funds a research post at party HQ.

58 'Liberalism and Labour', reprinted in J.M. Keynes, *Essays in Persuasion*, London, 1931, p.343.

59 Quoted in Stephen Ingle, 'The Liberal Democrats and the 1992 Election' (paper delivered at the 1992 conference of the Political Studies Association Specialist Group on Elections, Public Opinion and Parties).
60 'The Role of a Third Party', leader, *Financial Times,* 21 September 1994.
61 See, for example, Audit Commission, *Local Authority Performance Indicators*, March 1995.

Part Two

Inside the Party

CHAPTER 5

Party organisation

Stephen Ingle

From the earliest days of the study of political parties in Britain and elsewhere, fears have been expressed concerning their steady deterioration; parties would inevitably come to dominate and not to serve their constituencies.[1] Rank-and-file members of parties would become disillusioned and eventually alienated and as a consequence parties would cease to be mass organisations and become instead cadre organisations whose only business would be to fight elections.[2] Indeed, in 1957 Downs famously argued that American parties had already become teams of entrepreneurs selling candidates and policies, striving by whatever means to maximise their market share of votes. Kirchheimer[3] later declared that mass parties driven by an ideology were becoming obsolete and were giving place to 'catch-all' parties – election-winning machines. He elucidated a number of developments which supported his view, amongst them a decline in membership and consequently of the role of individual members; a strengthening of the role of the leadership, and finally a weaker relationship with the electorate.

A number of factors in the alleged decline of political parties have been identified, amongst which the nature of party organisation is clearly crucial. The perceived force and relevance of party ideology will have a profound impact upon organisation – as indeed upon every feature of party activity – but this chapter focuses more specifically upon the organisational structure of the Liberal Democrats, including the parliamentary party, in order to assess its strengths and weaknesses and to make some judgements upon what the organisation tells us about the democratic vitality, so to speak, of the party. If the Liberal Democrats, whose entire *raison d'être* is built upon the concept of the participating community, has become a shell dominated by professionals, then the future for traditional political parties in Britain is indeed a bleak one. Certainly, party leader Paddy Ashdown has shown a general awareness of the dangers of a breakdown in trust between political parties and the electorate. He wrote: 'A gap is opening up between government and governed in Britain ... without a fundamental change to the way we conduct our politics, which amounts to finding a new settlement between the

113

politician and the citizen, we cannot reconstruct a sense of common purpose as a society.[4] If the Liberal Democrats are serious about bridging the gap between politicians and people then the party organisation is the most obvious forum in which a new and more mutually supportive relationship might be structured. Indeed, the preamble to the constitution states the party's dedication to liberty, community and diversity and declares that the state's job is to empower people to 'take part in the decisions which affect their lives'; as Ashdown argues, 'if the people are working properly then the country will work properly.'[5] The preamble goes on to declare that the objective of the party's federal framework is to retain 'as much power as [is] feasible' in the states and the regions, hoping to create a flourishing system of democratic local government. It is in this manner that the party claims to be working for 'a sense of partnership and community'[6] which it would like to be considered its hallmark, and thus to be working to re-establish that trust between voter and party, the absence of which is a cause of such anxiety elsewhere.

The history of Liberal Democrat organisation is necessarily short and recent. Its most noteworthy features are its distinctive federal structure and its absolute commitment to participative politics. The federal structure gains further salience from the fact that the Liberal Democrats plan to create a federal structure of government for Britain, and perhaps the way in which federalism operates within the party might tangentially offer some guide as to how it would impact on the government of the nation. Another aspect of Liberal Democrat organisation which needs to be considered, if only briefly, is the extent to which serious conflicts of identity remain between former Liberals and Social Democrats.

In practice the Liberal Democrats, following on the much older traditions of the Liberal party itself, declare a positive commitment to enmesh their philosophy of participation within the formal organisational structure of the party. They claim to do this in the following general ways:[7] the tradition of one member one vote for the party leader, (recently copied more or less by Labour but not by the Conservatives) and president; the representation of both genders on all decision-making bodies; the use of proportional representation (single transferable vote) in party elections; a commitment to subsidiarity (the taking of decisions at the lowest level consonant with general party efficiency) through decentralisation to the state parties, the regional and local parties.

Before the merger of the two parties the Liberals had already moved towards a federal structure but time did not allow the many problems that emerged to be satisfactorily addressed. The Scottish Liberal Party operated in many respects as an autonomous unit but the policy committee of the national party, with prime responsibility for policy and indeed for strategy, was often perceived by the Scots to make federalism more a myth than a reality. The desire for federalism had arisen chiefly in Scotland, though Welsh Liberals were generally supportive. The position of England had always posed a major problem by virtue of its disproportionate size and wealth, and in order to 'square' England the new federal structure which emerged from the negotiations between the Liberals and Social Democrats incorporated twelve English regional organisations.[8] This new arrangement had to accommodate the existing structures of the two parties, but this proved to be far less of a problem than might have been envisaged.[9]

The merger negotiations establishing the English regions (potentially one of the more contentious issues) proved successful. There has been no renegotiation of regional boundaries, despite the relocation of some local parties into other regions. English regional parties can, if they choose, seek the status of state parties. None has so far done so, though some, with the Yorkshire region in the van, claimed to be considering such a development in the immediate post-merger period of 1988–89. Like all the regions (and the states), Yorkshire was concerned with mismanagement from party headquarters at Cowley Street, especially financial mismanagement. At the March conference in 1989 a motion of no-confidence was moved in the federal party's administrative competence, especially its financial competence. The vote of no-confidence was thought by many present to have been passed on a show of hands but there had followed a demand from the platform for a recount. As the party was about to unravel before members' eyes, a point of order was raised by party president Ian Wrigglesworth who declared that if the motion were passed on the recount then he and the executive would be obliged to resign: the motion was duly defeated and the day was saved, but misgivings in the states and the regions did not disappear immediately, though the pressure for regions to become states did.

Structure of organisation

In order to belong to the Liberal Democrats it is necessary to belong to a local party or to a specified associated organisation (SAO)[10] representing youth and/or students. However, potential members living abroad may join a state party directly. Membership may be revoked by material disagreement (conduct not in keeping with fundamental values of the party or which brings the party into disrepute; standing against an official party candidate or supporting another political party). Thirty members may form a local party, provided such an organisation is based upon at least one parliamentary constituency. If, however, a local organisation represents more than one constituency when a parliamentary candidate is selected, then provided there are thirty members from that constituency within the local party, it is they who are responsible for selecting the candidate. Each local party (indeed each constituency if it has more than thirty members in the local party) is entitled to send representatives to the federal and state conferences. As is logical from the above, local parties may decide to divide but only on the basis of at least thirty members per constituency.

The constitution of the local party is subject to the federal and state constitutions, and these latter must prevail in any dispute. Any local party with a membership which remains below thirty for six months will be automatically suspended. The state party can suspend a local party 'if events have taken place or are about to take place which are or may be seriously detrimental to the local party or to the party as a whole' (more of this later).

The local parties, then, are directly represented at federal conference and the strength of representation depends upon size of party: up to two representatives from local parties of between 30 and 50 members but up to eleven for parties with memberships of 401 to 450, plus an additional member for every 100 members. Standing orders provide for consultative sessions at the September conference in which any member may speak, though, as is customary, it is the responsibility of the particular session chair to select speakers. They may also speak in full conference, with the conference committee's permission. In theory, then, it is relatively easy for ordinary members to have a public input into the party's policy-making procedures. At an earlier stage in the process they may submit evidence to any party policy working group or even become a member of such a group.

The federal conference normally meets twice each year and is organised by a federal conference committee (FCC), consisting of the party president, the chief whip, one representative of each state party, two members of the federal executive, two members of the federal policy committee (FPC), the chief executive of the federal party with another staff representative (non-voters) and twelve members elected by federal conference itself. FCC is enjoined to ensure the correct balance between state and federal policy debates in the final agenda.

As for the pivotal FPC, its principal task is to approve party policy papers, culminating in the drawing up (in conjunction with the parliamentary and European parties) of the general and European election manifestos. It also has the secondary, and seldom used, function of making interim policy on topical issues (and this policy has later to be formally approved by conference). FPC has the additional function of making detailed policy of the kind needed to implement the broad policy outlines adopted by conference. It consists of: the party leader, a representative of the parliamentary party, three MPs representing respectively English, Scottish and Welsh constituencies, a Liberal Democrat peer, the party president, three elected local councillors, two representatives of the Scottish and Welsh state parties, and fifteen activists elected annually by conference. The FPC chair is elected by the parliamentary party and must be an MP, almost invariably the party leader. It has the power to set up policy working groups which have a remit to consult as widely as possible and to prepare policy papers.

The most important of the party committees, however, is the federal executive (FE). The FE comprises the party president as chair, the party vice-presidents, the party leader, two MPs, one peer, two leading councillors, one representative from each state party, fourteen members elected by federal conference, and five non-voting members (the chief whip, the chair of finance and administration, the federal chief executive and a staff representative and finally the chair of FPC). The FE sets up a finance and administration committee, which liaises with the membership and finance units at headquarters, and a campaign and communications committee (CCC) which liaises with the campaigns and elections unit. Chaired by an MP, almost invariably the leader, CCC meets about every second month. Its role is chiefly a coordinating one. Its meetings comprise about twenty, an informal mixture of members and officers. Each year CCC selects a single policy area for development within the party (health in 1995) on which it then encourages discussion so as to move policy forward. This structure has recently been strengthened by the appointment of a director of strategy and planning who chairs a small core group which oversees and better coordinates CCC's activities. CCC's role in planning general election strategies is crucial; it was CCC which recommended the basic party strategy for the 1992 general election, for example the concentration on the five 'E's (electoral reform, environment, Europe, economic policy and, perhaps most successfully, education) as distinctive Liberal Democrat policies, the playing of the 'Ashdown card' and the concentration of effort and resources on targeted, winnable seats.

The FE also has the formidable power to conduct consultative ballots of all party members 'on any fundamental question where, in its judgement, the values and objectives of the Party are in issue or it is otherwise in the essential interests of the Party'. Thus, for example, the FE could, in principle, thwart a conference decision which went against party ideology. This is a residual power, however, and an expensive one to bring to bear in terms of finance, time, energy and party unity.[11]

The well-being of the party organisational structure is the responsibility of the president, 'the principal public representative of the party', who is elected by the membership on a postal ballot for a fixed term of two years. He or she chairs the FE, sits on the FCC and the FPC and its more important sub-committees. The president's role in assuring the effectiveness of the party organisation and of representing the party hierarchy to activists is thus of major importance, but he or she should not be compared with the party chairman of the Conservative Party. Each of the state parties designates one of its officers to be vice-president and to assist the president in his or her tasks.

Any problems in interpreting the constitution are settled by reference to an appeals panel consisting of eighteen members, nine of whom are elected by FE (and must include at least three women) and three by each state party. The chair is chosen by the panel itself from among those elected from FE. The panel has responsibility for adjudicating any dispute over the interpretation of the constitution, any disputes between federal and state parties or between regional and state parties.

This, then, is the basic structure of the federal party (see Fig. 5.1, page 131). The structure of the two state parties in Scotland and Wales is broadly similar. The two state parties have their own constitution, leader and officers and policy-making structure. They hold two conferences each year, making it difficult for members to find time to play a full part in federal conferences. The electoral decline of the Welsh party, however, allows much less scope for autonomy than is the case with the Scottish Liberal Democrats (SLD). Leader of the SLD is Jim Wallace MP and the current president is Sir Russell Johnston MP; the party has a full-time staff in Edinburgh comprising a chief executive, an administration officer, a campaigns officer (partly funded by the Association of Liberal Democrat Councillors, ALDC) and a press officer. There are additional part-time staff. The Welsh party, led by Alex Carlyle MP with Martin Thomas as president, has, by contrast, only one full-time administrator. Very clearly stated amongst the objectives of the 'Edinburgh Constitution' is the commitment to the establishment of a parliament in Scotland. The Scottish party jealously guards such autonomy as it enjoys and finds it difficult on occasions to subordinate itself to the federal (especially as this is sometimes seen as synonymous with English) policy objectives.

The English state party, however, is crucially different. The constitution of the English party informs us that the party does not 'as yet' have a structure for determining state party policy and that as a consequence these powers have been vested in the federal party. In fact the 'as yet' is misleading since the autonomy of the English party appears to be declining, not growing; the state party headquarters' staff, for example, up to eleven before the reorganisation of 1993, is now skeletal. Staff and functions have been transferred to the federal party. Another significant difference regarding England is the existence of the regional party structures. These parties have the power to make policy on matters which relate exclusively to the regions. They can, if they choose, draw up a regional manifesto for use in general elections provided that this manifesto is consistent with federal policy. An added function of the regional parties is to ensure that local organisations conduct themselves in a manner consistent with Liberal Democrat ideology and policy and to take action against any that might not – though in such cases the local party has a right of appeal to the state party against subsequent suspension.

At the apex of the English state structure is the English Council, which consists of the chair of each of the twelve regions together with members elected annually by each region and by the SAOs representing youth and/or students in England on the basis of one for each 500 members (or part thereof). Council meets at least twice a year, with one meeting being the annual general meeting. The council has formal responsibilities upwards to the federal party and downwards to the local parties and SAOs. For example, it negotiates financial arrangements with the federal party and determines the amount of membership income to be remitted to the regions and the level of grants to SAOs. It has certain fundraising responsibilities and also elects the English representatives to any federal body.

Between meetings English state affairs are overseen by the English Council Executive (ECE), presided over by the chair of the council, with one representative of each region and youth/student SAO and an equal number elected by council, the council treasurer, a staff representative with prescribed voting rights and three further co-opted (non-voting) members. The ECE organises meetings of council, keeps and maintains accounts for the state party and employs staff. A more formidable potential power is to require the vacation from office of the officers and executive members of any regional party which ECE deems to have acted or to be about to act in a way 'seriously detrimental to the Party'. If it took such action, ECE would be required to convene a regional conference to elect a new executive and appoint new officers.

These arrangements are held in place by a panel elected by the English Council, with one representative from each region and a designated chair. The panel is responsible for adjudicating any dispute concerning the interpretation of the articles of the state constitution, disputes between the state and regional parties, between regional and local parties or between regions. Apart from such cases in which the federal constitution allows a right of further appeal, the panel's decisions are 'final and binding'. This then is the party structure with its intricate interlocking mechanisms designed to maximise subsidiarity and to make it workable within the structure of a modern national party.

Party leader

The leader of the Liberal Democrats is elected by all members of the party, and an election is called when the incumbent seeks it, or on the death or incapacity of the leader, if the leader loses his or her parliamentary seat, or resigns or declares the intention so to do, or when a majority of members of the parliamentary party pass a vote of no-confidence in the leader or when the party president is in receipt of a requisition calling for such an election signed by seventy-five local parties (or SAOs). Provided the leader is not a member of the government, a leadership election must be called within the lifetime of each parliament. History suggests that a Liberal Democrat leader is in the job till death, incapacity, resignation, loss of support in the parliamentary party or the party at large, or loss of his or her seat in a parliamentary election. Until such time, a party leader enjoying a favourable public image has considerably greater influence in the affairs of the party than even the leaders of the major parties. Activists have frequently said somewhat archly that the best way to discover their party's policy on an issue is to listen to Ashdown on the television; exactly the same criticism was made of Steel, Thorpe and Grimond in their respective days as leader. It is an interesting paradox, however, that in a party dedicated to maximising participation, leaders from Grimond onwards have had a reputation for dominating their parliamentary colleagues and party structures.

The leader's dominance, however, is not based upon his or her status in the party constitution: it is the consequence of his media image and more general contribution to the political life of the nation, in no area more than in parliamentary debate. The leader's statements on major issues are invariably reported by the media. Moreover, in most major debates Ashdown is the only Liberal Democrat certain to speak. For example, on 23 July 1993 the House debated a Labour amendment to a government motion of confidence – clearly a crucial debate – in which, following the opening speeches by the prime minister and the leader of the opposition, twenty-one others spoke, Ashdown being the only Liberal Democrat.

To all intents and purposes, the leader *is* the party on such occasions.[12] These pressures make it inevitable that the Liberal Democrat leader will occupy a dominant role in the party, even by the standards of British party leaders. Nevertheless, it is clearly advantageous for a minority party seeking to maximise its coverage in the media that its leader can show a self-confidence and calm assertiveness; it is equally clear that these characteristics will reinforce the tendencies towards dominant leadership.

Policy-making

The defining characteristic of Liberal Democrat policy is that it is formally made by conference in accepting or amending policy papers or policy motions from local and regional parties.[13] The life story of a policy paper might be as follows: it originates in a conference or FPC decision (FPC's aim is to publish policy papers in all major aspects of policy during the course of a parliament) and a policy working group and chair is then appointed by FPC, with due attention being paid to gender, age and geographic balance. Relevant SAOs and AOs (Associated Organisations),[14] such as the Association of Liberal Democrat Councillors (ALDC), party agents, candidates, Liberal Democrat trade unionists, women and youth groups, are invited to contribute. FPC provides a remit and evidence is taken. A consultation paper is then drawn up by the group, identifying major issues and suggesting policy options consonant with party principles.

The consultation paper is then scrutinised and circulated for discussion among local regional and state parties and thereafter discussed at a consultative session of the next conference. The consultation paper is also scrutinised by environmental, equal opportunity and costings groups. The final draft of the consultation paper is then forwarded to FPC for approval and then is sent off to all conference representatives together with the conference agenda. At this final pre-conference stage, policy motions referring to the consultation paper are drawn up by FPC and conference representatives and local parties are asked to submit amendments. At last, at the relevant September conference, consultation paper, policy mission and amendments are debated and further amended and thus become party policy.

This constitutes a properly participative, if somewhat convoluted *modus operandi* but should be seen in the context of a party which needs to balance its commitment to participation with a proper concern for general electoral appeal, which needs to balance the agenda of party activists with the more realistic approach of parliamentary spokespeople. These problems are common to all modern democratic parties and the balances are never easy. For the Liberal Democrats, however, a third balance needs to be struck – between a commitment to a federal structure and the need for decisiveness in policy formulation. There are clear advantages to the process of policy-making which the Liberal Democrats have established: it brings the great benefit of wide consultation with interested parties, with individuals and groups with expert knowledge, and thus the added advantage of making policies which command wide support.

Conference itself has inherited something of a reputation for being unbusinesslike, a criticism which David Owen made of the Liberals before the merger. Liberal conferences in the past were undeniably prone to Byzantine procedures, and some of this reputation has rubbed off onto the Liberal Democrats. Writing about the amended constitution approved at conference in 1993, for example, Simon Hoggart described 'a magnificent Baroque version of a Liberal resolution, a Salzburg Cathedral among motions, bedecked with sections, clauses, sub-clauses, codicils and curlicues'.[15] It would be wrong not to recognise a serious and, as we are about to see, sometimes justified criticism amidst the hyperbole. It would be equally wrong, however, not to acknowledge the improvements to conference procedures which followed the merger.

The Brighton conference of 1994 was said to have depressed and angered the leadership by its outcome. A high profile debate was held on the monarchy in which many speakers advocated republicanism. It is true that the motion in favour of abolishing the monarchy was defeated but press coverage was generally unfavourable. Worse, however, from the party's image perspective, was the debate on drug misuse. The press reported conference as having passed a motion in favour of decriminalising the use and possession of cannabis.[16] In fact, conference adopted an amendment seeking the establishment of a royal commission on drug misuse empowered to consider a range of strategies *including* decriminalising the use and possession of cannabis. It is true that this last strategy was not much welcomed by the leadership and its inclusion was the result of an amendment passed by 426 to 375 but the motion could not be fairly described as favouring or recommending decriminalisation. As if these debates were not injury enough, the leadership was defeated on the issue of a party commitment to a minimum wage.

Ashdown's displeasure at this turn of events was plain for all (including media representatives) to see. The conference's deliberations – or some would say the leadership's over-reaction to them – certainly had an immediate effect: party support in the opinion polls fell by 4 per cent within a month.

There was concern within party hierarchy. In the *Reformer* it was argued: 'The minority of party activists – especially those on the conference committee – who see the conference as an opportunity to put the parliamentary party in their place and to debate fringe issues of peripheral importance, need to return to planet earth. Our members don't deliver leaflets, week in week out, to see their efforts blown by a burst of self-gratification by a few.'[17] The article concluded: 'The party needs to manage the proceedings better – not to stifle democratic debate, but to allow conference to be an effective forum, concentrating on the main issues and communicating our policies to the country.' The deputy chairman of Conservative Party Michael Dobbs, also expressed his belief that the conference had damaged the Liberal Democrats' image (and by implication improved his own party's).[18] It might nevertheless be argued that the party leader was at least partly responsible for the adverse media coverage of the Brighton conference by making his displeasure apparent.

On some occasions, the defence debate in 1986 Liberal assembly, for example, conference could be said to have been right to disregard the platform's strong advice to support the compromise European (joint French and British) nuclear capacity. Its unwillingness to do so caused David Steel evident displeasure. If a party committed to liberal democracy were not able to debate issues such as drug misuse and the monarchy then perhaps the balance would have swung too far towards perceived electoral acceptability. If the leadership wishes for public demonstrations of party support then its proposals must be watertight and enjoy wide support and it must encourage and not stifle sensibly expressed concern about contentious matters. Liberal Democrat conferences will not be dominated by the parliamentary leadership.

Recognising the need to ensure the effective organisation of conference, Ashdown appointed a director of strategy and planning (to whom reference has already been made), part of whose task would be to foresee and avert possible embarrassments. The Glasgow conference of 1995 was more thoroughly prepared, more tightly managed and much more successful in terms of media coverage.On the whole it would be reasonable to emphasise that Liberal Democrat conferences are more business-like than those of the old Liberal Party.

Candidate selection

Candidate selection in Scotland and Wales is organised through a candidates' committee, which draws up a list of approved candidates for parliamentary and European elections, coordinates procedures for selection and adoption, publishes criteria for the assessment of candidates, trains them and makes rules governing the selection and adoption of candidates. In England it is formally the regions which operate candidate committees and provide candidates lists for parliamentary and European elections and they, in turn, coordinate with the state party. In addition, however, there exists a federal joint candidates' committee, chaired by the chief whip and with state representatives, which meets at least once a year to oversee the operations at state level. The state/regional party has to take account of previous work for the party, and of gender, ethnic and age balance in drawing up their lists. It can remove names from the list if individuals are thought no longer to support Liberal Democrat values, or to have behaved in an unsuitable way, or to have become unfit through poor health and so on.

Shortlists of two or four must include at least one member of either sex and of five, at least two. 'Due regard' is required by the party constitution for ethnic representation. Hustings meetings are arranged for all candidates on the shortlist and all who belong to the local party at the closing date for applications are able to vote. Every member receives through the mail a copy of the shortlist, with notification of hustings. All who come to hustings or who submit a request will receive a ballot paper. The reselection of a candidate requires a two-thirds majority of the local executive, while sitting MPs require endorsement by a majority at a general meeting.

Although, in the event, only two women MPs were elected, the Liberal Democrats nevertheless fielded 144 women candidates in the general election of 1992, for the second successive election the highest number for any party (105 in 1987).[19] The party was less successful in terms of ethnicity, fielding only 6 candidates of black/Asian origin – 2 fewer than in 1987. (This compared with 9 for Labour and 8 for the Conservatives.) The party candidate in Bethnal Green resigned before the election, because, she alleged, of a 'a high level of racism in the party'.[20] In terms of age, although the median age of candidates of all the three major parties is similar (mid-40s), a greater proportion of Liberal Democrat candidates are young. Thirty-seven per cent were under forty, compared with 29 per cent for Labour and 32 per cent for the Conservatives. It would be fair to conclude that the selection procedures, more explicit in terms of securing fairer gender representation, have also been more successful. Indeed, if we consider the far larger measure of Liberal Democrat representation, that on local councils, we see that approximately 30 per cent of all Liberal Democrat councillors are women.[21]

Parliamentary party

The leader of the party is *ipso facto* leader of the parliamentary party, of which everyone who takes the Liberal Democrat whip is automatically a member. The parties in both the Lords and the Commons may (and do) also appoint chief whips and deputy leaders. The party in the European Parliament consists of only two MEPs who have joined the 52-strong Liberal Democrat and Reformist Group.

In 1994 the Liberal Democrat parliamentary party in the House of Commons took a new approach to the organisation of their parliamentary responsibilities . The party moved away from the idea of individual MPs seeking to shadow ministers in government departments to a system of shared responsibility within a number of teams, sub-committees of the parliamentary party covering wider areas of parliamentary activity. The intention was to increase the level of flexibility within the parliamentary party and to improve the party's collective effectiveness within the House. However, for logistical reasons, the practice of nominating individual spokespersons for the purposes of parliamentary debates was not abandoned, but it connotes something rather different from past practice. The remodelled 'frontbench' comprised: Ashdown as leader; Maclennan as party president; Beith as deputy leader in the Commons with responsibilities for the co-ordination of the work of the party's committees; Kirkwood as chief whip in the House of Commons; Hughes as deputy Commons whip; Campbell as convener of the foreign affairs, defence and overseas development committee; Bruce as convener of the Treasury, economic and environmental affairs committee; Beith as convener of the home affairs committee; Lord Jenkins as leader in the House of Lords; Baroness Seear as deputy Lords leader; Lord Harris as chief whip in Lords.

It has to be admitted that critics were not universally impressed by the changes. David McKie declared that 'there are few in [Ashdown's] ranks about whom you could safely say that ... they might be worth watching' as skilled parliamentary performers.[22] McKie argues that the modern parliamentary party compares unfavourably with its more colourful predecessors, when the Commons was graced with Liberals of genuine public stature such as Grimond, Thorpe, Steel, Freud and Smith, not to mention Owen, Jenkins and Williams in the days of the Alliance. It is almost certainly the consequence of a style of candidate selection which, as we have seen, tends to favour those with a good record on a local council or in local party affairs and thus to produce, in McKie's words, a sound but pedestrian parliamentary party.[23] Small though it is, the parliamentary party suffered its own crisis of discipline when, in 1992, David Alton resigned the whip over the issue of abortion. Although he returned to the fold in 1993 he asked not to be given any responsibility in the new structure because he wanted to devote his time to retaining his seat, unfavourably modified by boundary changes.

The Liberal Democrat party in the House of Commons is small and cannot claim to exercise much influence. Twenty Liberal Democrats were elected in 1992 and they have been joined by four by-election victors.[24] When House of Commons select committees were reconstituted, in the summer of 1992, the party was represented on only three of the key departmental committees: Menzies Campbell on defence, Alan Beith on Treasury and civil service and Malcolm Bruce on trade and industry. Robert Maclennan had a place on the Public Accounts Committee. There were no party representatives at all on home affairs, foreign affairs, education, environment, health, agriculture or science and technology. The party commands only three of the twenty opposition days in which it can initiate debate. It is principally for these reasons that McKie's comments have resonance: the party can wield influence in the House of Commons chiefly as a consequence of the personality of its spokespersons.

Bearing in mind these limitations the party has nevertheless sought to establish its distinctiveness as a party of opposition by attacking the government on issues of principle but not 'for the sake of opposition'. This position has frequently been derided both by the government and by the Labour opposition, and on no issue-area more than on Europe, where both of the major parties attacked the Liberal Democrats for inconsistency. In fact, Europe offers a conveniently visible example for exploring both the party's consistency and the reasonableness of its claim to operate a policy of 'principled opposition' as the following three cases show.

First, the Liberal Democrats earned Conservative displeasure when they supported a Labour amendment which sought to provide that the United Kingdom's representatives on the European Parliament's new committee of the regions should be elected by local authorities and not government nominees. That displeasure intensified when the government was defeated by twenty-two votes, despite support from the Nationalists.

Secondly, the Liberal Democrats earned Labour's displeasure when, in November 1992, the government won a paving motion to proceed with its Bill to legislate on the Maastricht Treaty by three votes, having been supported by the Liberal Democrats. Defeat for the government, said Labour (implausibly), would have led indirectly to the government's being brought down. Labour was particularly angered by the Liberal Democrat's refusal to support an amendment requiring delay in ratification pending the Edinburgh summit. Ashdown decried Labour opportunism, and the party succeeded in restricting the vote to the substantive issue. This was one of several occasions in the passage of the Maastricht Bill when Liberal Democrat support helped Major's government to carry the day.

Thirdly, the Liberal Democrats earned further Labour opprobrium when the party supported the government on the European Union Finance Bill in 1994. Labour had proposed an amendment not to sanction any increase in the United Kingdom's contribution to the EU budget 'without action by the government to curb fraud and waste in Europe'. Again the Liberal Democrats accused Labour of opportunism and the government secured a comfortable majority of twenty-seven.[25]

Although the government and the opposition Labour party would find it hard to agree, it is possible to discern the application of 'principled opposition' in these three examples. Moreover, the idea of a Labour opposition seeing it as a patriotic duty to bring down an unpopular government at any cost does not match the facts. In the vote to institute a referendum on the ratification of the Maastricht Treaty, moved by the Labour Eurosceptic Bryan Gould, the Liberal Democrats voted against the government but the motion was defeated by Labour's front bench supporting the government. On the whole it is probably fair to conclude that the Liberal Democrat party in the House of Commons has operated in a reasonably distinctive and consistent manner in seeking to provide 'principled opposition'.

In the House of Lords fifty-four peers take the Liberal whip of whom some thirty-five to forty can be considered active. They meet every Thursday at 2.30 p.m. with either the leader or deputy leader in the Lords taking the chair. At these meetings the Liberal Democrat lords may be addressed by the relevant Commons spokesperson. The party in the lords, additionally, has its own committees, on more conventional lines than those in the Commons, but the entire party in the Lords is supported by only three paid officials, and so Liberal Democrat peers feel there is a limit to what they can accomplish. Short of assistance, cramped for space, they nevertheless concentrate resources on producing their own amendments to legislation rather than simply responding to Labour's. Moreover, Lords' procedures grant the Liberal Democrats the right to speak third in debates, in recognition of their status as third party (a right they do not enjoy in the Commons).

Liberal Democrat peers, should they become chair or deputy of House committees, can become influential figures in the Lords; Baroness Seear recently chaired the social affairs committee with considerable distinction, for example. Others brought considerable knowledge and experience in public affairs to bear: the late Lord Bonham Carter, for example, was influential in all matters relating to civil rights and foreign affairs. In set-piece debates, major speeches by Lord Jenkins, the party leader in the Lords, are certain to have an impact, but he has not been regularly very active in the life of the Lords. Other Liberal Democrat peers may be intermittently influential. This is true of the dozen or so hereditary Liberal Democrats who claim some particular field of expertise and whose contribution to the affairs of the House has been almost solely in that policy area.

It should be remembered that the Liberal Democrats play a more influential role generally in the Lords because of the pivotal importance of the third-party and cross-bench vote. Indeed, between them Liberal Democrats and cross-benchers can usually expect to hold the balance of power in the Lords (though not necessarily on a major issue) and Labour's influence, without their support, is limited. A recent analysis[26] of members attending on an 'average day' indicated that 46.1 per cent were Conservative, 22.1 Labour, 11.7 Liberal Democrat and 18 per cent cross-bench. Some peers[27] argue that the Liberal Democrat opposition to the Conservative government in the Lords, just as in the Commons, is more consistent than that of Labour because the latter is not often prepared to send a disputed Bill back to the Commons a second time. Labour peers might argue that it would be constitutionally improper to do so but Labour would also surely be constrained by the knowledge that Conservative peers might more easily and regularly do the same to them when next they form a government. The Liberal Democrats have the luxury of no such constraint. Whatever the constitutional arguments, Liberal Democrats would claim that they were let down by Labour on an issue such as mandatory life sentences for murder, which their lordships accepted, having originally rejected; not a party matter, they claim, just bad legislation.

Party organisation and community politics

It would be inappropriate to complete this analysis of Liberal Democrat organisation without making specific reference to the concept and practice of community politics in so far as they clearly affect party organisation. Community politics is a form of politics which seeks to identify and empower local communities. It seeks to work beyond the formal structures of local authorities and thus represents the ultimate example of subsidiarity; the taking of decisions at the lowest level consonant with efficient and effective government. Liberal Democrats define a community as follows: 'A *community* is a group of individuals with something in common: nationality, neighbourhood, religion, work, workplace, victimisation, hobbies and mutual interests are a few obvious examples. The members of a community have some interests in common, something which enables them to identify, one with another.'[28] The practice of community politics has been, at least in part, and probably in large part, responsible for the successes of quite a few of the current 5,400 Liberal Democrat councillors and many of their predecessors over the past twenty years. Originally, community politics was associated with the more radical elements of the Liberal party and indeed was seen as subversive, a counter-culture mobilised by radical groups like the Association of Liberal Councillors (ALC) against the party leadership. However, by the mid-1980s the poachers, generally speaking, were becoming the party's gamekeepers, and community politics had become mainstream liberal democracy. Even the more traditional SDP, despite the misgivings of David Owen, felt able to take the ideology to its bosom. The championing of the notion of community was in some senses making a virtue of necessity, for the Liberals had to build up local power bases and this was best done by concentrating on local issues,[29] but it had a powerful ideological resonance as a context for the idea of citizenship developed by, among others, David Marquand. 'The city, the polis,' he suggested, ' belongs to and is fashioned by its citizens; they must not hand over their obligation to honour and defend it to some charismatic leader or remote bureaucracy'.[30] Ashdown developed this notion in his books *Citizens' Britain*, published in 1989, and *Beyond Westminster,* published in 1993, and its centrality to the party's perception of its distinctiveness is clear. From the organisational perspective its importance is equally clear, for it sets the concept of subsidiarity at the core of organisational structure.

We need to establish at first how seriously it is taken. There is some debate concerning the extent to which devolution to local communities had taken place in Liberal Democrat authorities. The inner London borough of Tower Hamlets had probably gone furthest in setting up local structures, though these had not developed very far beyond the administrative as opposed to the political. The goal of creating genuine 'urban parish councils', for example, had not been achieved. Nor indeed in any of the other forty or so councils which Liberals control has a full politically devolved structure been put in place. There were plans to create mini town halls in Liverpool had the party won power and these institutions, an important first step, have been created in Kingston, while Richmond and Sutton have done much to make their administrations more accessible. Tower Hamlets, however, pioneered the 'one stop shop' system, in which one office in each of the borough's seven designated communities would deal with all public enquiries about local authority services. The local party felt able to conclude that the new system brought 'a new resource to the community at a very local level ... [bringing] the council closer to the people'.[31] A crucial aspect of the Tower Hamlets case, then, was that the authority was considered by the party to be at the cutting edge of community politics.

Tower Hamlets, however, came to public notice for quite other reasons and these can be seen to raise fundamental questions about the nature of community politics and the idea of citizenship. As a consequence it is necessary to set out the course of events. Certain *Focus* leaflets distributed in the early 1990s in one of Tower Hamlets' communities, the Isle of Dogs, had called for priority in the borough's development areas to be given to 'sons and daughters' of Isle of Dogs families and not to homeless (Asian) families. The local Labour MP wrote to Ashdown in March 1991 asking him to dissociate the federal party from these leaflets and received no reply. In fact the local Liberal Democrats had obtained a copy of her letter and used it in a leaflet, declaring that it proved that Labour was against the council's policy of 'Island homes for Island people'.[32] This traditional dockland community had seen an influx of Asian families to comprise something like 20 per cent of the population,[33] and this in an area notoriously short of public housing. That the influx of Asian families was perceived locally as a major problem is substantiated by the 1993 local government by-election victory (by seven votes) of the British National Party in the island ward of Millwall. Accused of racism, the local Liberal Democrats claimed that up to 75 per cent of local party members were from ethnic minorities and that Bangladeshi party members helped to deliver the leaflets in question. 'If we're banned from talking about issues that affect local people, we will not be representing the people of Tower Hamlets' argued the co-author of the offending leaflet. Worse was to follow when another leaflet appeared, depicting a black boxer who appeared to be threatening a white woman pensioner.

The party established an inquiry into these incidents, chaired by Lord Lester, president of the Liberal Democrat Lawyers Association, and containing members of the London regional party, a representative of the ALDC (who sat on an inner-city council outside London) and an independent member nominated by Commission for Racial Equality. The inquiry found that three local members had 'pandered to racism' and should be expelled, with the right of appeal. Indeed, one of the three had distributed an entirely bogus 'Labour' leaflet in 1990 'seeking to exploit racial prejudice'. The report concluded: 'It is politically inept and likely to bring the Liberal Democrats into disrepute if public statements are made which can be fairly and reasonably described as racist ... In the context of the Isle of Dogs, appeals to Islanders or those who endured the Blitz, as distinct from homeless people, are likely to be understood as appeals to white people ... It is likely to be self-defeating, encouraging a political climate in which deprived white voters will express resentments at what they perceive as unfair favouring of ethnic minorities.' [34]

The report endeavoured to address the wider problem of community politics, claiming that the essentially pluralistic, inclusive nature of community was its dominant, indeed defining characteristic. 'When power is spread, it is in everyone's interests to use their power to maintain the civil liberty of others,'[35] it argued, going on 'The Liberal vision of community politics is dependent upon the universal safeguard of civil liberties. Unless a community respects, and upholds the liberty of the individual, of minority groups, and indeed of majority groups, no community ... can enhance the experience of each and every individual who makes it up.'

Here is the crux of the issue. The Isle of Dogs case is being considered here not because its populist, allegedly racist politics can be seen to be typical of community politics or of local Liberal Democrat councils; the opposite would be nearer the truth; but because the case raises fundamental questions about the organisational and ideological implications of community politics. The *a priori* assumption of traditional liberalism was man's rationality. Following from this, local communities, of all human associations, should be the most likely to act rationally: that is why Liberal Democrats seek to empower them. The community of the Isle of Dogs defined itself, or was defined by some of its elected representatives, in a manner which other Liberal Democrats considered to be selfish, irrational and indeed immoral, because of its latent or overt racist attitudes. When communities act like this, they do not, for Liberal Democrats, constitute a healthy community. Yet it can equally well be argued that it is precisely because they constituted a community, bound by wartime experiences and by the effects subsequently of inferior and insufficient housing, that they reacted so strongly to an influx of incomers. If it is conceded, and after Tower Hamlets it must be, either that communities can act irrationally or if not, that what constitutes a community must be decided by some external agent (the party) according to clear rules, then the centrality of rationality and its organisational corollary subsidiarity must surely be reconsidered. The party did indeed set up an enquiry to review the nature of community politics and it was concerned, among other things, to distinguish community politics as the mobilisation of local grievances (especially to win local elections) from some undefined wider vision. It is arguable, however, that Tower Hamlets has uncovered a paradox: to empower only such communities as the party defines as communities clearly constitutes a departure for traditional liberalism and constrains the modern versions of community politics and citizenship.

One outcome of the Tower Hamlets case was the subsequent inclusion in the party membership card of a 'clause four' type definition of liberal democracy, taken from the preamble to the federal constitution. It reads: 'The Liberal Democrats exist to build and safeguard a fair, free and open society, in which we seek to balance the fundamental values of liberty, equality, community and in which no-one shall be enslaved by poverty, ignorance or conformity.' If this statement may be seen as an acknowledgment that such a balance is the product of nurture and not nature then its organisational implications may eventually prove substantial.

Conclusions

Having completed the analysis of Liberal Democrat organisation, we may now return to the questions with which we began. Let us begin with the easy ones. How effectively has the party amalgamated (in organisational terms) Liberals and Social Democrats and how successful is the federal structure? To begin with the former, in their study *Liberal, Social Democrat or Liberal Democrat,*[36] Bennie, Curtice and Rüdig conclude that, to all intents and purposes, in terms of membership and ideology, they are 'all Liberal Democrats now'. Much the same could be said concerning the structure of party organisation. The story of the organisational compromises which followed merger have been examined in depth elsewhere.[37] Yet tensions remain, and the more successful Tony Blair is perceived to be in modernising the Labour party, the less likely these tensions are to be soothed. In 1993 a new journal the *Reformer*, established chiefly by former Social Democrats, came into being. Charles Kennedy chairs the editorial board which includes Shirley Williams and Ian Wrigglesworth. Early editions of the journal identified a concern with the alleged strongly pro-market policy of the leadership and declared a commitment to ensuring that the party 'sets out a clear and active role for the state in creating a dynamic economy and extending individual opportunity. It rejects any false impression that we are a laissez-faire party ...'. More disturbing for party unity is the fact that the journal claims to be looking to Labour's modernisers, claiming that 'a common front of the mind is beginning to take shape'.[38] Yet at Brighton in 1994 a new Liberal Democrat Urban Campaign Network was established precisely to fight Labour more actively. This group sought to counter what some perceived to be the shift of the party agenda towards Labour, promoted by former Social Democrats. However, this matter should be kept in perspective. As the urban campaign convener argued, is there an active SDP wing in the party? No, 'just one or two feathers'.[39]

Turning now to assess the success of the federal structure, it is possible to discern some potential problems, though their seriousness can only be guessed at. Organisationally, though not ideologically, the Scottish Liberal Democrats (SLD) form a party within a party.[40] Liberal Democrats would want to argue that this is precisely what organisational federalism implies, but this reasoning is disingenuous. Federations come under pressure; indeed they sometimes fracture. In 1994 a major contribution to the uncertainties of the debate at Brighton on decriminalising cannabis stemmed from the fact that the conference of the SLD had already declared support for decriminalisation. It is pertinent to consider what sense the British voter would make of Liberal Democrats in Scotland being in favour of decriminalisation but English and Welsh Liberal Democrats opposed. More important for party unity was the obvious rift in 1992 between the federal leadership and the SLD over support for a putative Labour minority administration which promised to legislate on a Scottish parliament but not on proportional representation. Ashdown's declared intention to vote down such a government would, had it ever been put into effect, probably have split the party. This tension is exacerbated by the preponderant size and financial strength of the English party. As has been suggested, from a Scottish perspective the federal party is frequently perceived as synonymous with the English state party.

Realists at party headquarters believe that the structure of power and influence within the party has more to do with financial resources than constitutional theories. In addition to the 20 per cent of their subscriptions which headquarters returns to the regions and the states (and the proceeds of their lotteries), the regions and the states, the SLD included, need funding from headquarters to survive, and in effect that means from the English party. The SLD, as we have seen, has its own bureaucracy in Edinburgh. The Welsh party and six of the English regions have offices (though two are private houses). Several of the English regions enjoy a sense not of autonomy by any means, but of identity. This is particularly true of regions with parliamentary (and now European) representation. However, there is a tension between regions naturally wishing to take responsibility for more of the administration but lacking the necessary computer hardware to take best advantage of the kinds of computerised service that the headquarters can provide.

It is difficult to generalise on the strengths and the weaknesses of the Liberal Democrat federal organisation. The party has consistently done better in local than general elections and this supports the notion of strong local organisation. The party has also shown an unusual ability to maximise its vote in winnable by-elections, which speaks much for its strategic acumen and ability to concentrate its forces. Considering the financial and manpower resources available to the party in comparison with those of its major opponents, it is difficult not to recognise the achievements of those who have given all their energies to building up an organisation to support the cause of the Liberal Democrats. On the other hand, federalism can as easily be a force for disunity as for democratic subsidiarity and the hugely ill-balanced Liberal Democrat model contains some potentially dangerous anomalies. For example, the SLD with a membership of less than seven thousand returns no fewer than nine MPs. Precisely contrary generalisations should be made about the SLD to those made about the English party; in Scotland relatively small, localised support is used to optimal electoral advantage, yet a relatively small adverse swing could be highly damaging to the SLD and thus to the Liberal Democrats at large. In England a sizeable adverse national swing need hardly affect the party's performance in winning seats. The position of the English state party too is anomalous, with the party having experienced endogenous growth into the federal party. Some in the party would argue that the abolition of the English state party and the adoption of state functions by the English regions would strengthen federalism (an intriguing prospect if the Liberal Democrat structure holds any lessons for the government of the United Kingdom at some time in the future). Finally, the anomaly of the Welsh state party needs to be addressed, for Wales has declined from a major Liberal heartland to a Liberal Democrat no-man's land, with only one Welsh MP and few members.

It is impossible to assess the success of Liberal Democrat federalism. Liberal Democrats are wedded to the notion ideologically and administratively and, after all, the party has made huge strides since the dark days of 1989. We cannot be sure that these facts are connected, or indeed, if they are, *how* they are connected, but we can be sure that the oxygen of electoral success at any level tends to respirate the system of a political structure and its lack might well have the opposite effect.

Finally, it surely must be agreed that, with approximately 100,000 members, the Liberal Democrats have built a party which encourages popular participation and makes such participation feasible. Popular participation in the party's policy-making processes, a conference system which enhances popular debate, an administrative structure which not only encourages but requires widespread participation, and finally a system of politics which seeks to empower ordinary people in a thoroughgoing manner which, in their periods of dominance, the major parties have not equalled in fifty years. In short it might be said that the problem for the Liberal Democrats today, how to manage, coordinate and set parameters for an active, ambitious, motivated occasionally populist, but growing mass membership, is the opposite to that envisaged for modern political parties by Downs, Kirchheimer and others. It is a problem that many western parties would like to have to confront.

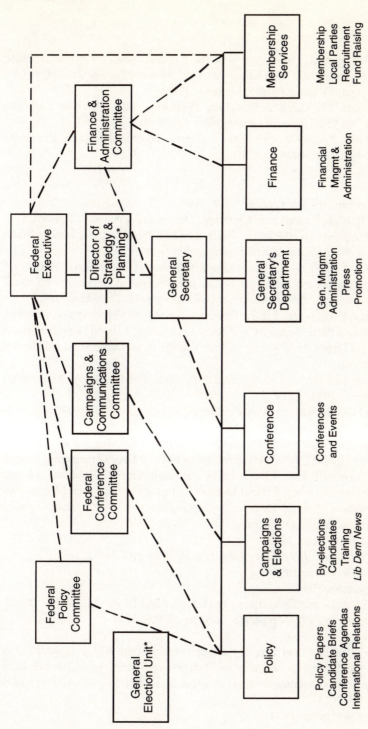

Figure 5.1 Liberal Democrat committees and HQ structure

*Report directly to the leader and linked with the Chair of Campaigns & Communications and the Federal Executive

Notes

1 See M.V. Ostrogorski, *Democracy and the Organisation of Political Parties*, Macmillan, London, 1902, and Robert Michels, *Political Parties*, Jarrold, 1915.

2 See M. Duverger, *Political Parties*, Methuen, 1986.

3 O. Kirchheimer, 'The Catch-all Party', in Peter Mair (ed.), *The West European Party System*, Oxford University Press, 1990, pp.50–60.

4 Paddy Ashdown, *Beyond Westminster*, Williamson Memorial Lecture, University of Stirling Publication, 1994, pp.2,3.

5 *Ibid.*, p.3.

6 *Ibid.*, p.5.

7 Liberal Democrats , *Policy Briefing No. 2, 1994.*

8 The twelve English regions are: Chilterns, Devon and Cornwall, Eastern, East Midlands, Hampshire and the Isle of Wight, London, Northern, North West, South East, Western, West Midlands, and Yorkshire and Humberside.

9 R. Pitchford and T. Greaves, *Merger: The Inside Story*, Hebden Royd, 1989.

10 The party recognises the following SAOs: the powerful Association of Liberal Democrat Councillors, the Association of Liberal Democrat Trade Unionists, Ethnic Minority Liberal Democrats, Liberal Democrat Agents and Organisers Association, Liberal Democrat Parliamentary Candidates Association, Liberal Democrat Youth and Students of England and Wales, Scottish Young Liberal Democrats, and Women Liberal Democrats.

11 Robert Garner and Richard Kelly, *British Political Parties Today*, Manchester University Press, 1993, p.219.

12 Paul Silk and Rhodri Walters, *How Parliament Works*, Longman, 1995, pp. 177–81.

13 Liberal Democrat Party, *Policy Making Process,* Policy Briefing No. 44, 1994.

14 AOs recognised by the Liberal Democrats are as follows: Green Democrats, Liberal Democrat Christian Forum, Liberal Democrat Engineers and Scientists, Liberal Democrat European Group, Liberal Democrats Peace Group, Liberal Democrats Against Apartheid, Liberal Democrats for Lesbian and GAY Action, Liberal International, One World Democrats.

15 *Guardian,* 22 September, 1993.

16 *Keesing's UK Record: 1994,* Circa Publications, 1994, pp.170–71.

17 *Guardian,* 30 December 1994.

18 *Ibid.*, 23 September 1994.

19 Byron Cridle, 'MPs and Candidates', in D. Butler and D. Kavanagh, *The British General Election of 1992*, Macmillan, London, 1992, p.219.

20 *Ibid.*, p.120.

21 Women comprise 29.45 per cent of the membership of the ALDC to which over 60 per cent of all Liberal Democrat councillors belong. There is no reason to believe that the proportion of women amongst all councillors would be different. (Figures provided by ALDC.)

22 *Guardian,* 19 September 1994.

23 *Daily Telegraph,* 3 August 1993.

24 The party won three stunning by-election victories in Newbury and Christchurch in May and July 1993 respectively and Eastleigh in June 1994.

25 *Keesing's UK Record: 1994, op. cit.*, pp.207–8.

26 See D. Shell and D. Beamish, *The House of Lords at Work,* Oxford University Press, 1993.

27 Baroness Seear, for example, in interview with the author.

28 T. Greaves and G. Lishman, 'Theory and Practice of Community Politics', quoted in *Political Speech and Race Relations in a Liberal Democracy,* Liberal Democrats, 1993. Report of an enquiry into the Tower Hamlets Liberal Democrats publication of allegedly racist election literature between 1990–1993.

29 See S. Mole, 'Community Politics', in V. Bognador, *Liberal Party Politics,* pp.258–74.

30 D. Marquand, *Guardian,* 16 August 1990.

31 *Service Beyond a Smile, Case Studies of Liberal Democrat Approaches to Customer Care in Local Government,* Customer Care Series No. 2, n.d .

32 *Guardian,* 20 September 1993.

33 *Daily Telegraph,* 18 September 1993.

34 *Guardian,* 17 December 1993.

35 *Race Relations in a Liberal Democracy, op. cit.*, p. 19.

36 Paper presented to the EPOP conference, University of Lancaster, September 1993.

37 See R. Pitchford and T. Greaves, *op. cit.*

38 *Guardian,* 17 September 1993.

39 *Ibid.,* 16 September 1994.

40 For a full account of the SLD and federalism see Peter Lynch, 'Third Party Politics in a Four Party System: The Liberal Democrats in Scotland,' unpublished monograph, 1995.

CHAPTER 6

Party members

Lynn Bennie, John Curtice and Wolfgang Rüdig

Introduction

It is now apparent that the Liberal Democrats represent a sustained threat to the established two party system of British politics. With a membership of approximately 100,000 the party has established a substantial membership base since the merger between the Liberal Party and the Social Democratic Party (SDP) in 1988.[1] In local government at least, the party can no longer be considered a minor party. After the 1995 local elections the Liberal Democrats could claim both more councillors elected and more councils controlled than the Conservatives. But who are the Liberal Democrats? What do they believe in? What are their views on pacts and coalitions? How active really are they? What has happened to the divisions that existed between the old Alliance parties? Before now, little has been known about the answers to these questions. Yet finding them out has clearly become important to understanding the possible future of British politics.

In this chapter we address those questions by presenting results from the first nationwide survey of members of the Liberal Democrats ever to be undertaken. Conducted by post in the spring and summer of 1993,[2] the survey enables us first of all to look at the social profile of Liberal Democrat members. We examine their age distribution, their sex and education, their occupations and religion, and we consider their perceptions of class. Secondly we report on their experience of being party members. How many active Liberal Democrats are there? Do they believe that the party is serving them well? Are they likely to remain members? Thirdly, we look at members' attitudes towards a number of major political issues. We ask, how pro-European is the party membership? Where does it stand on economic issues? What are the social attitudes of Liberal Democrats? How do their views on issues like capital punishment compare with those of the general public? We also consider the extent to which the policy differences between Liberals and Social Democrats have been healed. Finally, we look at Liberal Democrats' views on party strategy and the future of the party. What are their attitudes towards pacts and deals with Labour? Where possible we also compare our survey findings with data on the other British parties and the general electorate at large.

A social profile: who are the Liberal Democrats?

As Britain's newest political party one might anticipate that the Liberal Democrats would have the youngest membership, but the survey results reveal that this is not the case. As Figure 6.1 shows, as many as one in three of the respondents to our survey were over 65. In contrast less than one in five Labour Party members fall into that age group.[3] However, over 40 per cent of Conservative Party members fall into that category, making the Conservative membership the oldest of all Britain's political parties.[4] Perhaps not surprisingly, the oldest group of Liberal Democrats were those who had previously been members of the Liberal Party, of whom as many as 40 per cent were over 65.

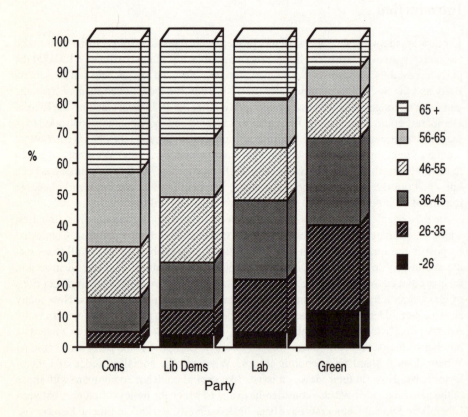

Figure 6.1 Age of party members (1993)

A party always appears healthier if it has a young age profile. If a party has an age profile like that of the Conservatives, two in three of whose members are aged over 55, it would appear to be in danger of losing a large proportion of its members in the foreseeable future. However, we should be wary about drawing such a conclusion. All the major political parties are underrepresented amongst the under-35s. Only the Greens have a distinctively younger membership, yet this does not appear to have helped them in building up a stable membership base.[5] In fact, our evidence indicates that older persons can provide a valuable recruiting ground for new members. We find that older people are more likely to stay in the party than younger recruits. Of those Liberal Democrats who had not previously been members of either of the two old Alliance parties and who are over 65, three-quarters say they will definitely renew their membership. In contrast, less then 50 per cent of 'new' members aged 25 or younger say they will renew. Nevertheless, the Liberal Democrats must be disappointed that they have not been more successful at winning recruits amongst young people than Labour have, despite Labour's electoral difficulties during the 1980s.

In fact, not least of the reasons that the Liberal Democrats' age profile is not younger is that although it is a new party the majority of its members are not in fact new to centre party membership. Over 60 per cent of its members had previously been a member of one of its two predecessor parties, the Liberals and the SDP,[6] while only just over one third joined the party in the five years between the time of the merger and our survey. The ballast of the new party evidently comes from members of the old Alliance parties who have remained faithful with it through the ups and downs of merger negotiations and name change.

If the Liberal Democrats have not been particularly successful at recruiting the young, they have had more success than Labour in recruiting women. Only 39 per cent of Labour members are women, compared with 47 per cent of Liberal Democrats. However, despite the fact that the Liberal Democrats, like Labour, have been concerned to promote the role of women within the party organisation, they are still less successful than the Conservatives in recruiting women, who constitute as many as 49 per cent of Conservative members.[7] However, none of Britain's political parties fully reflect the gender profile of the general population: according to the 1991 census, women represent 52 per cent of the British population.

The Liberal Democrats are certainly the most highly educated group of major party members.[8] No less than 43 per cent completed their continuous full-time education after the age of 18 and just under a half have studied for a degree. In contrast, just under one in five Conservative members completed their education after the age of 18 and less than one in three Labour members have a degree. This concentration of the educated middle class amongst the Liberal Democrats' numbers is reflected in its voters as well-educated members of the salariat, that is, people in salaried professional or managerial occupations, who in the electorate as a whole give more support to the Liberal Democrats than any other identifiable group.[9] It should perhaps then be no surprise that despite its middle-class membership the party should have campaigned at the 1992 election for a one penny increase in taxation to finance increased education spending and that the party continued this campaign theme into the 1995 local elections.[10]

Most organisations – with the notable exception of trade unions – are disproportionately middle class in their membership. Even in the Labour Party only just under one in three are members of the working class, and nearly half belong to the salariat. However, no less than just over two in three Liberal Democrat members in our survey indicated that they had an occupation belonging to the salariat. Using occupation as an objective indicator of class, the Liberal Democrats appear to be even more middle class than the Conservatives. Only 55 per cent of Conservative members belong to the 'salariat'. Meanwhile, just one in eight of Liberal Democrats has a manual occupation: only a little higher than amongst Conservative members. As many as 19 per cent are self-employed: nearly double the proportion in the electorate as a whole and more than the Conservative Party membership, just under 13 per cent of whom are self-employed.[11]

The party's middle-class character might seem inconsistent with its stance in favour of increased taxation. However, as many as 49 per cent work for a nationalised industry, the government or some other part of the public sector, while 46 per cent work for a private company or are self-employed. Amongst the electorate as a whole, in contrast, there are two private sector workers for every one in the public sector.[12] Liberal Democrats are very much part of the public sector middle class.

One of the historical roots of the Liberal Party was religious nonconformism and nonconformists have long been more likely to vote Liberal Democrat than other voters.[13] The legacy of nonconformism can also be seen amongst the Liberal Democrats' membership. As many as 18 per cent of Liberal Democrats claim allegiance to one of the nonconformist denominations compared with 7 per cent of the electorate as a whole. Even so, the Liberal Democrats are not a party of nonconformists – Anglicans are by far the largest religious group in the party, constituting one in three of all members. Meanwhile, irrespective of their denomination Liberal Democrat members are more likely to be seen in church than the average voter – nearly one in four claim to attend church once a week compared with one in eight of the electorate.

On the whole Liberal Democrats are serious competitors with the Conservatives for the title of the most middle class party in Britain. They are highly educated and they are likely to belong to the salariat. However, Liberal Democrats are distinctive in terms of their exceptionally high levels of education and the numbers who work in the public sector. Indeed, the Liberal Democrat members appear to come from a particular section of the middle class, the better educated in society who choose employment in one of the caring professions in the public sector. This distinctive social background of Liberal Democrat members certainly corresponds with the party's policy of increasing taxes to support more public spending on education.

Activism: what is it like being a Liberal Democrat?

Members are vital to the Liberal Democrats. Lacking major funding from either big business or trade unions, the party is reliant upon its members not only for finance but also as a manpower resource. One of the hallmarks of the community politics style of campaigning promulgated inside the Liberal Party is extensive local campaigning using hand-delivered leaflets. Liberal Democrat by-election campaigns are now famous for their bussing in of large numbers of party workers from around the country.

How active is the general membership of the party? Not perhaps as much as the image of the party suggests. Just under a half of all members responding to the survey say that they do not spend any time at all in party activity in the average month outside of election times. Even amongst the remainder, a half spend three hours a week or less. Perhaps not surprisingly the burden of running the party falls on a small number of people: 6 per cent of our respondents reported spending twenty or more hours a month on party affairs.

These levels of activism are no higher than those in the Labour Party where exactly 50 per cent of the membership is normally inactive.[14] However, both opposition parties' members are much more active than are Conservative members, and the balance and concentration of activity amongst Liberal Democrat members rather different from those of Labour Party members (Table 6.1).

Liberal Democrats are a little more likely to say that they frequently deliver leaflets than are Labour Party members.[15] In contrast, they are less likely to engage frequently in some of the more traditional forms of local party activity such as attending meetings and canvassing. The style of Liberal Democrat campaigning does indeed appear to have a distinctive character to it.

That distinctive style is also reflected in the party's commitment to fighting local elections. No fewer than one in five party members have been a candidate for the party in local elections. The Liberal Democrats may be a minority party at Westminster, but its membership can hardly be regarded as being insulated from the feelings of the electorate.

Clearly, one challenge for any party with a substantial 'passive' membership is maintaining the members' contact with, and commitment to, the party. In many respects the party seems to have had some success with this, although its national publications are regarded a little lukewarmly. Asked to mark these out of seven, only 38 per cent were prepared to give them a score of six or seven for interest, and as few as 25 per cent for persuasiveness. Even so, as many as 85 per cent felt that the party did enough to keep them informed: 78 per cent receive a newsletter from their local party and only 5 per

Table 6.1   What activists do: percentage saying they have been frequently active in the past five years

	Lib Dem	Lab	Con
Displayed election poster	64	65	19
Delivered election leaflets	62	57	22
Donated money to party funds	38	33	30
Attended party meeting	36	42	17
Canvassed voters	30	36	10
Stood in an election	16	9	3

cent have no contact with their local party at all. Two-thirds read the party newspaper, *Liberal Democrat News*. Just one-fifth believe that the party leadership pays little attention to the views of ordinary members.

The party is certainly keeping in contact with its membership so far as money-raising is concerned. No fewer than 88 per cent had received an appeal for money from the federal level of the party in the previous twelve months. One of the innovations that the SDP brought to British politics was the construction of a computerised national membership list which can be used to make direct mail appeals. The Liberal Democrats are clearly exploiting this facility – and indeed more of its members report giving money frequently to the party than do either Labour or Conservative members.

We have seen that the level of activism in the party is similar to that of the Labour Party. It is not so clear that the membership's depth of commitment to the party is the same. One of the weaknesses of the Liberal Democrats' electoral position is that their voters tend to feel less emotional attachment to the party than do voters for Conservative or Labour and in consequence are less likely to be loyal to the party in the polling booth. This lack of emotional appeal is also apparent amongst the party's membership. Only one in three say that they would call themselves a 'very strong' Liberal Democrat. In contrast over a half of Labour members say that they are 'very strong' Labour.

Furthermore, there is also evidence of a decline in the level of activism in the party in recent years. Almost one in three members (30 per cent) said they were less active in the party now than five years ago[16] while only one in five said they were more active. Consistent with this, whereas 55 per cent of those Liberal Democrats who were members of the Liberal Party or the SDP prior to the merger said they were at least fairly active in their former party, only 40 per cent of them said they were at least fairly active in the Liberal Democrats now. Meanwhile, the level of activity reported by all those who are currently members of the Liberal Democrats is lower than that reported by all former members of the two predecessor parties.[17]

One possible interpretation of these results is that some Liberal Democrat members have still not recovered their enthusiasm for the party in the wake of the party's early difficulties.[18] However, Seyd and Whiteley's surveys of Labour and Conservative members have also found a similar reported fall in the level of activism compared with five years previously. The level of party membership in Britain has been in steady decline since the 1950s so perhaps all parties are suffering from a growing disillusionment with political parties, a disillusionment from which even the Liberal Democrats are unable to escape.

A more prosaic explanation is also possible. Given the age profile of Liberal Democrat members – and party members in general – ill health can be expected to have reduced the ability of some to maintain their level of activism over a period of five years. As many as one in four of those who said they were not very active or not at all active indicated that the reason for this was bad health. It may be that not too much should be made of the apparent fall in activism.

One acid test of the real level of commitment to a party amongst its members is whether or not they intend to remain members. Just over 75 per cent of our respondents said they intended to renew their membership when it next became due, while another 18 per cent said that they probably would. Only 5 per cent said that they were likely to leave or indeed had already left. Of course, those who are thinking about leaving were probably less willing to respond to our survey, but even so it seems likely that the party has a reasonably stable membership base. It certainly compares favourably with the Greens' membership in the wake of their European election success. When surveyed in the autumn of 1990 only 64 per cent of Green members said they intended to renew their membership, while just over 12 per cent said they had left or were on the point of leaving.

Why were those who were not sure that they would renew their membership dissatisfied? In most cases the reasons were personal, such as age or ill health (20 per cent) or not being able to afford the cost (19 per cent). However, the party's handling of one important political issue emerged as a significant source of dissatisfaction. This was its decision to support the government on the bill which implemented the provisions of the European Union's Treaty of Maastricht. Because the Conservative government could not rely on the support of some of its Eurosceptic backbenchers, the support of the Liberal Democrats in the so-called paving debate in the autumn of 1992 was decisive in permitting the progress of the bill at that stage. No less than one in five of possible leavers cited this action as the reason that they might leave. The Liberal Democrats are often seen as the most united of all the parties on Europe, with a clear pro-union stance. The Liberal Party was, after all, the first party to favour Britain joining the EC while disagreement with Labour's then anti-EC stance was one of the reasons that the 'Gang of Four' left to join the SDP.[19] However, on this evidence there seems cause to inquire into the current attitudes of Liberal Democrats a little further. Is this opposition to the party's support for the Maastricht Bill simply explained by opposition to the Conservative government? Or is it in fact indicative of a degree of anti-European sentiment within the party?

Political attitudes: what do Liberal Democrats believe?

There is further evidence in our survey that the Liberal Democrats are not as enthusiastic about a strong Europe as is often supposed. Given a wide set of options for Britain's future role in the EU, only 47 per cent favoured either the formation of a single European government or an increase in the powers of the EU, while as many as 44 per cent favoured either the withdrawal of Britain from the EU or at least a reduction in the European Union's powers. Liberal Democrats are, it seems, scarcely more pro-European than the electorate as whole, 41 per cent of whom were in favour of a stronger EU at the time of the last election and 43 per cent a weaker one.

This result does not appear to be a fluke of question wording. In response to a completely different question only 55 per cent of Liberal Democrats said the government should make Britain part of a federal Europe while 36 per cent were opposed. This compares with 21 per cent of Conservative party members who are in favour of a federal Europe and 64 per cent who are against.[20] Although in contrast to the Conservatives, therefore, Euro-enthusiasts are the larger group in the Liberal Democrats and Eurosceptics are in the minority, it would appear that Europe is capable of dividing the Liberal Democrats just as it does the Conservatives.

Apart from its pro-European stance, another distinctive feature of Liberal Democrat policy is its commitment to domestic constitutional reform. Surprisingly, support for this is not overwhelming in all respects either. Eighty-eight per cent favour a Bill of Rights and no less than 93 per cent are in favour of proportional representation, but support for a change of electoral system is not necessarily accompanied by a rejection of British-style single party government. Only 35 per cent feel that coalition governments are the best form of government for Britain while one-quarter actually disagree, the rest believing it does not make much difference either way.

Meanwhile, support for official party policy on devolution begins to look particularly weak. The Liberal Democrats and its predecessor parties have long favoured some form of devolution to the English regions as well as to Scotland and Wales. Yet only 60 per cent agree that the government should 'create separately elected Parliaments for Scotland and Wales, and elected regional assemblies for England' while as many as 30 per cent were opposed.

In contrast to Europe and constitutional reform, economic policy has rarely been seen as one of the party's distinctive cards. It is in this area of policy where the party has been perceived as a centre party, but our survey suggests that centre-left would be a more accurate description of the party membership. In the first place, a considerable proportion of the party clearly believes that the government has an important interventionist role to play in the economy, including the ownership of key sections of industry. Nearly two in three believe that 'major public services and industries ought to be in state ownership', putting the party well to the left on this issue. Consistent with this stance, over half believe that the 'public enterprises privatised by the Conservatives should be returned to the public sector' while less than a quarter are opposed.

So far as taxation and spending are concerned, the membership is overwhelmingly in favour of the latter, even if this means raising the former. No less than 95 per cent favour increasing 'public spending on education and training even if it means raising taxes', while 96 per cent oppose reducing taxes 'if it means reducing spending on health and social services'.[21] These results represent a wholehearted endorsement of the party's 1992 commitment to spend more on education by raising income tax. Education and health spending are of course popular throughout the electorate so perhaps these results are not as spectacular as they might seem. Moreover, as we have already seen, Liberal Democrats are likely to work in the public sector so we might expect them to support spending in these areas. However, as many as 51 per cent of Liberal Democrats endorse the much more radical statement that 'income and wealth should be redistributed towards ordinary working people', while only 18 per cent are opposed. As many as two-thirds believe that 'ordinary working people do not get their fair share of the nation's wealth'. There can be little doubt that for the most part Liberal Democrat members wear their hearts to the left and are more likely to have something in common with Labour members than the Conservatives. It would appear that Paddy Ashdown's decision as party leader in May 1995 to indicate that his party would not be willing to work with the Conservatives after the next election but only with Labour was at least in tune with the political attitudes of his party members.

Table 6.2. Party members' views on the role of government

	% agree		
	Lib Dem	*Lab*	*Con*
Income and wealth should be re-distributed towards ordinary working people	51	88	26
The government should spend more to get rid of poverty	91	99	81
The government should encourage the growth of private medicine	11	4	52
The government should put more money into the NHS	93	99	80
Reduce government spending generally	35	21	60

As Table 6.2 indicates, Liberal Democrat members are consistently closer to Labour members than the Conservatives on issues of income redistribution and general government intervention, although they are less likely to favour government spending than Labour Party members. Thus, on socio-economic issues, the Liberal Democrat membership can accurately be described as centre-left.

It is only when it comes to the generation rather than the production of wealth that Liberal Democrats reveal any semblance of the traditional nineteenth-century Liberal belief in the virtues of the market. Forty-six per cent believe that 'the production of goods and services is best left to a free market' while only 27 per cent disagree. Even then only 31 per cent agree that 'private enterprise is the best way to solve Britain's economic problems' while 36 per cent do not.

We have seen that on socio-economic issues Liberal Democrat members lean towards the left and this is also where they see themselves. Asked where they would place themselves on a left–right scale, in relation to British politics as a whole, over half put themselves to the left of centre and less than one in five to the right (Figure 6.2). Not that many put themselves on the far left – the average Liberal Democrat sees him or herself as just to the left of centre.

In terms of self-perception, Labour Party members are much more likely to place themselves on the far left than Liberal Democrats and, as we would expect, Conservatives see themselves as definitely to the right. Liberal Democrats place themselves closer to Labour members than Conservative members. So, when we consider both the self-perceptions of members and their declared policy preferences it is clearly more accurate to describe the Liberal Democrats as Britain's centre-left party rather than its centre party. So here also, Paddy Ashdown's abandonment of equidistance, that is a willingness to work after an election with either the Conservatives or Labour, in favour of declaring a preference for Labour appears to be in accordance with the views of the membership.

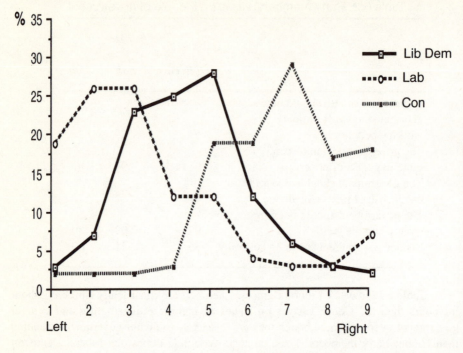

Figure 6.2 Placement on left–right scale

Nevertheless, the Liberal Democrats have maintained some distinctive characteristics. In line with the Liberal tradition, Liberal Democrat members are critical of class divisions in society. Class identity amongst Liberal Democrats does not approach the levels evident in the two major parties. As many as 48 per cent of our respondents claimed they never thought of themselves as belonging to a particular social class, compared with only 28 per cent of Labour members and 38 per cent of Conservatives. Nevertheless, when forced to choose between working class and middle-class, 69 per cent of Liberal Democrat members put themselves in the middle-class category, thus reinforcing the party's middle-class image.

Overall, the political attitudes of Liberal Democrats fit well with the tradition of social liberalism as propounded by Hobhouse and Hobson rather than the classical liberal approach of *laissez-faire* economics.[22] Liberal Democrat members regard state involvement in the economy as necessary and indeed desirable. They reveal a distrust for private monopolies and support the principle of income redistribution through taxation and welfare spending in the belief that this provides an opportunity for individual self-development. This was most apparent in their support for increased spending on education. We can safely conclude that the social liberal tradition is alive and well in the attitudes of modern-day Liberal Democrats.

Social attitudes: how 'liberal' are the Liberal Democrats?

Central to both classical and social liberalism is the promotion of individual rights. If, as we have already suggested, social liberalism has affected the views of Liberal Democrats, we might also expect Liberal Democrats to reveal a strong concern for civil liberties, albeit within the context of a responsible state. Given their relatively high levels of education, one would also expect party members to be fairly libertarian on contentious social issues such as the death penalty.

The survey results allow us to compare some of the social attitudes of Liberal Democrat members with those of the general population. Indeed we do find that Liberal Democrat party members are, on the whole, more 'liberal' than the electorate at large (Table 6.3).

Liberal Democrat members are certainly more liberal than the electorate when it comes to restoration of the death penalty; they are also more tolerant of unconventional behaviour and they are more likely to defend the right to protest. On these issues, the Liberal Democrat members definitely come down on the side of individual rights. However, on the issue of homosexuality, Liberal Democrats do not appear to be significantly more tolerant than the wider population.

Unfortunately it is more difficult to establish whether Liberal Democrat members are also more liberal than Conservative and Labour members because the latter have been asked relatively few questions about social issues. True, it seems safe to assert that they are more liberal than Conservative members, who indeed appear to be less liberal than the electorate at large. For example, 69 per cent of Conservative party members support the reintroduction of the death penalty. As many as 56 per cent of Conservatives believe

Table 6.3 The 'liberal' in Liberal Democrat

	% agree	
	Lib Dem	*BES '92*
Death penalty should be reintroduced for murder	29	45[23]
People should be more tolerant of the unconventional	57	48
Young people do not have respect for traditional values	54	68
Anti-democratic parties should be allowed in general elections	36	20
People should be allowed to protest against the government	88	62
Homosexual relations are wrong	29	27

Source: BES '92: British Election Study 1992

that 'When it comes to a family, a woman's place is in the home' compared with only 23 per cent of Liberal Democrats. Equally, no less than 91 per cent of Conservatives believe that 'restrictions on immigration into Britain are too loose and should be tightened', while only 57 per cent of Liberal Democrats *dis*agreed that 'restrictions on immigration into Britain are too tight and should be eased'.

It is far less certain that Liberal Democrat members are more liberal than their Labour counterparts. The one strand of evidence we do have certainly suggests otherwise. No less than 42 per cent of Labour members agree that immigration restrictions should be eased compared with only 18 per cent of Liberal Democrats.[24] Otherwise we have to make inferences from the attitudes of party identifiers where a recent analysis of authoritarianism across a broad spectrum found that it was Labour rather than Liberal Democrat identifiers who were the least authoritarian.[25] While, on the whole then, the Liberal Democrats do live up to their reputation of 'libertarianism', it is doubtful whether they have made the stance their own.

Healing the Liberal–SDP divide

The party apparently has divisions on Europe and devolution that one might not have anticipated. How far has it succeeded in healing the very real differences between its two predecessor parties? Its start was certainly inauspicious as the two camps argued about what the party should be called. What of the situation now?

Our analysis reveals few signs of the policy divisions that existed between former Liberals and former Social Democrats. The most acrimonious debates between the two former Alliance parties were about nuclear weapons and nuclear power stations, with the Social Democrats more inclined to support both than the Liberals (Table 6.4). Indeed, those Social Democrats who joined the Liberal Democrats are still more pro-nuclear than the former Liberals, but only on civil nuclear power is the difference at all substantial.[26]

There are few signs of substantial differences on other issues either, but ironically such as there are suggest that the SDP was a little closer to being a liberal party on the Continental European pattern than was the former Liberal Party. Former Social Democrats are a little *less* likely to be on the left on socio-economic issues than former Liberals but *more* likely to take a liberal stance on moral issues. For example, only 45 per cent of former Social Democrats believe that the privatised industries should be returned to the public sector compared with 55 per cent of former Liberals. Meanwhile only 20 per cent of former Social Democrats favour the reintroduction of the death penalty for murder compared with 26 per cent of ex-Liberals.

Former Social Democrats are outnumbered by former Liberals by nearly four to one in the party. In addition, those Liberal Democrats who did not belong to either of the two old parties are more commonly similar in their attitudes to former Liberals than former Social Democrats.[27] The scars of the 1980s appear to have healed, but the temper of the new party is much closer to that of the former Liberal Party than that of the SDP.[28]

Table 6.4. Liberal and SDP differences

	% agree Former members of		
	Liberals	*SDP*	*Neither*
Close all nuclear power stations	62	45	59
Abandon nuclear weapons as a deterrent	62	52	53
Britain should have nothing to do with nuclear weapons	33	26	30
Government should spend less on defence	61	63	59

Strategy: what is the future for the Liberal Democrats?

The Liberal Democrats may have largely put the divisions of the 1980s behind them but many commentators now argue that the party faces a new challenge in the 1990s. The revival of the Labour Party under the leadership of Tony Blair has led to some interesting questions being raised about the future strategy of the Liberal Democrats. On the one hand, Blair's 'New Labour' party appears to have moved towards the Liberal Democrats on many policy issues. This raised doubts about whether the policy positions of the Liberal Democrats were any longer distinctive and, as already mentioned, required the Liberal Democrats to re-examine their policy of equidistance between the Conservatives and Labour. Some indeed argued that given Labour's new-found popularity, there was real risk of the Liberal Democrats being squeezed out of the party political game. On the other hand, the Conservative Party has won four general elections in a row. Even when it fights a general election in the teeth of an economic recession it appears to be difficult to dislodge. Labour still seems to have some fundamental electoral weaknesses and could be incapable of winning an overall majority. At the same time, as the failure of the SDP indicated, Labour's working-class base is difficult to dislodge. Thus the apparently logical thing for the Liberal Democrats to do would be to enter into an electoral pact with Labour and mobilise the anti-Tory majority.

The Liberal Democrats debated this issue at the party's 1992 conference. They passed a resolution which called for dialogue with other parties (not just Labour) but ruled out a national electoral pact. The party seemed to wish to keep the entrance to cooperation open but avoid putting up large signposts advertising to the public where it was. One fundamental problem for the party is of course that many of its voters say that they prefer the Conservatives to Labour – indeed by no less than 45 per cent to 39 per cent in England at the time of the last election – and any electoral pact or close cooperation with Labour could frighten those voters into the Conservative camp. Indeed, although a number of local electoral deals and understandings were made with Labour before the county council elections in 1993, the Liberal Democrat leadership was subsequently keen to emphasise that it had reached post-election understandings on how to run councils with Conservatives as well as Labour.

We have already seen, however, that on socio-economic issues Liberal Democrat members lean towards the left and do not simply lie in the centre. This was also where they saw themselves on the left–right scale. This positioning of themselves on the left–right scale is also reflected in their feelings about the Conservative and Labour parties. We asked our respondents to score each party on a 'feeling thermometer', that is to give it a rating out of 100 indicating how 'warm and sympathetic' they felt towards the party. If they felt very warm and sympathetic they would give the party a score close to 100 while if they were cold and unsympathetic they would give the party close to zero. We found that on average Liberal Democrats proved to be considerably more warm and sympathetic to Labour than to the Conservatives. The average score given to the Conservatives was just 19, indicating that most Liberal Democrats feel decidedly cool and unsympathetic towards the Conservatives. Feelings towards Labour are not warm, but at 37 the average Labour score was considerably higher.[29]

Thus some of the ingredients necessary for cooperation with Labour do appear to be present. On both policy issues and in terms of general feelings Liberal Democrats appear to have considerably more in common with Labour than the Conservatives. Further, only a minority of party members feel that they can achieve political power on their own – less than one in four said that they felt that a majority Liberal Democrat government is likely within the next ten years, while nine in ten think that the party is likely to hold the balance of power. But just how far are Liberal Democrat members prepared to go?

Quite a long way it seems (see Table 6.5). Informal discussions between members of the two parties before an election would appear to be so widely supported that it is no longer likely to be worthy of comment. However, even on formal talks, proponents outnumber opponents despite the unease some Scottish Liberal Democrats have expressed about their experience in the Scottish Constitutional Convention.

There also appear to be majorities of nearly two to one in favour of striking a deal with Labour *after* the next election in the event of a hung parliament. So just as we saw earlier on attitudes towards the role of government, it would seem that Paddy Ashdown's move away from equidistance between Conservative and Labour is also in line with party feeling about what its future strategy should be. Interestingly, there is rather more support for forming a coalition government with Labour than supporting a minority Labour government. Perhaps some members with long memories look unfavourably upon the experience of the Lib/Lab Pact in 1977–78. Others may feel that a coalition government would give the Liberal Democrats a better chance to negotiate for and implement some of its policy priorities and ensure that it is not outmanoeuvred. What is clearly not acceptable, however, is a national electoral pact. This is opposed by a majority of more than two to one. This dream of some commentators is evidently a non-starter.

On the other hand, the door to electoral pacts is not entirely closed. Only 40 per cent say that the party should *never* enter into a pact with Labour. Well over half of our respondents were prepared to support 'locally negotiated pacts in which Liberal Democrats did not fight some constituencies at the next election while Labour did not

Table 6.5 Collaboration with Labour?

	Support %	Oppose %
Informal policy discussions	75	12
Formal policy talks	41	34
Locally negotiated general election pacts	57	28
National general election pact	23	58
Support Labour minority government	48	28
Join coalition government with Labour	56	24

oppose Liberal Democrats in others'. It should perhaps be borne in mind that there are precedents for such deals. Local pacts with the Conservative Party enabled Liberal MPs to be elected in Bolton and Huddersfield in the 1950s. The Liberal Democrats did not stand against the two SDP MPs, John Cartwright and Rosie Barnes, who defended their seats at the last general election. Such deals offer the prospect of reaping some of the rewards of a national pact while enabling the national party leadership to distance themselves from claims that they imply a willingness to work together in government after the election. It would certainly seem that should the party leadership wish to permit such pacts it would not meet undue resistance from the majority of Liberal Democrat members.

Other evidence in our survey also suggests that the leadership may have considerable room for manoeuvre in determining party strategy. We asked our respondents to say whether they agreed or disagreed with a number of statements designed to reflect long-standing debates in the Liberal Democrats and the old Alliance parties about party strategy. Many party members support both sides of the debate. One such debate, for example, is whether the Liberal Democrats should be a centre party or a radical alternative to the Labour Party. No less than 59 per cent agreed that 'the Liberal Democrats should be a centre party in between the Conservatives and Labour'. At the same time, however, 70 per cent agreed with the objective that Jo Grimond set for the old Liberal Party that 'the Liberal Democrats should aim to replace Labour as the main opposition party in British politics'.

Another such debate has been between those who have emphasised the need for a 'community politics' approach based on local campaigning and those who favour concentrating on the world of Westminster and the national media. Sixty-four per cent agreed that 'the Liberal Democrats should place greater emphasis on local campaigning', but 68 per cent also agreed that 'the Liberal Democrats must concentrate their efforts on national level issues if they are to win power'. Thus to some extent the Liberal Democrat membership is inclined to face both ways on some of the strategic choices that confront it. In those circumstances the members are likely to take whichever direction the party's leadership decides.

Conclusion

This chapter contains much that is good news for the Liberal Democrats. It suggests that the divisions between the Liberals and the SDP have been healed. The Liberal Democrat membership is as active as that of the Labour Party while the party seems to be maintaining contact with a large proportion of its passive membership. In short, the problems that surrounded the party's birth do indeed appear to have been put behind it.

However, we have also identified new challenges and difficulties that could face the party should it approach the threshold of power. Its membership is not as united on some of the party's key policy positions, most notably on Europe and on devolution, as might have been expected and appears to have the potential to split. While the party does seem relatively willing to cooperate with other parties to secure power, there is a clear danger that the preferences and attitudes of its membership could put it at odds with the views of its electorate. For, far from being in the centre of British politics, the membership of the Liberal Democrats is clearly on the left of centre and would find it more congenial to strike a deal with Labour than with the Conservatives. In recent elections, however, the party's electorate has been of a more Conservative persuasion. Paddy Ashdown has done well to lead his party back into the central political game after the disaster of the 1989 European elections, but it will take just as much political skill to avoid the pitfalls that could accompany political success in future.

Appendix 1

THE SURVEY*

A twenty-page questionnaire was sent to a random national sample of 2,478 members of the Liberal Democrats immediately after the county council elections and the Newbury by-election held in the first week of May 1993. The survey was followed two weeks later by a reminder postcard, and a second questionnaire two weeks after that, to those who had not yet responded. A total of 1,675 completed questionnaires were returned. This represents a response rate of 68 per cent, slightly higher than in the two recent surveys of Labour and Conservative Party members, and only a little below that achieved in high quality face-to-face surveys of the general population such as the British Election Study.

The sample was selected from the database of members of the Liberal Democrats resident in Great Britain held at the party headquarters at Cowley St. Members were defined as those who had paid a subscription within the fifteen months prior to 30 March 1993. The list was ordered alphabetically within three groups according to whether the member was recorded as previously being a member of the Liberals, the SDP or neither, and then every thirty-third name was selected using a random starting point. Thirty questionnaires were returned because the respondent was dead, gone away, etc. and these have been excluded from the calculation of the response rate.

Parallel surveys of former members of the Liberal Democrats and members of the Liberal party and the SDP who had never joined the Liberal Democrats were also conducted at the same time as this survey of current members.[30] In addition, we conducted a survey of a sample of Liberal Democrat conference attenders in September 1993, the results of which will be reported later.

* This survey was financed by the Economic and Social Research Council, under grant no. R-000-23-3450. We are grateful to the council for their financial support, but it has no responsibility for the views expressed here. We are also grateful to Graham Elson, Keith House and the staff of the Liberal Democrats Membership Services department for assisting us in the selection of the sample and the administration of the survey, but, equally, they have no responsibility for the views expressed here, for the content of the questionnaire or for the conduct of the survey.

Notes

1 Membership statistics from the Liberal Democrats, Cowley Street, London.
2 Further details of the survey are presented in the appendix.
3 All figures for Labour Party members quoted in this chapter are taken from P. Seyd and P. Whiteley, *Labour's Grassroots*, Clarendon, 1992.
4 All figures for Conservative Party members quoted in this chapter are taken from P. Whiteley, P. Seyd and J. Richardson, *True Blues: The Politics of Conservative Party Membership*, Clarendon, 1994.
5 Figures for the Green Party are taken from W. Rüdig, L. Bennie and M. Franklin, *Green Party Members: A Profile*, Delta Publications, 1991.
6 The Liberal Democrats' membership records distinguish between those who were previously members of the Liberal Democrats, the SDP and those who were not a member of either. The response rate amongst these three groups differed and in particular was lowest amongst 'new' members who are on average less active. The results of the survey have been weighted to correct for this differential response and the figures quoted here and elsewhere in this chapter are based on this weighting. However, the Liberal Democrats' record of who was previously a member of one of the predecessor parties is known not to be entirely accurate and so in calculating figures for past membership we have relied on respondents' self-reports of their previous party membership and weighted these by past membership as recorded by the party itself. This procedure produces the following estimate of previous party membership: Liberal 48 per cent, SDP 13 per cent, new 39 per cent. Our figures contrast with the party's own estimate of the time that 50 per cent of their members were new.
7 In the Green Party, 47 per cent of all members are women.

8   Note, however, that Green Party members, two in three of whom have studied for a degree, are even more highly educated than Liberal Democrats.

9   See A. Heath, R. Jowell and J. Curtice, *How Britain Votes,* Pergamon, 1985, and A. Heath, R. Jowell, J. Curtice, G. Evans, J. Field and S. Witherspoon, *Understanding Political Change: The British Voter 1964–87,* Pergamon, 1991.

10 However, we should note that as many as 30 per cent of Liberal Democrats attended an independent fee-paying school for at least part of their secondary education. It seems likely that experience of public schooling is at least as common amongst Liberal Democrats as amongst Conservatives, 23 per cent of whose last secondary school was a private fee-paying school.

11 An identical proportion of the Greens, 19 per cent, are self-employed. Less than 5 per cent of Labour members are self-employed.

12 All figures for the electorate in this chapter are taken from the 1992 British Election Study. See A. Heath, R. Jowell and J. Curtice with B. Taylor (eds), *Labour's Last Chance? The 1992 Election and Beyond,* Dartmouth, 1994.

13 J. Curtice, 'Great Britain: Social Liberalism Reborn?', in E. Kirchner (ed.), *Liberal Parties in Western Europe,* Cambridge University Press, 1988.

14 The level of activism amongst Liberal Democrats does, however, seem to be higher than it was amongst the Greens in the wake of that party's breakthrough in the 1989 European elections. In autumn 1990, 32 per cent of Green members said that they had been fairly, very or extremely active over the past twelve months. In this survey 37 per cent of Liberal Democrats said they were at least fairly active.

15 Although the question reported here referred to election leaflets, it is clear that this activity is not necessarily confined to general elections. In response to a separate question about local party activity, 59 per cent said they had helped to deliver local party leaflets in the past twelve months. In contrast, only around one in four had helped at coffee mornings or occasionally attended party meetings.

16 As the survey was administered in the spring of 1993, five years ago would refer exactly to the period when the Liberal Democrats were founded.

17 The apparent decline in long-term centre party activity is discussed in W. Rüdig, J. Curtice and L. Bennie, 'The Membership Dynamics of British Centre Parties: From Liberals and Social Democrats to Liberal Democrats', in J. Lovenduski and J. Stanyer (eds), *Contemporary Political Studies 1995,* Vol. 1, Political Studies Association, 1995.

18 Note also that as many as 56 per cent of our respondents said that the party's general election performance was not as good as they had expected.

19 For details of the formation of the SDP see Ian Bradley, *Breaking the Mould: The Birth and Prospects of the Social Democratic Party,* Martin Robertson, 1981.

20 Although Labour Party members were not asked directly about Britain becoming part of a federal Europe, only 16 per cent of Labour members agreed with the statement 'Labour should resist further moves to integrate the European Common Market' with 72 per cent in disagreement.

21 Ninety-two per cent of Labour members but only 26 per cent of Conservative members would 'increase taxes and spend more on health, education and social

benefits'.

22 See J. Curtice, *op. cit.*

23 This figure is the proportion agreeing with the statement, 'Britain should reintroduce the death penalty'. Note also that combining the answers to questions which asked about the use of the death penalty in three different circumstances, Ahrendt and Young found that in the 1993 British Social Attitudes Survey no less than 65 per cent favoured the death penalty in at least one of the three circumstances. See D. Ahrendt and K. Young 'Authoritarianism Updated', in R. Jowell, J. Curtice, L. Brook and D. Ahrendt (eds), *British Social Attitudes: the 11th Report,* Dartmouth, 1994.

24 Equally, 37 per cent of Green Party members also adopt this view.

25 See D. Ahrendt and K. Young, *op. cit.*

26 Note also that there is little evidence here that unilateralism is strong in the party, even amongst former Liberals only one in three of whom endorse the view that 'Britain should have nothing to do with nuclear weapons'. In contrast, when asked the same question in 1990 nearly three-quarters of Labour members favoured this position.

27 For example, 52 per cent of new members believe that the privatised industries should be returned to the public sector while 34 per cent favoured the reintroduction of the death penalty for murder.

28 For a fuller analysis of what has happened as a consequence of the merger see W. Rüdig *et al., op. cit.*

29 Note in the light of our earlier comments that the temper of the party is closer to that of the former Liberal Party than to the SDP that the average score given to the old SDP was 56 but that for the Liberal Party, 71.

30 For some of the results of these surveys see L. Bennie, J. Curtice, and W. Rüdig, Liberal, Social Democrat or Liberal Democrat? Political Identity and British Centre Party Politics', in D. Broughton, D. Farrell, D. Denver and C. Rallings (eds), *British Elections and Parties Yearbook 1994,* Frank Cass, 1995, and W. Rüdig, J. Curtice and L. Bennie, 'The Membership Dynamics of British Centre Parties: From Liberals and Social Democrats to Liberal Democrats', in J. Lovenduski and J. Stanyer (eds), *Contemporary Political Studies 1995,* Vol. 1, Political Studies Association, 1995.

CHAPTER 7

Factions and groups

Vincent McKee

Assessments of factionalism within any party must take account of that party's constitution and internal culture. Such an examination is all the more necessary in the case of the Liberal Democrats, because these factors have substantially affected the development and conduct of factions and groups. The Liberal Party[1] provided an accommodating framework for autonomous groups, whereas the SDP was less accommodating.[2] The place and legitimacy of actions and groups were thus a contentious matter during the drafting of the party constitution, on account of the different cultures of the former Alliance partners. The question of legitimacy was raised by the American political scientists Frank P. Belloni and Dennis C. Beller, who noted that whereas parties and interest groups are an accepted part of the political process in western parliamentary democracies, factions have not gained the same respectability.

> The significance attributed to parties, and to a lesser extent, interest groups, is partly due to the greater obviousness of the structure and the activity of these organisations, in contrast to that of factions. And while the party has achieved the greater measure of such legitimacy, both party and interest group are now widely regarded as playing positive roles in the political process. It is just such perceived legitimacy that factions continue to lack.[3]

This chapter examines the nature of factions and groups in the Liberal Democrats and assesses their relevance to internal debates and power structures in the party. How the Liberal Democrats accommodate and manage group activity is the key question. It is also important to consider the extent to which factionalism is a consequence of the Liberal Democrats' constitution, policy direction and party culture. Generally, the constitutional and party organisation have taken priority over policy issues in internal

The author wishes to thank Mr David Allworthy of Liberal Democrat Head Office, London for providing material on membership and other activities of the party.

party debates, and divisions have centred around those questions, embellished by ideological currents. The emergence of ideological forums like LINk (Liberal Information Network) and Social Democratic Voice testifies to a degree of pluralism that is both inevitable and healthy for the party.[4]

Models and approaches

There are, broadly speaking, two models of party power. One is that of Roberto Michels, who argued that parties are controlled by influential elites, among which is the party bureaucracy.[5] The oligarchical authority of elites exceeds that of even the party leader, while rendering checking mechanisms irrelevant. Significantly, Michels, who was writing in the early years of the century, said little about constitutions, which were rare to parties of his time; nor did he pay much attention to grass-roots activists. Alternatively Maurice Duverger (1954) presents the democratic perspective of a *members' party*, where participatory mechanisms ensure a fair degree of rank and file activism.[6] Such enabling devices check leadership, and limit the influence of elites. Factions and groups are a potent manifestation of pluralism and democratic culture. The pluralist factor is significant in terms of power politics because this is an effective check against central regulation and authoritarian leadership. This chapter argues that factions and groups within the party do strengthen the accountability of the Liberal Democrat leadership, while also curbing party elites. It also demonstrates how the party constitution accommodates various independent and autonomous groups, who make a considerable input to policy and decision-making. Giovanni Sartori felt internal competition to be desirable and healthy, within limits.

> Parties cannot be, nor should they be monoliths. It can be conceded that fractionism might have a positive value. But the vindication of fractionism must be when appropriate, well justified.[7]

A framework for the analysis of factions and groups should be both broad and flexible. According to Rose, who regards internal discipline as a prime criterion for distinguishing between sub-party organisations, these groups may be considered in three categories.[8]

Single cause groups represent an extension of pressure group activity, and target party policy-makers. Many, though not all, take an ideological cum strategic position in party debates. *Tendencies* are composed of activists holding 'a stable set of attitudes', political predispositions, and, over time, a range of policies, according to David Hine in an article that drew upon the Rose thesis.[9] Central cohesion exists along with corporate structure, but not to the level of rivalling official party organisation. Significantly, tendencies rarely experience long lifetimes without incurring corporate and objective changes along with membership turnover, often in response to changing party events. *Factions*, by contrast, are solidly organised groups, extolling discipline, self-awareness, stability and loyal membership. This guarantees ideological and corporate cohesion, thereby underlining the difference in stability compared with tendencies. In addition to Rose's categories, the present author suggests a fourth category, the *institutional lobby*, which includes only official party bodies, such as auxiliary, research and staff groups, and the party press. It often assists one cause or another in party conflicts, but outside periods of internal division tends to serve the leadership regime of the time.

There are alternative perspectives on factionalism which have some relevance to this study. The American political scientist and historian, William N. Chambers, viewed factions as pre-party units in an evolutionary process.[10] Factions, he argued, are embryonic parties in that they constitute an element of the national political elite, with programmes, structures, members and leadership. Their existence is, of necessity, short-lived; they being prominent only for the duration of an election or single issue debate. Chambers was not greatly concerned with single issue groups, whose activities he viewed as an extension of outside lobbying, and easily accommodated under the umbrella of factions and pluralistic parties. This thesis has some relevance to Owenites within the post-merger SDP and Jenkinsites in Michael Foot's Labour Party (1980–83). It is otherwise inappropriate for understanding factionalism within British parties,[11] including the Liberal Democrats, which are parliament-orientated and accommodating of a range of single issue and wider ideological groups.

Ralph Nicholas viewed factions as essentially leadership–client bodies.[12] He defined factions as leader–follower groups, whose roles are dictated less by ideology and more by the bonds of loyalty and common purpose engendered by fraternal fellowships. Leaders depend on the fidelity of followers, in the legislature and within the party, while those followers can expect to benefit from patronage and offices falling within their leader's gift. Nicholas further contends that real political competition is based on factions, whose appeal to members' individual interests exceeds that of parties. Therefore at certain junctures, factional allegiances assume priority. Nicholas views factions as a product of conflict, thereby ensuring at least two factions in any party. However, factions also lack the corporate structures of parties, and endure only for as long as there is an effective leader and *raison d'être*.

The Nicholas thesis has much to commend it, especially with regard to charismatic leaders – past and present – holding established followings within their respective parties. Examples include the Powellites, Bennites and Haughey's faction in the pre-1979 Fianna Fail and Reverend Gerry Faldwell's Moral Majority crusade within the American Republican Party. However, Nicholas' thesis is not wholly applicable to British parties generally or the Liberal Democrats specifically. The idea that factions are constructed on the strength of mutual self-interest bonds is rather sweeping and underestimates the appeal of ideology in group loyalties. Also, several ideological factions like the Tribune Group, the Monday Club and the Chard Group all manage without dominant leaders.[13] Furthermore, Nicholas makes little distinction between the various levels of factionalism, thereby ignoring the degree of cohesion and structure characterising tendencies and factions.

Although the respective scholarly works of Sartori, Nicholas and Beller and Belloni on factionalism offer alternative frameworks, nevertheless Rose's formula defines and categorises the different layers of sub-party organisation in a fashion relevant to this study. The chief concern is with applying a framework that is suitable to the groups under examination. Most are single issue campaigns, with a few tendencies, inclusive of elitist fellowships, plus certain institutional lobbies, but–to date–no factions of the Rose definition. This framework offers a basis for analysing the types of body that the Liberal Democrats have generated over the course of their brief existence.

Character of the party

The constitution of the party engendered a strong leadership culture, which is more a Social Democrat than a Liberal legacy. It embraces the conventional assumption of a leader's primacy in policy articulation and presentation, while assuming the party's duty to provide orderly support.[14] Significantly, as with the SDP and the Liberal Party, the Liberal Democrats' constitution also confers special recognition on select policy and ancillary organisations, e.g. students, trade unionists and women. Recognition is at the discretion of the Federal Executive, and is consistent with SDP practice of encouraging malleable specialist groups. Generally a constitution can ensure either rank and file sovereignty or leadership control. The Liberal Democrats' constitution is eclectic in combining leadership authority with rank and file checks, but with the balance tilted towards the former. This analysis is supported by the following evidence.

First, the overall party character exudes coherence and discipline, both of which are necessary for electoral credibility.[15] These traits have been born as much of necessity–specifically early electoral disasters that threatened the party's existence–as has the constitution. Secondly, an important indication of balance has been the growing plurality of party groups and campaigning activists. There are now many unofficial groups concerned with single causes like the environment, animal welfare and health, as well as broader ideological tendencies campaigning on both strategic and programmatic fronts.

There is still a lack of clarity about the party's ideological direction, thus ensuring a continuation of earlier jousting between Liberals and Social Democrats. The combined efforts of prominent Liberals like Baroness Nancy Seear, former Liberal president Viv Bingham and radical councillor Tony Greaves, along with groups like LINk pushing for the adoption of an unequivocal Liberal identity have encountered opposition from Social Democratic quarters. The opposition has come from Jenkinsites on the Federal Executive, grass-roots campaigners like the former Social Democratic Voice (1989–93) and currently the leftist Chard Group. Additionally, there have been a growing number of 'mixed' organisations like the recently disbanded Beveridge Society and newly launched *Reformer* magazine, whose supportive bands of Jenkinsites and social liberals ensure a definite left-of-centre ethos. These lobbys are more easily squared with Social Democratic than traditional Liberal politics; although, as Curtice argues, social Liberals–who predominated in the Liberal Party of the 1970s and 1980s–also occupy centre-left ground.[16]

Local politics

Liberal Democrat strength in local government has been a positive inheritance from

Alliance and pre-Alliance days, the Liberals having developed a substantial base in town halls across the country throughout the 1970s and 1980s. This base has expanded to 5,035 councillors across Britain, with control of 54 councils, thus making it the country's second largest local government party behind Labour.[17] Inevitably such a heavy concentration of councillors in a party with only 24 MPs and 2 MEPs has ensured prominent recognition for councillors' interests in federal organisation and policy-making. The party constitution reserves two Federal Executive places for councillors, with three similar places reserved on the Federal Policy Committee. There has also been a substantial councillors' presence on all the federal committees. There were three councillors on the Federal Executive (1991–93), five on the Federal Policy Committee, three on the Conference Arrangements Committee (no reserved places), and a further three on the Finance and Administration Committee.

Predictably, the party's local government strength has boosted the Association of Liberal Democratic Councillors (ALDC). This semi-autonomous organisation – a Liberal inheritance – has long appealed to radical Liberals, especially at conference. It has been a principal protagonist of community politics programmes, thereby prioritising local campaigning in search of a national breakthrough. The style of its campaigns and radical approach of key activists like Tony Greaves and Gordon Lishman have caused strains with leadership.[18]

In the Liberal Party, ALC (as it then was) played a major role in policy-making while formulating campaigning strategy in the regions and on councils. Because of its high numbers of councillors and the unique platform offered at town halls, the organisation became a focus for radicals and other anti-establishment types. In the process, it became identified with various radical campaigns, such as environmentalism, Liberal CND and animal welfare. During the Alliance, some of the loudest rumblings against cooperation with the SDP came from radicals within this organisation. Moreover, after merger, Liberal radicals found a sympathetic base in ALDC, though avoiding the confrontational posturing of earlier times. The association's failure to pursue a coherent political programme over recent years may be partly attributed to the stable culture generated by Paddy Ashdown's leadership. Another reason is that organisational pressures resulting from the party's ever-increasing town hall strength prevents ALDC being as ideologically active as in earlier days.

ALDC operates from a headquarters at Hebden Bridge, Yorkshire, while enjoying additional independence and income from the sale of publications and revenues generated by its three thousand members. Previously it had a substantial input to the former Hebden Royd Publications, which in 1990 was replaced by Liberal Democrat Publications (Dorchester-based) as the party's official publishing division. This move has meant a diminution in ALDC's role in policy-making, although it continues to have a major input to party strategy debates. Its (inflation-linked) grant in 1993 came to £72,500. Generally, over the short lifetime of the Liberal Democrats, ALDC has reached a *modus vivendi* with the party establishment, allowing it to retain its traditional character in return for a positive profile.

Official organisations

The party constitution recognises two types of ancillary organisation, one being the specified associated organisation (SAO) and the associated organisation (AO). Recognition criteria for AO/SAO status is specific, and at the Federal Executive's discretion. It is usually conferred on organisations 'having a common link of interest ... [and whose] membership is limited to members of the party or non-members who support the fundamental values and objectives of the party'.[19]

By June 1994 eleven groups had received AO status from the Federal Executive. They were Green Democrats, Liberal Democrat Christian Forum, Liberal Democrat Eastern Europe Group, Liberal Democrat Engineers and Scientists, Liberal Democrat European Group, Liberal Democrat Health Association, Liberal Democrat Peace Group, Liberal Democrats Against Apartheid, Liberal Democrats for Gay and Lesbian Action, Liberal International [British Group] and One World Democrats.

AOs are specialist lobby groups led by activists whose initiatives stimulate party debates. Membership levels are small (rarely rising above 150), income is self-generated and publications vary from group to group, while officers and activities are usually centred on London. From the party's viewpoint, AOs constitute reliable fellow travellers who can be trusted to devise policy proposals without challenging leadership. Moreover, the patronage of party MPs, peers and other celebrities augments their malleability. So too does the threat of withdrawal of AO status, with all the lost privileges that would incur. The malleability issue is significant because independent organisations like the Chard Group have incurred displeasure from the party establishment. The group's application for AO status was refused by the Federal Executive in summer 1993. Clearly Chard's campaigns–especially over electoral cooperation with Labour–did not appeal to the party establishment, while its officers were viewed with unease.[20]

SAOs are similar to AOs, save that they are specified and protected by the constitution. In June 1994, there were seven SAOs, namely Liberal Democrat Parliamentary Candidates Association, Liberal Democrat Agents Association, Liberal Democrat Youth and Students, Liberal Democrat Women, Association of Liberal Democrat Trade Unionists, Association of Liberal Democrat Councillors and Liberal Democrat Ethnic Minorities Association. They are ancillary organisations, politically malleable, save for ALDC, and useful to the efficient workings of the party machine. With the exception of councillors and youth, the others are small in membership (rarely rising above 300) and London-orientated. They are promoted through party literature and conference facilities, while certain groups, i.e., Students and Women, are accommodated at head office. The latter two organisations are also recipients of Federal Executive funding to the tune of £25,500 and £2,500 respectively.[21] Additionally, SAOs are represented at Federal and other conferences, and entitled to present motions.

Several organisations are close to the party establishment, by way of officers sitting on Federal Executive or holding senior positions at head office. This relationship is underpinned by leadership patronage, e.g. Paddy Ashdown is president of the Parliamentary Candidates Association, while party parliamentarians attend SAO conferences and fringe meetings. This mixture of constitutional obligation, leadership sponsors and privileged status ensures conformity by minimising the capacity for dissent. The exception to this rule is the ALDC, whose radical character pre-dates the Liberal Democrats and which is not dependent on leadership approval for either prominence or projection.

Generally, both AOs and SAOs are, excepting ALDC, subject to regulation and approval by the party executive. Their specialisms make for diversity and informed debate, while members have risen from their ranks to the party's upper echelons. These official organisations contribute to the plurality of Liberal Democrat politics, while also ensuring both expertise and scrutiny in policy-making. They may be too dependent on party establishment favour, however, to be genuinely independent. Such a role belongs to the fringe of unofficial organisations.

Unofficial organisations

As the party has developed, so the number of unofficial groups has increased, with varying effects on the character of Liberal Democrat politics. Aims and causes vary, as does the influence of specific groups. Significantly, some are more open than others in their lobby activities. Generally, the unofficial fringe may be divided into three categories. First are lobby groups, whose activities are the life-blood of any democratic party. Secondly, there are ideological tendencies, which challenge orthodoxy in the party. Both types lack 'associated' status, but enjoy *de facto* recognition as legitimate associations. Third are the elite fellowships which are influential and exclusive.

In June 1994, there were seventeen informal groups acknowledged by head office. They were: the Beveridge Society,[22] Chard Group, City Liberal Democrats, Liberal Democrats Action Group for Electoral Reform, Liberal Democrat Animal Protection Group, Liberal Democrat Campaign for Land Value Taxation, Liberal Democrat Education Association, Liberal Democrat Friends of Israel, Liberal Democrat History Group, Liberal Democrat Humanist Association, Liberal Democrat Lawyers, Liberal Philosophy Group, Liberal Democrats Against Bloodsports, Liberal Democrats Inter-Faith Forum, Liberal Information Network (LINk), Liberal Summer School, Lloyd George Society.

Lobby groups

Most but not all groups are single issue lobbyists concerned with advancing their particular cause at conference, to the Federal Executive, Federal Policy Committee and general membership. They organise fringe meetings, publish newsletters, advertise and proselytise through the weekly *Liberal Democrat News*, and actively seek patrons from among party parliamentarians and enjoy the party establishment's approval. The size and profile of the groups varies according to scope, resources and membership. For example, City Liberal Democrats (membership 100) are chiefly concerned with recruiting business figures into the party, and also with advising parliamentary spokespersons on economic policy. LINk, with a combined total of 500 members and registered supporters, holds monthly meetings around London and Manchester and provides a forum for ideological debate through its pamphlets and booklets. Most groups originated in the Liberal Party, but there have been some Social Democratic groups, such as Social Democratic Voice (1989–93). The number of organisations inherited from the former Alliance parties, such as City Group, Friends of Israel and the animal welfare lobby suggests a continuity of political concerns extending through the Alliance into the new party.

Since 1992, the increasing debate over animal rights has ensured a high profile for the Green Liberal Democrats and its sister organisations Liberal Democrats against Bloodsports and Liberal Democrats Animal Protection Group. Given the party's traditional penchant for animal welfare and environmental causes, this concern has enabled grass-roots campaigners to take the initiative, thus forcing the leadership onto the defensive. Significantly, in 1994, a new pro-hunting lobby emerged, the Liberal Democrats Forum for the Countryside, which enjoys support among party councillors and activists in rural areas. Equally significant is the resourceful style of its campaign, which seems not to be limited by either money or up-to-date research. It remains to be seen whether this group will attempt to reverse party policy on hunting, the manner of such a campaign and its impact on party conference.

Two journals are worthy of special mention. The radical monthly, *Liberator*, serves as a voice for Liberal radicals inside and outside the party. It has assumed a greater importance since the demise in 1992 of another independent Liberal organ, the policy journal, *Radical Quarterly*. In September 1993, *Reformer* was launched. With an editorial board which includes Shirley Williams, David Marquand and Sir Ian Wrigglesworth, its contents give more reflection of party establishment thinking.[23]

Whatever may be the distance between unofficial groups and the party establishment, their informal status gives them considerable freedom. This was the consolation available to the Chard Group following Federal Executive's rejection of their application for AO status in June 1993. The rejection left Chard, LINk and other independent groups free to campaign without the obligation of keeping favour with the party establishment. Moreover, the party leadership is prevented from regulating the activity of the groups, as happened in the SDP.

Ideological tendencies

Most of these organisations are ideological in character, specifically LINk, Chard, the Liberal Philosophy Group, the Lloyd George Society and the former Social Democratic Voice. They are each concerned with ideological projection, and it is Liberal ideologues who have made most of the running. By contrast, Social Democratic campaigners have been less assertive, more accepting of their relatively small numbers at grass roots and willing to submerge their identity behind social Liberal causes like fiscal reform, civil liberties and European integration. Also, their enduring penchant for elite sets, rather than grass-roots campaigns – a consistent feature of the Jenkinsites since Labour Party days – had carried on into the Liberal Democrats.[24]   This trend is demonstrated by Jenkinsite reluctance to associate with grass-roots campaigners like Social Democratic Voice and the Chard Group. Instead, their preference has been for operating exclusive fellowships like the A1 circle, whose activities are examined subsequently. They are less beholden to the party leadership and have adopted a more contentious profile. Some have set themselves against the party establishment, but not to the point of total alienation, while the scope of activity varies from group to group, depending on resources, membership and strategy.

LINk is the longest-running vehicle for the propagation of ideological Liberalism. The group was established in 1983 to promote a distinctly Liberal view within the Alliance, and has continued its campaign into the Liberal Democrats. Policy debates and pamphlets have been one method, but there have also been public forums with prominent speakers from other parties, such as Calum Macdonald (Labour/Liberal Democrat cooperation) and Frank Field (poverty). The group enjoys the advantage of being an established organisation, with abundant Westminster patronage from Paddy Ashdown, Archie Kirkwood, Simon Hughes and Nick Harvey, all of whom are official sponsors. Moreover, several prominent LINk activists have been absorbed into the hierarchy, including Duncan Brack (Liberal Democrat director of policy until January 1995), Virginia Morck (former Chief Candidates Officer at HQ), and Alan Leaman (Policy Advisor to Paddy Ashdown until 1993, and Director of Planning and Strategy since 1995). Although this high-level patronage and access to the establishment may enhance the appeal of the group at grass roots and boost its importance as a debating forum, LINk has actually declined since the merger in 1988. Perhaps it is difficult for radicals to retain their sharpness when moving into the party establishment, while the organisation is also constrained. Such experiences are not confined to either LINk or the Liberal Democrats. The muted radicalism of Labour's Tribunites over recent years is largely owing to successive Tribune leaders, Michael Foot and Neil Kinnock. Equally, Conservative free market zealots, once the 'wild men' of Edward Heath's leadership tenure, came into more orthodox settings during the Thatcher years.

Social Democratic Voice, for some two years between 1989 and 1992 provided the only campaigning body for grass-roots Social Democrats. It was launched at the 1989 federal conference at Brighton by activists, mostly former SDP mergerites, worried at the predominance of Liberals in the new party. They feared that unless the banner was raised then the already slim Social Democratic character would be subsumed in a revamped Liberal Party. Founders included several former officers of the SDP's centre-left Limehouse Group, along with Charles Kennedy MP as patron. Social Democratic Voice raised a membership of over one hundred, ran conference fringe meetings, and published several policy pamphlets emphasising the equality theme alongside Liberal concerns with liberty. Its main thrust was to seek an explicit acknowledgement of Social Democratic values, especially in economic policy and international policies. Though treated with respect by the party establishment, its campaign achieved only modest gains, resulting in a transfer of energies to the Beveridge Society, *Reformer* magazine and Chard Group respectively in Autumn 1993.

Three problems bedevilled the best efforts of Social Democratic Voice. First, was the relatively small numbers of former SDP activists joining the merged party. According to a membership report in 1992, only 12 per cent of the Liberal Democrats' English membership had previously belonged to the SDP, as opposed to 36 per cent ex-Liberals and 52 per cent of no previous party.[25]   This relatively low proportion of former SDP membership limited the group's appeal from the outset. Secondly, was the ambiguous Social Democratic identity, which overlapped with the Owenites and certain streams on the Labour right. Among some Liberal radicals there existed a barely disguised hostility towards Social Democratic values, and from this quarter emerged an insistence on Liberal symbols for characterising the party. The name battle of 1988/89 and eventual dropping of 'Social Democrat' from the party's long title testified to an identity struggle, and one that resulted in the Social Democratic character, with tacit leadership approval, being quietly scuttled. Thirdly, and most crucially, was the refusal of the Jenkinsite cadre including Jenkins, Williams and Marquand, to give their support. Instead, Jenkinsites preferred the conviviality of the A1 circle to having any links with Social Democratic Voice, thereby leaving it on the margins. This experience highlights the ever-recurring dichotomy between elite lobbyists and outside campaigners, which is a feature of factional politics in most centre-left parties.

The Chard Group, with two hundred members, constitutes the party's most effective left-of-centre campaigning organisation.[26]   Although variably composed of Social Democrats and leftist Liberals, in fact the group's left-wing programme puts it squarely in the anti-establishment orbit. What is really significant about Chard is the cogency of its campaigns, which exceed the bounds of conventional Liberal Democrat politics. In addition to organising fringe meetings and promoting its case by way of published essays and pamphlets, Chard has also staged policy seminars and marched under its own banner in TUC demonstrations in 1993. Chard officers, specifically chairman Richard Denton-White, and treasurer Humphrey Deveraux have challenged for places on the Federal Exective and Policy Committee (1993 federal elections), but without success. This high-profile campaign forms a conscious strategy by Denton-White aimed at forcing the leadership into adopting clear left-of-centre policies.

Predictably, the Liberal Democrat establishment has steered a firm distance from the Chard Group, refusing its application for Associated status and labelling the group as maverick and its chairman as eccentric.[27] There is also the absence of Liberal Democrat MPs as patrons, plus a reluctance by parliamentarians and Federal Executive members to address Chard meetings or consort with them publicly. An exception is the former Stockport Social Democrat MP Tom MacNally, himself a Federal Executive member, who addressed Chard's Chichester seminar on City regulation in November 1993. Chard events have also attracted outside speakers like Labour's Frank Field and Richard Thomas of the centre-left Institute for Public Policy Research. The reality is that Chard caters for a left-wing school which is campaign-oriented and Social Democratic in outlook, without the Jenkinsite elitism. However, its programme contains more symbolism than policy, and it remains to be seen how far this trait will mature. More generally, it remains to be seen how far the party's plurality extends, in accommodating radicals from the Social Democratic and Liberal schools.

Elite fellowships

In addition to campaigning and ancillary groups, the party accommodates a small network of exclusive associations. These groups are usually of informal type, small in numbers, but composed of senior policy-makers and academics. From spring 1992 until 1994 there was the *Beveridge Society* that aimed to conduct research and publish pamphlets emphasising the redistributive and welfare themes of social Liberalism. Its founders consisted of some eighty members drawn largely from the remnants of the SDP's Tawney Society and associated Liberal quarters.[28] They included Sir William Goodhart, Roger Liddle, Tom MacNally and Lord Richard Holme, while patrons included Lord Jenkins, Lord Rodgers, Baroness Williams and Baroness Seear. Significantly, most former leading members have served on the Federal Executive or Federal Policy Committee. This was an establishment body, providing a forum for parliamentarians, academics and policy-makers, which underlines the extent to which an elite structure has emerged in the party. It failed to recruit a substantial ordinary membership, which may have limited its development in the party. Moreover, there were alternative outlets for reformist opinion, such as the *Reformer* magazine, the Lloyd George Society, LINk and the Chard Group. Finally, the return to Labour of some leading Social Democrats reduced the organisation's pool of prominent ideologues.[29]

Another elitist association is the *Gladstone Club*, which is composed mainly of businessmen, lawyers, academics and economists. Their convenor is Roger Pincham, a former Liberal chairman. Gladstonian activities are centred around monthly meetings at the National Liberal Club in London, where visiting speakers are frequently national figures like Nancy Seear and formerly Jo Grimond. It also runs seminars and publishes pamphlets, which are aimed at party and public policy makers. The Gladstone Club is essentially an inside lobby group seeking to influence economic policy in contrast to Chard's attempts to influence strategy from the outside.[30]

By far the most exclusive party fellowship is A1–a code for *Alliance First'*. This group has been inherited from the Alliance, where it was concentrated around a Jenkinsite coterie. Its select membership has included key Jenkinsites such as Jim Daly; Roger Liddle, Clive Lindley, Sir William Goodhart, David Marquand and Sir Ian Wrigglesworth, and Liberals of like mind such as Roger Pincham and Richard Holme. During the Alliance this group operated informally as an exclusive dining club, but from its ranks came funding for the merger campaign group.[31] That organisation was basically Jenkinsite, but also contained some Liberal members and operated in the Liberal Party. Interestingly, A1 sources produced funds to mount the successful 'Yes to Unity' campaign of summer 1987 inside the SDP.[32] Since the Liberal Democrats' inception, A1 has continued in a low-key role, acting as a voice for the Jenkins set at leadership levels. Its current membership is drawn from non-parliamentarians, but the practice is to invite MPs and peers to dinner gatherings. Various leadership figures have attended, including Nancy Seear, Roy Jenkins, Shirley Williams, Charles Kennedy and others. No rallies are held or membership lists published. Indeed, its influence centres around an elite circle from which have emerged Social Democratic nominees for party president and federal committees.

While elite dining clubs are not unique to the Liberal Democrats, A1's role is of special interest. First, its existence and activities are surreptitious, which hardly squares with the party's principle of open government. Secondly, it is not merely a dining club but an exclusive brotherhood with privileged access to leadership and the capacity to manipulate the federal party agenda. Thirdly, given A1's record of funding select causes, e.g. the Alliance merger campaign, it is to be wondered which select Liberal Democrat initiatives will be similarly endowed from the same quarter. The inclusion of so many A1 'fellows' on the *Reformer*'s editorial advisory board is significant.[33] More generally, the character and behaviour of A1 demonstrate the continuing role of Jenkinsites within the Liberal Democrats, and also their continuing taste for elitist clandestine politics.

Conclusions

The evidence here suggests that the Liberal Democrats have firm structures and a pluralistic culture, with competing groups and interests. These developments have resulted partly from the constitution, partly from the evolving culture of limited leadership, and partly from electoral pressures for survival. The constitution stands as a compromise charter, striking a balance between grass-roots activism and effective leadership. It imposes a basic discipline in pursuit of cohesion. However, beyond the latter, power is diffused, with appropriate checks limited the concentration of power on the central bureaucracy and Westminster leadership. This balance emanates in no small way from the Alliance experience of opposite extremes. The constitutionally limited leadership of David Steel, who was unable to control Liberal Assembly and grass-roots activists at certain key points, was counterpoised by an over-centralised SDP, led by the autocratic David Owen.[34] Accordingly, the party's constitution provides something close to Duverger's model of a participatory movement, with an accountable leadership and active outlets for grass-roots initiatives.

Independent groups appear to enhance the party's internal democracy and have generated a mixture of pressure groups, policy study groups, campaigning lobbies and a few ideological dissidents. While Michels' oligarchical model seems generally inappropriate to the Liberal Democrats, powerful elites are not entirely absent. The elusive A1 fellowship and other influential elites like the Gladstone Club and the former Beveridge Society, which may be likened to what Duverger called magic circles monopolise policy-making, choose candidates for party offices and seek to influence the leader.[35] Notwithstanding the influence of those fellowships, no omnipotent body exists with the power cited by Duverger and Michels. Moreover, among existing elites there is competition for influence and party positions, thus adding to the plurality of life at the party's higher echelons. The latter includes rival candidates' slates between pro-leadership supporters and radicals, for recent Federal Executive elections. This is equally true of the various ancillary and semi-official organisations harbouring under the party's wing. These groups serve a utility purpose while making an input to policy-making as well as providing parliamentary and other middle ranking personnel.

Thus the Liberal Democrats have learnt to live with a network of diverse voices from within. These have ensured a plurality of interests in a party not totally dominated by leadership. While groups vary in kind, their activities are the life-blood of an effective and growing third party. Moreover, such groups offer a link between the internal power politics of the party and outside campaign lobbying. Doubtless this factor enhances the general quality of policy debates as well as their value to the party's policy-makers.

Policy lobbying aside, sectarianism has not come to dominate Liberal Democrat politics. Indeed, the party's pluralist culture appears to be tempered by voluntary restraint on three counts. First, as recruitment figures show, only a small percentage of members hold group associations. The great majority stay aloof from ideological tendencies and play only a modest part in single issue groups. Actually, it is only at conference time that these groups make much contact with rank-and-file members. Secondly, as befits a campaigning third party, greater urgency is given to electoral tasks than to internal argument. The Liberal Democrats, having been born in the most inauspicious circumstances, have been careful of their image, lest the experience of near-annihilation in the 1989 European elections be repeated.[36] That factor alone has generated caution among ordinary members, who have preferred to keep a distance from factional politics. Thirdly, Paddy Ashdown's leadership appears to enjoy strong support among a cross-section of the membership. His leadership of the party from near-collapse in 1989 to a respectable performance in the 1992 general election, four subsequent by-election gains and local government electoral successes of 1993, 1994 and 1995 add up to an effective captaincy. Finally, Ashdown has avoided divisive attachments, embraced both the traditions of the merged party and maintained an effective media persona. All these factors show the Liberal Democrats to be enhanced by a leader with optimism and authority.

It remains to consider how effective groups have been in taking policy and strategic initiatives. The constitution accommodates lobbies from various quarters, including conference, the Federal Executive and Federal Policy Committee, as well as the state and regional organisations. Given that most major powers are concentrated on those authorities, it is thus to them that lobby groups have directed their campaigns. By necessity, all independent groups are organised along federal lines, including the ideological tendencies competing for influence at central levels. This suggests that, notwithstanding the party's federal structure, real power is concentrated at the apex of the federal party, with the state and regional parties counting for little in making strategy and policy.

It would seem that there are two categories of factional organisation, *insiders* and *outsiders*. The insiders are so-called because they enjoy either the ear of the leadership and the party establishment, and thus access to policy-making. That category includes those official organisations (AOs and SAOs) like the councillors (ALDC) and European lobby, along with elite fellowships like A1. Significantly, with the exception of ALDC, all other insider organisations are either sponsored by MPs or peers or otherwise dominated from Westminster, which is in itself a guarantee of influence. Outsiders represent dissident groups challenging policy or strategy from the outside, without substantial assistance from parliamentarians or the party establishment. The Chard Group, *Liberator* magazine and the former Social Democratic Voice lack influence with the leadership but have less responsibility and more freedom of action.

The issue of factionalism cannot be totally divorced from a party's standing in the wider political stakes, specifically its proximity to power. In that respect, recent electoral advances by the Liberal Democrats in local government have brought the party closer to the various realms of civic power than either the Liberals or the SDP before them. Moreover, it suggests that the perceptions of McKenzie and Rose that third party politics was inconsequential can no longer be sustained. Even Ingle's treatise of 1987 was pessimistic about the prospects of a serious third party role at any level of British politics.[37] Developments since 1993, however, hold positive, if uncertain omens. Equally uncertain is the effect this has upon the party's internal politics, including alignments and policy battles on which group tensions feed.

Until now, the Liberal Democrats have been preoccupied with ensuring their own survival and development. Their factional politics have reflected those priorities. The emphasis may shift towards external goals, which in turn may well generate a new and bolder level of factionalism, itself feeding off the carrots of public office. Such a spectacle is a possibility for the future, but remains some distance from the party's present experiences. There is even the potential for large-scale secessions in the event of a major centre-left realignment. Then the extent of the party's ideological diversity and the complexity of its internal politics would become clear.

Notes

1   John Curtice, 'Great Britain Reborn: Social Liberalism Reborn?', in E. Kirchener (ed.), *Liberal Parties in Western Europe*, Cambridge University Press, 1988.
2   Vincent McKee, 'Factionalism in the SDP, 1981–87', *Parliamentary Affairs*, Vol. 42, No. 2, 1989.
3   Dennis C. Beller and Frank P. Belloni, 'The Study of Party Factions as Competitive Organisations', *Western Political Quarterly*, Vol. 29, No. 4, 1989.
4   V. McKee, *Parliamentary Affairs*, op. cit.
5   Roberto Michels, *Political Parties*, introduction by S. Lipset, Collier, 1962.
6   Maurice Duverger, *Political Parties*, Methuen, 1986.
7   Giovani Sartori, *Parties and Party Systems*, Cambridge University Press, 1976, p.106.
8   Richard Rose 'Parties, Factions and Tendencies in Britain', *Political Studies*, Vol. 12, No. 1, 1964.
9   David Hine, 'Factionalism in West European Parties: A Framework for Analysis', *Journal of West European Politics*, Vol. 5, No. 1, 1982.
10 William N. Chambers, *Political Parties in a New Nation: The American Experience 1776–1806*, Oxford University Press, 1963, p. 29.

11 V. McKee (i) *Parliamentary Affairs,*1989; (ii) Fragmentation on the Labour Right 1975–87'; *Politics,* Vol. 11, No. 1, 1991).

12 Ralph W. Nicholas, 'Factions: A Comparative Analysis', in M. Banton (ed.), *Political Systems and the Distribution of Power,* Tavistock Publications, 1965.

13 Patrick Seyd, 'Factionalism within the Conservative Party: The Monday Club', *Government and Opposition,* Vol. 7, No. 4, 1972; *The Rise and Fall of the Labour Left*, Macmillan, 1987, Chap. 2; V. McKee, 'Conservative Factions since 1945'; *Contemporary Record,* Vol. 3, No. 1, 1989.

14 H. Drucker, 'All the King's Horses and all the King's Men, The Social Democratic Party in Britain', in W. E. Paterson and A. H. Thomas, (eds), *The Future of Social Democracy,* Clarendon, 1986; V. McKee, *Parliamentary Affairs, op. cit.*

15 In the European Parliament elections of June 1989, the Liberal Democrats scored only 6.2 per cent of the vote (no seats), coming fourth behind the Greens (15 per cent).

16 J. Curtice, *op. cit.*

17 Figures correct as of 31st December 1995.

18 For an insight into the thinking of Liberal Radicals, see Rachael Pitchford and Tony Greaves, *Merger: The Inside Story,* Hebden Royd, 1989; John Stevenson, *Third Party Politics since 1945: Liberals, Alliance and Liberal Democrats*, Blackwell/ ICBH 1993, Chaps. 4–7.

19 Liberal Democrat Constitution, Article 13.1.

20 Interview, V. McKee with Richard Denton-White (Chairman of Chard Group), 18 October 1993; Profile on Denton-White and Chard by Zerbanoo Gifford, *Liberal Democrat News*, 26 November 1993.

21 Liberal Democrat Federal Treasurer's Report, spring 1994.

22 By autumn 1994, the Beveridge Society had been wound down.

23 The *Reformer*'s editorial board members were listed in the inaugural issue as: David Boyle, Simon Bryceson, Tim Clement-Jones, Malcolm Dean, Bridget Fox, Sir William Goodhart, Mike Hancock, Chris Huhne, Alan Leaman, Professor David Marquand, Linda Murray, Rabbi Julia Neuberger, John Shipley, Matthew Sowremimo, Graham Watson, Baroness Shirley Williams and Sir Ian Wrigglesworth.

24 V. McKee, *Politics*, 1991.

25 Liberal Democrats Council for the Regions of England–Regional Membership Summary–Report by Keith House and David Allworthy (Membership Officers), 27 June 1992.

26 Interview with Denton-White plus a variety of internal Chard organisational and policy documents 1992–95 to which the author was granted access.

27 The author gained this impression from discussions with a number of senior party officers and Federal Executive members. The Gifford profile, *Liberal Democrat News* (1993), reinforced this view.

28 Interview, V. McKee with Anna Hodgets (secretary of the Beveridge Society), 12 October 1993.

29 Roger Liddle's likely return to the Labour Party is being spearheaded by a book on trade union reform co-written with Labour parliamentarian, Peter Mandelson.

30   Interview, V. McKee with Roger Pincham (chairman of the Gladstone Club), 10 May 1990. Also, the author was granted access to club meetings, plus Gladstonian newsletter and general documentation.

31   Interview, V. McKee with Clive Lindley, convenor of A1 (Alliance First), 4 June 1991; Unpublished Diary of Clive Lindley, Vol. 3, 1982–83; V. McKee, 'Factionalism among the Social and Liberal Democrats: Preliminary Assessments', *Radical Quarterly*, 17 September 1990, pp. 17–26; V. McKee, 'British Liberal Democrats: Structures and Groups on the Inside', in Patrick Dunleavy and Jeffrey Stanyer (eds), *Contemporary Political Studies*, PSA, 1994, pp. 1001–1022,

32   Interview with Clive Lindley; Lindley Diary, Vol. 3.

33   A1/Jenkinsite associates on *Reformer* editorial board included William Goodhart, David Marquand, Shirley Williams, Ian Wrigglesworth and Julia Neuberger.

34   J. Stevenson, *op. cit.*; V. McKee, *Parliamentary Affairs, op. cit.*

35   Duverger, *op. cit.,* pp.151–7.

36   V. McKee, *Op*, Cit., 1990.

37   Stephen Ingle, *The British Party System*, Blackwell, 1987, Chap. 8.

Part Three

Party Competition

CHAPTER 8

Political strategy

Don MacIver

Introduction

Political parties are always concerned about presenting their ideas, projecting their image, maximising their support and gaining political power. When an ambitious party which believes it has distinctive and original ideas has been denied power for decades, these matters become an obsession. This may explain why no other British party is so concerned, indeed obsessed, about political and electoral strategy as the Liberal Democrats. Moreover, probably no other party has such a keen, well informed and continuous debate about strategy throughout its organisation.

Liberal Democrats feel that the quality of their ideas, research, policy innovation and campaigning, not to mention their work in local government is not sufficiently recognised or appreciated and fails to bring them either the political credit or the parliamentary representation they deserve. The interest in strategy, therefore, reflects a concern to rectify this, to develop public awareness of the party's activities, raise its status, increase its influence and its share of power. It also reflects a determination to change the widespread perception that third parties in a two party dominant system were necessarily ineffective, permanently marginalised and without influence, merely a repository of protest votes.[1]

There are ways in which a third party can enhance its position. It can work with the major parties, exercising influence and negotiating a share of power, as the FPD has done in Germany. This is not a realistic option in Britain because the electoral system rarely produces a hung parliament and the Liberal Democrats have not yet been able to create a pattern of support which would produce such a result.[2] Alternatively a third party can simply challenge the other parties and increase its own share of the vote at their expense, as has happened in Britain, especially in local government, where this has been a moderately effective strategy for the Liberals and the Liberal Democrats.[3]

This strategy may also enable a third party to replace one of the major parties either by a steady build-up of support over a long period or in consequence of a major external intervention which damages one of the parties or disrupts the two party electoral pattern.[4] The Liberal Democrats seek to incorporate all these elements in their strategy.

The major problem facing the Liberal Democrats was that they have major party ambitions riding on minor party resources.[5] They always knew that their attainable objectives were constrained by their resources and opportunities as well as their ambitions. Before they could transform the party system they knew that they had to transform their own situation. They had to build a secure base of electoral support which they could only do by developing an effective campaigning capability and this required an efficient political organisation. Such an organisation could only be created by expanding their membership in order to generate the corps of activists and the income to sustain and operate it.

They had the advantage of inheriting from their Liberal antecedents an already well-tried approach to third party politics. This provided them with a ready-made political tradition and a set of perceptions, ideas and practical guidelines which gave them a particular view of their own role in the political system, as well as an understanding of the issues and problems facing them as a third party. This approach has three distinct components which can be identified as realignment, community politics and political cooperation, each of which has a separate origin and particular application. The party continues to deploy them separately but has also tried to combine them in an integrated campaign strategy. The origin and rationale of these strategies and their contribution to the development of Liberal Democrat campaign management are now considered.

Realignment

From the beginning the leader of the Liberal Democrats declared that his party's ultimate objective was to become the major alternative to the Conservatives as a party of government.[6] Thus Paddy Ashdown committed himself to a posture and style of third party politics which had been invented by Jo Grimond when he articulated the realignment of the left strategy in the 1950s. The realignment strategy was originally inspired by the belief that Liberal ideas were the only possible basis for effective opposition to Conservatism and that this could be provided only by the Liberal Party. It was based on the twin assumptions that the conditions which led to the decline of the Liberal Party in the inter-war years could be reversed and that the Labour Party could be split and sections of its support won over.[7] Although in many respects Grimond's vision may have been quixotic, it rallied the remnants of the Liberal Party, gave the party a new sense of purpose, provided inspiration for those sections of the electorate who were interested in Liberal ideas and attracted the attention of political commentators.

Since the 1950s the idea of realignment has been the principal motive force of third party politics in Britain. Its most bullish version would have the Liberal Democrats and their ideas providing the basis of a new centre-left movement as the Liberals did in the Alliance. A more realistic version sees the Liberal Democrats as a significant and politically influential, but relatively small component of a centre-left coalition.

While the idea of realignment thus raises some questions about the future of the party system, it also reveals a fundamental dichotomy within the Liberal Democrats about the nature of the party, the direction of its development and its relationship to other parties. On one side are the radicals who believe their party is a radical alternative to both the major parties; on the other are the centrists who see it as a centre party, which can construct a middle way between the major parties. The radicals believe the party must challenge the old parties and establish itself by its own efforts without being tainted by their failures, while the centrists feel that much can be gained by negotiating and working with other parties. There is general agreement in the Liberal Democrats about some form of realignment as an ultimate goal, but the precise nature of that realignment and the means of accomplishing it are contested issues. The issue here is between those who see realignment as a 'long march' taking many years, even decades to accomplish, and those who think there can be a 'quick fix'.

For Grimond, while the realignment strategy did not necessarily exclude the possibility of alliances and coalitions with other parties, it was primarily a strategy of challenge which was intended to win support for the Liberal Party and the Liberal message. For the radicals this meant ensuring that there was a full list of candidates in general elections, that all by-elections were vigorously contested and every possible support and encouragement were given to fighting local government elections. This has created a commitment to political campaigning and fighting elections which is now a major feature of the culture of the Liberal Democrats. Elections are perceived as opportunities to project the party, raise its profile and enhance its status in respect of news coverage and election broadcasts. For the more enthusiastic exponents of this approach, its appeal lies in its emphasis on the distinctive values of the party, the radicalism of its message and the excitement of the contest.[8]

On the other hand, the centrists and the advocates of realignment by negotiation, such as David Steel, believe that the main object is 'to break up the monoliths of the old parties' and use Liberal Democrat values to save Britain 'from the polarised extremes of right and left'.[9] Thus the strategy should be understood as one of compromise and negotiation which should exploit every opportunity of creating a 'moderate' alternative to Conservatives and Labour. This strategy, they believe, is more likely to succeed than that of the perpetual challenge of the radicals, which would simply condemn the Liberal Democrats to another generation in the wilderness. The radicals, most of whom eschew the centre party conception, tend to suspect that the negotiation strategy is a sell-out and a betrayal of their radicalism. This distinction between radical and centrist conceptions of the party and its political role has roots in the remaking of the Liberal Party in the 1950s and 1960s and, through the agency of the Alliance, has been intensified in the new party.

There are thus two significant dichotomies within the Liberal Democrats, first on the nature of the party and second on the approach to realignment and the strategy for achieving it. The issues of realignment strategy within the party, then, are contested in a framework produced by the two dimensions of radicalism – centrism and long march – quick fix. This framework reveals four different approaches to realignment within the party which may be identified as long march centrist, long march radical, quick fix radical and quick fix centrist (see Figure 8.1), each of which has a group of supporters within the party.

Long march centrists look to an extended attrition of public opinion with a slow build-up of support eroding the position of the other parties to a point where the structure of party politics is irretrievably altered. They are now a relatively rare breed amongst activists and leading figures in the party, but probably include some of the more passive members. Long march radicals see themselves as more active and more committed than the centrists and cheerfully accept the prospect of years of membership work and campaigning in by-elections and local elections until they have established a secure political base. For them the effort is its own reward and it is truly better to travel hopefully than to arrive disappointed. They are the most strongly supported of the four groups and include such well-known figures as Tony Greaves, Gordon Lishman, Liz Lynne and probably a majority of Liberal Democrat councillors, not to mention the bulk of local activists.

By contrast, the quick fix radicals hope for a major election breakthrough which would demonstrate the vitality of Liberal Democrat ideas and enable them to create a new political coalition for a programme of radical reform. They are a relatively small group, although they have included some distinguished individuals, probably incuding Jeremy Thorpe, who believed that 'one more heave' would make the breakthrough.[10] They now include LINk, possibly Paddy Ashdown and a number of MPs like Simon Hughes, who, while wishing to protect the separate identity of the Liberal Democrats, see the value of working with other parties, provided that acceptable arrangements can be made. The quick fix centrists, on the other hand, hope to find themselves in a pivotal position from which they could negotiate the introduction of proportional representation, which they believe would transform the prospects of the party and the future of the party system. They include David Steel, Richard Holm, Charles Kennedy and the Jenkinsites and are strongly represented at the national level of the party amongst MPs and parliamentary candidates and may still be the second largest group, although probably less well supported than they once were.

Conception of the party

Centrist	Radical	View of realignment
Long march centrist	Long march radical	Long march
Quick fix centrist	Quick fix radical	Quick fix

Figure 8.1 Approaches to realignment

The long march radicals are associated with a distinctive strategy, community politics, which they regard as a badge of identity and a political creed, if not the true faith. The quick fix centrists are also identified with a distinctive strategy called political cooperation, which they see as the most advantageous role for the party and the most rewarding approach to realignment. Community politics and political cooperation are the two most significant strategies inherited by the Liberal Democrats from the Liberal Party.

Community politics

The Liberal Party survived the lean years after the Second World War because of the concentration of Liberal support in certain areas at levels well above that which the party could expect in the country at large. The Orpington by-election victory in 1962, which many Liberals at the time regarded as a breakthrough, came after several years of grass-roots campaigning and local election advances. This led many Liberals to believe that it would be possible to reconstruct the Liberal Party and restore its position in British politics by building new concentrations of support on the basis of effective and well directed local campaigning. They recognised that Liberal electoral advances would depend on recreating a Liberal tradition and the habit of voting Liberal in areas where organised Liberalism had all but disappeared. This in turn entailed a major effort to renew the organisation, membership and campaigning activities of local Liberal parties. This belief in the effectiveness of grass-roots organisation and campaigning as a route to political power was the motor of the 1960's revival and the inspiration of the community politics strategy, which was adopted by the Liberal Party in 1970.[11]

Although in many respects it was inspired by 1960's radicalism, community politics was also an affirmation and embodiment of well-established Liberal ideas and principles.[12] Indeed, the enthusiasm of the Liberals and now the Liberal Democrats for community politics stems very largely from the belief that it uniquely expresses the underlying values and political style of their party. Liberalism has always been concerned with freedom, but modern Liberalism, since the late nineteenth century, has also been concerned with justice, conceived as a composite of equality, fairness and rights. As a philosophy, therefore, community politics is concerned with the distribution and the exercise of power, that power is exercised in the interests of people rather than elites and institutions, and that voters are not alienated from the making of public policy. It makes a trenchant and forceful critique of both state socialism and Conservative patrician elitism on the one hand, and of rotten borough local government on the other, that has never been effectively countered. It incorporates a philosophy of empowerment, of giving power to individuals and communities to enable them to protect and promote their own interests. Different powers are appropriate to different sorts of community and Liberal Democrats, therefore, have a programme of decentralisation which comprises both regional devolution and strong local government. Community politics is thus an approach to politics which includes a political philosophy, a critique of alternative approaches, a policy programme, a campaigning strategy and a technique for its implementation in everyday political action.

As a political strategy, community politics is based on the ideas of agitation, participation and mobilisation. It is intended first to heighten people's awareness of their own communities and the problems and needs that exist within them; and secondly, to encourage people to take and use power themselves. Following these principles the Liberal Democrats have created vigorous community politics groups in many parts of the country which have provided them with a large and generally reliable base of support in local government and enabled them to challenge the conventional wisdom that local issues and local action make little difference to the outcome of elections. The main instrument of the community politics strategy is the *Focus* newsletter,[13] which is produced by local Liberal Democrat campaigners and circulated several times a year in a recognised local area, such as a ward. It carries news of the local community, local political campaigns, relevant council business and gives the Liberal Democrat point of view on issues and policies. Critics dismiss this as an inefficient and time-consuming activity which does not necessarily win support for the party and may even alienate it. According to these critics, the political theory on which community politics is based is poorly understood by those who practise it; it is thus reduced to a mere technique for gaining political advantage by the manipulation of local grievances, which can easily be mishandled by the unwary, as in Tower Hamlets.[14]

If the main purpose of the community politics strategy was to raise the profile, increase the campaigning effectiveness and advance the electoral fortunes of the the party, it has had considerable success. It has also brought other benefits. Through the practice of community politics, activists gained a new enthusiasm for campaigning, learned new approaches and techniques and acquired an understanding of the nature of communities and how to address their needs. It enhanced the capability of the party nationally and locally by producing generations of new activists with the experience, skill and sensitivity to win public confidence and hold on to electoral support. It became an unrivalled means of presenting and promoting Liberal ideas, emphasising community as opposed to class and sectional interests, contrasting 'hands-on' commitment to the doctrinaire remoteness of the other parties.[15] Community politics, then, is a distinctive style of politics which has attracted considerable attention to the Liberal Democrats and enabled them to project a clear political image.

There are those in the party, however, who regard community politics as a primarily local strategy and, while advances at local government level are welcome, they are not sufficient. Their major criticism of community politics is that it has not enabled the party to win more parliamentary elections and significantly increase its representation in the House of Commons. Their expectation was that community politics would develop a base of support and a habit of voting which could be converted into votes for a Liberal Democrat candidate at parliamentary elections. They also believed that by taking control of district and county councils, they would demonstrate that Liberal Democrats could exercise power and thus make the party more credible to voters at parliamentary elections. Finally, they thought that links could be created between local and national issues which could be exploited at parliamentary elections, while the techniques of community politics could be adapted and applied to parliamentary campaigns, particularly at by-elections and target seats in general elections. They argue that these links between local and national levels have failed to materialise and there is not much evidence of correlation between local government success and parliamentary success. While the party's strength in local government is mainly in the home counties and the south west and in a broad band from Merseyside to Northumberland in the north with significant pockets elsewhere, its parliamentary strength is mainly in the Celtic fringe and the west of England. For those who are anxious to advance the fortunes of the party in parliament, therefore, community politics has not yielded the results expected of it. Some have complained that the strategy has established a perception of the Liberal Democrats as a local party rather than a national one, creating a glass ceiling, which prevents the conversion of local government majorities into parliamentary majorities.

Paddy Ashdown and others have forcefully denied the existence of a glass ceiling and argue that disciplined campaigning and effective engagement in the issues will eventually bring success. They would point out that the Liberal Democrats and their predecessors have had a long run of spectacular success at by-elections, established themselves as the first party of opposition in many constituencies in the 1980s and achieved a modest success in the European elections in 1994. All these advances, they claim, are largely owing to the effectiveness of community politics.

Community politics may be reviewed from time to time, but it has powerful and committed advocates in the party, including many of the professional staff, several MPs and a considerable number of the Federal Eexecutive. The most significant and articulate lobby for community politics, however, is the Association of Liberal Democrat Councillors (ALDC), which was established to provide back-up information, advice, training and campaign materials to local parties engaged in community politics. The staff and most of the leading members of ALDC are committed to the realignment of the left and, over the years, they have persuaded many others that there is no quick fix way of achieving it.

Political cooperation

While the community politics strategy has always been associated with the grass roots of the party, where it has been nurtured and developed, the cooperation strategy originated in the parliamentary party leadership and has been particularly associated with David Steel.[16] It was inspired by Grimond's ideas about realignment of the left and was actually conceived as a way of operationalising them. Where community politics is a strategy of challenge and contention, however, the cooperation strategy is more ambiguous and more complicated, offering the prospect of two parties cooperating and even sharing power to accomplish the objectives which they had in common. This would not preclude competition between the parties, and Liberal Democrats intend to secure the election of as many MPs as possible in order to maximise their influence in Parliament.

The key assumptions of the cooperation strategy are that, while the Liberal Democrats are not likely to gain a parliamentary majority on their own, a hung parliament is a strong possibility and, in such a situation, the Liberal Democrats could expect to play a significant role. The strategy comprises two distinct though not necessarily conflicting approaches. These may be described as, first, parliamentary cooperation, which includes participation in a governing coalition or simply maintaining a minority government by parliamentary agreement; and secondly, electoral cooperation which includes any kind of arrangement, formal or informal, with other parties at elections. The problem with the strategy is that it opens deep divisions amongst Liberal Democrats about the nature and image of their party, the direction it should take and their views about relations with other parties.

Within the party, therefore, the political cooperation strategy generates considerable controversy. In the first place, it is said to limit the ambitions and the prospects of the party, condemning it to a perpetual third party status, offering 'a balanced niceness rather than a forthright alternative'.[17] Secondly, many Liberal Democrat radicals believe that the idea of political cooperation characterises their party as a centre party, which they strongly repudiate. Some, particularly amongst former Liberals, also feel that the independent assertive radicalism which they believe should be the hallmark of the party, has been diluted or even discounted in favour of a more bland and moderate image.[18] Thirdly, there are those who think that the pursuit of coalition or power sharing has become an end in itself rather than a means to an end, with the consequence that efforts to project the party as an independent force with a distinctive political position fail to gain credibility.[19] Fourthly, the fact that the Liberal Democrats are the lead opposition in both Conservative and Labour held seats, complicated by their expressed willingness to share power with either of these parties, further intensifies these difficulties and undermines the primary objective of realignment.[20] The cooperation strategy thus mercilessly exposes the difficulties facing the Liberal Democrats in a political system where politics means 'picking sides'.[21]

A further problem facing advocates of the cooperation strategy is that there is little practical experience on which to assess its validity. The Liberal/SDP Alliance was considered by many, including its architect David Steel, to be a classic example of cooperation, but it created immense difficulties for both partners and few would now regard it as a model for the future. The most recent experience of parliamentary cooperation, the Lib/Lab pact, is seen by some as a missed opportunity, by others as simply a misjudgement, but by few as a triumph and it is in any case now beyond the direct political memories of most leading Liberal Democrats.[22] It is clear, nevertheless, not only that Liberal Democrats would welcome a power-sharing role, but also that they have tried to create opportunities to perform it. Much thought has been given to the problems of governing without a majority, but even the very consideration of the issue creates problems.[23] It exposes the negotiating weaknesses of the Liberal Democrats and highlights the dilemmas they face in choosing with whom to cooperate: dilemmas which are not resolved by devices like 'equidistance' or declarations that they will cooperate with any other party to end confrontational politics. Nor are they likely to be resolved by insisting on proportional representation as the condition of political cooperation, for example in a hung parliament.

Liberal Democrat enthusiasm for proportional representation (PR) could be regarded as an acceptance by the party that it is unable to win a general election under the present electoral system, facing potential Liberal Democrat voters with the 'wasted vote' dilemma. The Liberal case for PR has always been based on the unfairness of the electoral system which gives the Liberal Democrats a consistently poorer ratio of MPs to their popular vote than other parties. The argument for PR, however, assumed the political preferences of the electorate were relatively static, whereas, if Liberal Democrat support continues to rise and to concentrate in certain areas, as it has done in the 1990s, then there might come a point where the number of Liberal Democrat MPs more accurately reflects the strength of the party's popular support. Having said that, however, long sufferance at the hands of the existing electoral system has made the party's belief in PR a matter of principle for which it has now built up a considerable level of public sympathy and acceptance. If the party had the opportunity to introduce it and then failed to do so, many believe that it would lose credibility. For these reasons alone, therefore, the Liberal Democrats may now insist on PR as a prerequisite to cooperation. It has always been considered in the past as a condition of coalition, but attitudes in the party now appear to be firmer.[24]

The question remains of with whom the party should cooperate. Within the party this is a delicate matter because many believe that there is a great deal to be lost by leaning publicly towards one or other of the major parties.[25] The question has been resolved by adopting a position officially described as equidistance, meaning that the Liberal Democrats are independent of both the other parties, but willing to work with either of them in appropriate conditions. There is some support in the Conservative Party for PR, but on the face of things at least, the Conservative Party rejects the idea of cooperation. The Labour Party makes similar disclaimers, but it is more likely to accept both PR and cooperation simply because of the arithmetic of recent election results. This arithmetic has enabled the Conservatives to win successive parliamentary elections since 1979 with narrow constituency pluralities, largely by default of a divided opposition.

In 1992 a swing of just over 1 per cent away from the Conservatives would probably have produced a hung parliament and created a coalition situation. In the European Parliament elections of 1994 a swing of about 1.5 per cent away from the Conservatives would have cost them up to ten seats. Of the first two dozen parliamentary seats that would be most likely to fall to the Liberal Democrats, most (about twenty) are now Conservative held. Similarly, the overwhelming majority of Liberal Democrat MPs face a primarily Conservative challenge. Moreover, Liberal Democrats' best prospects are in Conservative marginals rather than Labour marginals. In all these situations Labour can prevent the Liberal Democrats winning, but not win itself. Labour candidates are themselves faced by a reciprocal Liberal Democrat threat in many of their own marginals. By taking votes and seats from the Conservatives, the Liberal Democrats relieve the pressure on Labour and enhance the possibility of a Labour or a Lib/Lab government. Thus the real battle for the Liberal Democrats is with the Conservatives, who are most likely to block a Liberal Democrat advance. On these terms Labour are in many respects natural allies rather than enemies. If cooperation means anything, then, it must mean cooperation with Labour.

Developing an integrated campaign strategy

The objective of the Liberal Democrats was to achieve office through either coalition or realignment or perhaps through a single party majority in the long run. In December 1988, a few months after the creation of the new party, the Federal Executive reaffirmed that the strategy outlined by the leader, to aim to become the alternative to the Conservatives, was the correct strategy for the longer term. In pursuit of these objectives the only strategies readily available to the party at first were community politics and political cooperation. The Federal Executive gave consideration to how these could be better coordinated and how a new strategic framework could be gradually evolved which could absorb them both.[26]

The Federal Executive expressed a preference for crisp and simple themes which would create a clear image and identity for the party. It stressed that the party 'must take sides' on major issues and adopt strong distinctive and relevant positions. In an apparent downgrading of the political cooperation approach, it ruled out pacts with other parties and any possibility of campaigning for the balance of power. Instead it noted the need for clear objectives, professional use of resources, effective communication, and radical policies. It took a favourable view of the principle of targeting parliamentary seats and applying the techniques of community politics in parliamentary campaigns. It emphasised the interdependence of campaigning at all levels and the need to integrate them effectively.[27]

In the early years of the party the efforts to develop an integrated campaign strategy encountered a number of problems, deriving largely from the party's origins. The turbulent and acrimonious end of the Alliance followed by the prolonged and undignified demise of the SDP left a poisoned legacy to the Liberal Democrats. The new party faced a humiliating decline, an acute financial crisis, an identity problem and a serious lack of credibility. Its share of electoral support dropped sharply, it lost ground in local elections, it lost by-elections which it could have won and its results in the 1989 European Parliament elections were disastrous. This collapse in performance was matched by a collapse in morale as the party experienced a fall in membership, a crisis of political identity and a fading of its public image. Fortunes began to improve in 1990 as Paddy Ashdown's leadership began to make an impression, but plans were already in hand to recover and strengthen the party's position.[28]

These plans addressed two issues. First, the recovery of the party's electoral support followed by the development and consolidation of regional strongholds, where the party could concentrate support and win seats. The hope was that this would enable it to make a breakthrough in these regions and gain enough seats to impair the ability of the other parties to generate majorities in the British electoral system. These areas include the Highlands, the Scottish borders, parts of Wales, the west of England and the West Country, but there are others in rural England, the suburbs and even the inner cities. The principal objective has been to build a strong and effective organisation in these areas with the campaigning capability and electoral support to enhance the chances of victory.

The second issue was the need to sharpen the party's image which had been seriously damaged by the squabbling which characterised its creation. It was felt that the party had an original and distinctive political position which was reflected in its policies on most issues and that this must be clearly defined and projected in its publicity and campaigning. The Policy Committee took the view that one of the party's major resources was 'the talents and expertise and imagination of the hundreds of policy experts within the party' and that 'this wealth of knowledge' should be channelled into a definition of the party's fundamental values and beliefs.[29] This resulted in the production of a paper entitled *Our Different Vision* which was intended to deal with the complaint that people did not know what the party stood for and to sharpen the image and raise the profile of the party in the media and the public at large. The themes developed in this paper became the basis for preparations for the 1992 general election campaign. It was agreed that the party should concentrate on a few selected issues which would create a distinctive position which could be easily conveyed to the electorate.

By and large the Liberal Democrats had three major objectives in the early 1990s. The first objective was to secure the future of the party, which meant holding on to its seats and share of the vote, fighting a good election campaign and being seen to do so and demonstrating that they were a real force in British politics. The second objective was to establish the Liberal Democrats as the *only* third party and a real challenge and alternative to the major parties which meant outstripping all the minor parties (the Greens, the Liberals and the SDP), creating a clear political identity and projecting a strong and distinctive image. The third objective was to renew the strength and effectiveness of the party which meant ensuring the vitality and unity of its organisation, the credibility of its claims and policies and the quality of its leader's performance. The Liberal Democrats hoped that the election campaign would enable them to address the problems which had attended the party since its birth and finally resolve them.[30]

The party began to prepare for the general election in June 1989 with a report from the Campaigns and Communications Committee which stressed the need for a clear party strategy. The strategy which emerged focused on a small number of key issues, targeted a few winnable seats and promoted the leader as much as possible. By October 1990 the Policy Committee began work on the manifesto, which it intended to be 'radical, convincing and distinctive'.[31]

One of the unifying features of the campaign strategy was the selection of key issues and target seats. The key issues were the operationalisation of the party's efforts to achieve a distinctive identity and image. These key issues, which became known within the party as the five' E's were electoral and constitutional reform, education, environment, economic policy and Europe. The five 'E's were an attempt to show what the distinctiveness of the Liberal Democrat approach meant in practice and to establish Liberal Democrat 'ownership' or primacy within certain policy areas. Targeting was intended to improve on the relatively poor results of national campaigning in the past and thus overcome the problem of having an even spread of support by developing concentrations of support which were potential strongholds. Targeting meant emphasising local issues and applying the methods and techniques of community politics which, its exponents believed, had been fully proven in local elections and by-elections. The promotion of the leader was simply a reflection of the wholehearted belief within the party that Paddy Ashdown was their strongest asset.[32]

The strategy which the Liberal Democrats developed for 1992 included three other lines of attack.[33] First, that the 'wasted vote' problem, which had so beset the Alliance and the Liberals in the past, should be dealt with by taking the attack to the major parties and highlighting the opportunities and votes they had wasted while in power. Secondly, that the Liberal Democrats should contest every seat in order to maximise their share of the national vote. Thirdly, that they should run a forward and aggressive public relations campaign and seek to ensure good media coverage. There were two points concerned with the defence of what were seen as Liberal Democrat weak spots. The first was the question of political cooperation and how they would handle a hung parliament and a balance of power situation. The second was how they would respond to the Conservative charge that the Liberal Democrats were simply a Trojan horse for a Labour government.

Support in opinion polls appeared to rise during the campaign, but the Liberal Democrats ended with a reduced share of the vote and a net loss of seats compared with 1987. While this result was disappointing, they took comfort from a high profile campaign which afforded ample opportunity to present their ideas. They projected a strong image, which made some impact. They offered a distinctive programme, emphasising education, environment and constitutional reform more than any of the other parties. Their most realistic expectation probably was that their campaign would bring them to the notice of the electorate and that the result would provide a base on which they could build support for the future. In this respect they had some cause for encouragement. Even before the campaign ended, the *Guardian* dismissed Labour's claims to victory with the verdict that 'Mr. Ashdown is the only winner of this campaign. ... The movement and the arguments have all come from the Liberal Democrats. They are the movers and shakers.'[34]

Reassessing cooperation

In their own view the Liberal Democrats are not only a party of ideas, like the old Liberals, but a potential party of government, even if only in a coalition. During the 1992 election campaign, however, they made an unmistakable and possibly premature bid for a share of power which may have been counterproductive. This bid may have driven some sympathetic electors to the Conservatives, as many Liberal Democrat activists believed. Paddy Ashdown blamed voters' fear of Labour for the late swing, a 'visceral fear' that was acknowledged by the Labour leadership.[35] Despite these disappointments and the partial recovery of the Labour Party, however, the 1992 election did establish the Liberal Democrats as a significant national party. Moreover, their position continued to consolidate and strengthen, their greatest successes being in local government. They made significant local election gains in 1993, 1994 and 1995, substantially increasing their influence at this level and now exercising power or a share of power in more counties and districts than ever before. After the 1995 elections they were in control of more local authorities than the Conservatives.

Whether or not the 1992 election campaign was a success (itself a matter of debate within the Liberal Democrats), it failed by and large to resolve the vexed question of party strategy. There were perhaps fewer supporters of political cooperation after the election than before it and possibly also an awareness of the need to refine the application of the community politics approach. As for the integrated campaign strategy, its exponents believed that it had been a success, but the sceptics argued that it demanded more in coordination and resources than the party could realistically manage.[36] Paddy Ashdown rang some alarm bells with the Chard speech, calling for a new attempt at the realignment of the left starting with a 'coalition of ideas' to oppose the Conservatives.[37] Many senior party members and professionals endorsed Ashdown's view but demurred at its timing and formulation. The fear was expressed at a very high level that Labour would now be even more encouraged to move onto Liberal Democrat ground and take over 'our agenda lock, stock and barrel'.[38] There was a call to keep the policy agenda moving forward and to open a new debate on strategy within the party so that all members had a chance to contribute to the development of the party's position. The result of this was a broad-based and wide-ranging consultative exercise on strategy followed by a full airing of the issues at party conference. This revealed an overwhelming preference amongst members for a distinctive and independent Liberal Democrat approach, challenging the other parties, rejecting any special deals with Labour and reserving political cooperation for situations where Liberal Democrats could have a share of power.[39]

This debate set the tone for the party's approach to political cooperation over the next three years, placing the emphasis on the independence of the party while welcoming opportunities to work with other parties for common purposes. At the 1993 party conference Paddy Ashdown declared that the Liberal Democrats were on 'the verge' of a 'big time' and should not betray their principles in the quest for votes. Any realignment, and by implication cooperation, on the left of British politics must wait until the outcome of the reform and modernisation process in the Labour Party was clear.[40] At the 1994 conference, when Paddy Ashdown clearly signalled his willingness to abandon equidistance, perhaps in the following year, he emphasised that his decision would depend on how far and how quickly the Labour Party moved.[41] During 1994 and 1995, with the accomplishment of equal membership voting rights, the reform of Clause Four and the apparent success of Tony Blair's new leadership style, the Labour Party's rigidities seemed to become less pronounced. This first caused Liberal Democrats concern that Blair's shift to their ground would cost them support but then led them to a renewed interest in the possibilities of cooperation, with considerable evidence that this was reciprocated by the Labour Party.[42] By the end of 1994, Liberal Democrat and Labour councillors were working together in coalition administrations in about twenty local authorities, while some constituency Labour parties showed a willingness to make common cause with the Liberal Democrats against the Conservatives.[43]

Inter-party dialogue received a considerable boost from the invitation to the Liberal Democrats to contribute to the work of the Labour Party's Commission on Social Justice and the reciprocal invitation to the Labour Party to participate in the Liberal Democrat-sponsored Dahrendorf Commission on the economy.[44] Tony Blair called for 'a dialogue of ideas' and expressed his willingness to work with the Liberal Democrats in a hung parliament. He did not take a 'tribal view' of relations between the parties of the left and he appealed to the Liberal Democrats to work more closely with the Labour Party.[45]

A newly formed group of Labour MPs, seeking to promote political cooperation, urged the Liberal Democrats to 'come off their absurd perch of equidistance' and form a 'popular front of the mind' against the Conservatives.[46] These overtures received a cautious welcome from Paddy Ashdown who said that, while Labour would be judged by its actions rather than its words, the two parties should cooperate where they agreed on policies and political objectives.[47]

Others, like Alan Beith and Simon Hughes, took the same view but were more insistent about the independence of the party and more cautious about moving closer to Labour. There was in fact considerable resistance to any relaxation of equidistance, on the grounds first, that the difference between the two parties was a 'fundamental difference of philosophy'; secondly, that moving too quickly could split the party, and thirdly, that it might cost the party the support of voters who were attracted by its distinctive image and policies.[48] After the 1995 local elections, however, relieved that they were continuing to advance in their target areas despite the revival of the Labour Party, some Liberal Democrats took a complaisant view of equidistance, arguing that they could now afford to abandon it. Moreover, there was a growing chorus in the press advocating a convergence with Labour, some arguing that the Liberal Democrats had a responsibility to construct a left of centre coalition to get the Conservatives out.[49]

A certain divergence of view was emerging within the party on this issue, with long march radicals in favour of maintaining the party's independence and quick fix centrists urging a closer relationship with Labour.[50] By the summer of 1995 there was mounting evidence that the party at national level was ready to relax its stance on equidistance and that the leadership was preparing to move to a position from which it would be possible to cooperate with the Labour Party. The chosen strategy was to emphasise the party's distinct identity and exclude any possibility of cooperation with the Conservatives, leaving open the question of working with Labour.[51] In addition to a new policy paper, position papers were being prepared on such topics as making coalition government work, negotiating in a hung parliament and enhancing the political power of third parties. Moreover, a discrete but widely based consultation was undertaken on political cooperation with Labour, partly to inform the leadership of opinion in the party and partly to prepare for a full debate on party strategy at the annual conference in September 1995.

Conclusion

Once they had overcome the initial setbacks and the difficulties which attended their early years, the Liberal Democrats made significant advances in electoral support. They have already reshaped the structure of party politics at the local government level, and they are gradually building substantial regional strongholds at the parliamentary level. Indeed, the Liberal Democrats now claim to be the only truly national party in the sense that they have a significant share of the vote in all regions of the country. They also have an expanding membership and an increasingly effective organisation, which enables them to take better advantage of this growing support. Their progress now fuels speculation not only about their own prospects but also about the future development of the party system. Both of these depend to some extent on how other parties perform and on the contingencies of political events and the opportunities they provide. The Liberal Democrats' acute consciousness of the importance of political strategy, however, increases the probability that they will effectively exploit such opportunities and maximise their potential.

The Liberal Democrats inherited a serious concern about political strategy from the Liberals, and the keen interest and high priority given to it at all levels of the party were clearly demonstrated during the post-election consultation exercise in 1992. This exercise helped to crystallise the elements of the party's strategy and gave some clear pointers to the emphasis and direction it is likely to assume. The belief that sincere commitment to a challenging statement of Liberal ideas and policies was in itself a sound basis for electioneering was in essence the strategy of Jo Grimond. This has now given way to a more calculated, self-critical and goal-oriented approach to campaigning, without losing sight of the importance of ideas or the needs of people and communities. In this new and constantly evolving approach to strategy, community politics has become, if anything, more important. The theories and techniques developed over the past thirty years have been refined and applied as appropriate to a range of situations from local campaigning to parliamentary by-elections and general election targets. Political cooperation has waxed and waned in importance over the years, but it too has now been absorbed into a comprehensive and integrated political strategy.

Political cooperation, however, remains at the heart of the problem facing the Liberal Democrats as a third party. Skilful, well directed and dedicated campaigning could raise the profile and the political influence of the party; it could also increase its electoral support and thereby its parliamentary strength; and it could ensure that the growth of support for the party is not a transient phenomenon. Ambition and commitment may spur the party to greater successes, but political change and realignment are likely to be gradual. Replacing the Labour Party is much too sanguine an ambition in the short or medium term and may never be a realistic one. Even at its lowest ebb in the mid-1980s, the Labour Party held about ten times as many parliamentary seats as the Liberal Democrats or the Alliance. It would be more realistic, therefore, for the Liberal Democrats to work for a new centre-left political formation, on the assumption that 'realignment... is a long-term tendency of our time'.[52]

This need not involve any formal arrangement with the Labour Party or any relaxation of electoral competition, but it probably would require an understanding, based on common political interests, to work together in certain defined circumstances. Such circumstances would arise in the event of a hung parliament or any other situation in which no party had a majority. Then political cooperation would become a necessity. There would be considerable risks as well as potential rewards, and there could be a high price. The Liberal Democrats do represent a particular blend of political values, attitudes and policy preferences whose adherents could be alienated by certain kinds of arrangement with Labour. Liberal Democrat leaders and activists, who develop and direct strategy, tend to be generally left of centre on the broad range of public policy. Liberal Democrat voters, however, while being generally to the left on social policy, tend to be more right of centre on economic and defence issues. Some of this support could be alienated if the Liberal Democrats in a coalition compromised these policies. Thus Liberal Democrats might yet find that, since political cooperation demands careful and judicious management, it could in practice lose as many votes as it gains and might even cost them votes across the whole range of their electoral support.

Notes

1 This perception, endemic in the British press until the 1990s, is also well supported in the academic literature. See M. Duverger, *Political Parties*, Methuen, 1986; R. MacKenzie, *British Political Parties*, Heinemann, 1963; R. Rose, *The Problem of Party Government*, Penguin, 1974; G. Sartori, *Parties and Party Systems*, Cambridge University Press, 1976 .

2 Jeremy Josephs, *Inside the Alliance*, John Martin, 1983, pp. 214–224.

3 H. Stephenson, *Claret and Chips: The Rise of the SDP,* Michael Joseph, 1982, pp.98–100; P. Pulzer, *The Slow Death of Labour*, Unservile State Papers, No. 32, Hebden Royd, 1985; R. Rose, 'A New Type of Party System', *Daily Telegraph*, 11 June 1983; I. Crewe, 'Is Britain's Two Party System about to Crumble?', *Electoral Studies*, Vol. 1, 1982.

4 Peter Pulzer, *op. cit.*; David Steel, *Labour at 80: Time to Retire*, Liberal Publications Department, 1980.

5 Jo Grimond once said that the Liberal Party was like a car with 'a magnificent body of policy but too small an engine'; Jeremy Josephs, *op. cit.,* p.14.

6 *Guardian*, 6 June 1988; cf. 'Ashdown should go for Labour's Blood', *Sunday Times*, 29 June 1988.

7 Jo Grimond, *The Liberal Challenge*, Hollis and Carter, 1963, pp.293–317; cf. Roy Jenkins, *Partnership of Principle*, Secker & Warburg, 1983, pp.23–6.

8 The best examples are the pamphlets and campaign guides published by The Association of Liberal Councillors (ALC), now the Association of Liberal Democrat Councillors. See, for example, G. Lishman and T. Greaves, *The Theory and Practice of Community Politics*, ALC, 1980. T. Greaves, *How to Fight Local Elections and Win,* ALC, 1978; J. Smithson, *Community Campaigning Manual,* ALC, 1977. See also general election agents' manuals prepared by Chris Rennard, Liberal Democrats campaigns director.

9 David Steel, *Against Goliath*, Pan 1991, pp.268–9; Stuart Mole, *The Decade of Realignment: The Leadership Speeches of David Steel, 1976–1986,* Hebden Royd, 1986.

10 See, for example, Tim Clement-Jones, 'Targeting for Breakthrough', *Liberal Democrat News*, 19 May 1995.

11 Liberal Assembly resolution, *Guardian*, 26 September 1970.

12 David Thomson, *The Shock Troops of Pavement Politics? An Assessment of the Influence of Community Politics in the Liberal Party*, Hebden Royd, 1985; G.

Lishman and T. Greaves, *op. cit*; Peter Hain, *Community Politics*, Platform Books, 1976; Jo Grimond, 'Community Politics', *Government and Opposition*, Vol. 7, No. 2, 1972.

13 D. Thomson, *op. cit.*, pp.15–18.

14 Steve Platt, 'The Liberals in Power', *New Statesman*, 11 September 1987; *Minutes of the Federal Policy Committee 1990–95, passim*; *Political Speech in a Democracy*, Liberal Democrat Publications, 1993.

15 Michael Meadowcroft, *Liberalism and the Left*, Liberator Publications, 1982, pp.25–9.

16 Jeremy Josephs, *Inside the Alliance*, John Martin 1983, pp.5–6.

17 Michael Meadowcroft, Liberalism and the Righ*t,* Liberator Publications, 1983, p.4.

18 Such views were frequently expressed from the inception of the political cooperation strategy; for example, a resolution of Liberal Party Council on 16 July 1983, recorded disappointment that the Alliance Programme for Government did not express the clear radical commitment of the Liberal Party. David Steel was frequently at odds with Party Council; David Steel, *Against Goliath, passim.*

19 See Rachel Pitchford and Des Wilson in the *Guardian*, 22 January 1988.

20 Stuart Weir, 'Split Loyalties', *New Statesman*, 26 October 1990; Sarah Baxter, 'Spot the Difference', *New Statesman*, 15 May 1992; Martin Rosenbaum, 'Pact to the Future', *New Statesman*, 28 May 1993.

21 Stuart Mole, *op. cit.*, p.21.

22 David Steel, *A House Divided*, Weidenfeld and Nicholson, 1980; James Callaghan, *Time and Chance*, Collins, 1987; A. Michie and S. Hoggart, *The Pact,* Quartet Books, 1977.

23 V. Bogdanor, *No Overall Majority*, Constitutional Reform Centre, 1986; V. Bogdanor, *Multi-party Politics and the Constitution*, Cambridge University Press, 1983.

24 See Steel on coalition, *Guardian,* 6 June 1983, and Ashdown, *Guardian*, 18 March 1991.

25 W. Wallace, 'Take Your Partner', *Guardian*, 6 April 1992.

26 *Minutes of the Federal Executive*, FE 26/6/89.

27 *Ibid.*, FE 15/12/88.

28 *Ibid.*, FE 8/1/90

29 *Papers of the Federal Policy Committee*, FPC 90/23.

30 Des Wilson to the Federal Executive, *Minutes of the Federal Executive*, FE5/11/90 and Des Wilson, 'Report on the Election', *Papers of the Federal Policy Committee*.

31 Paddy Ashdown to the Federal Policy Committee, *Papers of the Federal Policy Committee*, FPC 28/10/90.

32 *Minutes of the Federal Executive*, FE 30/11/93.

33 Des Wilson, 'Report on the Election', *Papers of the Federal Policy Committee.*

34 *Guardian*, 6 April 1992.

35 Paddy Ashdown reported by Stephen Castle in the *Independent*, 17 April 1992 and Patricia Hewitt reported by Sarah Baxter in the *New Statesman*, 15 May 1992.

36 *Minutes of the Federal Executive*, FE8/6/92.

37 *The Times,* 5 May 1992. Cf. *The Times*, 11 May 1992.

38   Minutes of the Federal Executive, FE 16/5/92.

39   *Guardian*, 12 and 14 September 1992.

40   *Ibid.,* 24 September 1993.

41   *Ibid.*, 29 September 1994. Ashdown welcomed Blair's leadership, but demanded a clearer commitment on policy. *Guardian*, 8 August 1994 and 15 September 1994.

42   Michael White in the *Guardian*, 8 August 1994 and Patrick Wintour in the *Guardian*, May 1995. Cf. *New Statesman*, 12 May 1995.

43   The model for these was a particularly successful informal understanding between Labour and Liberal Democrat councillors in Berkshire. See Peter Hetherington in the *Guardian*, 21 September 1994. On the other hand, there were cases of Labour joining the Conservatives to keep the Liberal Democrats out.

44   On receiving the invitation to contribute to the Commission on Social Justice, Paddy Ashdown said that 'the Labour Party should be invited to participate in our consultation exercises, when appropriate'. *Minutes of the Federal Policy Committee,* FPC/93/12, 28 January 1993.

45   *New Statesman*, 28 April 1995. Cf. *Guardian*, 6 July 1995.

46   *Guardian*, 8 May 1995. This was followed by a counter-move, led by Jack Straw, to undermine cooperation with the Liberal Democrats. *Guardian*, 29 May 1995.

47   *Guardian,* 29 April 1995.

48   *Ibid.*, 8 May 1995.

49   For example, Hugo Young in the *Guardian*, 6 May 1993; David Marquand in the *Guardian*, 15 May 1994; Andrew Rawnsley in the *Observer*, 14 May 1995.

50   Cf. leading article in the *Reformer*, July 1994, statement by William Rogers, the *Guardian,* 8 August 1994, and views of the ALDC, *Liberal Democrat News*, 25 November 1994.

51   *Minutes of the Federal Policy Committee*, FPC 95/25, 13 May 1995. Cf. *Guardian,* 26 May 1995.

52   Martin Jacques, *Sunday Times*, 18 July 1993.

CHAPTER 9

Who votes for the centre now?

John Curtice

The organisational structure of centre party politics in Britain underwent a revolution in the 1980s. At the beginning of the decade the principal alternative to the Conservatives and Labour was provided by the Liberal Party who could trace a continuous organisational history back to 1859. By the end of the decade the Liberals had dissolved themselves into a new party, the Social and Liberal Democrats. In the meantime the Liberals shared the centre ground with the Social Democratic Party (SDP) which was formed following a split in the Labour party.

Has this revolution at the top been matched by change at the bottom? What impact, if any, did the elite manoeuvrings of the 1980s have on the character of centre party support? Are those who vote for the Liberal Democrats different in character from those who used to vote for the Liberals, or have all the changes of the 1980s left the Liberal Democrats with similar psephological constraints and opportunities to those of its predecessors?

The Liberal inheritance

There is certainly much reason to believe that the Liberal Democrats would not wish their support to be similar in character to that of the Liberals. Nearly all research and commentary on the Liberal vote in the 1960s and 1970s came to the conclusion that the character of its support left the party at a distinct disadvantage in comparison with their Conservative and Labour opponents.[1] Three key problems could be identified.

First, the party largely lacked any distinct social basis of support. Whereas Labour's electoral strength was concentrated amongst the working class and the Conservatives were strong in the middle class, the Liberals drew their support more or less evenly across the social spectrum. The party itself made a virtue of its classlessness, but in so doing it appeared to be trying vainly to override a social cleavage which had existed since the beginning of the twentieth century.

191

In fact the Liberals' support was not quite so classless as was sometimes claimed. The party consistently did somewhat better amongst middle-class voters than working-class ones. Indeed, Heath *et al.* noted that support for the centre appeared to be as middle class as support for the Conservatives, albeit that Liberal voters tended to belong to a different part of the middle class than Conservatives.[2] The Liberals appeared to do particularly well amongst those who had been in receipt of higher education, perhaps because such education appeared to encourage support for liberal values more generally.

Further, it was also possible to discern remnants of the nineteenth-century cleavage based on religion. Before the rise of the Labour party after the First World War, the Liberals had been identified with those of a non-conformist persuasion who favoured the disestablishment of the Anglican Church in England and Wales. Even in the 1970s, non-conformists, and especially Methodists, were more likely to vote Liberal, although they constituted only a small minority of all Liberal voters.[3]

Secondly, the party's vote was geographically evenly spread. Given its relatively low share of the vote, this placed the party under a severe disadvantage under the first-past-the-post electoral system. It meant, for example, that in February 1974, when the party won nearly one-fifth of the vote, that while it came second in 148 constituencies, it came first in only 14.

Support for the Conservative and Labour Parties varied from constituency to constituency because, first, their support was concentrated in a particular class and, secondly, constituencies varied considerably in the proportion of each class that they contained. Further, Labour, for example, did well in predominantly working-class constituencies not only because such constituencies contained more of the party's 'natural' supporters, but also because even middle-class people were more likely to vote Labour if they lived in a predominantly working-class constituency. The Liberals, in contrast, did not benefit from any of these processes.

Thirdly, support for the party was relatively volatile. Compared with both the Conservatives and Labour, far more of the party's supporters at one election were more likely to defect to another party at the next election, irrespective of the overall level of the popularity of the party. True, these losses were compensated for by new recruits to the cause, but their support was likely to prove equally fickle.

Not least of the reasons for this pattern was that many people who voted Liberal did so in order to protest against the current policy or performance of the party they normally supported,[4] rather than because they were positively attracted to the Liberals. All the party needed was a sufficiently attractive image to make it an acceptable vehicle of protest.

As a result, the party's support was not only fickle, but incoherent. In 1974, for example, it attracted the support of Conservatives who were opposed to their party's support for the Common Market, and the votes of Labour supporters who were upset at their party's threat to pull out. There was far less agreement amongst Liberal supporters about what should be done in any particular area of policy than was true of Conservative and Labour supporters.[5]

The impact of the SDP

This picture was modified only marginally following the formation of the Alliance with the SDP in 1981. In particular, despite being formed as a result of a breakaway from the Labour party, the SDP failed to attract more working-class voters to the centre than the Liberals had succeeded in doing. Indeed, the increase in Alliance support in 1983 compared with that for the Liberals in 1979 was twice as big amongst members of the salariat (salaried professional and managerial workers) than amongst the working class.[6] Moreover, if we look at those who said they identified with the SDP in 1987, we find that only 26 per cent were working class compared with 32 per cent of those who identified with the Liberals.

There was also some evidence of a difference between the ideological structure of the Alliance vote and that of the old Liberal party. Heath *et al.* argued that political values in Britain could best be summarised as lying along two dimensions. The first, the left/right dimension, was about attitudes towards equality and the role the government should play in the economy. Conservative and Labour voters were sharply distinguished from one another on this dimension, with Labour voters strongly in favour of government intervention and greater equality and Conservative voters equally opposed.

However, there were also differences between Conservative and Labour voters on the second, liberal/authoritarian dimension. On this dimension were aligned attitudes towards a range of issues including nuclear weapons, the welfare state and law and order. Conservative supporters were less keen on welfare state spending, regarding some of its beneficiaries as scroungers. They took an equally punitive attitude towards criminals, while they wished to retain the nuclear weapons as a deterrent against external threats. Labour supporters, in contrast, were keener on welfare spending, adopted a more liberal attitude to issues such as the death penalty and were less keen on nuclear weapons.

More importantly, for our purposes, Heath *et al.* argued that if we took this two-dimensional view of British political attitudes we found that the Alliance vote was neither simply an ideologically incoherent protest vote nor just a centre vote. Rather the Alliance was particularly strong amongst those voters who were in the centre or even on the right of the left/right dimension but at the same time were towards the liberal end of the liberal/authoritarian dimension. In contrast, when the Liberals surged in 1974, the party's support came equally from all ideological quarters.

This concentration amongst centre-right liberals appeared to offer the Alliance an opportunity to carve out for itself a distinct niche in the political marketplace. The centre-right liberal ground had been vacated by both the Conservatives and Labour, yet the proportion of the electorate that occupied that position was growing. Further, centre-right liberals appeared to be more loyal in their support for the Alliance than the party's other voters. The SDP itself may not have changed the character of British centre party politics, but the growing polarisation of Conservative and Labour, one of whose consequences had been the formation of the SDP, had apparently given the Liberals and the SDP together a new opportunity to establish the centre as a major player in the British political system.

As the Alliance discovered to its cost, however, its support was just as evenly spread geographically as that of the old Liberal party. Indeed, if anything, it was more so.[7] As a result, despite coming just two points behind Labour in terms of votes in 1983, the Alliance trailed by no less than 186 in terms of seats. This, as much as anything, accounted for the failure of the Alliance to disturb the continued dominance of the House of Commons by the Conservatives and Labour.

The Liberal Democrat vote

What, then, of the Liberal Democrats? How far does the picture we painted of the Liberal and Alliance vote still hold? Has the formation of a new party been accompanied by at least some modification of the party's electoral base?

We shall discover that there appear to have been a number of important changes. At its first showing in 1992 the Liberal Democrat vote proved to be at least as concentrated sociologically, geographically and ideologically as the centre vote was at any time in the history of the old Liberal Party. Although the Liberal Democrats still suffer from a number of disadvantages, not least a more volatile electoral base, the character of its support suggests that it potentially poses a more robust challenge to the two-party system than did any of its predecessors.

SOCIAL BASE

We look first at the social base of the Liberal Democrat vote. In Table 9.1 we show the level of the party's support in each social class and at each educational level in the 1992 general election and compare it with the pattern of support for the Alliance at the previous general election in 1987.

We hardly acquire the impression of a vote evenly spread across social strata. Rather, the Liberal Democrat vote was distinctly higher amongst the salariat and the better educated than in other social groups. As we noted earlier, a similar pattern had been apparent in the Liberal and the Alliance vote, but it was marginally stronger in 1992 than in 1987 and appears to have been as strong as at any time since 1964.[8] For example, Liberal Democrat support in 1992 was eleven points higher in the salariat than amongst the working class; in 1987 the equivalent gap in Alliance support was only seven points[9]. It is perhaps doubtful whether the Liberals ever were a truly classless party. The Liberal Democrats certainly do not seem to be.[10]

In one intriguing respect the Liberal Democrat vote appears to have cast off its Liberal legacy. Support for the Liberal Democrats amongst nonconformists was just 15 per cent, three points *lower* than among Anglicans and four points lower than amongst those who profess no religion at all. Even in 1987, support for the Alliance amongst non-conformists was no less than eleven points *higher* than amongst Anglicans. Just why the Liberals' long-standing association with nonconformism should apparently have disappeared is far from clear,[11] but it seems possible that the organisational translation from Liberal to

Table 9.1 Social base of Liberal Democrat support: percentage
voting Liberal Democrat in 1992 (Alliance in 1987)

Social class	1992	1987
Salariat	23	28
Routine non-manual	16	22
Petty bourgeois	17	19
Foremen and technicians	14	24
Working	12	21
Highest educational qualification		
Degree	34	37
Higher education below degree	23	26
'A' level	17	26
'O' level	18	20
CSE or less	12	21

Source: British Election Study 1987 and 1992. Social class is based on the scheme devised by John Goldthorpe and detailed in J. Goldthorpe, *Social Mobility and Class Structure in Modern Britain,* Clarendon, 1987, and A. Heath, R. Jowell, J. Curtice, G. Evans, J. Field, and S. Witherspoon, *Understanding Political Change: The British Voter 1964–87*, Pergamon, 1991. Percentages are based on those reported having voted at the relevant election.

Liberal Democrat may have helped to break one of the few remaining threads linking modern Liberalism with its Victorian past.

GEOGRAPHICAL BASE

Given that no more than one in ten voters professes to belong to one of the non-conformist denominations, this change in support by non-conformists is of little import to the party's electoral prospects. However, any change in the geographical pattern of its support is another matter: and there have been two important changes since the system gave the Alliance so little reward for its 26 per cent of the vote in 1983. Both have helped to increase the geographical concentration of Liberal Democrat support.

The first change is the emergence of a regional concentration of Liberal Democrat strength in the south west of England. Across the nation as a whole, support for the Liberal Democrats in 1992 was eight points lower than that recorded by the Alliance in 1983; but in the south west it was only two points lower. The Liberal Party always had a few areas of strength in Devon and Cornwall, but the Liberal Democrats now have a far more substantial bridgehead in the region, securing seats in Avon, Gloucestershire and Somerset as well as Devon and Cornwall. Even in the relatively unpropitious circumstances of 1992, it was able to win nearly one-third of the vote across the whole region, a figure only remotely matched elsewhere in the handful of seats in the Highlands of Scotland.

Some of this success appears to have come at the expense of the Conservatives. Conservative support in the south west dropped by nearly four points between 1983 and 1992 , more than in any other part of Great Britain. The region largely missed out on the fruits of the economic boom of the mid-1980s and has also experienced political controversy over a number of local issues, most notably the price of water. The Liberal Democrats appear to have been able to turn these factors to their advantage and may have begun to be identified as the party best able to advance the interests of the region in much the same way that the Labour Party has become identified as the party of the north of England, or the Conservatives, the party of the south east.[12]

The Liberal Democrats have profited in the south west at the expense of Labour too. The Liberals always derived some profit from tactical voting in those constituencies where they managed to secure a good second place. Most commonly this involved acquiring the support of Labour voters who were keen to ensure the defeat of the local Conservative MP.[13] Equally, some voters were reluctant to vote for the Liberals because they did not feel they had a chance of winning under the first-past-the-post electoral system. Nowhere was this more true than in seats which were marginal between the Conservatives and Labour.[14]

Still, the number of tactical voters, and the number of seats that they swayed were relatively small. Heath *et al.* estimated that no more than 6 per cent of voters voted tactically in the 1980s.[15] Further, any increase in the number of tactical voters was, they argued, not the result of any increase in the propensity of voters to vote tactically, but simply that more voters lived in constituencies where it made sense to do so. Nevertheless, and this brings us to the second important change in the geography of the Liberal Democrat vote, analysis of both the election results themselves and of survey data collected after the 1992 election suggested that tactical voting had been more prevalent than previously and had had a greater impact as well; one estimate put the number of tactical voters at 9 per cent.[16] Some of this involved Liberal Democrat voters switching to Labour, but equally, and in the south west especially, the Liberal Democrats appear to have succeeded in squeezing Labour. Arguably, all four of the seats they gained from the Conservatives at the election were only won thanks to tactical voting.

The Liberal Democrats not only did relatively well in their strongest region in 1992, but also did best in some of their better prospects within that region. All of this helped to ensure that the party's vote was less geographically evenly spread in 1992 than in any election contested by the Liberals or the Alliance since February 1974, the first election to be fought by the Liberals on a nationwide basis.

These trends were confirmed by the results of the 1994 European Parliament elections. In the three previous rounds of these elections the Liberals and the Alliance had failed to win a single seat in the European Parliament. In 1994, however, despite winning a lower share of the vote (17 per cent) than was secured by the Alliance in 1984, the Liberal Democrats won two seats, both of them in the south west. Their vote became even further concentrated in the region while the party benefited from further tactical voting, this for the first time in a European Parliament election. Indeed, so strong was this trend (and, equally, so heavy was the concentration of Conservative losses in their areas of previous strength) that overall, the Liberal Democrat vote was no more geographically evenly spread than the Conservative vote. One of the apparently safest generalisations in British politics – that the centre vote is geographically more evenly spread than that for the two main parties – was overturned for the first time in a modern British election.[17]

The Liberal Democrats are, then, better equipped than their predecessors to cope with the barriers that the first-past-the-post electoral system establishes against third parties. If the party were to repeat the Alliance's 1983 performance now, but with its vote distributed as it was in 1992, it could expect to win 38 seats rather than the 23 that were won on that occasion. A weaker Conservative performance, and the rewards would be even greater. It is doubtful, though, whether this change has anything to do with the formation of the new party. The increasing geographical concentration of support in the south west began to appear in the 1987 election when the Alliance was still in existence. Building as it does upon a traditional Liberal base, the new geography of centre party voting in Britain arguably has occurred despite rather than because of the merger.

IDEOLOGICAL BASE

What of the ideological pattern of Liberal Democrat support? What has happened to the bridgehead of support that the Alliance appeared to be developing amongst centre-right liberals? One of the problems faced by the Liberal Democrats compared with the Alliance is that both Labour and the Conservatives are now thought to be closer to the ideological centre than they were in the 1980s. Even before the 1992 election, Labour had conducted its policy review resulting in a substantial shift to the right on issues such as nationalisation and nuclear weapons, while the Conservatives had made themselves appear less extreme by exchanging John Major for Margaret Thatcher. Since 1992, further moves to the right by Labour under the leadership of Tony Blair, coupled with Labour's adoption of a wide-ranging programme of constitutional reform, suggested that the ideologically distinctive space of the Liberal Democrats was being eroded.

Fortunately we are in a position to replicate some of the analysis which led Heath *et al.* to argue that the Alliance vote was not simply a centre party vote.[18] In Table 9.2 the electorate is divided according to their attitudes towards two issues. The first, designed to measure Heath *et al.*'s left/right dimension, is nationalisation and privatisation. On the left we place those who in 1992 were favour of the nationalisation of at least some parts of the economy which were then in private hands. On the right we place those who favoured the further privatisation of enterprises which were then state-owned. In the centre are those who do not want any change to the status quo.[19]

The second issue, used to measure the liberal/authoritarian dimension and displayed vertically, is attitudes towards taxes versus services. At the top we place those who would like to increase taxes and spend more on heath and social services. At the bottom are those who want lower taxes and less spending while in the middle are those who want little or no change.[20] So, combining the two scales, those in the top left-hand box

Table 9.2 Ideological base of Liberal Democrat voting

percentage of voters voting Liberal Democrat 1992
(compared with percentage voting Alliance 1983)

In favour of	*More nationalisation*	*Status quo*	*More privatisation*
Higher taxes and	18	27	22
more spending	(+3)	(-7)	(-6)
No change	10	15	11
	(-9)	(-22)	(-7)
Lower taxes and	12	15	8
less spending	(-2)	(-4)	(7)

Sources: British Election Study 1992; A. Heath, R. Jowell and J. Curtice,
How Britain Votes, Pergamon, 1985, Table 10.4.
Note: Figures in parentheses show the percentage voting Alliance in 1983.

are those who are both in favour of nationalisation and want more spending and higher taxes. Then, within each cell of the table the main entry shows the proportion of those with each combination of attitudes on the two dimensions (excluding non-voters) who voted Liberal Democrat. Thus we can see that 18 per cent of those in favour of both more nationalisation and higher spending voted for the Liberal Democrats in 1992.

Much of the pattern identified by Heath *et al.* in the 1983 Alliance vote also appears to have been present in 1992. Liberal Democrat voting was highest amongst those who were in the centre or on the right on the nationalisation issue but took a liberal attitude towards welfare spending. Indeed, Liberal Democrat voting was not particularly high amongst those in the ideological centre. Despite the narrowing of the ideological distance between the Conservatives and Labour, the Liberal Democrats still appear to have been able to retain a distinct ideological space for themselves in 1992.

Indeed, as an examination of theAlliance entries in Table 9.2 reveals, the ideological space occupied by Liberal Democrat voters in 1992 was arguably even more distinctive than that occupied by Alliance voters in 1983. These figures compare the percentage who voted Liberal Democrat in 1992 in that cell with the proportion voting Alliance in the equivalent table for 1983. They show that Liberal Democrat voting fell by far the most heavily amongst those in the centre on both dimensions. Never before has Britain's supposedly centre party been so relatively weak amongst those in the ideological centre. Meanwhile the Liberal Democrats were actually stronger amongst those in Labour's traditional heartland, that is those in favour of more spending and more nationalisation, than the Alliance were in 1983.[21]

In short, the Liberal Democrats in 1992 looked more like a pro-welfare, state-spending party rather than a centre party. One of the distinctive features of the Liberal Democrats' campaign in 1992 was a call for a one penny in the pound increase in income tax to be spent on education. This appeal would appear not to have been without consequence for the character of the party's support in 1992.

However, the association between Liberal Democrat voting and ideological liberalism goes well beyond the specific issue of welfare state spending. This can be seen if we use more elaborate and robust measures of left/right and liberal/authoritarian values than were available in the 1983 election study.[22] Position on the left/right dimension is measured by combining respondents' answers to five items which tap their attitudes towards equality and the extent to which the government should intervene in the economy.[23] Similarly, position on the liberal/authoritarian dimension is measured by five items which focus on the balance that the respondents strike between the freedom of the (unconventional) individual and the right of society to impose order.[24] Note that none of the items taps attitudes towards the welfare state.

Although position on the liberal/authoritarian dimension is measured very differently in Table 9.3 from the way it was in Table 9.2, we again see that irrespective of whether they are on the left, the right or in the centre, those of a more liberal ideological persuasion were more likely to vote Liberal Democrat in 1992 than the rest of the electorate. The party's liberal base is thus more than a response to the party's pro-tax-and-spend position in the 1992 election. Meanwhile we again see that the party was not particularly strong in the ideological centre.

However, Table 9.3 does suggest one modification to the picture painted by Heath *et al.* On the measure of the left/right dimension used here, it appears that the Liberal Democrats do relatively well amongst those on the centre-left rather than on the centre-right. We appear again to have evidence of the Liberal Democrats' ability to make inroads into Labour's traditional ideological territory.

Table 9.3 Ideological base of Liberal Democrat voting
in 1992: an alternative view

Position on liberal/authoritarian scale	Position on left–right scale		
	Left	Centre	Right
Liberal	25	31	11
Centre	16	19	9
Authoritarian	16	24	9

Source: British Election Study, 1992.

Continued weaknesses

Our description of who votes Liberal Democrat is rather different from the traditional one of who voted for the old Liberal Party. Support for the party is not classless, but is distinctly stronger amongst the educated middle class than in the less well educated working class. The party is not simply a vehicle of protest or the voice of the ideological centre; rather it has a particular appeal to those of a liberal rather than an authoritarian persuasion. Further, rather than having a geographically evenly spread vote, the party has developed an area of concentration in the south-west of England.

However, we should not overdraw the contrast. The Liberal Democrats may be more successful *amongst* the middle class, but they are not the party *of* the middle class, the majority of whom still vote Conservative. Similarly, Labour easily outpolled the party amongst liberals on the centre-left, and the Conservatives still won nearly half of the vote in the south west in 1992. The party may have particular areas of strength, but nowhere has it yet become the party which is most strongly identified with a particular constituency.

Not surprisingly, then, we find that many of the traditional weaknesses of the Liberal and the Alliance vote were still apparent in 1992. Most notably, the party's vote is still relatively volatile. Of those who voted for the Alliance in 1987 and did not stay at home in the 1992 election, only 55 per cent cast a ballot for the Liberal Democrats. In contrast, the Conservatives retained 84 per cent of those who voted for them in 1987, and Labour 87 per cent.[25] Even those who supposedly have an emotional attachment or identification with the party do not necessarily vote for it. Only 77 per cent of those who said that they identified with the Liberal Democrats voted for the party in 1992; in contrast, nine in ten Conservative and Labour identifiers supported their party. Like the old Liberal Party, the Liberal Democrats are like a hotel at a busy airport, convenient for a one-night stopover but not somewhere people wish to stay.

The party still lacks some of the incentives that Conservative and Labour voters receive to remain loyal to their party. Lacking a constituency all of their own, we find that Liberal Democrat voters are less likely than Conservative and Labour voters to find social reinforcement for their views. For example, in 1992, only 33 per cent of 1992 Liberal Democrat voters reported that the person with whom they spoke most often about important matters was also a Liberal Democrat. In contrast, no less than 45 per cent of Labour voters said that they spoke to a Labour supporter while 58 per cent of Conservatives said they spoke to a Conservative. Meanwhile, the first-past-the-post electoral system still encourages the perception that a Liberal Democrat vote is a wasted vote. Those who said they would have voted Liberal Democrat in 1992 but did not do so because they thought they had no chance of winning in their constituency constituted no less than 4 per cent of the total electorate.[26]

Conclusion

What can our examination of the character of Liberal Democrat support tell us about the party's prospects for the future? In particular, what does it tell us about how the party might respond to the most important challenge which appears to face it: the resurgence of a Labour Party keen to occupy the ideological centre ground?

Our analysis suggests that Labour may not be capable as inflicting as much long-term damage on the Liberal Democrats as some commentators have suggested. For all three constituencies which we have identified as areas of Liberal Democrat strength, all serve to give the party's support a rather different character from that of Labour's.

First, on the sociological front, Labour is still far stronger amongst the working class than the middle class. The Liberal Democrats in contrast are predominantly a middle-class party, and thus are always likely to be better placed to win over disaffected Conservatives. Secondly, in geographical terms the Liberal Democrats are strongest where virtually all the spoils to be won are from the Conservatives rather than from Labour. Labour is second to the Liberal Democrats in only a handful of constituencies anywhere in the country, and vice versa. Increasingly, the two parties have come to dominate the non-Conservative vote in different parts of the country. So far as winning seats is concerned, the Liberal Democrats and Labour are not really in competition with each other but rather both parties' prospects depend on profiting from Tory misfortune.

On the third front, the ideological one, the Liberal Democrats emerge as a liberal party, not a centre party. Labour, in contrast, proved to be no more popular in 1992 amongst liberals than they were amongst authoritarians. As Labour switches to the centre not only on left/right issues but also on such issues as the welfare state and law and order, it could leave open new opportunities for the Liberal Democrats to build upon their relative strength on the second dimension. We have already seen that in 1992 the party was particularly successful amongst those who wanted more spending on the welfare state. Labour's continued reluctance to commit itself to higher taxation, for example, could well give the Liberal Democrats the opportunity to pursue that constituency further.

We should be wary of pursuing this analysis too far, however. In looking at the character of the Liberal Democrat vote we have been looking at the long-term structure rather than the short-term flux. As Table 9.1, for example, illustrates, when the centre vote falls, it tends to fall everywhere. If, for example, the Liberal Democrats have an unpopular leader or Labour a popular one, then voters everywhere are likely to take notice. All we can do here is to identify the potential for long-term growth or harm. Whether it will be realised will depend on the actions of politicians.

Notes

1   See, in particular, D. Butler and D. Stokes, *Political Change in Britain* (1st edn), Macmillan, 1969, Chap. 14; P. Lemieux, 'Political Issues and Liberal Support in the February 1974 British General Election', Vol. 25, 1977; J. Alt, I. Crewe and B. Särlvik, 'Angels in Plastic: The Liberal Surge in 1974', *Political Studies*, Vol. 25, 1977; H. Himmelweit, P. Humphreys, and M. Jaegar, *How Voters Decide*, Open University Press, 1985; J. Curtice, 'Liberal Voters and the Alliance: Realignment or Protest?', in V. Bogdanor (ed.), *Liberal Party Politics*, Clarendon, 1983.

2   A. Heath, R. Jowell and J. Curtice, *How Britain Votes*, Pergamon, 1985.

3   J. Curtice, 'Great Britain: Social Liberalism Reborn?', in E. Kirchner (ed.), *Liberal Parties in Western Europe*, Cambridge University Press, 1988.

4   P. Lemieux, *op. cit.*

5   B. Särlvik and I. Crewe, *Decade of Dealignment*, Cambridge University Press, 1983.

6   A. Heath *et al.*, *op. cit.*

7   J. Curtice and M. Steed, 'An Analysis of the Voting', in D. Butler and D. Kavanagh, *The British General Election of 1983*, Macmillan, 1984.

8   See A. Heath *et al.*, *op. cit.*, Table 5.2.

9   Of course we should be very wary about drawing inferences from relatively small changes in the difference between two figures, both of which are subject to sampling error, but the evidence in Table 9.1, which is based on two separate cross-section studies, is corroborated by the results of the 1987–92 panel survey also undertaken as part of the British Election Study. This survey reinterviewed in 1992 respondents who had previously been interviewed as part of the 1987 cross-section study. It showed that voting for the Liberal Democrats was ten points higher in the salariat than in the working class in 1992 whereas Alliance voting was only seven points higher in 1987. Meanwhile the gap between those with a degree and those with a CSE or less widened from 12 points to 21.

10 In fact no less than 64 per cent of the Liberal Democrat vote was cast by members of the salariat or routine non-manual class, slightly higher than the 62 per cent of the Conservative vote that came from those two classes. Labour, in contrast, drew just 35 per cent of its vote from those two groups.

11 Even if we look at party identification rather than vote, there are still clear signs of a weakening of the centre's link with non-conformism. Just 18 per cent of non-conformists identified with the Liberal Democrats, only 4 percentage points more than amongst Anglicans. In 1987 the equivalent gap was ten points. If the difference between the two groups had narrowed in respect of vote but not of party identification we might reasonably have argued that the 1992 pattern between Liberal Democrat voting and religion was likely to prove temporary. The evidence about party identification suggests this is less likely to be the case.

12 J. Curtice and M.Steed, 'The Results Analysed', in D. Butler and D. Kavanagh, *The British General Election of 1992*, Macmillan, 1992.

13 M. Steed, 'The Results Analysed', in D. Butler and D. Kavanagh, *The British General Election of October 1974*, Macmillan, 1975, pp.34–2.

14 A. Heath, R. Jowell, J. Curtice, G. Evans, J. Field, and S. Witherspoon, *Understanding Political Change: The British Voter 1964–1987*, Pergamon, 1991.

15 A. Heath *et al.*, *op. cit.*, Chap. 4.

16 J. Curtice and M. Steed *op. cit.*; G. Evans, 'Tactical Voting and Labour's Prospects', in A. Heath, R. Jowell and J. Curtice with B. Taylor (eds), *Labour's Last Chance? The 1992 Election and Beyond*, Dartmouth, 1994.

17 J. Curtice and M. Steed, 'An Analysis of the Results', in D. Butler and M. Westlake, *The 1994 European Election in Britain*, Macmillan, 1995.

18 A. Heath *et al.*, *How Britain Votes*, Chap. 10.

19 Respondents were presented with an eleven point scale and asked the following: 'Some people feel that government should nationalise many more private companies These people would put themselves in box A. Others people feel that government should sell off many more nationalised industries. These would put themselves in Box K. And other people have views somewhere in-between, along here (POINT LEFT A–F) or along here (POINT RIGHT, K–F). In the first row of boxes please tick whichever box comes closest to your own views about nationalisation and privatisation.' Respondents who placed themselves in any of boxes A–E are classified in the table as in favour of nationalisation, those who placed themselves in G–K are regarded as in favour of privatisation, while those who put themselves in box F in the middle are described as in favour of no change.

Note that the question used here to measure the nationalisation/privatisation issue is slightly different from that used in A. Heath *et al.*, *How Britain Votes*, Chap. 10, because the question they used was not included in the 1992 election survey. However, the 1983 survey did include the question used here (albeit administered as a 21- rather than an 11-point scale) and if we replicate Heath *et al.*'s analysis for 1983 using that question we get similar results to those that they published. Thus the change of question does not render our comparison with 1983 invalid.

20 Respondents were asked: 'Some people feel that government should put up taxes a lot and spend much more on health and social services. These people would put themselves in Box A. Other people feel that government should cut taxes a lot and spend much less on health and social services. These people would put themselves in Box K. And other people have views somewhere in-between, along here (POINT LEFT A–F) or along here (POINT RIGHT K–F). In the first row of boxes, please tick whichever box comes closest to your own views about taxes ands government spending.' Respondents who ticked any of boxes A–E are classified as in favour of higher taxes and more spending, those who ticked any of boxes G–K are regarded as in favour of less taxes and lower spending, while those in box F are described as in favour of no change. The question is exactly the same as that used in the equivalent tables in Heath *et al.* (1985) except that it was administered as a 21-point scale.

21 This finding is repeated if we use attitudes towards the death penalty as an alternative measure of respondents' position on the liberal/authoritarian dimension rather than

taxes versus services. (See A. Heath *et al.*, *How Britain Votes*, p.155). This also shows that Liberal Democrat support in 1992 amongst those opposed to the death penalty and in favour of nationalisation was higher than Alliance support in 1983, whereas in all other groups Liberal Democrat voting was lower than 1983 Alliance support.

22 A. Heath, R. Jowell, J. Curtice and S. Witherspoon, *End of Award Report to the ESRC: Methodological Aspects of Attitude Research*, SCPR, 1986; A. Heath, G. Evans and J. Martin, 'The Measurement of Core Beliefs and Values: The Development of Balanced Socialist/Laissez-Faire and Libertarian/Authoritarian scales', *British Journal of Political Science*, Vol. 24, 1994; G. Evans and A. Heath, 'The Measurement of Left-Right and Libertarian–Authoritarian Values: A Comparison of Balanced and Unbalanced Scales', *Quality and Quantity*, Vol. 29, 1995.

23 The five items are: (1) ordinary people do not get their fair share of the nation's wealth; (2) there is one law for the rich and one for the poor; (3) there is no need for strong trade unions to protect employees' working conditions and wages; (4) private enterprise is the best way to solve Britain's economic problems; (5) it is the government's responsibility to provide a job for everyone who wants one. Respondents were invited to indicate their agreement or disagreement with each item along a five-point scale ranging from 'agree strongly' to 'disagree strongly'. Each respondent's scale score is simply the sum of his/her score on the individual items, except that the scores for right-wing propositions are inverted. This results in a range of scores from 5 to 25. Those with a score of 11 or less have been classified here as left-wing, those with a score of 16 or more as right wing, with the remainder placed in the centre. This has the effect of dividing the sample into approximately three equal groups.

24 The items are as follows: (1) young people today don't have enough respect for traditional British values; (2) censorship of films and magazines is necessary to uphold moral standards; (3) people should be allowed to organise meetings to protest against the government;(4) homosexual relations are always wrong; (5) people in Britain should be more tolerant of those who lead unconventional lives. The respondent's scale score is derived in the same way as on the left/right scale. Respondents with a score of 11 or less were classified as authoritarian and those with 15 or more as liberal.

25 Calculated from A. Heath *et al.*, *Labour's Last Chance?*, p.290.

26 G. Evans, in A. Heath *et al.*, *Labour's Last Chance?*, *op. cit.*

CHAPTER 10

The electoral record

Colin Rallings and Michael Thrasher

Writing about the Liberal Party, one observer noted, 'the party's electoral strategy has been at the core of its whole strategy'.[1] Few would disagree if the same description were now applied to the Liberal Democrats. Some parties give a high priority to raising or altering political consciousness, others campaign on a single or narrow band of issues, but the Liberal Democrats are, first and foremost, a party sustained by election adrenalin. Frequently marginalised between elections, the Liberal Democrats appear to comprise a party of nomads who, when one election is over, immediately pack up their belongings, break camp and continue their journey on to the next hustings. Parliamentary by-elections provide a perfect illustration of this. Victory will nourish the party for weeks, even months, providing the energy needed in the struggle to break the stranglehold of two party politics. Failure, however, either because of the party's own shortcomings or because of unfavourable circumstances, means that an opportunity to attract nationwide publicity and to transform the pattern of British politics will be lost.

It is fitting, therefore, that the Liberal Democrats should be assessed and judged on the effectiveness of their election strategy. It is equally appropriate that any assessment be set alongside the record of the party's predecessors. Over the long term, of course, the Liberal Democrats must be compared with the Liberal Party which last formed a government on its own eighty years ago. Over the short term, Liberal Democrat performance can be compared with the alliance between the Liberals and the Social Democratic Party (SDP) which spanned the 1983 and 1987 general elections. Those parties displayed different strengths and weaknesses. The Liberals enjoyed strong organisation but were weak in ideological identity, while the SDP were a party boasting ideas and rhetoric but with little or no organisational substance, especially at grass-roots level. With their subsequent merger and reincarnation as the Liberal Democrats it was believed a strong political message could be underpinned by an organisation with a clear and well-directed electoral strategy.

The purpose of this chapter is to examine the electoral strengths and weaknesses of the Liberal Democrats. The problem, however, is finding the most appropriate way of measuring performance. In the vanguard of most modern parties are the 'spin-doctors' whose pre- and post-election announcements are specifically designed to place the party in the most favourable light in the hope that outside observers concur with that view. On these terms it might not matter that a party has sustained seat losses because overall vote share has remained firm. Another day, another election, and the emphasis switches to votes and not seats. Our purpose here, however, is to take a wider view to see how the parts relate to the whole. For the Liberal Democrats the immediate national electoral strategy must surely be to hold the balance of power in a hung parliament from which position they would be better able to negotiate some measure of electoral reform. Other possibilities exist, of course, but with these the fate of the Liberal Democrats lies more with the actions of other parties and less upon their own efforts. Optimists within the party may hope for majority government but unless Conservative and/or Labour self-destruct then such an outcome is remote and should form no part of an effective electoral strategy.

We assess the Liberal Democrat strategy in the light of five different types of electoral contest. These are the 1992 general election, various local elections, parliamentary by-elections, their local government equivalents and finally European elections. For each of these types we consider the nature of the Liberal Democrats' electoral strategy. The party cannot call upon a loyal band of voters in quite the same way as can the Conservative and Labour Parties. For that reason the Liberal Democrats are the victims of electoral context, unable to dictate the course of an election and largely reliant for their successes upon the weaknesses of other parties. Nevertheless, translating protest votes into seats under a winner-takes-all electoral system requires skill and the Liberal Democrats have evolved an increasingly effective strategy in recent years. An essential element in this strategy has been to link the local and the national. The party expects that victories in local council elections and other 'second-order elections'[2] will help to generate success at the parliamentary level. A sense of the scale of the task ahead can be seen from the party's performance at the last general election.

The 1992 general election

Although it was held during an economic recession, the 1992 general election brought the Conservatives their fourth consecutive victory. Labour, tipped by the polls to win or at least to become the largest party, failed for the sixth election running to exceed 40 per cent of the popular vote, finishing almost eight points behind the Conservatives. For some, the part played by the Liberal Democrats in this election was decisive. Dunleavy, for example, has argued that party leader Paddy Ashdown made a crucial mistake the weekend before the election in suggesting that a Labour minority government would result in economic catastrophe unless a deal with the Liberal Democrats was negotiated.[3] In the days following, some late swing to the Conservatives was detected, fuelled no doubt by that party's campaign message that a vote for the Liberal Democrats would lead to a Labour government.

Was 1992 a successful general election for the Liberal Democrats? Not, certainly, in terms of share of the vote. Polling less than 18 per cent of the vote the party fell further behind the peak of 25.4 per cent won by the Alliance in 1983. Once again Labour appeared to be the main beneficiaries of this decline. Before the election, Liberal Democrats had emphasised that they and not Labour were the main challengers to the Conservatives. Following the 1987 general election the Liberal Democrats were second in 230 Conservative-held seats compared with Labour being second in 142. In 1992 the Liberal Democrats were often unceremoniously brushed aside by the national swing to Labour. They emerged in second place in just 145 Conservative constituencies, well behind Labour who were second in 188. Even worse for the Liberal Democrats, of Conservative seats vulnerable to a 5 per cent swing they were second in just 19 compared with 70 for Labour.

Despite a drop of 4.8 per cent in their vote and a reduction in the number of second-places, the Liberal Democrats still succeeded in winning 20 parliamentary seats in 1992, only slightly fewer than the Alliance had won with a larger share of the vote in 1983 and 1987 (Table 10.1). The party had apparently succeeded in ameliorating the worst effects of the electoral system. How had it done this? Some insight can be gleaned from an examination of the standard deviation in their vote. The more evenly a party's vote is distributed the smaller the standard deviation. For a third party attempting to break the hold of two party politics an even vote distribution in a first-past-the-post electoral system means less prospect of translating votes into seats. In 1983 and 1987 the standard deviation of the Alliance vote had been 7.3 and 8.9 respectively. By 1992 the standard deviation had risen to 10.2, still lower than that for the Conservatives and Labour but suggesting the variation in the Liberal Democrat vote was growing more pronounced across the country.[4] Although many Liberal Democrat votes were still effectively wasted, it appeared that the party had become more successful at targeting winnable seats.

An indication of the increasingly variable pattern in the distribution of the Liberal Democrat vote can be found in Table 10.2. In some parts of Great Britain, most notably Scotland and Wales, the Liberal Democrat vote virtually halved compared with what the Alliance parties had achieved in the early 1980s. In Scotland, however, this was not to the detriment of the party's ability to win seats. Elsewhere there was less dramatic but

Table 10.1 Parliamentary votes and seats 1983–1992

	1992		1987		1983	
	%vote	Seats	%vote	Seats	%vote	Seats
Conservative	41.9	336	42.2	375	42.4	397
Labour	34.4	271	30.8	229	27.6	209
All/Liberal Democrat	17.8	20	22.6	22	25.4	23
Other	5.9	24	4.4	24	4.6	21

still consistent decline. Only in the south west, where the Alliance had achieved its highest shares of the vote and which had traditionally been a region of strength for the Liberals, did the Liberal Democrat vote show signs of holding up. In 1992, and despite the break-up of the Alliance, the Liberal Democrats not only protected their seats in the region but also captured the Conservative constituencies of Bath, Cheltenham, Cornwall North and Devon North. By defying the national trend and with an average Conservative to Liberal Democrat swing of just over 5 per cent in these four seats, the effectiveness of an electoral strategy which involved an ever more specific targeting of individual constituencies was demonstrated. In several other constituencies the party experienced some near misses. The Conservatives held onto St Ives but saw their majority decline to less than 3 per cent with a swing to the Liberal Democrats of 5.8 per cent. In Somerset, Paddy Ashdown comfortably held Yeovil while Liberal Democrat candidates performed well in the neighbouring constituencies of Somerton, and Frome, and Taunton, again registering swings in excess of 5 per cent.

The Liberal Democrats also performed a little better than average in the south east where their vote fell by 4.6 per cent compared with 1987. Curtice and Steed, however, reveal considerable variation even within this region with the Liberal Democrat vote falling by less than 2 per cent in constituencies situated along the south coast and by less than 3 per cent in the Thames Valley. This intra-regional variation is so marked that it is possible to divide the area such that a party might do well in one but not in the other. The Liberal Democrat vote in 1992 correlates with the 1987 Alliance vote in a south east triangle of constituencies, but across the country as a whole there is no such correlation. Moreover, in other clusters of constituencies, for example, to the north and east of London, the electorate has proved reluctant to support the Liberal Democrats. The evidence from a regional analysis of the 1992 vote led Curtice and Steed to speculate that, 'Maybe the increasing Liberal Democrat strength in the South West and the far South of England,

Table 10.2 Alliance and Liberal Democrats in the regions

	1992 % share	1992 Seats	% change 1992/87	% change 1992/83
South east	20.4	1	-4.6	-7.0
South west	31.4	6	-1.6	-1.8
East Anglia	19.5	0	-6.2	-8.7
East Midlands	15.2	0	-5.8	-8.9
West Midlands	15.0	0	-5.8	-8.4
Yorks & Humbs	16.8	0	-4.9	-8.8
North West	15.8	2	-4.8	-7.8
North	15.5	1	-5.5	-9.5
Wales	12.4	1	-5.5	-10.8
Scotland	13.1	9	-6.1	-11.4

and their loss of support in some of their isolated pockets of support elsewhere, is part of a growing identification of the Liberal Democrats with one particular part of the country.'[5]

One of the more important lessons of the 1992 general election for the Liberal Democrats, therefore, was that with a more specific targeting of individual constituencies they could, in terms of parliamentary seats, effectively withstand a decline in their popular support nationwide. The recovery in Labour's fortunes came at the expense of the old Alliance vote but the Liberal Democrats were successful in defending their vote in large parts of the south west and some areas of the south east. Whether this is sufficient to support the argument that the Liberal Democrats have become a regional party remains to be seen. What cannot be denied is that in 1992 the Liberal Democrats proved the effectiveness of an electoral strategy which concentrates more on the regions than on the country as a whole. Labour's new public standing has meant that the Liberal Democrats can no longer rely on disgruntled voters transferring from that party or on former Conservatives seeing the Liberal Democrats as the only home for protest votes. The days of plenty enjoyed by the Alliance appear, temporarily at least, to be over. The Liberal Democrats must make a reduced level of electoral support go a long way. We will now see whether the evidence from local elections is similar to that from the last general election.

Local elections

Following their victory in the Orpington parliamentary by-election in 1962 the Liberals thrived in local elections, making a total of 567 net gains that year and by the following year controlling twenty local councils.[6] Such gains could not be consolidated, however, and the local government base became depleted. When local government was reorganised in the early 1970s Liberal candidates, despite continued, if intermittent successes in parliamentary by-elections, failed to make a big impression. Indeed, the party had majority control in just one council (Eastbourne) out of more than five hundred new authorities.[7] Only one out of every twenty-four councillors across Britain was a Liberal. The Liberal revivals sparked by parliamentary by-election victories during this period were certainly not grounded in a strong local electoral or organisational base.

The Liberal Democrats, in contrast, believe that success must be built from the bottom up. Despite the development of the philosophy of community politics, neither the Liberals nor the Alliance managed to achieve a significant breakthrough in the level of the parties' local government representation. Today, however, the Liberal Democrats have over five thousand councillors, control 51 councils in Britain and play a critical role in scores of others where no single party enjoys an overall majority. They have relegated the Conservatives to the third party in British local government. These developments are even more remarkable given the Liberal Democrats' troubled beginnings and the impact this had on the party's competitiveness in local contests.

In January 1988 the Liberals and SDP voted for merger. Launched in March of that year the new party found the headlines dominated by David Owen's decision to lead a

Table 10.3 Liberal Democrat performance in local elections
in England, 1988–1994

		% share	*% in seats contested*	*Seats won*	*% seats won*
1988	Districts	18.5	25.7	234	12.9
	Mets	13.9	17.2	69	8.3
1989	Counties	20.1	25.9	439	14.6
1990	Districts	18.5	27.8	335	18.7
	Mets	13.5	18.8	66	8.0
1990	London	14.1	16.2	229	12.0
1991	Districts	22.7	33.7	1,972	19.5
	Mets	18.6	22.4	107	12.9
1992	Districts	21.1	25.3	266	14.5
	Mets	17.3	19.0	100	12.1
1993	Counties	29.3	33.8	833	27.8
1994	Districts	29.7	35.3	583	32.1
	Mets	22.8	25.9	132	15.5
	London	22.1	23.9	327	17.1

rump SDP. Opinion polls suggested that its electoral support was evaporating fast. A MORI poll conducted at this time gave the Liberal Democrats a derisory 6 per cent –one point ahead of Owen's SDP. These combined scores were just half the rating the Alliance had enjoyed in 1984 when the particular set of local elections due in May 1988 had last been contested. Such a setting was far from an ideal preparation for those elections but, despite a decline in both vote share and council seats, the actual number of losses sustained was not great. Why, when the Liberal Democrats had lost considerable support in the polls, were they able to avoid a more damaging loss of support? Were the polls simply wrong or had the Liberal Democrats already begun to display an ability to defend and even win local council seats despite the wider national tide running against them?

Although the polls suggested that Owen's SDP was as popular as Ashdown's Liberal Democrats, the election results told a different story. Across England and Wales the SDP fielded just 282 candidates–six times fewer than the Liberal Democrats. A mere 4 SDP councillors were elected compared with over 300 Liberal Democrats. The average vote share for Liberal Democrat candidates in the shire districts was 25.7 per cent (Table 10.3), for the SDP just 11.7 per cent. In a number of wards, candidates from the two parties competed. In such wards, the Liberal Democrats were twice as popular as the SDP in the shires and six times more popular in the metropolitan boroughs. In local elections at least, therefore, the SDP, regardless of what the polls might have intimated, were no match for the Liberal Democrats. Indeed, the Liberal Democrats' national equivalent vote share in these elections was 17 per cent–three times their opinion poll rating. Thus began the pattern of a sizeable gap between the Liberal Democrats' popularity as suggested by opinion polls and their support in local elections.

A more difficult test for the Liberal Democrats came in the following year's 1989 county council elections. On the last occasion these authorities had been elected in 1985 the Alliance was enjoying buoyant opinion poll ratings (about 28 per cent), had won one in five of the 3000 seats available in the 39 English counties, finished just 2 per cent behind Labour in the popular vote and was instrumental in causing a sharp rise in the number of hung county councils. Even allowing for some underestimate of Liberal Democrat strength by the polls, it seemed inevitable that the party must lose perhaps two-thirds of those county councillors elected under the Alliance label in 1985.[8] True, the Liberal Democrats did falter, but their loss in seats was small compared with what might have been. In total the party lost 193 seats in England, but these were partially offset by more than 80 gains. Opinion polls had become a poor guide to the Liberal Democrats' electoral performance and results showed that the swing of the electoral pendulum in their case was not uniform.

The county council elections demonstrated Liberal Democrat strength in the shires, but their support in metropolitan England was not put to the test until May 1990. This set of elections took place amidst considerable government unpopularity over the poll tax. The Conservatives suffered badly but the protest vote went chiefly to Labour. Liberal Democrats, perhaps partly because of their practice of targeting winnable wards and partly because Labour was viewed as having won the right to represent dissatisfaction over the tax, contested a far lower proportion of seats than had the Alliance four years previously. In the London and metropolitan boroughs, for example, the party fielded candidates for just 63 per cent of available seats. In turn this affected their overall vote share. In the capital they polled 14 per cent–almost 10 per cent lower than the Alliance in both 1982 and 1986. However, their share of seats (229 seats, 12 per cent) was virtually identical to the situation in 1986 (249 seats, 13 per cent) as the party's strategy of ignoring lost causes and focusing campaigning activity on vulnerable wards began to reap dividends.

In metropolitan Britain and in those shire districts with elections there was a similar story. Although the Liberal Democrat vote declined by some 10 per cent compared with the Alliance, their share of seats fell by less than 4 per cent. The Liberal Democrats had begun to overcome an important effect of the electoral system. Liberals, and to a lesser extent the SDP, had amassed votes only to see a low return in seats. The Liberal Democrats, with a more bespoke campaigning style, reduced the number of 'wasted votes' and learnt how to safeguard their own areas of strength. So successful was this approach that the party added the London boroughs of Tower Hamlets and Sutton to the growing number of authorities under their control. Much of this electoral terrain was not, on the face of it, to their liking–inner city wards where Labour was strong. The poll tax which so dominated the elections was an issue suited to Labour's national campaigning style. Despite such circumstances the Liberal Democrats emerged from these elections in far better shape than might have been expected for a party whose opinion poll rating was still less than double figures.

The 1991 local elections presented the Liberal Democrats with possibly their biggest test to date in two important respects. First, the sheer number of seats would stretch the party's slender resources to the limit. Across England and Wales there were contests for over eleven thousand council seats, and finding sufficient numbers of candidates proved difficult. Secondly, this particular local electoral cycle was widely regarded as a dummy run for a general election. Mrs Thatcher, for example, had used the same set of contests in both 1983 and 1987 to judge the national electoral mood and had called a general election shortly afterwards on both occasions. For the Liberal Democrats it would be their last real opportunity before a general election to convince voters that despite their upheavals they were still a credible force in British politics.

The Alliance had contested just half the wards in England in 1983, boosting their presence to two-thirds of contests in 1987. In 1991 the Liberal Democrats were only able to match the 1983 figure. Moreover, in many wards with multiple vacancies the party fielded only a single candidate. In large areas of the country potential Liberal Democrat voters were left with a choice of abstention, using less than their full quota of votes, or of dividing their support amongst other parties. The party was presented with a difficult problem: they had to be perceived as a national electoral force with less than a national electoral presence. They were helped by survey findings such as those presented by MORI. As well as asking the usual general election voting question the pollsters had asked respondents how they might vote in specifically local elections. The Liberal Democrats, whose putative general poll rating languished at 15 per cent, showed a recovery to 21 per cent following this line of questioning.[9]

This approach resulted in a remarkably accurate poll forecast. The nationwide vote shares subsequently turned out to be Conservative 37 per cent, Labour 39 per cent with the Liberal Democrats on 21 per cent. It would be wrong to describe these results as a triumph, but the Liberal Democrats' electoral strategy of targeting wards was rewarded. Despite their vote share in the shires declining from 27 per cent in 1987 to 23 per cent in 1991 they made a net gain of almost five hundred seats. Across the country, the party's share of seats rose from 16 per cent in 1987 to 19.5 per cent in 1991.

Some striking examples of this electoral strategy at work can be seen from the results in individual local authorities. In East Devon, for example, the Liberal Democrats' vote share fell by 10.3 per cent, largely a function of contesting fewer wards, but the party's seat share rose by 6.7 per cent. In West Wiltshire, the party's vote share declined by 1.7 per cent despite fighting an additional seat, but none the less their share of seats rose by 35 per cent. Overall, in 128 out of 332 local authorities the Liberal Democrats' vote fell but their share in seats either remained static or increased. Clearly, the Liberal Democrats, unlike the Alliance, had developed a sophisticated local electoral strategy.

The 1992 general election demonstrated that the Liberal Democrats could withstand a decline in electoral support without too much damage to their numerical strength at the parliamentary level too. In an important sense this skill had been nurtured in local election contests. The 1992 local elections followed closely on John Major's general election victory and brought significant Conservative gains at Labour's expense. By the autumn, however, withdrawal from the European Exchange Rate Mechanism undermined Conservative support and the government approached the 1993 county council elections with trepidation. In fact the results saw the worst Conservative performance in the shires since local government reorganisation in the 1970s. Some counties, including Dorset, Kent and Norfolk, were without a Conservative majority for the first time in more than a century. The battle honours went to the Liberal Democrats, who with more than eight hundred councillors, almost doubled their representation. Majority control in Cornwall and Somerset was achieved, further consolidating advances in the far south west. One of the most remarkable aspects of these elections, however, lay in the party's success at converting votes to seats. With 27 per cent of the vote the Liberal Democrats were 1 per cent behind the Alliance share in 1985 but that had only brought one-fifth of the seats. In 1993 the Liberal Democrats made a critical breakthrough in securing a 1 per cent higher share of seats than votes. How had they achieved this?

An analysis of each party's share of the vote at the 1989 and 1993 county council elections allows an assessment to be made of their average gain and loss. Applying these figures to each 1989 division result shows what the outcome would have been for each party if there had been a uniform swing. What this exercise reveals is that the Conservatives would have lost 100 seats rather than the 470 they did lose and that the Liberal Democrats would have made only 150 gains rather than the 380 they achieved. Were Liberal Democrat candidates simply the beneficiaries of tactical voting or had the party itself created the conditions for such a favourable distribution of results? In order to rule out the possibility that the forecasting error was purely a function of changing patterns of party competition, i.e. seats changing hands because one party or another did not have a candidate, we analysed only those 1,605 English county divisions where the three major parties competed in both 1989 and 1993.

Tactical voting appears to have played only a secondary role. In Conservative/Liberal Democrat marginals, defined as those seats where the Conservative majority was 20 per cent or less, tactical voting would have revealed itself with a better than average Liberal Democrat rise and a squeeze on the Labour vote. Across all seats where the 1989 contest had finished with the Conservatives in first place and the Democrats as runner-up the Democrat vote rose by 10.7 per cent. In the marginal seats the rise was lower at 9 per cent–the opposite of what was expected. The Labour vote, far from being squeezed in the marginals rose at a faster rate overall. Whatever the factors accounting for Liberal Democrat success in 1993, therefore, tactical voting was not amongst them.

Overall there was a 6 per cent swing from Conservative to Liberal Democrat in the county elections. Inspection of 233 seats the Liberal Democrats gained from the Conservatives in 1993, however, indicated much greater swings. In those seats the average vote changes were Conservative -13.5 per cent, Labour -3.4 per cent and Democrat +20 per cent. The average Conservative majority in 1989 in these same seats had been 17.4 per cent with a maximum of 52.9 per cent. In short, many of the Liberal Democrat victories were in seats which could not be classed as marginal at all nor was the swing within the expected range. Furthermore, in 49 of these cases the Liberal Democrats had actually finished in third place in 1989 and so had had to leapfrog Labour to win the seat. Where the Liberal Democrats had overtaken both Labour and Conservative the average rise in their vote share was some 31 per cent. Although swings in local elections are frequently higher than in national elections, such changes are extreme. Variations of this magnitude suggest an important aspect of Liberal Democrat strength lies in the ability of the party's local activists correctly to identify vulnerable seats and to launch a well targeted campaign almost irrespective of the party's previous electoral strength.

The Conservative humiliation in the 1990 local elections had been widely viewed as contributing significantly to Mrs Thatcher's fall from power.[10] Four years on and the Conservatives were more unpopular then they had been at the height of the poll tax controversy. Although Labour were expected to capitalise on Conservative unpopularity, the position of the Liberal Democrats had changed substantially. Unlike 1990, the Liberal Democrats became the focus of a massive protest vote. Labour's national equivalent vote share was 40 per cent, some three points lower than it had been in the poll tax elections. The Liberal Democrats, however, improved even on their county election performance and with 27 per cent were just 1 per cent behind the Conservatives and back to the levels of popularity enjoyed by the Alliance. Once again, the party performed better than the opinion polls suggested and, once again, seat forecasts based on an assumption of uniform swing proved wide of the mark.

Since their establishment in 1988, the Liberal Democrats have developed a strong local electoral base. This has resulted in the party winning more seats and controlling more councils than either the Liberals or the Alliance. Despite the party not matching the popular support achieved by the Alliance in the first half of the 1980s, the Liberal Democrats have proved a more successful party. From the beginning the party became more selective about which local wards were contested. In the early years the pattern of contestation had less to do with a definable electoral strategy and rather more to do with scarce resources in terms of both finance and members. In recent years the party appears to have made a conscious decision to focus its campaigning strength in areas where other parties, chiefly but not exclusively the Conservatives, have shown vulnerability. The consequence has been that the party's vote is now much less widely dispersed than before. What was once a sizeable gap between vote and seat share has now narrowed considerably, even to the point in recent elections where the proportion of seats won has exceeded that for votes.

Parliamentary by-elections

Parliamentary by-elections have been as crucial to the fortunes of the Liberal Democrats as they were to the Liberals. Famous Liberal successes in the late 1950s and early 1960s prompted further activity which saw their national vote almost double between the 1959 and 1964 general elections. In the early 1970s the Liberals enjoyed a considerable run of success, beginning with victory in Rochdale in October 1972 followed by gains in Sutton and Cheam (December 1972), Ripon and Isle of Ely (July 1973) and Berwick-upon-Tweed in November 1973. Such victories provided an important base for the Liberal's general election performance in February 1974 when their vote rose by 12 per cent on the 1970 election. A third phase of crucial by-election victories began in October 1981 when, following endorsement a month before at the Liberal Party assembly of the plan to form an alliance with the SDP, the term 'Alliance' was first used on posters in the successful bid to win Croydon North West.[11] This victory was quickly followed by those of Shirley Williams in Crosby and Roy Jenkins in Glasgow Hillhead. A few months before the 1983 general election Simon Hughes captured the safe Labour seat of Southwark and Bermondsey on a record 42 per cent swing. These examples all serve to demonstrate the importance of by-election victories to the old Liberal Party in their pursuit of general election success.

Discussion of the Liberal Democrats' by-election performance can usefully be divided between the period from their establishment in 1988 up to the 1992 general election and the period following. In their first four years the Liberal Democrats succeeded in gaining just three seats out of 23 by-elections. One significant cause of the Liberal Democrats' lack of success in an arena of electoral politics where their predecessors had excelled was the rumbling discord and rivalry with the old SDP. Dr Owen's core of anti-mergerites succeeded in fielding candidates against Liberal Democrats in eight of the first ten by-elections of the 1987 parliament. In some cases SDP candidates did sufficiently well to undermine any chance of the Liberal Democrats themselves capturing a seat. In Epping Forest, for example, the Conservatives retained the seat with a slim majority over the second-placed Liberal Democrat. In fourth place, with 4,077 votes (just 427 fewer than the Conservative majority) was the SDP candidate. Without the distraction of candidates from two parties which eighteen months before had fought a general election together, the electorate might well have taken a completely different view of the likely electoral outcome–and adjusted their votes accordingly.

More damaging still was the by-election in Richmond, Yorkshire, held in February 1989 following Leon Brittan's appointment as a European Commissioner. The Liberals had contested the seat at the previous general election on behalf of the Alliance and it was seen as winnable, requiring only a 17 per cent swing. The Liberal Democrats again found themselves competing against an SDP candidate with, on this occasion, an established local political profile. The campaign reflected more the tensions between the opposition than the prospect of a Conservative defeat. In the event the result was doubly frustrating for the Liberal Democrats. First, the joint Liberal Democrat/SDP vote would easily have surpassed that of the Conservative who rather gratefully retained the seat. Secondly, the SDP finished as the runner-up and with over five thousand more votes than the Liberal Democrats.

Richmond threatened to derail the Liberal Democrats' development and certainly affected the party in the short-term. Although the continuing SDP had long ceased to have much presence in local elections, parliamentary by-elections did give it a platform for survival without the necessity of a proper organisational base. Nemesis was slow in coming, but each by-election performance tended to be even worse than the last. Less than three months after Richmond, Labour gained the Vale of Glamorgan from the Conservatives as candidates from the Liberal Democrats and the SDP each lost their deposits. A month later the two parties' combined vote in Glasgow Central was less than that of the Green Party candidate. In May 1990 three candidates from the former Alliance stood against each other in the safe Labour seat of Bootle. The Liberal Democrats easily won this side-show, with the SDP candidate polling just 155 votes–fewer than the Greens, fewer than the Liberal Party and, worst of all, considerably fewer than Lord David Sutch standing as the Monster Raving Loony candidate. The following week David Owen officially dissolved the SDP.

With the SDP's demise the Liberal Democrats were now free to contest by-elections on just one front. Their chance came in Eastbourne and the party could not have hoped for a better opportunity. The Liberals had taken control of the local council in 1973 and consistently polled well in the authority over a period of twenty years. The constituency required a relatively modest swing of 15 per cent to fall to the Liberal Democrats, though the by-election contest was complicated by the fact that it had been caused by the IRA's assassination of the sitting MP, Ian Gow, and the possibility of a sympathy vote for the Conservatives. The Liberal Democrats proved to be fortunate in facing a Conservative candidate widely regarded as inexperienced and unable to cope with media pressure. That fact, together with a strong Liberal Democrat party organisation, combined to create the conditions for success and give the party a winning majority of more than 4,500 votes.

This first by-election gain for the new party proved to be of more than symbolic significance. It boosted the party in the polls and renewed talk of a new Liberal Democrat revival of the 1990s to rival those by the Liberals in the 1960s and 1970s and the Alliance in the early 1980s. Liberal Democrat candidates were to gain two further Conservative seats in this parliament. In March 1991 a Conservative majority of almost twenty thousand was overturned on a 24.8 per cent swing in Ribble Valley. Later that year, the Liberal Democrats were victorious in Kincardine and Deeside in Scotland with a lesser swing of 11.4 per cent. This last victory illustrates the difficulty caused by the organisational disruption of the party's formative years. The Democrats' first by-election victory had not occurred until more than half way through the parliament. Their last win came with a general election less than six months away. This meant that the party's by-election momentum had been held in check by continuing arguments within the party itself and with former colleagues from both the SDP and the Liberals opposed to the merger. When victories finally occurred, the party was already facing the prospect of a pre-election recovery in Conservative fortunes and had little time in which to consolidate its hold on individual constituencies. Therefore, it came as no great surprise when at the general election all three by-election gains reverted to Conservative control.

The first by-election after the 1992 general election was held in Newbury in May 1993. As with Eastbourne, the seat was centred on a local authority with a history of strong Liberal Democrat representation. Indeed, the party had seized overall control of the council in 1991. The Conservatives were defending a majority of 18.6 per cent over the Liberal Democrats with Labour, polling just 6 per cent in 1992, a distant third. With only a small third party vote to squeeze, the Liberal Democrats' best chance of success lay in converting former Conservative supporters. Prospects were helped considerably by the dramatic decline in the government's popularity following withdrawal from the European exchange rate mechanism and devaluation of sterling. The by-election in Newbury was held on the same day as the county elections and the Liberal Democrats won a majority of some 38.2 per cent. The Conservative to Liberal Democrat swing of

28.4 per cent was amongst the highest at any by-election and served to demonstrate that, unlike the previous parliament, the Liberal Democrat by-election machine had already begun to work.

That machine was called into action again in Christchurch in July 1993. Another seat in the south of England, another seat where the Liberal Democrats had finished in second place at the general election but, unlike Newbury, an area where the party had not established a strong local government presence. That said, the Conservatives were in poor shape to contest a by-election. Their humiliation in the county elections had left them with control of a solitary county, Buckinghamshire, and hope only lay in their large majority. The task before the Liberal Democrats, therefore, was to capture the Conservatives' fifteenth safest seat without the benefit of a well organised and active local party. A feature of the Liberal Democrats' campaigning style, however, is their ability to mobilise rank-and-file activists prepared to move temporarily into a constituency to canvass and campaign vigorously. They were helped by a delay in calling the by-election. On the eve of election most commentators believed the Liberal Democrats would win but few anticipated the enormous swing of over 35 per cent.

Two gains turned into three when yet another Conservative seat in southern England, Eastleigh, had a by-election in June 1994 following the death of Stephen Milligan. His majority had been 23 per cent but with the precedents of Newbury and Christchurch appeared vulnerable. What made Eastleigh interesting, however, was that Labour's vote in 1992 had been just 7 per cent behind the Liberal Democrats and the party had also done reasonably well in local elections, polling 30 per cent in the 1990 contests. Labour's public view, stated by Jack Straw before the by-election had been called, was that they and not the Liberal Democrats were best placed to win the seat. In the event the Liberal Democrats justified their favouritism, winning with 44.3 per cent of the vote. The Conservatives were pushed back into third place by Labour.

Indeed, Labour's ability to limit the squeeze on its own support in Eastleigh was indicative of a new and worrying development for the Liberal Democrats. The electorate seemed no longer to think of Labour as an unelectable party, and the belief that they would blindly support the Liberal Democrats against the Conservatives regardless of the circumstances of the contest became more difficult to sustain. Simultaneous with the contest for Eastleigh were four other by-elections, all in Labour-held seats. Unusually, in all of these Labour's vote share increased. In one, Newham North East, the Liberal Democrat candidate announced he was joining the Labour Party. Naturally, this had the effect of undermining the party's vote there but, significantly, the Liberal Democrat share of the vote also fell in two other constituencies. Public support for Labour was to increase further following the outcome of the race for the Labour Party leadership in July. The so-called Blair factor began to be felt.

The first real test of the effect of this new presence on the Liberal Democrats came in December 1994 with a by-election in the Dudley West constituency. A Conservative seat widely regarded as a Labour target, the Liberal Democrats had a defensive agenda of, first, sustaining their general election vote as far as possible and, secondly, hoping that many disenchanted Conservatives cast their protest vote for their candidate. The outcome proved disappointing for the Liberal Democrats, both in terms of the swing of

29 per cent from Conservative to Labour which rivalled that of their own recent wins and because their own vote share fell by 3 per cent. Dudley West was the tenth by-election of the parliament, and although the party had gained three seats, in half the contests their vote share had actually fallen. Moreover, the result in Dudley also appeared to suggest that the Liberal Democrats no longer had a monopoly on causing by-election upsets and that Labour, with a new leader aiming to take the party towards the centre ground, would make life more difficult for the Liberal Democrats in the future.

Local by-elections

Although the Liberal Democrats derive a great deal of national publicity from victories in parliamentary by-elections these tend by definition to be sporadic. For more sustained media attention the party has had to rely upon the far more frequent local government by-elections. Based in Hebden Bridge, the Association of Liberal Councillors was extremely active in the 1980s in persuading local party groups that local by-election success was crucial in raising morale amongst activists and generating favourable media publicity. Renamed the Association of Liberal Democrat Councillors (ALDC) the organisation continues this process. The party's own newspaper *Liberal Democrat News* (and the Liberal Democrats are the only party to have such a publication) carries a weekly report of by-election results from around the country, provides forewarning of pending contests and appeals for help in campaigning.

Local government by-elections, therefore, can be used as an essential tool for gauging the overall health of the party and in assessing the nature and purpose of its electoral strategy. For example, the inter-party acrimony after 1987 was reflected in a series of poor by-election performances. Throughout 1985 the two parties of the Alliance contested 91.4 per cent of 451 local by-election vacancies, more than either Conservative or Labour. In 1988 the Liberal Democrats fielded candidates in 80 per cent of by-elections and by 1990 they were contesting only two-thirds of vacancies. More recently, however, the rate of contestation has risen again: to 87 per cent in both 1993 and 1994. Contesting seats, of course, merely reflects the level of organisation and state of morale within a party. In order to assess electoral success, details on vote share, seat gains and losses and the like should be examined.

Any assessment of the Liberal Democrats in this arena of electoral competition should contrast the party's performance with that of the Alliance. Have the Liberal Democrats inherited all the qualities and overcome the weaknesses of that earlier effort? Within the Alliance the respective contributions of the Liberals and SDP were unbalanced. In the two-year period beginning in June 1983, for example, Liberal candidates made net gains of 122 seats while their SDP partners could manage less than 50. Although Liberals contested more seats than the SDP, in the ratio of 6:4, the ratio for seats won was 4:1. In cases with three party competition the Liberal share was consistently higher than that of the SDP. In 1985, for example, Liberals averaged 40.5 per cent while SDP candidates were some eight points lower. While the Alliance collectively was doing well in these years the Liberals were consistently the senior party.[12] In terms of best practice, therefore, the Liberal Democrats would have wished in an ideal world to inherit the local by-election experience of the old Liberal party. Crucially, however, two factors combined to prevent this. First, the fall-out from the events in 1987 and 1988 adversely affected the ability to fight and win local by-elections. Secondly, Labour's recovery began to take hold and the struggle for by-election votes became more competitive.

Table 10.4 provides a clear illustration of these effects by comparing by-election results from 1983–87 with those from 1987–92. The 1987 general election forms a clear watershed in the respective fortunes of Labour and the Liberal Democrats. During the 1983 parliament, for example, the Liberals made net gains of some 162 seats while the SDP gained 98 seats. Although many of the seats came from the Conservatives, a significant proportion were won from Labour. After the 1987 election, however, the Liberal Democrats were never able to match this success. Their total of 28 net gains could not disguise the fact that in exchanges between themselves and Labour they suffered a net deficit of 6 seats. In contrast, Labour recovered from a total of 12 net losses between 1983 and 1987 to register 45 net gains from 1987 to 1992.

Table 10.4   Transfer of seats in local government by-elections

July 1983–June1987

	Gained by				Total
	Con	Lab	Lib	SDP	losses
Gained from					
Conservative	–	53	155	66	274
Labour	18	–	42	32	92
Liberal	17	18	–	–	35
SDP	4	9	–	–	13
Total gains	39	80	197	98	
Net gains/losses	-235	-12	+162	+85	

June 1987– April 1992

	Gained by			Total
	Con	Lab	LibDem	losses
Gained from				
Conservative	–	87	93	180
Labour	48	–	35	83
Liberal Democrat	59	41	–	100
Total gains	107	128	128	
Net gains/losses	-73	+45	+28	

Note: A party's gains should be read vertically, losses read horizontally.

From the 1992 general election to March 1995 there were more than a thousand local by-elections of which almost four hundred resulted in the seat changing party control. Overall, while Labour made 55 gains from Conservative, the Liberal Democrats gained twice as many. Moreover, for every seat Labour gained from the Liberal Democrats, two went in the other direction. Superficially, therefore, it would appear as though the Liberal Democrats had put their relatively poor performance behind them and had begun to recapture some of the by-election form shown in the Alliance years. Examined more closely, however, the figures reveal a different story. At the end of 1992, the Liberal Democrats had made net gains of 14 seats since the general election while Labour had incurred 20 losses. The following year, although Labour managed 2 net gains, the gap widened, with the Liberal Democrats registering 75 net gains. By 1994, however, the tide had turned, most especially after Tony Blair succeeded John Smith as Labour leader, and at the end of the year the two parties were inseparable with 39 gains each. It is, of course, too early to say whether these data represent the beginning of a trend, but for the Liberal Democrats, dependent as they are on by-election victories, it will be a cause for concern if a resurgent Labour party blocks their future advance.

European elections

In the first two sets of direct elections to the European Parliament in 1979 and 1984 the Liberal Democrats' predecessors performed well but were penalised heavily by the electoral system. In 1979 the Liberals obtained 12.6 per cent of the vote and in 1984 the Alliance scored 18.5 per cent, but on both occasions no seats were won. A month before the 1989 European elections the Liberal Democrats had achieved a creditable performance in the county council elections with a national equivalent vote share of 18 per cent. The prospect of the party emulating the Alliance's performance looked good. However, many voters disillusioned with the two major parties decided to ignore the Liberal Democrats in favour of the Greens. In the shires, where voters had been to the polls for both local and European elections, there was a dramatic change in Liberal Democrat fortunes. From 20.1 per cent in the English shire elections the party's vote slumped to just 7.5 per cent in the European contests while Green support rose from 2.1 per cent to 17.3 per cent in the same areas.

Such figures suggest that much of the support for the Liberal Democrats in the local elections transferred itself to the Greens in the space of a month. One possible explanation for this transformation lies in the importance of electoral context. The Liberal Democrats, much like the Liberals, have fared best in local elections where their campaigning style and brand of 'pavement politics' has tapped into concerns with neighbourhood. In contrast, the Greens have proved insufficiently organised to conduct similar campaigns and have failed at the local government level. The platform of the European elections in 1989, however, gave the Greens a perfect opportunity. The electorate appeared disillusioned with both Conservative and Labour, the Greens were campaigning in just 78 constituencies and not thousands of wards and their message of an environmental disaster facing Europe appeared appropriate for the time and context. [13]

Table 10.5 European elections, 1989 and 1994

| | *1989* | | *1994* | |
	% share	*Seats*	*% share*	*Seats*
Conservative	34.7	32	27.9	18
Labour	40.1	45	44.2	62
Liberal Democrats	6.2	0	16.7	2
Green	14.9	0	3.2	0
Other	4.1	1	4.8	2

Note : The number of seats increased between 1989 and 1994.

For the Liberal Democrats the 1989 European elections were a severe setback. Results clearly demonstrated the fragility of their electoral support, but longer term they also appeared in danger of becoming stereotyped as a party capable of doing well only in certain types of election. The 1994 contests therefore became a crucial test for the party. Following their triumph in 1989, support for the Greens dwindled considerably, but the fact that many commentators expected the Liberal Democrats to do well, particularly in the south of England, added to the pressure on the latter. Certainly they appeared well placed to inflict damage on a troubled Conservative government, and in the May local elections they gained seats and councils and recorded a nationwide vote of some 27 per cent.

Two obstacles to a Liberal Democrat bandwagon existed. First, there was the death on 12 May 1994 of the Labour leader, John Smith. Political and electoral hostilities were suspended for a time and this checked the Liberal Democrats' ability to take full advantage of the favourable publicity engendered by the local elections. Secondly, the reunification of Germany meant that the overall size of the European Parliament was increased, with Britain receiving an additional six seats. Both parties and electorate had to come to terms with new constituency boundaries and many calculations about the utility and direction of tactical voting were upset. Against the backdrop of a wave of public sympathy for Labour and the customary problems of campaigning on the doorstep across constituencies with half a million voters, the Liberal Democrats' vote share more than doubled compared with 1989 but still stuck a critical ten points lower than they achieved in the local elections barely a month previously.

In winning two seats, however, the party managed to do what neither the Liberals nor the Alliance had done. Those victories, in the Cornwall and West Plymouth and Somerset and North Devon constituencies, confirmed the Liberal Democrats' growing strength in the far south west. Arguably, had it not been for a candidate standing as a 'Literal Democrat' in the Devon and East Plymouth seat, the Liberal Democrats' might have won three seats. As it was, they showed that they could challenge the two main parties on the difficult terrain of European constituencies and that their strategy of targeting seats could have its rewards even when those seats were on a much larger scale. It could be argued, however, that in these European elections the Liberal Democrats flattered only to deceive. Had they continued the momentum of the local elections then the European contests might have brought as many as fourteen seats. Instead, their national vote share fell by some 10 per cent as Labour's rose. Once again, the electorate demonstrated that its inclination to support the Liberal Democrats was related to the electoral context.

Conclusion

The Liberal Democrats have met with different levels of electoral success in different electoral contexts. The 1992 general election was the new party's most critical test and there it deployed an electoral strategy which was evolved before and has since undergone further refinement. It is not a strategy without risk. Targeting winnable seats rather than seeking every available vote means the party might project the wrong image. The Liberal Democrats want to be viewed as a national party with national ambitions. At the same time, party campaign managers and the like know from the experience of the Alliance that there are no prizes for coming second under Britain's current electoral system. Any public statement that the party was concentrating its efforts in a handful of constituencies would inevitably lead to accusations that it had forsaken the prospect of winning power itself. At this point electoral strategy has to become divorced from public image.

The greatest success of the Liberal Democrats has been in overcoming the difficulties posed by the British winner-takes-all electoral system. In its previous incarnations the party has been heavily penalised in terms of its ratio of votes to seats. Spreading support thinly means that a party will not win many seats. In the Alliance's heyday, electors decamped in large numbers from both Conservative and Labour Parties but neither the Liberals and still less the SDP had an effective method for channelling this support to where it could be translated into seats. The Liberal Democrats, although never as popular as the Alliance, have proved much more effective at operating within the confines of an electoral system that traditionally works against third parties. Since 1988 the party has demonstrated in a range of local, national and European elections its strategy of concentrating its resources. This strategy has met with varying degrees of success.

What will the future bring? In terms of local government the Liberal Democrats have proved they have the capacity to win. In other electoral arenas their position is less assured. European elections appear unsuitable terrain with very large constituencies and an issue agenda that has side-stepped Liberal Democrat concerns. By-elections, both local and parliamentary, occur randomly and do not always favour the party. Moreover, they can be extremely competitive, with the Liberal Democrats now confronted by a much stronger Labour Party. The next general election promises to be critical for the Liberal Democrats. Should the pattern of 1992 be repeated, the party might well gain seats without a significant rise in its overall vote share. Should those gains occur where it already has a presence, for example in Scotland and the far south west of England, there is the complication that the Liberal Democrats will be viewed as a regional rather than a national party. Ironically, the party's electoral strategy might turn out to have short-term benefits but long-term costs.

Notes

1 Michael Steed, 'The Electoral Strategy of the Liberal Party', in V. Bogdanor (ed.), *Liberal Party Politics,* Clarendon Press 1983, p.75.

2 K. Reif and H. Schmitt, 'Nine Second-order Elections–A Conceptual Framework for the Analysis of European Election Results', *European Journal of Political Research,* Vol. 8, No. 1, 1980, pp.3–44.

3 Patrick Dunleavy, 'The Political Parties', in P. Dunleavy *et al.* (eds), *Developments in British Politics 4,* Macmillan, 1993.

4 J. Curtice and M. Steed, 'The Results Analysed', in D. Butler and D. Kavanagh (eds), *The British General Election of 1992,* Macmillan, 1993.

5 John Curtice and M. Steed, *op. cit.,* p.337.

6 William Wallace, 'Survival and Revival', in V. Bogdanor, *op. cit.*

7 C. Rallings and M. Thrasher (eds), *Local Elections in Britain: A Statistical Digest,* Local Government Chronicle Elections Centre, 1993.

8 'Huge Defeat Predicted for Tories', *Sunday Times,* 23 April 1989.

9 'Labour Set to Trounce Tories, Says Computer', *Sunday Times,* 28 April 1991.

10 D. Butler, A. Adonis and T. Travers, *Failure in British Government,* Oxford University Press, 1994.

11 D. Butler and D. Kavanagh, *The British General Election of 1983,* Macmillan, 1984, p.74.

12 C. Rallings and M. Thrasher, 'Party Competition and Electoral Volatility: The Case of Local By-elections, 1983–1987', *Local Government Studies,* Vol. 14, No. 6, 1988, pp.67–76.

13 C. Rallings and M. Thrasher, 'Exploring Uniformity and Variability in Local Electoral Outcomes: Some Evidence from English Local Elections 1985–1991', *Electoral Studies,* Vol. 12, No. 3, 1993, p.366–84.

CHAPTER 11

Power in the balance

Michael Temple

Introduction

The importance of local politics to the Liberal Democrats cannot be overstated. After the 1970 general election, with just six Members of Parliament, the Liberal Party appeared to be getting nowhere as a national force. In the aftermath of defeat, their assembly at Eastbourne that year passed a resolution which called for 'a primary strategic emphasis on community politics'. The resolution sparked the emergence of a new generation of activists determined to change British politics from the bottom-up by encouraging local communities to take control of local decision-making.[1] The Liberals started to concentrate more of their energies on contesting local seats, in an attempt to build local power bases as a future springboard to success in national elections. This activity has had a dominant role in both the continued existence of the party (under whatever appellation) and its revived electoral fortunes at both national and local level since the community politics resolution was passed. Liberal Democrat success at the grassroots has meant that the other main parties have had to follow suit or risk their local power bases diminishing, contributing to a revitalisation of local government electoral campaigning.

Throughout this period, a specifically 'Liberal' approach to local politics has been developed, often disparagingly referred to by their political opponents as 'pavement politics'. At the local level, Liberal Democrat politics are founded on ideas of community politics, debate and openness. This basis can present problems when the opportunity to put these principles into action arrives, because in the majority of cases Liberal Democrat groups attain a share of power in hung councils, where no one party has an overall majority of seats on the council. Therefore, deals have to be struck with parties whose basic principles can be at odds with those of Liberal Democrats and in which notions of open government have rarely been articulated. The realities of power might also affect the party's principles. Utilising questionnaire and face-to-face interviews with political and bureaucratic leaders in both hung and majority control councils, this chapter examines the success of Liberal Democrat groups in hung (or, as many in the party prefer to call them, balanced) local authorities.

The chance to govern

Over the past decade, the opportunities for Liberal Democrats to demonstrate their competence to govern have proliferated. The British political system, with little experience of the phenomenon at either local or national level, has had to accommodate an increasing number of hung local authorities. Identifying hung councils in Britain can be problematic, as local government results often fail to identify parties and both by-elections and changes of party allegiance are more frequent than at national level. Therefore, precise judgements on council composition are often difficult. Some councils are only nominally hung, in that there is a less partisan approach than is now the norm. For example, while no party has an overall majority in either Kennet District Council or Gwynedd County Council, their respective chief executives argue that the relevance of party groups is less important, and a more independent style of working prevails. Such councils do *not* consider themselves hung. There are also some strange interpretations as to what constitutes a hung council. For example, in Wolverhampton the chief executive has an unusual perception of the politics of coalition-making. Despite the clear arithmetic of Labour (29 seats), Conservatives (28) and Liberal Democrats (3), he argues that:

> Wolverhampton is *not* hung. The Conservatives and LibDems have formed a 'Majority Group', formally registered with me, which is opposed by the 'Labour Group'. So far as normal council service is concerned, the Majority Group acts like a normal controlling group. The LibDems and Conservatives sort out their differences (if any) *within* the group and not in front of officers. [original emphasis][2]

Despite the comments of the chief executive, Wolverhampton is clearly a hung council ruled by a formal coalition of Conservatives and Liberal Democrats. Such views give some idea of how difficult it can be to assess the politics of hung authorities.

This survey has classified as hung all those authorities where no one party or organised group of councillors has an overall majority. In most cases, this definition causes little trouble. The trappings of party politics (notably strict party discipline when voting) have gradually infiltrated nearly all political arenas in Britain.[3] While some councils may have more independent ways of working (such as Kennet and Gwynedd) and others may have large numbers of Independent councillors (such as Dyfed and West Oxford) they are still in effect hung and need to be included in any analysis. These four councils all have a substantial Liberal Democrat group. Indeed, in most hung councils all three main parties were potential participants in government. Only 5 of the 151 hung councils surveyed had no Liberal Democrat councillor, compared with 9 with no Labour member and two without a Conservative councillor.

Problems of identifying administrations

Hung national legislatures are a common occurrence in most western European democracies. In such parliaments, party lines are usually clear and whether a legislature is hung or not is readily apparent. Not only that, but pay-offs between coalition partners (whether in the form of cabinet posts or policy concessions) are usually easy to see. As with these national legislatures, hung councils necessitate the formation and maintenance of coalitions, however constituted, between political parties. They should provide us with readily observable evidence of party cooperation, especially in the form of office 'pay-offs', for example, committee chairs. However, besides the problems of identifying hung councils, discovering the administrative arrangements and pay-offs existing in hung councils can also be difficult. First, it is not unknown for the actors involved to disagree on the composition and nature of the administration; one leader's coalition is another leader's informal arrangement. Secondly, while it might be supposed that office pay-offs will be readily apparent, agreements to share chairs may be purely for technical purposes, with no agreement to cooperate legislatively. Thirdly, it has been noted that many 'partners' will not take committee chairs, preferring to extract policy concessions.[4]

When they are apparent, office pay-offs can provide some indication of possible policy deals; appointing a representative of a 'junior' coalition partner to an important committee chair can often be an indication that policy concessions have been made to the smaller party, although the senior party may be reluctant to admit this. In the main, policy pay-offs are even less easy to discover than office pay-offs. Political parties have a vested interest in hiding their policy deals with erstwhile and future rivals, especially if elections are approaching. Election campaigns demand a distinctive party programme, which policy agreements with another party may blur. Imminent elections are often a catalyst for the breakdown of alliances.[5]

Central party disapproval of coalition politics is another good reason for blurring the nature of any agreements. Local Labour and Conservative groups (in particular) who do cooperate with the Liberal Democrats may be in conflict with central instructions, and therefore reluctant to admit such arrangements publicly. However, while Clause 6 of Labour's model standing orders comes close to forbidding local pacts and some groups have acquiesced to central party pressure,[6] Labour has adopted a more pragmatic response in recent years. For local Labour groups, especially in the shire districts and county councils long held by Conservatives, the lure of office or a share of power after a long time in opposition is apparent, and the Liberal Democrats are often the only viable partner. The pressure group Labour Initiative on Cooperation (LINC), formed in May 1995, is actively encouraging greater cooperation between the two parties, aiming to build 'a radical consensus for change by constructive dialogue with all those who want to see new post-Tory politics'.[7]

While Conservative Central Office might feel it has little to gain nationally by proving the efficacy of coalition politics at any level of British politics, local Conservatives are noted for their independence and pragmatism. As the Conservative group leader in Rochdale put it, getting and then holding on to power is the 'only virtue' in politics; her group has a power-sharing arrangement with the Liberal Democrats.[8]

Local Liberal Democrat groups value their relative autonomy. Essex County Council's Liberal Democrat leader says he would terminate the power-sharing arrangement his group had with Labour if instructed to do so by party headquarters, but he appears to be the exception. As noted, community politics and local decision-making play a major role in the current prominence of the Liberal Democrats in local government, which prominence in turn has contributed to the revival of the party's fortunes at *national* level. Local Liberal Democrat groups are aware of the importance of their success to the national party and are unlikely to feel as constrained when seeking policy or office pay-offs in hung councils as the other main parties. After all, their national party has a great deal to gain by demonstrating that coalition politics can work. Despite leader Paddy Ashdown declaring that he will not do a deal with the Conservatives in the event of a hung parliament after the next general election,[9] the party is perfectly at home with the Conservatives at local level, as their formal coalition in Wolverhampton and power-sharing in Rochdale demonstrates. As we shall see, pragmatism can appear to be the dominant strategy of Liberal Democrats in hung councils.

Administrative arrangements in hung councils

Given the increasing pragmatism of the three main local parties, we would expect to find them all actively involved in a variety of political partnerships. Table 11.1 lists the administrative arrangements in hung British councils, taken from the replies of 151 hung councils polled from December 1993 to April 1994. The political composition of administrations shown in Table 11.1 demonstrate that local political parties in Britain are willing to seek agreement with partners from across the ideological spectrum, and that Liberal Democrats are to the forefront.

Liberal Democrats are the most active participants in administrations in hung councils, with greater involvement than either Labour and Conservatives. Excluding councils who replied that they had 'no administration' or 'no formal party groups', Liberal Democrats are involved in at least 75 of 120 administrations (62.5 per cent). Despite their similar levels of representation in the hung councils examined, Labour (with 62 administrations) and Conservative groups (61 administrations) appear to be less successful. Indeed, Liberal Democrat involvement is even higher than it at first appears.

Examinations of administrative formation in English local government note the extraordinary success enjoyed by the Liberal Democrats even when another party is heading a minority administration.[10] If these accounts are accurate, one would expect to find that the influence of the party is even greater than its participation in 62.5 per cent of hung councils indicates, for Liberal Democrats will be helping to maintain in office many of the 18 Labour, 14 Conservative and 4 Independent minority administrations listed in Table 11.1. Some parties *must* be supporting the minority party even if only negatively, by abstaining from voting against the party in control. Of the 50 minority administrations in Table 11.1, we have information on the 'support' party in 25 cases

Table 11.1 Administrative arrangements in hung councils

Arrangement	Number of administrations
Conservative minority administration	14
Labour minority administration	18
Liberal Democrat minority administration	14
Independent minority administration	4
All-party administration	27
Conservative/Labour	1
Conservative/Liberal Democrat	9
Conservative/Independent	6
Labour/Liberal Democrat	15
Labour/Scottish Nationalist Party	1
Independent/Liberal Democrat	3
Independent/Ratepayers	1
Labour/Liberal Democrat/Independent	2
Conservative/Liberal Democrat/Labour	1
Conservative/Liberal Democrat/Independent	4
No formal party groups	5
No administration	26

Source: survey of hung councils, December 1993–April 1994; $n = 151$.

(4 Conservative, 10 Labour, 8 Liberal Democrat and 3 Independent minority administrations).

Table 11.2 lists the support parties to those 25 minority administrations. Out of 17 minority administrations run by other parties, the Liberal Democrats are the sole support party in 7 cases, and part of the all-party support in another 4 councils. Given this, it is likely that Liberal Democrat administrative involvement in hung councils could be over 80 per cent, indicating a quite phenomenal level of influence in hung local authorities in Britain. From these responses, it seems that the Liberal Democrats are more likely than

Table 11.2 Support parties to minority administrations

Administration	Con	Lab	Lib Dem	Indep	All-Party	Other
Conservative	–	0	2	1	1	0
Labour	1	–	4	2	2	1
Liberal Democrat	0	4	–	1	2	1
Independent	1	0	1	–	1	0

Source: survey of hung councils, December 1993–April 1994 ; $n = 25$

any other party to support either a Labour or a Conservative minority administration in power. In Liberal Democrat minority administrations, Labour is the most likely support party and vice versa.

The relevance of 'equidistance' at local level

At national level it has long been recognised that the only likely coalition involving the big three parties would be some sort of arrangement between Labour and the Liberal Democrats. As one commentator points out:

> the main policy differences between the two parties now lie in the area of constitutional reform ... from the electoral point of view, [they] are perfectly compatible.[11]

The Liberal Democrat's abandonment of equidistance between the two big parties has now acknowledged this closeness. However, at local level a strategy of equidistance appears highly relevant, with the Liberal Democrats seemingly prepared to do a deal with whichever party or parties are prepared to negotiate. That said, previous studies have often found a propensity for Liberal Democrats to seek agreements with Labour rather than the Conservatives,[12] and both Tables 11.1 and 11.2 confirm a preference for Labour as a partner. However, the belief that, because the Liberal Democrats are much closer ideologically to Labour than Conservative at national level they are more likely to make deals at local level with Labour in order to push the Conservatives into opposition[13] is to understate the independence and ideological diversity of local Liberal Democrat politicians. Local Liberal Democrat groups are far more likely to differ ideologically from their national leadership than local Labour and Conservative groups. The fact that the majority who do see themselves as ideologically divergent argue they are more left-wing than the national party[14] might also suggest a predilection to support Labour.

However, although Liberal Democrats *are* involved in more two party administrations with Labour than with other groups, many local party groups are perfectly willing to come to an arrangement with both Independents and Conservatives. The tendency for Labour and the Liberal Democrats to work together locally may reflect a natural desire not to allow a long-term 'traditional ruler' to remain in power. The traditional ruler (overwhelmingly the Conservatives) tends to suffer from deals made by the two long-term opposition parties. As the Liberal Democratic group leader in Lincolnshire County Council put it: 'it is great to be in power after 100 years of Conservative rule'–his party has a formal coalition with Labour. Another Liberal Democratic leader in an ex-Tory council felt that, 'after 12 years shut out contemptuously in opposition, it is wonderful to be able to participate constructively'.[15] While the Conservatives *are* less successful than Labour in coming to an arrangement with the Liberal Democrats, if one included all-party administrations there would be very little difference overall in Liberal Democrat support for Labour or the Conservatives. The Conservatives are active participants in administrations in hung councils and still form a number of two party administrations with Liberal Democrats.

Labour and Conservative–an 'unholy alliance'?

Not only do the Conservatives form alliances with the Liberal Democrats, but they will also come to an arrangement at local level with their national enemies, cooperating with Labour in a number of multi-party governments. In Cleethorpes, while an all-party administration exists, Labour and the Conservatives (the two largest parties) share all the major chairs. While there is only one authority (Tandridge District Council) where the two parties work together formally to hold power, Liberal Democrats argue there are other cases where the two parties secretly cooperate. The party's literature complains such deals are a 'gigantic con trick on the voters', alleging that:

> Labour and Tory councillors in a string of local authorities across England have entered unholy 'Old Pals' pacts in order to exclude Liberals Democrats from power.[16]

There is some support for this belief, but the evidence is far from overwhelming. The Liberal Democrat group leader of a north east district council alleges that the Tories and Labour in his council have a 'tacit agreement' designed to allow Labour to keep minority control of the council. In Chorley, where a Labour minority administration rules, the Liberal Democrat group leader says there is really a 'secret coalition' between Labour and the Conservatives. He alleges that the terms of the deal are unknown and that decisions are pre-agreed between them, emerging only after a 'laughable token debate or shadow-boxing'; against this, both parties deny that there is a deal between them.

There are councils where Labour and the Conservatives clearly cooperate. The Conservatives in Hampshire recently offered to give £5 million to support Labour's spending plans in return for remaining in power.[17] In Devon, Labour and Conservative voted together in a no-confidence motion to defeat the Alliance minority administration in 1987. This was despite the absence of any alternative administration to assume control and despite over two years of, successively, a Labour/Alliance 'working arrangement' and then support from Labour for the Alliance budget. In effect, the county council was left to drift without effective political leadership until the elections of 1989 returned it to Conservative control.[18] That electoral outcome could be offered as a vindication for the Conservative tactics in Devon, at least in the short term, but the 1993 county council elections returned Devon to both hung status and to a Liberal Democrat minority administration in which neither of the two main parties holds committee chairs. The tactics of Labour and the Conservatives during 1985–89 have probably had an inhibiting effect on cross-party cooperation in Devon.

It is certainly the case that local Labour and Conservative groups often have a negative attitude towards coalition government and are unhappy about the power such a situation can give 'smaller' parties, especially the Liberal Democrats. When one of them does enter into a partnership which includes the Liberal Democrats, there may be a feeling that Liberal Democrats cannot be trusted to deliver the necessary council votes. For example, in Oldham a minority administration of 29 Labour councillors relies on the votes of 7 Conservatives to maintain control. The large Liberal Democrat group (23 councillors) is frozen out because of alleged personality clashes between them and Labour. The Labour leader's complaint that 'it is easier to work with the Tories [because] the Liberal Democrats are obsessively individualistic'[19] echoes not only a well documented history of Liberal reluctance to toe a party line[20] but also many allegations from frustrated local coalition partners. The Labour leader in Winchester, where the three parties share power complains:

> Liberal Democrats have no coherent policy or philosophy and are often split among themselves ... therefore, it is difficult to know in advance what policies can command majority support.

Gloucester's Labour leader (where the Liberal Democrats lead a minority administration with Conservative support) complains of the party's arrogance, and there can be a shared resentment of a party that is often seen as irresponsible and inexperienced.[21]

Normally, the extent of Labour and Conservative cooperation is difficult to assess, as any arrangement tends to be low key and (as in Chorley) sometimes denied altogether. There is no doubt of genuine hostility by Labour and Conservatives to local Liberal Democrat tactics in some areas. However, in the one case of Conservative/Labour power-sharing (Tandridge) listed in Table 11.1, the Liberal Democrats had previously shared chairs with both the groups but had withdrawn from the arrangement, so the two parties had entered into the arrangement by default. There is little substantive evidence to support the belief that Labour and the Conservatives are regularly acting in concert to prevent Liberal Democrats from exerting influence. If Labour and Conservative local parties are trying to exclude Liberal Democrats, the success of the party in hung councils suggests they are generally failing in that aim.

It must also be remembered that, despite the Midlands Independent councillor who believes 'local government is about common sense and community, not national party politics', local government is an important political arena and it is in the political interests of the two traditional rulers to prevent Liberal Democrats gaining power in whatever form. Liberal Democrat complaints overlook the fact that there is no reason, except perhaps the historically adversarial nature of their relationship, that the two large parties should not engage in cooperation (of whatever kind) to ensure local communities have what they regard as an administration capable of effective delivery of services. Liberal Democrat complaints of an 'old pals act' and an 'unholy alliance' often appear to have a whiff of sour grapes about them,[22] as if the Liberal Democrats are in favour of coalition politics only when they are not excluded from the partnership .

A movement away from minority rule

The term 'coalition politics' implies a degree of cooperation and formality that many of the arrangements in hung councils do not begin to approach; we need to be careful about our definitions of local coalition activity. Coalition studies (especially those from a theoretical perspective) have often tended to cite any instance of cooperation as a coalition. However, local leaders would never agree that abstaining from voting, thus allowing a minority administration to pass policy, means they have formed a coalition with that minority party. Like the participants, writers on hung councils tend to adopt a fairly rigorous definition of what constitutes a coalition or an administration. For example, in contrast to most *theoretical* studies of coalitional activity, Mellors questions whether the'loose, tacit, and often unstable agreements which exist at local level qualify for the term "coalition" at all'.[23] Therefore, we need a definition of the administrations that form which describes the actuality and is acceptable to the perceptions of local actors. Following Leach and Stewart, administrations were classified under four types:

1. *Formal coalitions,* with shared chairs and some policy agreements, usually with an agreed time limit.
2. *Power-sharing*, with shared chairs only.
3. *Minority administrations,* comprising one or (less usual) more parties,
4. *No administration* in place, for example, either no permanent chairs, rotating chairs or purely technical chairs.

Chief executives and group leaders were given the above classifications and definitions and asked to place their current administrations in one of the four categories. Respondents to earlier surveys often believed that what one Conservative called a return to normality would come at the following election, but many local politicians and chief executives are having to learn to live permanently with the politics of hung councils. A move towards more formal and clearly agreed relationships does appear to be happening. For example, Leach and Stewart found that two-thirds of all hung councils were controlled by a single minority party.[24] It is quite clear from Table 11.3 that this is no longer the case: just over a half (51.1 per cent) of all hung councils now have a formal coalition or power-sharing administration in control.

However, while it appears that power-sharing, practised in 39.5 per cent of hung councils, is now the most usual response to this situation, formal coalitions are still relatively rare. As Table 11.3 shows, barely one in nine administrations (11.6 per cent) are formal coalitions. Also, despite the decline of minority administrations, over one-third of hung councils are still run by a single party. In those councils where chief executives have said that 'no administration' best describes the situation in their authority, there is often all-party cooperation, albeit usually in the form of an agreement to rotate the chairs or have purely technical chairs. The important point that the difference between a 'power-sharing' arrangement of all parties and 'no administration' may be merely one of definition needs to be kept in mind. Also, in Redbridge the official response was that there was 'no administration' in charge of the council, yet all the chairs were held by Labour, which was the largest minority party. Such problems of interpretation and definition are inevitable but do not obscure the rise in what are clearly coalitions. It is also the case that, as one would intuitively expect, the Liberal Democrats are disproportionately represented in the ten formal coalitions listed in Table 11.3. Three of the party's seven formal coalitions are with Labour, two with Conservatives, one with

Table 11.3 Type of administration

Type	Number	% administrations
Formal coalition	10	11.6
Power sharing	34	39.5
Minority government	30	34.9
No administration	12	14.0

Source: survey of hung councils, December 1993–April 1994; $n = 86$.

Labour and an Independent group, and one with Independents. Two Conservative/ Independent and one Ratepayers/Independent administrations are the other formal coalitions.

The increasing numbers of coalition and power-sharing administrations may indicate a learning process at local level, with initial mistrust of local coalitions giving way to a greater political sophistication. On the other hand, it may merely indicate a greater openness by politicians about the realities of life in hung councils. In a political culture where coalition politics is seen as abnormal and distinct party platforms and identities seen as essential, cooperation with another party will tend to be hidden or informal. To a large extent, the high number of minority administrations found by previous surveys may have reflected an unwillingness to admit to coalition deals for many reasons. For example, if the often anticipated policy drift materialises, politicians may fear the electorate will punish their party at the next election for cooperating in an ineffective council, thereby preventing them regaining or gaining control of the council. In a political system where hung legislatures become the norm, the 'stigma' of formal agreement with another party must lessen.

The change from the norm of minority government towards more open power-sharing deals could be a reflection of what one local Conservative calls a recognition of the *realpolitik* of hung councils. That is, hung councils are here to stay, so like it or not, if you want power you will have to be prepared to take a share of it rather than the outright control most political parties would prefer. The Liberal Democrats, with their generally positive approach, appear ideally placed to benefit from the increasing number of hung councils. Moreover, the perception that their ideological position is in the centre must also benefit them.

Importance of a central position

The power that Liberal Democrats have in hung councils has been frequently demonstrated by academic research. For example, Mellors found that in twenty hung English county councils the then Alliance parties achieved extraordinary success in getting their budgetary proposals accepted. Despite being the largest group in only three of those twenty councils, their proposal was accepted in thirteen and they reached a compromise with another group in a further six; in only one county (East Sussex) did they lack influence over the budget set.[25]

While recognising that their greater willingness to negotiate was an important contributory factor, such a success was largely attributed to their central position. The importance of a central position to achieving objectives in hung situations has been frequently noted in formal studies of coalition behaviour.[26] When there are only three groups on the council, there is no winning and ideologically connected coalition that can form without the participation of the Liberal Democrats, if we accept the proposal that the scale will feature the parties left to right in the order Labour, Liberal Democrat, Conservative.[27] One examination of the importance of the median actor found that in councils where all the parties could be placed on an ideological scale, the Liberal Democrats were a member of *all* the extant coalitions, and highly successful in achieving their policy aims. Also, the Liberal Democrats were usually the most influential opposition party in minority administrations controlled by either of the two main parties.[28] In three-party systems, where the absence of an Independent group prevents Conservatives seeking what might be a natural alliance, Liberal Democrats are enormously influential in whether a minority administration or majority coalition forms.

Mellors also noted a general closeness between Labour and the Alliance over budgetary objectives, observing that the 'tactical compatibility' of Labour and the Conservatives in some counties when committee chairs were being allocated (offering some support for Liberal Democrat allegations of an 'unholy alliance') 'did not reappear at budget time'.[29]

As Table 11.4 indicates, it is clear that Liberal Democrat groups feel more influential than other groups in hung councils. Two-thirds of all Liberal Democrats saw themselves as very influential in budgetary matters, a far higher proportion than their political opponents. In further support of the proposal that the Liberal Democrats will tend to exercise a greater degree of budgetary influence, 36.1 per cent of Liberal Democrat leaders reported that the rate set was *identical* to their preferences, a far higher percentage than the other two main parties. These findings support the overwhelming impression that the Liberal Democrats take good advantage of the factors favouring their success in hung councils.

Table 11.4 Influence on rate precept by political party (responses of group leaders, %)

	Very influential	Quite influential	Not very influential	Not at all influential
Conservative (*n* = 37)	29.4	8.8	29.4	32.4
Labour (*n* = 30)	40.0	23.3	26.7	6.7
Liberal Democrat (*n* = 40)	65.0	12.5	12.5	10.0
Independent (*n* = 8)	50.0	37.5	12,5	0.0

Source: survey of hung councils, December 1993–April 1994: *n* = 86.

A positive attitude gives positive advantages?

For national success, the Liberal Democrats have to prove they are capable of governing, and the main opportunities to do so have come in hung local authorities. The open attitude of Liberal Democrat groups towards cooperation gives them an advantage over the two main parties when negotiations have to take place. For example, Leach and Stewart have noted that two of the characteristic mistakes of Labour Party strategy in hung councils (especially when they have formerly ruled the council alone) are an initial hostility towards doing deals and a belief that they can continue in power much as they have done in the past. Similarly, the archetypal Conservative mistake is to attempt to carry on ruling alone without any agreement on continuing support, perhaps reflecting an assumption, not uncommon in some shire counties, that they are either 'the natural party of government or that they have a kind of paternalistic "duty" to form an administration'.[30]

This is not to say that Liberal Democrats do not also make mistakes. For example, their position in the centre gives them considerable strength, yet they have sometimes overestimated their bargaining position. Their frequent belief that Labour and the Conservatives are too far apart to reach any coherent agreement overlooks the annoyance that the traditional ruling parties can feel at seeing a disproportionate amount of power going to a small party. In a number of cases the two main parties have reached a deal, usually allowing one or the other to rule alone, especially where there is a tradition of good relationships between them. However, politics is also about achieving your priorities, and their centralist position gives Liberal Democrats greater room to manoeuvre. If a Labour group is anxious for a core policy to be implemented, it is unlikely to receive a sympathetic approach from its Conservative rivals, and vice versa. In short, needs must, and the closeness of Liberal Democrat and Labour policies makes any agreement much easier to reach. The positive public attitude of Liberal Democrats towards consensus also helps.

Previous studies have noted that the Liberal Democrats believe that the quality of the policy process and the policies themselves have improved since their council became hung. Two out of three Liberal Democrats think decision-making has improved and seven in ten believe the policy made is better than before.[31] Of course, it has often been their first taste of power and the two main parties, especially when they have formerly ruled the council, have been far more likely to see decision-making as having deteriorated.[32] However, recent research indicates that while Conservative leaders remain overwhelmingly negative, a majority of Labour leaders now believe that both the quality of policies made and the quality of the decision-making process have improved. Unsurprisingly, Liberal Democrats remain positive about the process of government in hung councils.

Although it seems that support from Labour politicians for the new ways of working is increasing, the Liberal Democrat leader of Leicestershire County Council believes 'the other two parties (particularly the Conservatives) don't want a hung council to work and are therefore destructive instead of being constructive'. Apparently, Disraeli's dictum 'England does not love coalitions'[33] remains true for Labour and the Conservatives.

Liberal Democrats – an irresponsible attitude to government?

Even the Liberal Democrats, the party with the most to gain (at both national and local level) from proving that formal cooperation with other parties is a viable alternative to single party domination, tend to shy away from talking about coalitions. Euphemisms such as 'working arrangement' are sometimes used, perhaps because of bad memories of the Lib/Lab pact and the Alliance with the Social Democratic Party in 1983 and 1987. Some Liberal Democrats argue that formal across-the-board coalitions (the norm in most European countries) are 'unlikely to be worthwhile, not least because of the potential political damage of being seen as Tory or Labour shadows'.[34]

As we have said, Liberal Democrat politicians and publications often attack the lack of responsibility of their opponents in hung councils. However, the advice to local groups offered by their own publications could be seen as just as irresponsible. Local groups are advised to end formal arrangements 'as soon as it is no longer worthwhile ... choosing an appropriate issue and moment'.[35] If they can, groups are recommended not to 'vote consistently with one side'.[36] Thus, the party with the most to gain nationally from demonstrating that hung legislatures can provide stable and responsible government is engaged in promulgating the opposite impression in its advice to local politicians. Liberal Democrat strategy documents are candid about the need to adopt a pragmatic approach, advising local groups that:

> your ultimate political success will be measured by the policies you have implemented, not the partners you work with ... your partners' political colour will be less important than their willingness to work with you. This may seem heresy to those fighting a tyrannical Labour majority, or a gang of neo-fascist Tories. Of course, there will be times and places when it will be absolutely clear with which party you are to make common cause. But never get too cosy, never take it for granted, and always put Liberal Democrat priorities first. [37]

Of course, such advice can lead to Liberal Democrat groups being seen as opportunists who cannot be trusted: a not uncommon view among their potential partners. There is some support for the allegation that Liberal Democrat groups are inclined to jump from partner to partner as it suits them, thereby contributing to instability. While the Liberal Democrats are almost as likely to come to an arrangement with Conservatives as with Labour, they find it harder to maintain agreements with Conservatives than they do with Labour. Conservative/Liberal Democrat administrations last an average of 15.3 months compared with the 19.6 months of Labour/Liberal Democrat administrations. Conservative/Liberal Democrat administrations are even shorter lived than periods of 'no administration', indicating a fairly high degree of volatility.[38]

However, the greater longevity of Labour/Liberal Democrat administrations may merely indicate that, for ideological reasons, Labour has little choice but to cooperate with Liberal Democrats. Conservatives often have the added option of coming to an arrangement with Independent groups, who are arguably less likely to be sympathetic to Labour policies. If this is the case, then the longevity of Labour/Liberal Democrat administrations, compared with agreements between Conservatives and Liberal Democrats, can be easily explained. The relative longevity of Liberal Democrat minority administrations (nearly 27 months) can also be explained by this, as Labour will again have little choice ideologically other than to support the Liberal Democrats or lose influence.

Perhaps for reasons of both ideological position and general smallness of group, Liberal Democrats have found themselves the most likely of the three major parties to be accused of undermining administrative stability. Blowers argues that small alliance groups tend to behave in an opportunist way,[39] and others have noted a tendency for the Liberals to switch support at crucial junctures.[40] As we have seen, the party's advice to its local council groups (if followed) could also increase instability. It may be that any small party group wielding influence beyond its size causes instability. However, while Mellors notes that 'constantly regrouping voting coalitions' could benefit any small party in hung authorities, he maintains the Liberals have been 'especially adroit' at ensuring maximum policy pay-offs from their voting strength.[41] There is some evidence to support the proposition that small Liberal Democrat groups (rather than small groups in general) will tend to generate administrative instability.[42]

Liberal Democrats and greater democracy

Given their commitment to the concept of community politics, the continuing growth of councils where Liberal Democrat groups have either control or a share of power should mean much greater opportunity for public participation. Liberal Democrat publications equate local democracy with 'trusting the people' and provide comprehensive details of Labour and Conservative negative reactions to Liberal Democrat groups opening up local government.[43] Liberal Democrat campaign literature places much emphasis on the greater openness of councils where they hold or have a share of power.[44] Indeed, the party leader in Kettering has said that 'refusing to support measures which improve public participation in council matters' would be one factor which might cause his group to terminate the power-sharing arrangement they have with Labour.

In both majority control and hung councils, the Liberal Democrats claim to have introduced a wide range of consultative procedures, better services and greater openness, although their rivals are sceptical about these achievements. The claims and counter-claims concerning council performance are inevitably politically motivated. As Walker notes, a major problem of assessing local council performance is that much of the evidence available is 'anecdote and impression ... [and] hard evidence is lacking'.[45] Some objective measurement is possible through the Audit Commission's local authority performance indicators. Wolverhampton (run by a formal Conservative/Liberal Democrat coalition) and Stockport (which the Liberal Democrats control) both perform badly on a number of performance indicators. Admittedly, those indicators are difficult to assess and debatable indications of a local authority's success, but the fact that Stockport is in the bottom five of all councils in providing pre-school nursery places conflicts with the Liberal Democrats' stated aims.[46]

It does appear that Liberal Democrat councils initiate more open government and attempts at greater community involvement in decision making than Labour or Conservative councils. In Liverpool, for example, such initiatives were 'abruptly reversed' when Labour regained power.[47] In Newbury, which changed from Conservative to Liberal Democrat control in 1991, Swords and Thorne argue that:

> there was a clear and significant shift in strategy. Regarding involvement of the public, there was much more extensive consultation before decisions were taken, and the council was entering into partnership agreements with a wide range of other organisations in the community.[48]

Notwithstanding the fact that one of the authors is an officer working for Newbury District Council, Swords and Thorne present a positive picture of Liberal Democrat politics and some indication that their approach is different.

A number of Liberal Democrat-controlled councils have introduced a register of members' interests, public question times and allowed voters to petition council meetings.[49] However, the public sometimes appears unwilling to take up the opportunities for community participation at council and committee meetings often provided by Liberal Democrats. In councils where, for example, an opportunity for public questions at meetings was introduced, some councillors (including Liberal Democrats) did not think the innovation achieved very much. Attempts to achieve greater openness in decision making procedures may also be less successful than their instigators hoped.[50] However, the party's emphasis on community and constituency politics has probably driven the other two main party groups to take on a more active role in 'pavement politics'.[51]

The Liberal Democrats support setting up community, town and parish councils in urban as well as the rural areas where parishes are common. In 1990, a parliamentary bill by the Liberal Democrat MP Simon Hughes failed in an attempt to introduce parish councils into London. Some Liberal Democrat controlled hung councils have given considerable powers to local committees, although the most well known example of this involved Tower Hamlets where they had sole overall control. In this London borough, the ruling Liberal Democrats devolved power to seven neighbourhood committees, each with their own substantial budget to provide their local neighbourhood with services. The party argued that basing elected local democracy on such 'natural communities' would 'bring a breath of fresh air' into local government.[52] Despite their good intentions, subsequent political events raised concern at this development. The Isle of Dogs, one of the seven neighbourhood committees in Tower Hamlets, had responsibility for a budget of over £24 million. After its electorate had returned a councillor for the openly racist British National Party (BNP), local observers feared the possibility that the BNP would win control of the neighbourhood committee and proceed to use the budget to favour racist organisations.[53] In the event, the BNP failed to gain the seat predicted, but the doubts raised by such a possibility may cause some Liberal Democrat groups to regard decentralisation with rather less enthusiasm in future. Since Labour regained control of Tower Hamlets in 1995, the neighbourhood committees have been disbanded and a process of what the council calls 'recentralisation' has taken place. This provides further indication that other parties may be less committed to devolving power to local communities than the Liberal Democrats.

Despite the often negative view of such efforts reported above, the party's commitment to more open government and greater community involvement continues. The enthusiastic responses of Liberal Democrats in hung councils of 'greater democracy', 'more fairness and open government', 'greater communication' and 'the need to consider all opinions before making a decision' reflect a very real commitment to more democratic local government. It is clear that, whatever the difficulties in persuading the public to become involved, Liberal Democrats are attempting to broaden the base for decision making in local communities. Such enthusiasm may eventually inspire a traditionally apathetic public not only to become more involved in local government decision-making but also to develop a more favourable impression of multi-party government.

Conclusions

Liberal Democrats are extraordinarily influential when a council becomes hung. They show a willingness to seek new ways of working in order to reconcile changed circumstances: a willingness which is facilitated by their ability to bargain from a central ideological position. The success of the party at local level is indisputable, and the Liberal Democrats are involved in more administrations than any other party or group. Liberal Democrat groups will seek agreement with either of the two main parties, or Independents, depending on circumstances. The belief that they favour partnering Labour rather than Conservative is only partly true, although it does appear that Liberal Democrat groups find it slightly easier to maintain their administrative agreements with Labour. Liberal Democrats are also far more likely to achieve their budgetary aims and, overall, the party is generally the most successful of the three major parties in hung councils. On the negative side, councils with small and pivotal Liberal Democrat groups seem to experience greater administrative instability than the norm.

Hung councils, as well as being interesting in their own right, provide observers with a rich source of information on the responses of national politicians and bureaucrats to such a change. Local actors share the same political culture and many of the attitudes of their national counterparts.[54] However, those looking for pointers to behaviour in any future hung national parliament should note that local and national politics, whatever their similarities, engender different pressures and requirements.[55] Local Liberal Democrats have been able to reach agreement with both Labour and Conservative groups, but Paddy Ashdown's refusal to keep a defeated Conservative Party in office have made some sort of coalition with Labour the most likely option in the event of a hung parliament. However, any Labour/Liberal Democrat parliamentary coalition would have to be more stable than some of those at local level. The party must avoid allegations of irresponsibility–it has to prove its ability to rule in order to safeguard its future electoral prospects. Of course, a permanently hung Parliament is unlikely without electoral reform. Leicestershire's Liberal Democrat leader, unusually pessimistic for his party, believes that 'the political culture in Britain is not ready for coalition government' and that the Liberal Democrats have yet to convince people that 'majority rule is the antithesis of democracy'. Opinion polls indicate that his assessment is generally correct, in that there is still no broad popular movement for electoral reform in Britain. This may indicate a failure by Liberal Democrats to publicise the success of the more consensual decision making that has emerged in hung councils.

More sophisticated coalition politics are emerging and a greater appreciation of the possibilities of hung government is now evidenced. Local politicians are learning to co-operate with their former rivals, and there is overwhelming support for the new and more consensual ways of working from chief executives and from all politicians but the traditional rulers. However, Liberal Democrats still seem to shy away from developing long-term responses to hung government. Perhaps the party needs to reconsider the often rather negative advice it offers to local groups and start trying to seek more formal and long-term coalitions at local level. This would be in the party's long-term interests. Coalitions are still seen by most politicians and observers as alien to British politics, and in order to support Liberal Democrat calls for electoral reform, which would almost certainly mean future coalition government, the party needs to give coalition politics a good name. The Liberal Democrats must demonstrate that coalition politics can mean more effective, responsible, responsive and open government, and that task must start in hung local councils.

Notes

1 D. Wilson, *Battle for Power,* Sphere Books, 1987, pp. 13–16.
2 Unreferenced quotations and attributions come from the author's surveys and interviews with actors in hung councils during the period December 1993 to April 1994.
3 D. Widdicombe (Chairman), *Report of the Committee of Inquiry into the Conduct of Local Authority Business* , HMSO, 1986.
4 M. Laver, C. Rallings and M. Thrasher, 'Coalition Theory and Local Government: Coalition Payoffs in Britain', *British Journal of Political Science* ,Vol. 17, No. 4, 1987.
5 M. Temple, 'A Multi-method Approach to the Study of Local Coalition Duration', paper prepared for European Consortium of Political Research Conference, Leyden University, Holland, 1993.
6 N. Carter, *Is There Life After Hanging?,* Centre for the Analysis of Social Policy, Bath, 1986.
7 P. Wintour, 'Labour "working with Lib Dems on 20 councils"', *Guardian*, 8 May 1995.
8 *Independent*, 23 September 1994, p.11.

9   P. Ashdown, 'Why I Won't Let Major In', _Independent_, 26 May 1995.
10 C. Mellors, 'Non-majority British Local Authorities in a Majority Setting', in C. Mellors and B. Pijnenburg (eds), _Political Parties and Coalitions in European Local Government,_ Routledge, 1989.
11 V. Bogdanor, 'A Gamble Kinnock Must Avoid', _Guardian_, 3 March 1992.
12 S. Leach and J. Stewart, _The Politics of Hung Authorities_, Macmillan, 1992, p.125.
13 P. Kellner, 'Ashdown Should Tell the Truth–That He's in Labour's Camp', _Sunday Times_, 19 September 1993.
14 M. Temple, 'The Relevance of Ideological Position and Policy Closeness to English Local Coalition Pay-offs', _Local Government Studies_, Vol. 21, No. 1, 1995.
15 Where the councils of respondents are not identified, the author is respecting a request for confidentiality.
16 _Liberal Democrat News_, 29 May 1992, p.1.
17 _Independent_, 27 May 1993.
18 M. Temple, 'Devon County Council: A Case Study of a Hung Council', _Public Administration_, Vol. 71, No. 4, 1993, pp.517–18.
19 _Independent_, 23 September 1994, p.11.
20 D. Widdicombe, _op. cit.,_ Table 7.17.
21 S. Leach and J. Stewart, 1992, _op. cit.,_ pp.89–90.
22 See _Liberal Democrat News, passim._
23 C. Mellors, 1989, _op. cit.,_ p.9.
24 S. Leach and J. Stewart, 1992, _op. cit._, p.113.
25 C. Mellors, 1989, _op. cit.,_ Table 4.6, pp.105–7.
26 M. Laver and N. Schofield, _Multi-party Government: The Politics of Coalition in Europe,_ Oxford University Press, 1990, pp.111–22.
27 M. Laver and W. Ben Hunt, _Policy and Party Competition_, Routledge, 1993.
28 M. Temple, 1995, _op. cit._
29 C. Mellors, 'Towards a Framework for the Study of Local Coalitions: A Case Study of English County Councils', paper presented to European Consortium of Political Research Conference, Gothenburg, 1986, pp.18–21.
30 S. Leach and J. Stewart, 1992, _op. cit.,_ pp.83–90.
31 C. Rallings, M. Temple and M. Thrasher, 'Hung Up on Power', _Local Government Chronicle_, 28 January 1994, p.17.
32 C. Rallings, M. Temple and M. Thrasher, 'Governing with a Fragile Balance of Power', _Local Government Chronicle_, 25 November 1988.
33 _Oxford Dictionary of Quotations,_ Oxford University Press, 1985, p.184.
34 A. Stunell, _Thriving in the Balance,_ Association of Social and Liberal Democratic Councillors, Hebden Royd, 1991, p.14.
35 _Ibid.,_ p.14.
36 _Ibid.,_ p.19.
37 _Ibid.,_ p.16.
38 M. Temple, 1993a, _op. cit._
39 A. Blowers, 'The Politics of Uncertainty: The Consequences of Minority Rule in an English County', _Local Government Studies_, Vol. 13, No. 5, 1987, p.42.

40 S. Leach, *The Management of Hung Authorities*, Local Government Training Board Paper, 1985, p.16.

41 C. Mellors, 'Coalition Strategies; The Case of British Local Government', in V. Bogdanor (ed.), *Coalition Government in Western Europe*, Heinemann, 1983, pp.241–2.

42 M. Temple, 1993a, *op. cit.*

43 P. Burstow, C. Harrow, A. Stunell and T. Swift, *Changing Local Government for Good*, Association of Social and Liberal Democratic Councillors, 1993, pp.17–21

44 A. Stunell, *op. cit.*

45 D. Walker, 'Local Politics: Who Gives an X?', *Independent,* 4 May 1995, p.17.

46 *Ibid.*

47 R. Pinkney, 'An Active Political Strategy: Liberals in Power in English Local Government', *Local Government Studies*, Vol. 10, No. 3, 1984, p.83.

48 D.Swords and M. Thorne, 'Choosing the Best Way of Providing what People Want', in F. Terry (ed.), *Towards Restructuring: The Dimensions of Change in Local Government*, CIPFA, 1994, p.33.

49 P. Burstow *et al., op. cit.*, p.21.

50 M. Temple, 1993b, *op. cit.*, p.531.

51 S. Leach and J. Stewart, 'The Politics and Management of Hung Authorities', *Public Administration,* Vol. 66, No.1, 1988, p.51.

52 P. Burstow *et al., op. cit,*, p.18.

53 BBC1, *On The Record*, 13 February 1994.

54 R. Wendt, 'Decision Making in Central and Local Government in the Absence of Political Majority', *Public Administration,* Vol. 64, No. 3, 1986.

55 M. Temple, 'Power Distribution in Hung Councils', *Local Government Studies*, Vol. 17, No. 4, 1991, p.41.

Appendix

Preamble to the Constitution of the Liberal Democrats

The Liberal Democrats exists to build and safeguard a fair, free and open society, in which we seek to balance the fundamental values of liberty, equality and community, and in which no-one shall be enslaved by poverty, ignorance or conformity. We champion the freedom, dignity and well-being of individuals, we acknowledge and respect their right to freedom of conscience and their right to develop their talents to the full. We aim to disperse power, to foster diversity and to nurture creativity. We believe that the role of the state is to enable all citizens to attain these ideals, to contribute fully to their communities and to take part in the decisions which affect their lives.

We look forward to a world in which all people share the same basic rights, in which they live together in peace and in which their different cultures will be able to develop freely. We believe that each generation is responsible for the fate of our planet and, by safeguarding the balance of nature and the environment, for the long-term continuity of life in all its forms.

Upholding these values of individual and social justice, we reject all prejudice and discrimination based upon race, colour, religion, age, disability, sex or sexual orientation and oppose all forms of entrenched privilege and inequality. Recognising that the quest for freedom and justice can never end, we promote human rights and open government, a sustainable economy which serves genuine need, public services of the highest quality, international action based on a recognition of the interdependence of all the world's peoples and responsible stewardship of the earth and its resources.

We believe that people should be involved in running their communities. We are determined to strengthen the democratic process and ensure that there is a just and representative system of government with effective Parliamentary institutions, freedom of information, decisions taken at the lowest practicable level and a fair voting system for all elections. We will at all times defend the right to speak, write, worship, associate and vote freely, and we will protect the right of citizens to enjoy privacy in their own lives and homes. We believe that sovereignty rests with the people and the authority in a democracy derives from the people. We therefore acknowledge their right to determine the form of government best suited to their needs and commit ourselves to the promotion of a democratic federal framework within which as much power as is feasible is exercised by the nations and regions of the United Kingdom. We similarly commit ourselves to the promotion of a flourishing system of democratic local government in which decisions are taken and services delivered at the most local level which is viable.

We will foster a strong and sustainable economy which encourages the necessary wealth-creating processes, develops and uses the skills of the people and works to the benefit of all, with a just distribution of the rewards of success. We want to see democracy, participation and the cooperation principle in industry and commerce within a competitive environment in which the state allows the market to operate freely where possible but intervenes where necessary. We will promote scientific research and innovation and will harness technological change to human advantage.

We will work for a sense of partnership and community in all areas of life. We recognise that the independence of individuals is safeguarded by their personal ownership of property, but that the market alone does not distribute wealth or income fairly. We support the widest possible distribution of wealth and promote the rights of all citizens to social provisions and cultural activity. We seek to make public services responsible to the people they serve, to encourage variety and innovation within them and to make them available on equal terms to all.

Our responsibility for justice and liberty cannot be confined by national boundaries; we are committed to fight poverty, oppression, hunger, ignorance, disease and aggression wherever they occur and to promote the free movement of ideas, people, goods and services. Setting aside national sovereignty when necessary, we will work with other countries towards an equitable and peaceful international order and a durable system of common security. Within the European Community we affirm the values of federalism and integration and work for unity based on these principles. We will contribute to the process of peace and disarmament, the elimination of world poverty and the collective safeguarding of democracy by playing a full and constructive role in international organisations which share similar aims and objectives.

These are the conditions of liberty and social justice which it is the responsibility of each citizen and the duty of the state to protect and enlarge. The Liberal Democrats consist of women and men working together for the achievement of these aims.

Bibliography

Ashdown, Paddy, *Citizen's Britain: A Radical Agenda for the 1990s*, Fourth Estate, London, 1989.

Ashdown, Paddy, *Beyond Westminster: Finding Hope in Britain,* Simon & Schuster, London, 1994.

Ashdown, Paddy, *Making Change Our Ally*, Liberal Democrat Publications, Dorchester, 1994.

Ashdown, Paddy, 'Why I Won't Let Major In', *Independent*, 26 May 1995.

Behrens, Robert, 'The Centre: Social Democracy and Liberalism', in L. Tivey and A. Wright (eds), *Party Ideology in Britain*, Routledge, London, 1989.

Beith, Alan, *The Case for the Liberal Party and the Alliance*, Longman, London, 1983.

Beller, Dennis C. and Frank P. Belloni, 'The Study of Party Factions as Competitive Organisations', *Western Political Quarterly*, Vol. 29, No. 4, 1976.

Beller, Dennis C. and Frank P. Belloni (eds), *Faction Politics: Political Parties and Factionalism in Comparative Perspective*, ABC/Clio Press, Santa Barbara, 1978.

Bennie, L., J. Curtice and W. Rüdig, 'Liberal, Social Democrat or Liberal Democrat? Political Identity and British Centre Party Politics', in D. Broughton, D. Farrell, D. Denver and C. Rallings (eds), *British Elections and Parties Yearbook 1994*, Frank Cass, London, 1995.

Bentley, M., *The Climax of Liberal Politics, 1868–1918: British Liberalism in Theory and Practice,* Allen & Unwin, London, 1987.

Bernstein, G.L., *Liberalism and Liberal Politics in Edwardian England*, Allen & Unwin, London, 1986.

Beveridge, William, *Why I am a Liberal,* Herbert Jenkins, London, 1945.

Blowers, A., 'The Politics of Uncertainty: The Consequences of Minority Rule in an English County', *Local Government Studies,* Vol. 13, No. 5, 1987.

Bogdanor, V., *Multi-party Politics and the Constitution*, Cambridge University Press, Cambridge, 1983.

Bogdanor, V. (ed.), *Liberal Party Politics,* Clarendon Press, Oxford, 1983.

Bogdanor, V., *No Overall Majority*, Constitutional Reform Centre, London, 1986.

Bogdanor, V., 'A Gamble Kinnock Must Avoid', *Guardian*, 3 March 1992.

Brack, D., 'A Comparative Look at the SDP', *Radical Quarterly,* special edition, *Where Next?,* 1987.

Brack, D., *The Myth of the Social Market: A Critique of Owenite Economics,* LINk Publications, London, 1989.

Bradley, I., *Breaking the Mould? The Birth and Prospects of the Social Democratic Party*, Martin Robertson, Oxford, 1981.

Bradley, I., *The Strange Rebirth of Liberal Britain*, Chatto & Windus, London, 1985.

Britain's Industrial Future, Report of the Liberal Industrial Inquiry of 1928, reprinted by Ernest Benn, London 1976.

Budge, Ian *et al.*, *The Changing British Political System*, Longman, London, 1988.

Bullock, Alan and Maurice Shock (eds), *The Liberal Tradition from Fox to Keynes*, Clarendon Press, Oxford, 1956.

Burstow, P., C. Harrow, A . Stunell and T. Swift, *Changing Local Government for Good*, Association of Social and Liberal Democratic Councillors, Hebden Bridge, 1993.

Butler, D. E., *The British General Election of 1951*, Macmillan, London, 1952.

Butler D., A. Adonis and T. Travers, *Failure in British Government*, Oxford University Press, Oxford, 1994.

Butler D. and D. Kavanagh, *The British General Election of 1983,* Macmillan, London, 1984.

Butler, D. and D. Stokes, *Political Change in Britain*, Penguin, London, 1969.

Callaghan, James, *Time and Chance*, Collins, London, 1987.

Carter, N., *Is There Life After Hanging?*, Centre for the Analysis of Social Policy, Bath University, Bath, 1986.

Chambers, William N., *Political Parties in a New Nation: The American Experience, 1776–1809*, Oxford University Press, Oxford, 1963.

Clarke, P.F., *Liberals and Social Democrats,* Cambridge University Press, Cambridge, 1978.

Clarke, Peter, 'Liberals and Social Democrats in Historical Perspective' in V. Bogdanor (ed.), *Liberal Party Politics,* Clarendon Press, Oxford, 1983.

Crewe, Ivor and Anthony King, *The SDP: The Life and Death of the Social Democratic Party*, Oxford University Press, Oxford, 1995.

Curtice, John, 'Great Britain: Social Liberalism Reborn?', in E.J. Kirchner, *Liberal Parties in Western Europe,* Cambridge University Press, Cambridge, 1988.

Curtice, J., W. Rüdig and L. G. Bennie, *Liberal Democrats Reveal All*, Strathclyde University Papers on Government, 96, Glasgow, 1993.

Curtice, J. and M. Steed, 'The Results Analysed', in D. Butler and D. Kavanagh, *The British General Election of 1992*, Macmillan, London, 1993.

Cyr, A., *Liberal Party Politics in Britain*, John Calder, London, 1977.

Derry, John, *Charles James Fox,* Batsford, London, 1972.

Dodds, G. E., *Let's Try Liberalism,* Simpkin Marshall, Huddersfield, 1944.

Drucker, H. M., *Multi-party Britain*, Macmillan, London, 1979.

Drucker, Henry 'All the King's Horses and All the King's Men', in W.E. Paterson and A. Thomas (eds), *Social Democratic Parties in Western Europe*, Oxford University Press, Oxford, 1986.

Dunleavy, Patrick, 'The Political Parties', in P. Dunleavy *et al.*, *Developments in British Politics 4*, Macmillan, London, 1993.

Duverger, Maurice, *Political Parties*, Methuen, London, 1986.

Eccleshall, R. (ed.), *British Liberalism: Liberal Thought from the 1640s to 1980s*, Longman, London, 1986.

Eccleshall, R., 'Liberalism', in R. Eccleshall *et al.*, *Political Ideologies*, 2nd edn, Hutchinson, London, 1994.

Essays in Liberalism, (no author), Collins, London, 1922.

Europe, Cambridge University Press, Cambridge, 1988.

Freeden, Michael, *Liberalism Divided*, Clarendon Press, Oxford, 1986.

Gladstone, W. E., *Midlothian Speeches 1879*, Leicester University Press, Leicester, 1971.

Greaves, T., *How to Fight Local Elections and Win*, Association of Liberal Councillors, Hebden Bridge, 1978.

Green, T. H. *The Works of Thomas Hill Green*, Vol. 3, edited by R. L. Nettleship, Longmans, Green, & Co., London, 1888.

Grimond, Joseph, *The Liberal Future*, Faber & Faber, London, 1959.

Grimond, Joseph, *The Liberal Challenge*, Hollis & Carter, London, 1963.

Grimond, Joseph, *Memoirs*, Heinemann, London, 1979.

Hain, Peter, *Community Politics*, Platform Books, London, 1976.

Hamer, D. A., *John Morley: Liberal Intellectual in Politics*, Clarendon Press, Oxford, 1968.

Hamilton, M. B., *Democratic Socialism in Britain and Sweden*, Macmillan, London, 1989.

Heath, A., R. Jowell and J. Curtice, *How Britain Votes*, Pergamon, Oxford, 1985.

Heath, A., R. Jowell, J. Curtice, G. Evans, J. Field and S. Witherspoon, *Understanding Political Change: The British Voter 1964–87*, Pergamon, Oxford, 1991.

Heath, A., R. Jowell and J. Curtice with B. Taylor (eds), *Labour's Last Chance? The 1992 Election and Beyond*, Dartmouth, Aldershot, 1994.

Hine, David, 'Factionalism in West European Parties: A Framework for Analysis', *Journal of West European Politics*, Vol. 5, No. 1, 1982.

Hirst, Francis, *Richard Cobden and John Morley*, Cobden Club, Midhurst, 1941.

Hobhouse, L.T., *Liberalism* (1911), Oxford University Press, Oxford, 1964.

Hobson, J. A., *The Crisis of Liberalism: New Issues of Democracy*, P. S. King & Son, London, 1909.

Hobson, J.A., *The Crisis of Liberalism* (1909); edited with an introduction by P. F. Clarke, Harvester Press, Brighton, 1974.

Ingle, Stephen, *The British Party System*, Oxford, Blackwell, 1987.

Jenkins, Roy, *Partnership of Principle*, Secker & Warburg, London, 1983.

Jenkins, Roy, *A Life at the Centre*, Macmillan, London, 1992.

Josephs, Jeremy, *Inside the Alliance*, John Martin Publishing, London, 1983.

Joyce, Peter, *Towards the Sound of Gunfire*, Liberal Democrat Publications, Dorchester, 1994.

Kavanagh, D. and P. Morris, *Consensus Politics from Attlee to Major,* Blackwell, Oxford, 1994.

Kellner, P., 'Ashdown Should Tell the Truth – That He's in Labour's Camp', *Sunday Times*, 19 September 1993.

Keynes, J.M., *The End of 'Laissez Faire'*, Hogarth Press, London, 1926.

Keynes, J.M., 'Liberalism and Labour', reprinted in Keynes, *Essays in Persuasion*, Macmillan, London, 1931.

Keynes, J.M., *The General Theory of Employment, Interest and Money,* Macmillan, London, 1936.

Laver, M. and W. Ben Hunt, *Policy and Party Competition*, Routledge, New York, 1993.

Laver, M., C. Rallings and M. Thrasher, 'Coalition Theory and Local Government: Coalition Payoffs in Britain', *British Journal of Political Science*, Vol. 17, No. 4, 1987.

Laver, M. and N. Schofield, *Multi-party Government: The Politics of Coalition in Europe,* Oxford University Press, Oxford, 1990.

Leach, R., *British Political Ideologies*, Philip Allan, Hemel Hempstead, 1991.

Leach, S. *The Management of Hung Authorities*, Local Government Training Board Paper, Luton, 1985.

Leach, S. and J. Stewart, 'The Politics and Management of Hung Authorities', *Public Administration,* Vol. 66, No. 1, 1988.

Leach, S. and J. Stewart, *The Politics of Hung Authorities*, Macmillan, London, 1992.

Liberal Democrats, *Minutes of the Federal Executive Committee* and *Minutes of the Federal Policy Committee*, Liberal Democrat Headquarters, London.

Liberal Democrats, *Changing Britain for Good*, Liberal Democrat Publications, Dorchester, 1992 (general election manifesto).

Liberal Democrats, *Unlocking Britain's Potential*, Liberal Democrat Publications, Dorchester, 1994 (European election manifesto).

Lishman, G. and T. Greaves, *The Theory and Practice of Community Politics*, Association of Liberal Councillors, Hebden Royd, Hebden Bridge, 1980.

Luard, Evan, *Socialism without the State*, Macmillan, London, 1979.

MacCallum Scott, John H., *Experiment in Internationalism,* Allen & Unwin, London, 1967.

McKee, Vincent, 'Conservative Factions since 1945', *Contemporary Record*, Vol. 3, No. 1, 1989.

McKee, Vincent, 'Factionalism in the SDP, 1981–87', *Parliamentary Affairs,* Vol. 42, No. 2, 1989.

McKee, Vincent, 'Factionalism among the Social and Liberal Democrats: Provisional Assessments', *Radical Quarterly,* No. 17, September 1990.

McKee, Vincent, 'Institutions and Groups in the Liberal Democrats', in P. Dunleavy and J. Stanyer (eds), *Contemporary Political Studies*, Vol. 2, PSA, Swansea, 1994.

McKenzie, Robert T., *British Political Parties*, 2nd edn, Heinemann, London, 1963.

Marquand, David, 'Inquest on a Movement', *Encounter,* July 1979.

Marquand, David, *Russet-coated Captains: The Challenge of Social Democracy*, SDP, London, 1981.

Marquand, David, *The Unprincipled Society,* Jonathan Cape, London, 1988.

Meadowcroft, Michael, *Liberalism and the Left*, Liberator Publications, London, 1982.

Meadowcroft, Michael, *Liberalism and the Right*, Liberator Publications, London, 1983.

Meadowcroft, M., 'Eastbourne Revisited', *Radical Quarterly,* No.5, Autumn 1987.

Meadowcroft, Michael and David Marquand, *Liberalism and Social Democracy*, Liberal Publications, London, 1981.

Mellors, C., 'Coalition Strategies: The Case of British Local Government' in V. Bogdanor (ed.), *Coalition Government in Western Europe*, Heinemann, London, 1983.

Mellors, C, 'Towards a Framework for the Study of Local Coalitions: A Case Study of English County Councils', paper presented to European Consortium of Political Research Conference, Gothenburg, 1986.

Mellors, C., 'Non-majority British Local Authorities in a Majority Setting', in C. Mellors and B. Pijnenburg (eds), *Political Parties and Coalitions in European Local Government,* Routledge, London, 1989.

Michels, Roberto , *Political Parties,* introduction by S. Lipset, Collier, New York, 1962.

Michie, A. and S. Hoggart, *The Pact: The Inside Story of the Lib-Lab Government 1977– 1978* , Quartet Books, London, 1978.

Mole, Stuart, *The Decade of Realignment: The Leadership Speeches of David Steel, 1976–1986*, Hebden Royd, Hebden Bridge, 1986.

Morley, John, *Life of Richard Cobden*, Chapman & Hall, London, 1881. (This is the most widely available early edition of Morley on Gladstone, but not the first.)

Morley, John, *Life of Gladstone*, Lloyd's Popular Edition, London, 1908.

Muir, Ramsay, *The Liberal Way,* Allen & Unwin, London, 1934.

Nicholas, Ralph, W., 'Factions: A Comparative Analysis', in Michael Banton (ed.), *Political Systems and the Distribution of Power*, Tavistock Publications, London, 1965.

Owen, David, *Face the Future*, Oxford University Press, Oxford, 1981.

Owen, David, *Time to Declare*, Penguin, London, 1992.

Padgett, S. and W. Paterson, *A History of Social Democracy in Postwar Europe*, Longman, London, 1991.

Pinkney, R, 'An Active Political Strategy: Liberals in Power in English Local Government', *Local Government Studies*, Vol. 10, No. 3, 1984.

Pitchford, R. and T. Greaves, *Merger: The Inside Story,* Hebden Royd, Hebden Bridge, 1989.

Pulzer, Peter, *The Slow Death of Labour*, Unservile State Paper No. 32, Hebden Royd, Hebden Bridge, 1985.

Rallings, C., M. Temple and M. Thrasher, 'Governing with a Fragile Balance of Power', *Local Government Chronicle*, 25 November 1988.

Rallings, C., M. Temple and M. Thrasher, 'Hung Up on Power', *Local Government Chronicle*, 28 January 1994.

Rallings, C. and M. Thrasher, 'Party Competition and Electoral Volatility: The Case of Local By-elections, 1983–1987', *Local Government Studies*, Vol. 14, No. 6, 1988, pp.67–76.

Rallings , C. and M. Thrasher, 'Exploring Uniformity and Variability in Local Electoral Outcomes: Some Evidence from English Local Elections 1985–1991', *Electoral Studies*, Vol. 12, No. 3, 1993, pp. 366–84.

Rallings, C. and M. Thrasher (eds), *Local Elections in Britain,* Local Government Chronicle Elections Centre, Plymouth, 1993.

Reif, K. and H. Schmitt, 'Nine Second-order Elections – A Conceptual Framework for the Analysis of European Election Results', *European Journal of Political Research,* Vol. 8, No. 1, 1980, pp.3–44.

Rich, B., 'Why Alan Leaman Needs Three Shredded Wheat for Breakfast', *Liberator,* No. 227, March 1995.

Rodgers, William, *The Politics of Change*, Secker & Warburg, London, 1982.

Rose, Richard, 'Parties, Factions and Tendencies in Britain', *Political Studies,* Vol. 12, No. 1, 1964.

Rose, Richard, *The Problem of Party Government*, Penguin, London, 1974.

Rüdig, W., L. Bennie and M. Franklin, *Green Party Members: A Profile,* Delta Publications, Glasgow, 1991.

Rüdig, W., J. Curtice and L. Bennie, 'The Membership Dynamics of British Centre Parties: From Liberals and Social Democrats to Liberal Democrats', in J. Lovenduski and J. Stanyer (eds), *Contemporary Political Studies 1995*, Vol. 1, Political Studies Association, Belfast, 1995.

Russell, Conrad, *The Liberal Cause: The Three Century-long Tradition of Liberal Democrats*, Unservile State Paper No. 35, Hebden Royd, Hebden Bridge, 1990.

Samuel, Herbert, *Liberalism: An Attempt to Restate the Principles of Liberalism in England*, Grant Richards, London, 1902.

Sartori, Giovani, *Parties and Party Systems,* Cambridge University Press, Cambridge, 1976.

Schulz, H. J., *English Liberalism and the State: Individualism or Collectivism*, Heath, London, 1972.

Seyd, Patrick, 'Factionalism within the Conservative Party: The Monday Club', *Government and Opposition,* Vol. 7, No. 4, 1972.

Seyd, Patrick, *The Rise and Fall of the Labour Left*, Macmillan, London, 1987.

Seyd, P. and P. Whiteley, *Labour's Grassroots,* Clarendon, Oxford, 1992.

Smithson, J., *Community Campaigning Manual*, Association of Liberal Councillors, Hebden Bridge, 1977.

Southgate, Donald, *The Passing of the Whigs 1832–1886*, Macmillan, London, 1962.

Steed, Michael, 'The Liberal Parties in Italy, France, Germany and the UK', in Roger Morgan and Stefano Silvestri (eds), *Moderates and Conservatives in Western Europe*, Heinemann, London, 1982.

Steed, Michael, 'The Electoral Strategy of the Liberal Party', in V. Bogdanor (ed.), *Liberal Party Politics,* Oxford University Press, Oxford, 1983.

Steel, David, *A House Divided*, Weidenfeld & Nicolson, London, 1980.

Steel, David, *Labour at 80: Time to Retire*, Liberal Publications Department, London, 1980.

Steel, David, *Partners in One Nation*, Bodley Head, London, 1985.

Steel, David, *Against Goliath*, Pan, London, 1991.

Steel, David, *Britain's Industrial Future* (Liberal Summer School Committee, 1927), reprinted 1991.

Stephenson, Hugh, *Claret and Chips: The Rise of the SDP*, Michael Joseph, London, 1983.

Stevenson, John, *Third Party Politics since 1945: Liberals, Alliance and Liberal Democrats*, Blackwell, Oxford, 1993.

Stunell, A., *Thriving in the Balance*, Association of Social and Liberal Democratic Councillors, Hebden Bridge, 1991.

Swords, D. and M. Thorne, 'Choosing the Best Way of Providing What People Want', in F. Terry (ed.), *Towards Restructuring: The Dimensions of Change in Local Government*, CIPFA, London, 1994.

Temple, M., 'Power Distribution in Hung Councils', *Local Government Studies*, Vol. 17, No. 4, 1991.

Temple, M., 'A Multi-method Approach to the Study of Local Coalition Duration', paper prepared for European Consortium of Political Research Conference, Leyden University, Holland, 1993.

Temple, M., 'Devon County Council: a Case Study of a Hung Council', *Public Administration*, Vol. 71, No. 4, 1993.

Temple, M., 'The Relevance of Ideological Position and Policy Closeness to English Local Coalition Pay-offs', *Local Government Studies*, Vol. 21, No. 1, 1995.

Thomson, David, *The Shock Troops of Pavement Politics? An Assessment of the Influence of Community Politics in the Liberal Party*, Hebden Royd, Hebden Bridge, 1985.

Tivey, L. and A. Wright, *Party Ideology in Britain*, Routledge, London, 1989.

Vincent, A., 'The New Liberalism in Britain 1880–1914' in *Australian Journal of Politics and History*,

Vincent, A., *Modern Political Ideologies*, Blackwell, London, 1992.

Vincent, John, *The Formation of the Liberal Party 1857–1868*, 2nd edn, Harvester, Hassocks, 1976 .

Walker, D., 'Local Politics: Who Gives an X?', *Independent,* 4 May 1995.

Wallace, William, 'Survival and Revival', in V. Bogdanor (ed.), *Liberal Party Politics,* Oxford University Press, Oxford, 1983.

Watson, George (ed.), *The Unservile State: Essays in Liberty and Welfare*, Allen & Unwin, London, 1957.

Wendt, R., 'Decision Making in Central and Local Government in the Absence of Political Majority', *Public Administration*, Vol. 64, No. 3, 1986.

Whiteley, P., P. Seyd, and J. Richardson, *True Blues: The Politics of Conservative Party Membership,* Clarendon, Oxford, 1994.

Widdicombe, D. (Chairman), *Report of the Committee of Inquiry into the Conduct of Local Authority Business*, HMSO, London, 1986.

Williams, Shirley, *Politics is for People*, Penguin, London, 1981.

Wilson, Des, *Battle for Power,* Sphere Books, London, 1987.

Wilson, Trevor, *The Downfall of the Liberal Party 1914–1935*, Collins, London, 1966.

Wintour, P., 'Labour "Working with Lib Dems on 20 Councils"', *Guardian*, 8 May 1995.

Index